ETHICAL ISSUES IN SOCIAL WORK

ETHICAL ISSUES
IN
SOCIAL WORK

Edited by

SHANKAR A. YELAJA, D.S.W.

Professor of Social Work
Faculty of Social Work
Wilfrid Laurier University
Waterloo, Ontario, Canada

CHARLES C THOMAS • PUBLISHER
Springfield • Illinois • U.S.A.

Published and Distributed Throughout the World by
CHARLES C THOMAS • PUBLISHER
2600 South First Street
Springfield, Illinois 62717 U.S.A.

©*1982, by* CHARLES C THOMAS • PUBLISHER
ISBN 0-398-04620-4 cloth
ISBN 0-398-04621-2 paper
Library of Congress Catalog Card Number 81 14460

*With THOMAS BOOKS careful attention is given to all details of
manufacturing and design. It is the Publisher's desire to present books
that are satisfactory as to their physical qualities and artistic possibilities
and appropriate for their particular use. THOMAS BOOKS will be
true to those laws of quality that assure a good name and good will.*

Library of Congress Cataloging in Publication Data
Main entry under title:

Ethical issues in social work.

Bibliography: p.
Includes index.
1. Social service—Moral and religious aspects.
I. Yelaja, Shankar A.
HV41.E83   174'.9362   81-14460
ISBN 0-398-04620-4   AACR2
ISBN 0-398-04621-2 (pbk.)

Printed in the United States of America
SC-RX-1

CONTRIBUTORS

Professor David Adams

Associate Clinical Professor
Department of Psychiatry
McMaster University
Hamilton, Ontario L8N 3Z5

Dr. Conrad Brunk

Associate Professor of Philosophy
Conrad Grebel College
University of Waterloo
Waterloo, Ontario N2L 3G6

Dr. Jean Givannoni

Professor
School of Social Welfare
University of California
Los Angeles, California 90024

**Professors Harvey Gochros
and Wendell Ricketts**

School of Social Work
University of Hawaii
Honolulu, Hawaii 96822

Mr. James Gough

Department of Philosophy
University of Waterloo
Waterloo, Ontario N2L 3G1

Dr. Robert Litke

Department of Philosophy
Wilfrid Laurier University
Waterloo, Ontario N2L 3C5

**Professors Abrahm Monk
and Marcia Abramson**

School of Social Work
Columbia University
New York, N.Y. 10025

Mr. J. Dale Munro

Clinical Consultant
Oxford Regional Centre
Woodstock, Ontario N4S 7X9

Dr. John Thomas

Professor
Department of Philosophy
McMaster University
Hamilton, Ontario L8S 4K1

Dr. Ray Thomlison

Associate Professor
Faculty of Social Work
University of Toronto
Toronto, Ontario M5S 1A1

Dr. Raju Varghese

Assistant Professor
School of Social Work and
Community Planning
University of Maryland at
Baltimore
Baltimore, Maryland 21201

Professor Suanne J. Wilson

Department of Social Work
College of Arts and Science
East Tennessee University
Johnson City, Tennessee 37601

Dr. Shankar A. Yelaja

Professor
Faculty of Social Work
Wilfrid Laurier University
Waterloo, Ontario N2L 3C5

"It is not enough to do good;
One must do it in the right way"

—John Morley
On Compromise (1874)

"Ethics is in origin the art of recommending
to others the sacrifices required for
co-operation with oneself"

—Bertrand Russell
On Scientific Method in Philosophy (1917)

"Every science has for its basis a system of
principles as fixed and unalterable as those
by which the universe is regulated and governed.
Man cannot make principles; he can only discover them."

—Thomas Paine
The Age of Reason (1794, 1796)

"An ethical person is one
—who does not confuse vested interests with ethics
—who defines his conduct by ethics, and
—who imprisons his song-bird in a cage."

—Author unknown

PREFACE

The social work profession, like other helping professions, is embedded in normative principles. Principles that define and operationalize "right" and "wrong," "good" or "better," "one good at the expense of another" are the bases for professional intervention and decision making. Since every professional intervention begins with value premises, values are permanently affixed to social work. The problem, however, is that values are not without moral controversy. Should we support abortion on demand or should we protect the right to life of the unborn? Should we let the children determine what is good for them or should we let parents and social agencies make decisions on their behalf? Should I as a social worker intervene or not intervene in removing a child from parents suspected of abuse/neglect? Should I offer counsel to a client who is depressed and wants to take his life or should I respect his right to die? These are but a few of the situations that involve intense value conflicts and moral dilemmas.

Social workers are obligated to make professional judgments on such conflicts and dilemmas. Their intervention/nonintervention begins and ends with a moral valuation. Ethics is an inquiry into the *principles of human action* to determine criteria by which to formulate ultimate social goals, to choose between conflicting or competing values, and to determine which should have priority. The results of such considerations are gathered together as a body of principles referred to as "the ethics of a profession," e.g. ethical codes of social workers, doctors, nurses, etc. A maturing profession takes its responsibility for maintaining standards of ethical behavior at both individual and collective levels. A profession comes of age when its members formulate and monitor their behavior and actions. One of the prerequisites of client confidence and societal respect for the profession is its enforcement of an ethical code.

Social workers are recognizing the need to develop a greater awareness and consciousness of the ethics of their professional responsibilities. The U.S. National Association of Social Workers recently revised its code (adopted by the general assembly delegates in 1979 and put into effect July 1, 1980) to provide greater specificity and direction in observing ethical behavior in practice. In Canada, the Alberta Association of Social Workers is spearheading the movement to make ethical codes more precise and less paternalistic and global. The Canadian Association of Social Workers has appointed a task force to review its present ethical code. The American Orthopsychiatric Association is giving serious consideration to ethical issues in professional practice. Monitoring of professional practice to ensure that it is governed by ethical principles is also gaining acceptance in professional circles. These trends are indicative of the profession's seriousness in living up to its commitments.

There are encouraging signs that as a profession we are willing to confront the ethical issues and to put our house in order. Encouraged by recent developments in the profession, I decided to address the issues by way of compiling a book. In this book the emphasis is upon clarification of value dilemmas and ethical problems that social workers are confronted with in their day-to-day practice. The essential purpose here is to raise the level of critical awareness and the consciousness of professional ethics among social workers so that they may improve their practice decision-making process when value conflicts and ethical problems arise.

To accomplish this, an attempt is made to analyze values and ethics from many facets. The set of case studies reinforces this notion since extreme care is taken in each case to present various dimensions of an ethical problem or conflict. It is recognized, of course, that we are dealing here with very complex issues in professional practice. For many ethical issues and value conflicts there appear to be no clear-cut answers or solutions; a state of continuing tension on some value/ethical issues is inevitable. Discussion and analysis of issues in each chapter and the case studies in the appendix may, however, prove helpful in providing guidelines for a professional ethical code in a more human and personal way because issues discussed in various social work practice contexts touch upon the very core of what we do. It is hoped that individual chapters and the collection as a whole will aid social workers and related helping disciplines in developing a greater appreciation for an ethical practice base, and also lead to higher motivation for monitoring quality and standards for professional practice.

The organizational framework of the book was certainly influenced by the focus, emphasis, and purpose stated above. As such, each contributing author was provided with a statement on the guidelines, to be used in developing a perspective for individual contributions. Extensive revisions in many chapters were undertaken to achieve a unity of theme and purpose. However, a book of readings such as this one must be evaluated not by its ability to achieve integration and organization, but rather by its contribution toward the essential purpose.

If this effort can help stimulate further interest in social work values and ethics and is able to challenge social workers to respond by giving a higher priority to the ethics of their profession, it would have more than served its purpose.

Shankar A. Yelaja
Waterloo, Ontario

ACKNOWLEDGMENTS

E diting this book has been a personally challenging and professionally rewarding experience for me. A book such as this is
the product of collective efforts and cooperation. Working together
professionally on a common objective is an experience that has its
share of rewards, problems, and frustrations. There is, however,
no greater reward than to see the completed product. It is a joy
pure and simple.

I am grateful to contributing authors who wrote their individual chapters for the book. Without their collaborative efforts and
patience the book would not have transformed itself from a dream
into a reality. Several graduate social work students provided
valuable research assistance and I wish to thank all of them; Kim
Harper, Wendy Redekop, and Peter Quick deserve special mention. James Gough, a doctoral student in philosophy, University
of Waterloo helped me in more ways than one. Joanne Snider
Bauer typed parts of the manuscript. My colleagues at Wilfrid
Laurier University offered support and encouragement: Dean
Sherman Merle read parts of the manuscript; Professor Shaun
Govenlock and Dr. Robert Litke encouraged me to pursue the
ideas; Professors Conrad Brunk and Max Siporin were most helpful in commenting on the organization of the book and in suggesting
contributors; Professor Brunk also assisted me in editorial work.

The production quality of this book is entirely due to the
painstaking efforts and cooperation of Mr. Payne Thomas and his
staff associates at Charles C Thomas, Publisher. They have been
most helpful to me through various stages of manuscript preparation.

I am thankful to the National Association of Social Workers,
Canadian Association of Social Workers, Alberta Association of
Social Workers, and the British Association of Social Workers for
their permission to reprint codes of ethics. Mr. Robert Cohen of
the N.A.S.W. was very helpful in answering my numerous inquiries and in providing appropriate documents/reports needed in my

work. Gweneth Gowanlock, executive director of C.A.S.W., provided information on the history of social work ethical codes in Canada; and Gayle Gilchrist James, past-president of A.A.S.W., was most cooperative in sharing the current activities of that association in social work ethics.

A special debt of gratitude is owed to the Research Grants Committee of Wilfrid Laurier University for awarding me a book preparation grant that has proved indispensable in successfully completing the project. The continued support of Wilfrid Laurier University and its many resources has been a source of strength in my scholarly work.

My deepest gratitude to all!

S.A.Y.

CONTENTS

ETHICAL ISSUES IN SOCIAL WORK

Part I

Introduction: A Perspective
On Social Work Values And Ethics

Chapter 1

VALUES AND ETHICS IN THE SOCIAL WORK PROFESSION

SHANKAR A. YELAJA

INTRODUCTION

The social work profession, like other helping professions, is embedded in normative principles. Principles that define right and wrong, good or better, are the bases for professional intervention and decision making. Values are, therefore, permanently affixed to social work. The problem, however, is that values are not without moral controversy. Although there is consensus on some absolute social work values, differences on how to operationalize them in practice are enormous, causing tensions within the profession. The value conflicts are inherent in the philosophy and ideology of social work. Social workers have to recognize and accept the heritage of their values and ideology.

Ethics can be defined as an inquiry into the *principles of human action*. The goal is to determine criteria by which to formulate ultimate social goals, to choose between conflicting or competing values, and to determine which should have priority. The code of ethics of a profession represents a degree of consensus among its members on shared common values. Professional ethics is values in action or values in operation. An ethical code represents behavioral expectations or preferences that provide the social worker with a guide for professional conduct. One of the prerequisites of client confidence and societal respect for the profession is the formulation and enforcement of an ethical code.

A profession comes of age when its members concern themselves with the ethics of their profession, with the values held by the collective group, and with the ethical behavior of the individual

5

practitioners. In recent years the emphasis in social work has shifted from a focus on client morality to the ethical behavior and morality of the professionals themselves. This is the sign of a maturing profession. In this chapter I would like to consider the significance of values and ethics to the social work profession, and raise issues/problems the profession must address in its ongoing development of professional ethics.

Concepts: Morality, Values, and Ethics

Concepts of morality, values, and ethics require some clarification in order to maintain conceptual and practical distinctions. According to Milton Rokeach a value is "an enduring belief that a specific mode of conduct or end-state or existence is personally or socially preferable to an opposite or converse mode of conduct or end-state of existence."[1] The emphasis is on the preferred mode of action and the definition does not include such terms as "ought" and "should"; thus the concept of morality has been deliberately eliminated. In social work, however, values are not necessarily expressed only as preferable devices to something else; there is often also an implicit moral force behind them.

Max Siporin suggests that a value is "a motivational, affectively charged belief; an attribution of worth; preferential behavior that is directed toward desired goals." He goes on to say that we give meaning to our biases by making evaluations in terms of "ideals, norms and preferred means and ends—such as health, welfare, freedom, justice, equality."[2] There is an implicit and sometimes explicit expectation that social workers shall abide by certain values. For example, social workers are expected to work toward the elimination of social injustice, discrimination, etc. Thus, social work values include values that concern end-states of existence as well as those that have a moral force behind them.

Rokeach suggests that the concept of morality is considerably narrower than the concept of values. Moral values refer only to certain kinds of instrumental values—to those that have an interpersonal focus that, when violated, arouse pangs of conscience or feelings of guilt for wrong-doing (e.g. a social worker being totally dishonest in his dealings with colleagues or clients). However, there are other types of instrumental values that refer to more than standards of obligation. There are, for example, those that may be called competence or self-actualization types of values. These have a personal rather than interpersonal focus and do not seem especially concerned with morality. Their violation leads to feelings of shame resulting in personal inadequacy rather than to feelings of guilt about wrong-doing.

Ethics provide a guide for professional conduct that can be used as the principles of action. They are the rules and principles that govern how human values are put into practice. Professional ethics, as a discipline, help to determine criteria by which one can formulate ultimate social goals, to choose between conflicting or competing values, and to make a decision on which should have priority. The results of such considerations are gathered together as a body of principles referred to as "the ethics of a profession" (e.g. ethical codes for social workers, doctors, lawyers, nurses, etc.). Thus, ethics provide the guidelines that put into operation both interpersonal moral values and personal competence values.

VALUES IN SOCIAL WORK

Social Work as a Normative Profession

Certain characteristics often attributed to professional occupations, though not necessarily the exclusive monopoly of the professions, can be used as a tool in distinguishing professional from nonprofessional occupations. These attributes can also be used to highlight some of the problems that professionalization inevitably precipitates.

Ernest Greenwood observes that all professions seem to possess the following attributes: (a) a systematic theory; (b) authority; (c) community sanction; (d) an ethical code, and (e) a culture.[3] Inherent in a systematic theory is the necessity for research. Thus, professionalization often precipitates a division of labor between the theory-oriented person and the practice-oriented person. If properly integrated this cleavage should produce an accelerated expansion of theory, however; if not, many problems could potentially arise.

Professional authority refers to the relationship between the professional and the client in terms of the decision-making process.

Unlike in the nonprofessional occupation, where the *customer* is always right, the professional is often required to dictate what is good and evil for the *client.*

The sanction of the community is important because it confers power and privilege on the profession. Professions, for example, have control over their training centers through accreditation and frequently over the licensing. Since these powers and privileges are granted by the community, the profession must make a concerted effort to persuade the community that it will benefit by granting the monopoly. Problems arise when there are differences between the professional and community norms.

The code of ethics is meant to assist in overcoming some of these problems by imposing ethical behavior on the profession. Greenwood suggests that professionals are sometimes tempted to misuse their community-granted monopoly by protecting vested interests rather than the public weal, by charging exorbitant prices for their services, by diluting the caliber of their performance, or by frustrating internal forces for beneficial change. Normally such abuses of privilege and power are dealt with by internal regulatory procedures before their gravity prompts the community to revoke the profession's monopoly.

The professional culture consists of its values, norms, and symbols. Social values are the profession's basic fundamental beliefs; norms are its guides to behavior in social situations; and symbols are its meaning-laden items. This is one of the most important attributes of the social work profession.

A profession, says Max Siporin, "is characterized by a set of beliefs and by a collective conscience with which to make these beliefs stick."[2] In addition, there are certain prescribed models and standards by which to describe and measure reality and with which to make moral-evaluative judgments. These norms give legitimacy to behavior and reality and become social rules for individual conduct. Siporin further suggests that social work as a profession represents society's response to the social needs of people and that it is these needs themselves that have shaped the features of social work practice, its philosophical value system and body of knowledge, its practice theory, and its interventive repertoire.

The difference between social workers and other helping professionals lies in the distinctive value system, which is the main feature of social work as a normative profession. Normative values include the uniqueness and worth of the individual; self-determination; the existence and value of freedom; the existence of obligations; and beliefs about the "good" life and "good" societies, including social justice. Without community sanction there could be no social work as we know it.

Basic to this value system is a belief in humanism, science, rationality, professionalism, and social welfare. Professions derive their knowledge from systematic theory. Inherent in theory construction is scientific research. Social workers continue to hope that with a scientific base and method they might realize their moral humanitarian purposes in society even as the profession is institutionalized and bureaucratized in the social welfare system. However, in searching for a scientific base and method, the social work profession has tended to ignore the subject of moral philosophy. Rather, social workers have used a value-free science as their model, assuming that social workers could hold a set of values so self-evidently true that they could be morally neutral and merely enable people to fulfill their own needs and desires.

This value-free ideology may have resulted from the confusion between values and knowledge. Value refers to something preferred; knowledge is what is known. William E. Gordon[4] argues that this distinction is clear when applied to real objects, behaviors, and conditions, but it is confusing when applied to statements about them. Knowledge and value can converge by two routes: (a) the shifting of preference toward the confirmed (the scientifically oriented society); (b) the modification of the reality on which confirmation is based (the change-oriented society). The knowledge base of social work has been formulated toward confirmed and confirmable propositions. The location of the ultimate social work value in human realization and the focus of its contributing science on social functioning distinguishes between value and knowledge and leads to a separation of the role of social norm enforcer from the role of scientific professional.

The value-free ideology may also have been an outgrowth of the reaction to the moralism of the early philanthropists. For example, when social workers rejected the notion of the deserving poor, the definition of poverty was changed from a moral problem to a social problem. However, Muriel Pumphrey accurately observes that the former moralistic attitude was replaced by a highly abstract phraseology that tended to be aired on ceremonial occasions.[5]

Professional values imply that there is a consistent choice prevailing over the lesser values of income, power, and prestige, that is, professional social work values are those espoused in the code of ethics. Serious departure from adherence to these values would likely result in the excommunication of social workers from the profession. In actuality, the values that underpin the social work profession are not yet altogether formed, codified, or established.

Noel Timms suggests that the treatment of values in social work is based on a list-making approach.[6] This approach assumes that social workers uphold the same values and that these values can be listed in a text. However, this assumption has been criticized by many writers. G. Channon, for example, suggests that social workers do *not* share core values.[7] He bases this belief on a study that was undertaken to formulate value congruence and incongruence among seven social workers in a hospital setting. Methods of data collection were taped interviews to cover all facets of social work activities with clients, and observation and documentation regarding how social workers' activities were allocated for the support of the values under study. Of 112 values codified, only ten received consensus among social workers. Of these ten, four were associated with professionalism, two with organizational functioning, two with personal qualities, and two with client-worker relationships.

McLeod and Meyer, in a study to determine if social workers held common values, identified ten such common value dimensions, putting them on a continuum.[8] The ten dimensions delineated as the most preferred values of social workers were (1) individual worth versus system goals; (2) personal liberty versus societal control; (3) group responsibility versus individual responsibility; (4) security/satisfaction versus struggle/suffering and denial; (5) relative pragmatism versus absolutism/sacredness; (6) innovation/change versus traditionalism; (7) diversity versus individual autonomy; (8) cultural determinism versus inherent human nature; (9) interdependence versus individual autonomy; and (10) individualization versus stereotyping. They discovered that, with one exception, seven of these ten value dimensions were significantly related to levels of professional social work training. For persons committed to a religious faith, professional training was not a significant factor in molding value positions.

The same value dimensions were used by Linda Rosa in 1978 to determine whether or not the values upheld by social workers differed from those recognized by other professions. She found that social work faculty members adhered to these value dimensions more consistently than did arts and science faculty members.[9] However, another study by Meyer, Litwack, and Warren found that primary school teachers upheld nearly the same values as did social workers.[10]

An inherent problem in much of the research that attempts to define and measure social work values is that most studies do not distinguish between what the social worker believes and what he/she actually does. Timms suggests that it seems

> ... much more profitable to conduct the study of social work values not so much on the basis of the values social workers mention, but on what they actually do when faced with a choice between valued courses of action. The question to ask is not so much what things, concepts, states of affairs, do social workers value, but how much do they value them. And this can only be discovered when social workers have to put their values in some order of priority.[6]

Few efforts to clarify the agreed-upon values in social work have been completely acceptable. This does not mean, however, that the task should be abandoned. According to Gross, Rosa, and Steiner, some social workers feel that today's social work profession should tolerate ideological diversity, and that this may in fact be the mark of a maturing profession. The authors, however, express their fears at this prospect, believing it will encourage contradictory ethical positions and be used as a hollow excuse for abandoning critical thinking on moral issues.[11]

In accordance with this later notion, Charles S. Levy, in an article on personal and professional values, argues that there is a great need for a consistent and accepted statement of social work values. He says "professional practitioners are conflicted in their choices of action in relation to clients, first because of conflicts among their own personal values and secondly because of conflicts between their own and professional values. Uncertainty is but added to the fire of conflict when there is doubt about the professional values or about the consensus which exists about them."[12]

Levy suggests that values may be conceived along three basic dimensions, which account for all major value orientations shared by social workers related to their professional practice. The three dimensions are preferred conceptions of people, preferred outcomes for people, and preferred instrumentalities for dealing with people. Distinct from knowledge, and adequately refined, these categories of values might constitute a guide for planning and action in social work *practice* and *education*. The predictability of professional behavior that might then result would help define what society and clients could expect from the social work profession.

In summary then, the social work values on which there is consensus cluster around a positivistic/humanistic philosophy expressed in these norms:

- Human beings have innate worth and good qualities in themselves.
- Their dignity must be respected.
- They have a right to make decisions on matters affecting their quality of life.
- They are capable of change, growth, and continuing development.
- Constraints and limitations imposed by personal and social factors on their ability to change, grow, and adapt should be removed in order to help them lead a personally meaningful and socially useful life.

Although social work values and norms have remained steadfast in professional thinking, the operational meanings and instrumental choices for putting them into practice continue to raise controversies, thus creating value dilemmas and conflicts in professional practice.

Value Conflicts and Dilemmas

Value conflicts and dilemmas are inherent in social work practice. Detailed consideration is given to this topic in Chapter 2 of this book. Here some basic ideas are outlined as these relate to the concept of social work as a normative profession and the significant impact of values on social work.

Louis Lowy reminds us of the two core social work values: the worth, dignity, and uniqueness of the individual; and the right to self-determination by individuals, groups, or constituents in a community.[13] Is there potential for operationalizing the value premise of the two main values, i.e. uniqueness versus self-determination? In order to operationalize these values the social worker must always ask, "What does this action on my part communicate to my clients about my perception of their personhood?" Social workers must also select a balance between classification (labeling) and the responsibility to respond to clients as individuals. There is an inherent conflict between science's need to order/classify and the humanism of social workers. The social worker's stance has generally been to couple the concept of client self-determination (the client as the chief problem solver) with that of the social worker not being the fountainhead of all knowledge. The social worker has responsibility to contribute to the data base from which the client will choose, including facts, ideas, and value concepts. It is important to make clear that the worker is offering only part of the total available social experience.

However, as discussed earlier, there may be a wide gulf between what social workers say they believe and what they actually do. Tradition emphasizes, for example, how important it is for social workers to maintain a positive view of their clients. Research on the practice behavior of social workers helps to illustrate the problem. A study was conducted in which thirty-one social workers in a hospital were asked to list from five to eight adjectives they felt adequately described clients. They also were asked to rate each adjective as positive or negative. Twenty (60%) social workers described their clients negatively and only nine (29%) described them positively. Of the twenty negative descriptions three were *very* negative, whereas none of the positive descriptions was *very* positive. Thus, although social work texts encourage a positive view of clients, the majority of these workers described their clients negatively.

Value dilemmas also arise when social workers impose their values, either personal or professional, on the client, group, or community. In a 1978 article, I. Mamber compares social work to

Machiavelli's *The Prince*.[14] Social work, he suggests, is a philosophy of goodness. Machiavelli's *The Prince* is a science of power. The two seem far apart, but when social work is stripped of illusions and brought to reality via practice, it looks Machiavellian. The client has no rights. The social worker makes judgments about what is right and wrong for the client; as an authority figure the social worker makes value judgments about what is good for the masses. Social casework, therefore, is faced with a fundamental and perhaps insoluble value paradox. Social work poses for itself the ultimate end of a dignified and worthy human being; however, the methods it uses to accomplish that end are likely to be demeaning to the individual.

Henry Miller suggests that value dilemmas are inherent in the social welfare system as it exists, that one cannot minister to man's suffering without robbing him of his dignity.[15] He goes on to say we must realize the enormous investment social work has in offering services to clients who make no request for it, who have little choice about their involvement, and less comprehension as to what the involvement entails. The client is not free to withdraw from the circumstances or reject the advice and yet he/she may not necessarily share the social worker's goals.

Dale Hardman also discusses the problems that arise when social workers impose their own values on their clients.[16] He states that social workers impose middle-class norms on lower-class clients. The imposition occurs either consciously or unconsciously and in a covert as well as overt manner. Sometimes the influence of values and norms is subtle and goes unnoticed; at other times it is less subtle, direct, and out in the open. However, the criterion for supporting or rejecting a norm should be its functionality, no matter whether it is a lower-, middle-, or upper-class value. Hardman goes on to argue that the more you understand poor people, the more you will see the need for them to make basic changes in their life-style. The following must be changed to break the poverty cycle: time orientation, primary group relationships, father-dominance, several child-rearing practices, and fatalism. However, the following lower-class values should not be changed: closer, more intimate interpersonal relationships, interpersonal honesty, more emphasis on person than status, intense but ready solution of conflict, and interpersonal good humor.

In 1973 H. C. Foot and S. P. Russel-Lacy conducted an investigation with twenty-seven British trainee social workers to test the hypothesis that social workers are more likely to attempt to impose social values on working class than on middle-class clients.[17] A questionnaire was devised around two fictitious families in different socioeconomic circumstances. Twelve problems emphasizing various social values were presented in relation to family members. The trainees were required to rank the alternative solutions in order of preference. Solution choices included reflection (revealing client's own feelings and motives), indiction (pointing out consequences of behavior), and value imposition (suggesting what the client should do). Solutions involving value imposition, though not a predominant choice, were ranked significantly higher for a middle-class than a working-class family. Thus the study indicated that social workers also impose their values on middle-class clients.

The biggest problem with the middle-class orientation of social workers is the difficulty it often creates in developing a meaningful engagement with disadvantaged people in our society. The obstacle in overcoming the built-in middle class bias in the therapeutic situation is best explained by C. W. Mills:

> Present institutions train several types of persons—such as judges and social workers—to think in terms of 'situations'. Their activities and mental outlook are set within the existent norms of society; in their professional work they tend to have an occupationally trained incapacity to rise above series of 'cases'. It is in part through such concepts as 'situation' and through such methods as 'the case approach' that social pathologists have been intellectually tied to social work with its occupational position and political limitations. And, again, the similarity of origin and the probable lack of any continuous 'class experience' of the group of thinkers decrease their chances to see structure rather than a scatter of situations.
>
> The mediums of experience and orientation through which they respectively view society are too similar, too homogeneous, to permit the clash of diverse angles which through controversy might led to the construction of the whole.[18]

Social workers do impose their values on their clients. It is important to realize, therefore, how the conflicting values are prioritized. Consider, for example, the problem that often arises when professional values diverge from personal values. Charles

Levy points out that professional practitioners experience considerable strain because of uncertainty about the professional values by which they feel ruled and because of the extent to which they feel ruled by professional rather than by personal values.[12] The suggestion that practitioners lay aside their personal values in the performance of their professional function may be offensive to their integrity. The practitioner is entitled to represent his interests and honor his values providing he does not do so by exploiting his advantage over clients. One way to achieve this, says Levy, is to distinguish actions on behalf of the practitioner himself from actions in relation to his client.

Ruth Smalley points to another difficulty that arises when social workers prioritize their values. She notes that the social worker is obliged by his purpose as a professional to direct his energies toward realizing the purposes of the social agency that has employed him.[19] As a professional social worker he will seek to realize that purpose, through a process identifiable as a social work process. His professionalism requires of him affirmation of the purpose—social work purpose—as exemplified in the specific agency's purpose. Thus a value conflict may be unavoidable when the purpose of the employing agency is contrary to that of the social worker.

This is where ethics in social work becomes a matter of paramount significance. Ethical guidelines help resolve value conflicts and dilemmas in practice. They provide guidelines for professional conduct and behavior. Without such guidelines professional social workers would experience even greater stress and conflict.

ETHICS IN SOCIAL WORK

Historical Overview

Because of the ambiguities and conflicts inherent in what social workers do, they need a statement of ethical principles embodied in a code of ethics to guide their professional conduct. The code of ethics of any professional organization evolves out of an accumulated body of experience. It grows and develops in response to new professional situations and practice demands. Changes and uncertainties in practice are also reflected in the code. In the evolution of a given code informed consensus of a professional group of colleagues plays an important part.

Historically, the efforts of social workers in the United States to focus the profession's interest on an ethical code can be traced to two veteran social workers, Mary Van Kleeck and Graham R. Taylor, who prepared an article on the development of professional standards in social work for the May 1922 volume of the *Annals of the American Academy of Political and Social Sciences*.[20] The volume was organized as a special issue on ethical codes in the professions. Kleeck and Taylor noted that although social workers did not have a written code of professional ethics they nevertheless were guided by the ideal of service rather than by any thought of pecuniary gain. Frank Lowenberg chronicles the brief history of the social work profession in developing an ethical code:

> ... in the years following the appearance of *The Annals*, a number of attempts were made to produce a written code of social work ethics. Thus, in 1923, the American Association for Organizing Family Social Work discussed (but did not adopt) a code with thirty-eight paragraphs. Many of the items in this code are found in subsequent codes and still sound familiar to present day social workers (e.g., "The Social Worker's first duty is toward his clients, unless the performance of this duty jeopardizes the welfare of the community"). A year later the American Association of Social Workers appointed a National Committee on Professional Ethics. Many local AASW chapters discussed the need for a code of ethics, and some produced draft documents. In 1924, the Toledo Chapter became the first to publicize such draft code of ethical principles. Even though this brief code contained only very general principles, it spurred other chapters to produce their own versions ... the delegate assembly on the National Association of Social Workers adopted a code in 1960 and amended this code in 1967. The code had received a mixed response from practitioners. ... [21]

The National Association of Social Workers, following the submission of a report by the Task Force on Ethics, adopted a revised code of ethics, which was approved by the delegate assembly in 1979 and came into effect on July 1, 1980. The task force had recommended that the proposed revision to the code ought to remain within the general spirit and intent of the original code, which encompassed a basically sound and durable set of principles. The basic professional values have not changed, but new practice situations and demands require up-dated guidelines for professional behavior and conduct. The current ethical code of

N.A.S.W. (which appears in the Appendix) reflects a fairly high degree of consensus among social workers.

The efforts to develop an ethical code in Canada also go back to the 1920s. The Canadian Association of Social Workers was established in 1926 and then, as today, had as one of its primary purposes the encouragement and development of high professional standards. In fact, between 1928 and 1930, in the fledgling stage of the Association, one of the four national standing committees focused on service and standards. These standards pertained to an insistence upon standards of service to clients and on the desire to improve standards of service to the community. This led, in the decade between 1928 and 1938, to a National C.A.S.W. Committee on Ethics. A study project on ethics begun in 1932 by the Canadian Association of Social Workers resulted in the adoption in 1938 of the following simple Code of Ethics:

Preamble

It is assumed that a professional social worker is motivated by an interest in the well-being of humanity rather than personal gain or advancement; that he will have knowledge and competence in his field; and that he is a person of integrity and open-mindedness.

1. A social worker's essential responsibility is the welfare of his clients.
2. A social worker's relationship to his colleagues should be based upon honesty, fairness, open-mindedness and appreciation of the part each plays in the larger professional field.
3. A social worker should so control his personal activities that he does not impair his professional capabilities nor bring adverse criticism upon his profession.
4. A social worker owes his employing agency conscientious service and adherence to the policies and regulations of his organization, which includes a responsibility to work towards their improvement and development.
5. A social worker is responsible for undertaking and stimulating progressive study, interpretation and action with a view to improving professional services and community standards.

As the practice of social work changed, subsequent revisions of the code took place in 1940, 1956, 1960, 1964, 1970, and 1979. Further updating is currently underway in 1981; in fact, C.A.S.W.'s current by-laws require that the national Code of Ethics be reviewed and modified as necessary every three years.

In the early years of the professional association—the 1930s and

1940s—breaches of the code were considered by a national committee. With the development of a new C.A.S.W. code during the 1950s, breaches became the responsibility of a panel of experts at the local level with reference to national resources only if the issue was more complex than could be handled locally.

Since 1975, when C.A.S.W. became a federation of provincial and territorial member organizations, complaints about ethical issues and enforcement of ethical codes have fallen to provincial or territorial professional social work organizations. All of these member organizations have agreed, as a minimum, to abide by the current C.A.S.W. Code of Ethics; many have taken that document several steps further. More detailed versions have been developed by several provincial associations. These relate to unique professional social work and other legislation in that province and are seen as necessary in order to render the code enforceable under law.

Ideally, official codes of ethics are structured around the reality of the client-centered ethical principle. This is part of a more widespread interest in values, morals, and ethics, and an interest in constructing a code that is appropriate to the present time. The professional code begins with a concise statement of the client-centered ethic itself. This is followed by a list of the most frequent explicit themes of ethical dilemmas, each heading up an explanatory paragraph to include, when appropriate, key legal citations and references to relevant ethical commentary. The goal is not an encyclopedic mix of ethics, laws, and regulations but a concise guide with which the professional can be expected to be familiar and one that can be consulted for ethical guidance whenever necessary.

Ethical Principles in Social Work

The N.A.S.W.'s code of ethics views self-realization of all people as the goal of social work practice. It is a guide to deal with issues in a variety of situations and is based on the fundamental values of the social work profession, which include the worth, dignity, and uniqueness of all persons as well as their rights and opportunities.

The major principles in the N.A.S.W.'s code of ethics are (a) the social worker's conduct and comportment as a social worker; (b) ethical responsibility to clients, i.e. primacy of clients' interests; (c) ethical responsibility to colleagues; (d) ethical responsibility to employers and employing organizations; (e) ethical responsibility to the social work profession; and (f) ethical responsibility to society, i.e. promoting the general welfare of society.

The N.A.S.W. ethical guidelines suggest that the issue of social work conduct is centered around the idea of propriety, competence, professional development, the service obligation of the profession, integrity, scholarship, and research. This is closely related to the ethical responsibility of the social work profession where the ideas of maintaining the integrity of the profession, assisting the profession in providing community service, and developing knowledge for professional practice are central. All of these principles deal with the social worker's obligation to the profession and how that stands in relation to his/her obligation to the self.

In discussing the principle of obligation to clients, the N.A.S.W.'s code of ethics suggests that: (a) "The social worker's primary responsibility is to the client"; (b) "The social worker should make every effort to foster maximum self-determination on the part of the clients"; (c) "The social worker should respect the privacy of clients and hold in confidence all information obtained in the course of professional service"; and (d) "When setting fees, the social workers should ensure that they are fair, responsible, considerate and commensurate with the service performed and with due regard for the client's ability to pay."

In terms of the social worker's ethical responsibility to colleagues, the code suggests that colleagues should be treated with respect, fairness, and courtesy. When dealing with a colleague's clients, the code requires that full professional consideration should be used.

The code also suggests that a social worker has an ethical responsibility to employers and employing organizations. It states that social workers should strive to improve the effectiveness and efficiency of the services rendered, prevent discrimination in the organization's practices, and use the organization's resources only with scrupulous regard.

Finally, the social worker's ethical obligation to society is discussed in terms of his/her responsibility to promote the general welfare of society, i.e. the social worker, according to the N.A.S.W., should act to eliminate discrimination, ensure equal access to resources and services, expand choice and opportunity for people, and so forth.

How helpful is the ethical code in providing guidelines for professional conduct, especially when decisions involving conflicting or competing values have to be made? Alan Keith-Lucas suggests that there are basically two kinds of situations that necessitate consideration of ethical implications: (a) "good-bad" decisions that are obvious and can be controlled to some extent by a code of ethics; and (b) decisions between two or more courses of action, both of which are potentially good although perhaps in different circumstances, or two contradictory "goods" that cannot both be attained.[22]

The ethical code, it appears, is helpful in ensuring that certain bad practice decisions will not occur. Extreme violations of clients' rights are well protected. Ethical obligations of social workers to act responsibly toward their clients, colleagues, and employers are clearly stated. Where the code is less helpful is with respect to a decision involving the choice of two equally good alternative courses of action, that is, a choice resulting in sacrificing one good at the expense of another. Here the code leaves much room for improvement. Perhaps this kind of refinement can take place only after the profession has accumulated and developed principles derived from individual cases and has established legal/moral precedents to deal with them.

Furthermore, it is important that the ethical considerations present in situations and decisions involving different value conflicts be identified and that due respect be given to each side of the conflict involved. Where possible, norms should be established along with criteria that can be used when exceptions to these norms must be made. This is where a comprehensive code of ethics is valuable. Future refinements in the code might be considered along these lines.

Why Have an Ethical Code?

Social workers' responsibilities for ethical behavior and their obligation to maintain high ethical standards are especially critical given the characteristics of their clientele and the services provided. This becomes even more important as the number of autonomous, independent practitioners grows: the number of social workers in private practice, the consulting business, research, evaluation, and policy advisory positions, as well as those working with allied professions such as law, medicine, and psychology is increasing. Thus the need for a solid code of ethics is also increasing.

Even without this growing number of autonomous practitioners, there is still an obligation to maintain high ethical standards. This obligation is a direct result of social workers being employed by social agencies. As employees they not only represent the organization but also the profession. The protection guaranteed to clients through the agency's accountability to the public is not enough. A profession must provide its own accountability to the clients and consumers of service. Social work is not unique in terms of maintaining a dual identity as a profession and as employees of organizations. For example, teachers, nurses, engineers, architects, lawyers, and even doctors (if they are employed in an organization), all share the same duality. The employee status of the social worker does not in any way minimize his/her ethical responsibility.

A built-in regulative code compels ethical behavior on the part of its members. According to Ernest Greenwood, ethical codes are part formal and part informal.[3] He states that through its ethical code the profession's commitment to social welfare becomes a matter of public record, insuring for itself the continued sanction of the community. Professional codes are more explicit, binding, and systematic, possess more altruistic overtones, and are more public service oriented than nonprofessional codes.

There are two main areas of concern in professional behavior: the client-worker relationship and relationships among colleagues. Towards the client there must be emotional neutrality, and towards colleagues there must be cooperation, equality, support, the willingness to share knowledge and eliminate competition for clients. The practice of consulting and referral is also important because it involves professional colleagues in a system of reciprocity, which fosters mutual interdependence. Interdependence facilitates social control whereas chronic violation of professional etiquette arouses resentment among colleagues, often resulting in the cessation of consultation requests and referrals.

Social work as a profession raises many ethical and philosophical questions. There are not only practical, legal, and policy implications with which one must deal, but also situations, both within and outside the practice setting, that may lead the practitioner to violations in terms of ethical behavior. Therefore, procedures for handling these problems are essential to social work, and, as such, a particular code of ethics is often subscribed to as a central feature of professionalism.

Furthermore, professional codes of ethics are pertinent to the adjudication of grievances. A code of ethics provides the guidelines by which activities can be designed for handling complaints by and against the profession. For example, the N.A.S.W. has established procedures for handling grievances against members. These procedures are meant to "interpret the meaning of this code to the profession and the community, protect its members from irresponsible accusations of unethical conduct, and discipline those whose behavior is found to be in violation of the code on the basis of objective evidence weighed judiciously by peers." These procedures are also meant to provide "the machinery for unifying concepts of professional values through the examination of specific behavior in professional practice. Moreover, in a time when professions generally are under public scrutiny, it is increasingly important that members be held to high standards of professional conduct."[23] It is important that professions establish standards of ethical practice and enforce those standards to the best of their ability. It is only through such codes that the professional, the employer, the employing organization, and the public can be protected from harmful actions.

Before discussing enforcement procedures it is important to recognize some of the problems presented by codes of ethics. For example, although the specific statements of the N.A.S.W.'s code of ethics spell out the values of social work as they must be manifest in the social workers' professional behavior, in many instances there are conflicts between these principles. Many of these conflicts remain unresolved.

Problems and Issues in Social Work Ethics

The main problem inherent in social work ethics is that it is not a practical science and therefore few absolute standards can be

applied. Rather, social work ethics are based on a relative standard, taking into consideration the consciences of the client, the
social worker, the agency, and the cohesive factors of society.

A social worker must make decisions that are directly related to
ethics and from these decisions arise many conflicts. For example,
in discussing the role conflicts of many social workers, P. R. Day
notes that the profession is faced with difficult dilemmas in trying
to respond to confused and changing attitudes or expectations of
public policy.[24] Social workers have a dual allegiance as professional
people and as employees. Decisions about the needs of the individual and the welfare of the community raise complex issues
about the availability, perception, and communication of evidence.
Part of a social worker's dilemma arises when there are different
sources of authority with different interpretations of, and attitudes
toward, the evidence on which a decision is made. Because social
workers have knowledge of social conditions and injustice, they
cannot adopt a position of neutrality toward decisions adversely
affecting these issues.

Problems arise in regard to ethical decision making in other
areas as well. For example, F. Redlick and R. F. Mollica note that
with rare exceptions, psychiatric intervention can be morally justified only with the potential patient's informed consent.[25] Therefore decisions regarding medical ethics center around the right to
be treated, the right not to be treated, the civil rights of psychiatric
patients, the ethics of behavior control, the problem of conflicts of
interest in therapeutic goals, privacy, confidentiality, policy decisions, and the profession's relationship to the changing moral
value structure of society.

A study conducted at a large state hospital following a three-day
sick-call walkout by psychiatric aides suggests an example of ethical conflict requiring decision making. Findings reported by R. H.
Bohr, H. Brenner, and H. Caplan revealed that many social workers
and other hospital employees experienced severe conflict when
faced with the decision to provide for patients' immediate needs or
to join the strike, which might provide long-range benefits both to
patients and hospital personnel.[26] Significant variables included
the role and the age of the social worker. The study implies that
such ethical conflicts will become more of a problem for social

workers as traditional values clash with an emerging sophisticated awareness of how society's ills are caused and perpetuated.

The problems inherent in ethical decision making stem from the built-in conflict between ethical principles, and this inherent conflict is not new to the profession. In a close look at the history of morality in social work, Frederick Reamer suggests that concern with the morality of the needy can be traced to the formulation of the Elizabethan Poor Law in 1601 and the Poor Law Reform Bill in 1834.[27] Until the beginning of the Settlement House movement in the U.S. in 1886, the emphasis in social work was on the reasons the needy were morally inferior, irresponsible, unresourceful, and unambitious. Reamer states that in 1886 reform became more important and since the 1950s the major issues have centered on values considered central to the profession (i.e. client dignity and self-determination), and on the rules intended to serve as guides for social workers in dealing with their clients. This is where the main problem is today.

Contemporary social work ethics, Reamer states, have only the guiding principles set out by the N.A.S.W. There is no systematic outline that considers all the traditional issues as well as the ways in which moral philosophies have traditionally approached ethical questions. For example, the way in which an ethical principle should be selected in the first place concerns issues of metaethics. Reamer says further that the N.A.S.W. guidelines are based primarily on "practice wisdom" rather than on evidence available from research or from careful philosophical analysis. Practitioners, then, have traditionally been introduced to ethical values and principles as if their validity is self-evident. However, says Reamer, if ethical guidelines are to be adopted by practitioners, then they must be justified in a manner that is more compelling and persuasive than intuitionism. Values are not sacred simply because they have been asserted in the N.A.S.W. guide; they must be adequately justified.

Alan Keith-Lucas discussed some of the current ethical problems.[22] The degree of control social workers should exercise over their clients, for example, is one problem that has never been solved. Intrinsic to this notion is the idea of respect and right to self-determination, on the one hand, and the responsibility of the profession to prevent breakdown on the other. Keith-Lucas states that the pitfalls of the controversy are self-destructive behavior at one extreme and thought or behavior control at the other.

Another problem noted by Keith-Lucas is that of accountability. Though the profession generally accepts the notion of accountability, it is somewhat of an ethical quandry. The problem is summed up as follows: Should the profession be primarily accountable to its clients or to those (taxpayers and others) who foot the bill? Whose interests should be primary when disagreements occur? While the social worker might be desirous of being accountable to the client, society gives to the person who pays the bills the right to know how the money is being used.

Keith-Lucas further delineates the problems that are encountered when social workers assume advocacy roles. While recognizing the obligation to take an active interest in the problems of the powerless, the repressed, and dispossessed in society, the social work profession must remember that advocacy on the one hand generally means being an adversary on the other. When the issue revolves around a case of one party having denied the rights of another, the ethical nature of advocacy is clear. The problem enters in, says Keith-Lucas, when there are conflicting rights or when advocacy for one person or group means treating others without understanding or respect, or even with hostility. Then, the right of social work to align itself with certain segments of the population may legitimately be questioned.

Radical advocacy may also involve the social worker in conflicts with authority, jeopardizing either his own future as a social worker or his ability to continue to serve his clients with integrity.

Honesty, in terms of confidentiality, is often promised to clients when in fact their records are read by many. This might be done because it is seen as being for the client's own good or because the client is unable to face the reality of the situation. Other aspects of reality might also need to be concealed at times when another person's right to confidentiality is threatened.

Finally, a difficult ethical problem arises when the decision is to offer a service that falls short of what is really needed, on the grounds that poor service is better than none. Offering lesser quality may inhibit the development of a better service by placating the community or by diverting to others resources that are needed to give high quality service. However, if the service is not provided then needy people are left without assistance.

From this outline of conflict situations it can be seen that the development of a code of ethics is not the final solution to solving value and ethical dilemmas. In many cases the correct action depends on the particular situation. Thus, although the development of norms is important, the dynamics of the situation must not be forgotten. One method of approaching this problem might be the defining of what constitutes unethical behavior. For example, the ethical difference between lying to protect one's self-interest or the client's interests must be determined. Although the specific rules for determining unethical conduct are far from clear, they must evolve from practical experience—the case approach.

Charles Levy supports this ideal,[28] emphasizing that the social worker's ethical responsibility is strongly defined in the real-life situation. To understand the nature and extent of ethical responsibility and to identify guides to ethical conduct, the social work service situation should be scrutinized. Levy applies Weber's *ethics of responsibility*, which demand accountability for the foreseeable results of the practitioner's actions. From looking at the nature and components of the service situation it is possible to ascertain the implied professional obligations. The social work service situation includes everything between social work and the client in relation to that service plus all other acts and statements that pertain to or affect that service.

W. T. Stace, on the other hand, suggests a different perspective on the problem of defining ethical behavior.[29] He says social work has grown in a Christian civilization, that is, in a civilization evolving nearly 2,000 years on the soil of Christian monotheism. It is in this frame that all our moral ideas have their roots. Waves of religious scepticism have not seemed to alter this at all. The moral ideas of those who violently reject the dogmas of Christianity with their intellects are still Christian ideas. It is claimed that ethical absolutism is the product of Christian theology. For the absolutist there are two senses of the word *standard:* standards in the sense of sets of current moral ideas are relative and changeable, but the standard of what is actually morally right is absolute and unchanging. The absolutist makes a distinction between what actually is right and what is thought to be right. Therefore, though the problem of defining ethical behavior still exists in that one must decide what he/she thinks is right, the absolutist provides a framework for developing a universal code of ethics.

Monitoring and Enforcing Ethical Behavior

There are four routes that clients of a social agency can take in seeking redress for their complaints and grievances. The first is the ethical review board of a professional organization that handles formal complaints. Clients may also pursue a civil suit litigation through the courts; however, in this case they must be seeking compensation for damages. Furthermore, an informal representation to the social worker or to the social agency employing the worker may be made by the client. Where the agency in question is a government social service, clients may seek redress for their complaints through the Ombudsman's office where such a service is available.

In examining mechanisms that clients might use to seek redress, one must consider that the majority of clients of social service agencies are poor, inarticulate, ill-informed, and often under psychological and physical stress. Because of this, they are more likely to suffer in silence than to seek redress for any wrong done to them. They are already stigmatized and perhaps feel guilt or shame for using the services of a social agency. Clients may also feel very dependent on the social agency; thus, unless they have an advocate working on their behalf, they are not likely to make use of litigation. Therefore, the social worker's responsibility for monitoring and enforcing ethical behavior in order to maintain high ethical standards is especially critical.

The N.A.S.W. has outlined a number of procedures for the adjudication of grievances. Along with the code of ethics, it developed the *Standards for Social Work Personnel Practices*, which includes guidelines for the adjudication of grievances in the work place. It is hoped that the adjudication process will contribute to improved personnel practices. In addition, the Association has written *Procedures for the Adjudication of Grievances*, which provides that

... the chapter of which the complainant or respondent is a member has initial responsibility for jurisdiction over the complaint. It ensures that the procedures will be begun and the first judgments made by social work peers who know the culture of the community and the context in which the events precipitating the grievance have taken place. It also provides for the additional check and balance of an appeal process in two steps at the national level, where experienced members can view the matter with as much objectivity as possible. This guide is intended to compliment the official procedures by offering a rationale for the required steps in the adjudication process.[23]

The N.A.S.W. protects the public through its Committees of Inquiry. These committees provide a peer review of the ethical practice of its members, and thus offer a source of professional opinion about what constitutes ethical practice.

Finally, many social workers are members of unions that provide collective bargaining with both private and public employees. When an N.A.S.W. member is covered by a negotiated contract, the contract and its terms constitute legally enforceable conditions of work that take clear precedence over the voluntary process provided by N.A.S.W. Such contracts usually include procedures for handling grievances of employees; however, many of these mechanisms only cover grievances about working conditions, as opposed to ethical considerations. Therefore, ethical problems are covered by the N.A.S.W. adjudication procedures without contravening the rights of the union or the employer.

In a study of the N.A.S.W.'s procedures for handling charges of unethical conduct, an analysis was made of the 154 formal complaints of unethical behavior adjudicated by the Association between 1955 and 1977. Forty percent of all the complaints (ethical) over the twenty-two years were handled in 1976–77 alone. The central issues of firing, personnel practices, breach of contract, and policy-related issues comprised nearly 60 percent. Sixty-eight of the 154 complaints were rejected for failure to meet procedural requirements. Fifty-three percent of the complaints were brought by employees against their managers and 12 percent by managers against employees. Only 13 percent were brought by clients against social workers, with most of those occurring in the last five years. Sanctions were imposed in thirty-eight cases in which ethical violations were found.[30]

Professional Stress Due to Ethical Responsibilities

Social workers experience psychological stress due to ethical responsibilities in practice. If not resolved to one's personal standards and expectations, ethical problems can increase the stress level, causing a host of other problems. Social workers are increasingly recognizing the correlation between professional stress and ethical responsibility.

K. W. Watson believes that personal beliefs lie at the heart of social work, and that they are battered by the stress of the times.[31] He examines stress on three levels: the conspicuous, the dynamic, and the philosophical. The conspicuous is the obvious pressure due to the nature of the job, and the dynamic is related to the impact of clients' problems on social workers. The philosophical is based on the notion that social workers are increasingly feeling stress that can best be understood from a philosophical perspective. Watson maintains that professional social work roots lie in the religious-humanist conviction that man has value and that each has some degree of responsibility toward others. The dilemma is that although social work must rely increasingly on scientific method and technology to justify its value, in so doing this social work is moved a step further from the human values it espouses. Thus, much of the stress experienced by professional social workers is due to ethical responsibility.

CONCLUSION

The social work profession has come a long way in articulating its value base and in its efforts at formulating more precise ethical guidelines for practice. Social workers are developing greater consciousness about their own ethical professional behavior. They are examining ethical implications of decisions made in practice. This is happening in direct service to individuals, families, and groups, in work with communities, in policy and planning, and in social service administration. This is a very encouraging sign because without ethical foundation for practice social workers cannot insist on a claim that it is a true profession or command the respect of the society and clients they serve.

REFERENCES

1. Rokeach, M.: *The Nature of Human Values.* New York, The Free Press, 1973.
2. Siporin, M.: *Introduction to Social Work Practice.* New York, Macmillan, 1975.
3. Greenwood, E.: Attributes of a profession. In Weinberger, Paul (Ed.): *Perspective on Social Welfare: An Introductory Anthology.* New York, Macmillan, 1974, pp. 426ff.
4. Gordon, W. E.: Knowledge and value: Their distinction and relationship in clarifying social work practice. *Social Work, 10(3):* 32–39, 1965.
5. Pumphrey, M. W.: Transmitting values and ethics through social work practices. *Social Work, 6(3):*68–75, 1961.
6. Timms, N.: *Social Work: An Outline for the Intending Student.* London, Routledge and Kegan Paul, 1970.
7. Channon, G.: Value and professional social work: A field study. *Australian Social Work, 27(2):*5–14, 1974.
8. McLeod, D. and Meyer, H.: A study of values of social workers. In Thomas, E. (Ed.): *Behavioral Science for Social Workers.* New York, The Free Press, 1967, pp. 401–416.
9. Rosa, Linda: Personal and Advocated Values of Faculty Members. Unpublished independent study completed in the baccalaureate social work program. Syracuse, New York, Syracuse University, School of Social Work, April 1978.
10. Meyer, H., Litwack, E., and Warren, D.: Occupational and class differences in social values: A comparison of teachers and social workers. *Sociology of Education, 41(3),* 1968.
11. Gross, G. M., Rosa, L., and Steiner, J. R.: Educational doctrines and social work values: Match or mismatch? *Journal of Education for Social Work, 16(3):*21–28, 1980.
12. Levy, C. S.: Personal versus professional values: The practitioner's dilemmas. *Clinical Social Work Journal, 4(2):*110–120, 1976.
13. Lowy, L.: *Social Work With the Aging.* New York, Harper and Row, 1979.
14. Mamber, I.: Social work and The Prince. *Jewish Social Work Form, 14* (Spring): 82–96, 1978.
15. Miller, H.: Value dilemmas in social casework. In Glicken, M. (Ed.): *Toward Effective Social Work Practice.* New York, MSS Information Corporation, 1974.
16. Hardman, D. G.: Not with my daughter you don't. *Social Work, 20(4):*278–285, 1975.
17. Foot, H. C. and Russel-Lacy, S. P.: The imposition of values in social casework. *Social Casework, 54(9):*511–518, 1973.
18. Mills, C. W.: The professional ideology of social pathologist. In Horowitz, Irving (Ed.): *Power, Politics and People.* New York, Oxford Press, 1963.
19. Smalley, R. E.: *Theory of Social Work Practice.* New York, Columbia University Press, 1967.
20. Kleeck, Mary Van and Taylor, Graham R.: Professional organization of

social work. *The Annals of the American Academy of Political and Social Sciences, 101(190):*158–168, May 1922.

21. Lowenberg, Frank: Professional values and professional ethics in social work education. In Baer, Betty and Federico, Ronald (Eds.): *Educating the Baccalaureate Social Worker,* Cambridge, Mass., Ballinger Publishing Company, 1978, pp. 115–129.

22. Keith-Lucas, A.: Ethics in social work. *Encyclopedia of Social Work,* Washington, D. C., National Association of Social Workers, 1978, vol. 1, pp. 350–355.

23. *N.A.S.W. Chapter Guide for the Adjudication of Grievances: A Supplement to N.A.S.W. Procedures for the Adjudication of Grievances.* Washington, D.C., National Association of Social Workers, 1980.

24. Day, P. R.: Communication and social work roles. *Case Conference, 15(6):*239–242, 1968.

25. Redlick, F. and Mollica, R. F.: Overview: Ethical issues in contemporary psychiatry. *American Journal of Psychiatry, 133(2):*125–136, 1976.

26. Bohr, R. H., Brenner, H. I. and Kaplan, H. M.: Value conflicts in a hospital walkout. *Social Work, 16(4):*33–42, 1971.

27. Reamer, Frederic G.: Ethical content in social work. *Social Casework, 61(10):* November 1980.

28. Levy, C. S.: The context of social work ethics. *Social Work, 17(2):*95–101, 1972.

29. Stace, W. T.: The concepts of morals. In *Quest of Values: Readings in Philosophy and Personal Values.* San Francisco, Chandler Publishing Company, 1963, pp. 366–377.

30. McCann, Charles and Cutler, Jane Park: Ethics and the alleged unethical. *Social Work, 24(1):*5–8, January 1979.

31. Watson, K. W.: Social work stress and belief. *Child Welfare, 58(1):*3–12, 1979.

Part II

Clarification of Ethical and Value Conflicts in Social Work

Chapter 2

CLARIFYING ETHICAL CONFLICTS
THROUGH DECISION MAKING

ROBERT LITKE

INTRODUCTION

Decisions are based upon our preferences, and preferences are expressions of our needs, wants, inclinations, goals, ideals, etc. Decisions are rooted in our motivational and emotional functioning as well as in our intellects. Moreover, to a large extent, our motivational, emotional, *and* intellectual functioning does not require conscious effort on our part. The experience of competent adults is that we arrive at most decisions instantly or intuitively. We often cannot say immediately what considerations lead us to our decision, though we may have full confidence in it. The topic of this chapter, conflict in decision making, focuses on atypical cases, cases calling for conscious, deliberative, intellectual effort. It would be unfortunate if this mislead us into an overly intellectualized view of decision making.

To some extent at least, our preferences may be ranked in order of importance. Some are more comprehensive and others more fundamental in their contribution to the satisfaction of life. Each person has some conception of basic needs, which must be satisfied if a full human life is to be possible. For example, Maslow considers that persons have gratified all their basic needs only in the following case: "they have a feeling of belongingness and rootedness, they are satisfied in their love needs, have friends and feel loved and loveworthy, they have status and place in life and respect from other people, and they have a reasonable feeling of worth and self-respect."[1]

No doubt many would consider this a specification of "the good life," and focus more on physiological necessities and physical security when thinking about basic needs. What is clear is that individuals will have diverse views about the matter but everyone will have some conception about what is basic to the satisfactory conduct of his life. At the other end of things are a person's ultimate life goals.[2] These specify one's conception of what makes life worthwhile. Rokeach refers to these as terminal values and defines them as *preferred end-states of existence.*[3] Examples of terminal values are a comfortable life, family security, freedom, happiness, mature love, self-respect, wisdom.[3] In all, he proposes eighteen terminal values (the full list appears later in this chapter). Again, different individuals will probably have different clusters of ultimate life goals but everyone has some guiding conception. Together, basic needs and ultimate life goals would outline a person's vision of what makes life possible and worthwhile. These two sets of preferences are the most important ones: they function as the court of highest appeal when justifying decisions. For the most part we argue from them, not about them.

Bridging the gap between basic needs and ultimate life goals are various preferences, which can be seen as instrumental to achieving the latter. For example, Rokeach defines instrumental values as *preferred modes of behavior.*[3] The picture that emerges is this:

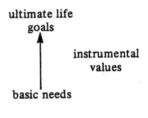

Structure 1

Much of the conflict experienced in decision making arises at the level of instrumental values.

For our lives to be satisfactory we need structure and direction. Without this we often would not know what to do; indeed, our lives would become impossible. Consider the case of a twenty-year-old man being brought into an emergency ward. He has been injured in a car accident and appears to be dying. Most of us would not know how to help this person. The emergency physician, on the other hand, has available a large number of procedures or techniques (modes of behavior). These would structure her behavior; they make a speedy and effective response possible. Furthermore, these procedures are employed in the pursuit of life and health. There is no question but to employ them immediately in the situation at hand. Our preference for life and health give direction to the physician's behavior. Now, what is true of the emergency ward is true of all life. Procedures or modes of behavior give structure to our lives and the associated beliefs about what is preferable serve to give us direction. Much of the time such preferred procedures allow us to achieve smooth efficiency in our response to the complex demands of life, which would otherwise not be possible.

On occasion, however, conflict arises. Suppose now that this same physician is called to another part of the hospital to treat an eighty-three-year-old woman who is apparently suffering from a heart attack. Suppose she is known to have had several heart attacks in the last two months and that she is in the hospital because she is dying from an unrelated painful terminal illness. To save her life is not to return her to health, as in the case of the car accident victim, but to return her to painful dying and perhaps subsequent heart attacks in the coming days. We would understand if the physician felt pulled both to save her life and to allow her to die. How should the physician proceed? Should she shorten suffering or prolong life? Both are worthy goals. In general, then, conflict is experienced when we are drawn to proceed in incompatible directions. The question in such cases is which preferences should be honored.

One of the functions of our intellect or reason is to devise techniques or procedures so as to more effectively pursue what our hearts desire, e.g. the complex array of current medical procedures. In this way we minimize failure in the pursuit of our preferences. Another function it serves is to help us determine what it is that we really do want in the face of conflicting wants— another way of minimizing failure. To do this our reason can devise what might be thought of as meta-procedures, i.e. procedures that help us decide which procedures to employ. That is what this chapter is about: decision-making procedures for cases of conflicting preferences. (Thus we may keep our supposition that all decisions come from the heart: it is reason's task to minimize failure in the pursuit of preferences by devising instrumental procedures of various kinds and levels.)

I suppose that one of the more important and interesting tasks we face in life is to put together an open-ended working model of ourselves-in-the-world that yields maximum satisfaction for us. (If that sounds like "narcissism of the seventies" or "unbridled egoism," I suggest that one read Bishop Butler's classic refutation of psychological egoism offered to the world in a sermon in 1726.) Such a model would consist of a coherent self-image and a coherent world-image telling us how we and the world are or should be. Additionally, it would contain complex sets of guidelines telling us how we should proceed in various contexts, given how we and the world are or should be. I would like to make several observations about such models.

First, each person must have his/her own working model and some idea of how it relates to those models others have. We differ from each other in important ways, e.g. in our conception of what makes life possible and worthwhile. It is foolish and sometimes catastrophic to adopt without thinking the model of someone else.

Second, the fact is that these models are predominantly covert. Little is immediately available to our conscious inspection unless we have taken the time to unearth this information. Watzlawick explains why this is so in terms of brain structure and hemispheric specialization.[4] Laing offers a parallel explanation in terms of rules and meta-rules and the processes of introjection and projection.[5] We are somewhat conscious of certain clusters of procedures to which our culture draws our explicit attention in various ways: rules of etiquette, codes of professional ethics, rules of morality, laws of the land, institutional regulations. Note that these are all instrumental values according to the scheme employed here and proposed by Rokeach. Presumably they have been devised by us to provide us with the structure and direction we need to better realize our ultimate life goals, whatever they are. Why else would we allow ourselves to be constrained by them? As we shall see shortly, they also can give rise to conflict.

Third, such a model calls upon and integrates the results of our emotional, motivational, and intellectual functioning. For example, values would be an important part of any such model. Rokeach points out that values have cognitive, affective, motivational, and behavioral components.[3]

Fourth, as we move into new areas of human experience we must work out fresh aspects of our working model so as to realize satisfaction in meeting the new demands we face there. This means being sensitive to our emotional system to see what it is that we want or need from the new settings, using our intellect to devise appropriate new procedures and to reorder priorities if necessary, and integrating all of this into our motivational system so that we can function effectively in the new settings.

To be very concrete, let us consider the situation of the fledgling social worker in a counselling agency. She or he must begin working out ways of functioning in the new setting that will be simultaneously sensitive to at least the following five sources of demand:

   (I) one's image of what it is to be a morally good person (private morality and public morality)
  (II) one's image of the competent therapist
 (III) one's conception of the good social worker (professional standards of competence and professional ethics)
 (IV) one's idea of being a responsible employee of the agency
  (V) one's image of being a good member of society (requirements of the law and good citizenship)

Each of these five items represents some aspect of what the person thinks is important and relevant to decision making in their new setting. Each embodies substantial preferences and so each is a source of constraint when trying to decide how to proceed. Thus, the new therapist must work out modes of behavior or ways of proceeding that will meet the multiple demands of each of these sources of constraint, for failure to do so spells failure. It will not be surprising then if the beginning social worker experiences conflict, being pulled to proceed in different directions. Even seasoned members of the profession (like the emergency physician) will occasionally be faced with cases which appear to demand that incompatible preferences be honored.

Such conflict is not to be shunned for it is an opportunity to work out a new corner of one's model of oneself-in-the-world. Impoverished models yield impoverished lives. I experience this in the lives of many of those who come to therapy. If this is true, then conflict should be welcomed; it is an opportunity to expand upon one's possibilities for a growing and satisfying life.

A DECISION-MAKING FORMAT

Whatever one's views about the nature or source of moral (or any other type of) obligation, it is in view of the expectable consequences of one's behavior that one should decide what to do. Moreover, this decision should be made in light of the known alternatives. Mature moral agents know full well that behavior is not to be judged good or bad in the abstract. It is to be assessed in light of what is or was possible in the concrete.

To be as concrete as possible, the following case will illustrate the steps in the decision-making format:

CASE STUDY:

You are the leader of an adolescent group in a counselling agency in a small town. It is being offered on a trial basis at your urging. Your perception was that the teenagers in the community were very badly equipped to deal with a number of serious problems they are currently facing. This has been corroborated by high school counsellors and by clergymen. Both the director of the agency and the chairman of the board have considerable misgivings about offering the group (these two pretty much determine which services the agency offers). One of their concerns is that the teenagers will not maintain confidentiality concerning what emerges in the group process. Since all group members come from the same small conservative community, this could be extremely embarrassing and possibly affect the level of financial support from the community, upon which your agency very much depends.

The group members also have some concerns. Most of them have espoused the belief that adults in positions of authority collude against them. The week before the group began, a physician told the parents of one of their friends that he was treating their son for venereal disease. The group members wonder whether you, as their leader, won't betray them as other adults have.

To build trust, you and all members of the group promised to maintain strict confidentiality. That done, Susan described how on two recent occasions her mother beat her when she was caught with marijuanna. She does have bruises on her face; you are inclined to believe her. Her mother is chairman of the board of your agency. You know the mother to be under very severe stress: her husband left her two weeks ago and the previous month her eldest son was sent to jail for drug trafficking.

In the wake of Susan's revelation, other members of the group started opening up, including Mary, one of the most troubled members. You have been told by a school counsellor (a) that Mary is pregnant, (b) that he was told this only after being sworn to secrecy by her, and (c) that she talked about running away or ending it all. Your hope is that Mary will eventually reveal her situation to the group or to you so that you can direct her to some individual counselling.

The law (in Ontario) is clear: you are required to report all suspected cases of child abuse to the proper authorities, in this case the Children's Aid Society. If you do not, you are subject to a fine of up to one thousand dollars. What should you do?

On the one hand, you promised to retain strict confidentiality, while on the other, the law requires that you make a report to the authorities. Now reporting this case may lead to the termination of the group by the agency or to the loss of group trust on the part of its members. In either event, the benefits of the group process will be lost or diminished for the present group members. We should not forget Mary and her unborn child. One should also think about those who would be denied help if future adolescent groups were not offered in the community because of this incident. Also, it would be unfortunate to jeopardize continuing financial support of the agency by creating or revealing a scandal concerning one of its most prominent members. Presumably such a loss would not only create a difficulty for agency staff but might well lead to a curtailment of services to the community at large. Of course, if it became public knowledge that one failed to comply with the law, that also may damage the reputation and support of the agency. What of the harm to Susan *and* her mother if the beatings did take place and if they continue in the months, perhaps years, to come? These are some of the initial pulls as reflection on the case begins.

I do not intend to examine all the complexities of this case in what follows. I leave that to the interested reader. I will simply draw on aspects of the case to illustrate how the decision-making format may be used. (The following format is drawn from presentations of Professor Rodney Allen,[6] Florida State University.)

Alternatives and Consequences

The first matter is to get a clear view of genuine options. All too often we put before ourselves two alternatives and then get locked into a simplistic either/or mind set. Discussion in small groups quickly generates a number of alternatives. By using one's imagination and by refusing to settle for just two choices, an individual can usually come up with a number of viable alternatives as well. The first question, then, is what are the main alternatives available?

Without trying to be complete, the following would seem to have some initial plausibility as alternatives:

A_1: You or the director simply make a report to the authorities.

A_2: You inform Susan that you or the director will be making a report to the authorities.

A_3: You explain the legal situation to Susan in the hope that she will release you from your promise of confidentiality.

A_4: You explain the whole matter to the group and let them decide what is to be done.

A_5: You lay everything before the director and let her decide what to do.

A_6: You do nothing at the present; you wait to see what develops.

A_7: You handle the matter internally; you insist that Susan and her mother come in for a joint session so as to determine whether there is a genuine problem of abuse.

The next matter is to determine what are the main expectable consequences of each alternative. These can be listed with each alternative:

A_2: (a) Susan will be upset and tell the other group members.

(b) The board and/or the director will terminate the adolescent group.

(c) The law will be complied with.

(d) It turns out that Susan's story was true; she and her mother receive needed help.

(e) It turns out that Susan's story was not true; needless embarrassment is suffered by all.

(n)

The same thing would be done with each of the other alternatives. Of course, consequences themselves have expectable consequences, and it is sometimes helpful to consider some of these as well:

A$_2$: (a) (i) Susan and/or other group members will accept your action when they understand the legal situation you were in.

(ii) They don't accept your action; the group stops functioning.

In turn, this latter consequence itself has the consequence that the likelihood of helping members of the group, including Mary with her pregnancy, is diminished. This is also a consequence of A$_2$(b). In schematic form we have this:

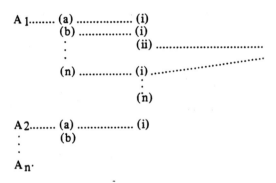

Alternatives	Consequences	Consequences of Consequences	Additional Consequences
A$_1$...... (a)	...... (i)		
(b)	...... (i)		
:		(ii)	
:			
(n)	...... (i)		
:			
(n)			
A$_2$...... (a)	...... (i)		
: (b)			
:			
A$_n$.			

Structure 2

I have used this type of decision-making format in classes in medical ethics for several years. One of the benefits is that it confronts us with the fact that we never know enough to make a completely informed decision. There are always alternatives that we did not think of; there will be consequences that we did not anticipate; of course, there are consequences of consequences of consequences . . . that are entirely beyond the reach of our knowledge. This should not, and indeed it does not, prevent us from making decisions and acting. The whole point of getting as clear as we can about alternatives and consequences is to minimize failure in the pursuit of our preferences. I expect that anyone who feels paralyzed by the lack of complete information has the mistaken view that reason *can* guarantee us success. It cannot. It can only help us eliminate known sources of failure. The first step in the decision-making format is to assemble what we know that is relevant to the case at hand. The best we can ever do is to act to the best of our knowledge.

Valuing

The second step is to bring our preferences to bear on what we know to be relevant. This is to be an undifferentiated judgment as to whether each consequence is desirable or not, without regard to the kind of preference being invoked. This information can be registered as a simple plus or minus following each consequence:

A_2 (a) Susan will be upset and tell other group members. $(-)$

   (b) The board and/or director will terminate the group. $(-)$

   (c) The law will be complied with. $(+)$

   (d) Susan and her mother will receive needed help. $(+)$

   (e) The story was false. $(-)$

Typically, each alternative will itself call conflicting preferences into play, i.e. have both pluses and minuses. We are accustomed to accepting disadvantages along with advantages when pursuing a line of conduct. Usually we know how to weigh the pros and cons. This format helps us get these clearly before us. What is more troublesome is deciding among several alternative lines of action where each has substantial advantages vis-à-vis each of the others. Again, what this format does is to clearly display the relevant information.

Candidate Decisions

In the light of the above information, you are now to decide which of the alternatives promise the best overall satisfaction of your preferences. This is not simply a matter of adding up pluses and minuses. Clearly, some consequences are far more weighty than others. By comparison, some will be seen to be just trivial.

It can happen at this point that a clear choice emerges. In fact, this is typically the case in normal experience. We do not find ourselves continuously facing serious conflict when deciding what to do. Sometimes interesting cases of ethical conflict do arise, however. In such cases two or more alternatives have substantial reasons for adopting them; to choose any one means sacrificing or ignoring important preferences. The next two steps in the decision-making format can help clarify how to decide in such cases. Even the case where a clear choice has emerged can benefit from the next two steps, for they help clarify how one could justify that choice. For the sake of illustration, let us suppose that the two most promising alternatives are these:

A_2: You inform Susan that you or the director will be making a report to the authorities.

A_6: You do nothing at the present; you wait to see what develops.

Instrumental Evaluation

To decide among substantial alternatives we have to look into their promise of satisfying important preferences. As noted in the chapter introduction, there are at least five sources of significant preferences at the instrumental level to which the social worker must be sensitive:

   (I) one's image of what it is to be a morally good person (private morality and public morality)
  (II) one's image of the competent therapist
 (III) one's conception of the good social worker (professional standards of competence and professional ethics)
 (IV) one's idea of being a responsible employee of the agency
  (V) one's image of being a good member of society (requirements of the law and good citizenship)

The task now is to see how each alternative meets these constraints. Here as before there is no claim to completeness.

A_2:I To inform the authorities without a release from Susan is to break a promise and to violate a trust, serious moral matters. On the other hand, it is to obey one's moral obligation to obey the law. If it turns out that Susan was telling the truth and if she and her mother receive help that prevents further abuse which would have otherwise occurred, then one has contributed to avoiding physical and psychological violence in this family and perhaps subsequent generations.

A_2:II As a counsellor your primary responsibility is to your clients. If making a report to the authorities results in the termination of the group by the agency or in irreparable damage to the group trust, you cannot serve your clients any longer. It appears that one has chosen to serve the law rather than them. On the other hand it may be that the Children's Aid Society can better help Susan (who is your client) and her mother than you could in the group context. It then appears that you have chosen to help Susan rather than the rest of the group, e.g. pregnant Mary.

A$_2$:III   In the codes of ethics of both the C.A.S.W. and the N.A.S.W., it is made absolutely clear that the social worker's primary responsibility is to clients (*see* Appendix B for copies of the codes). As we just saw in the previous paragraph, due regard for the law may mean disregarding the welfare of some of your clients. In addition to this, the N.A.S.W. code holds the social worker responsible to society in a more general way:

"The social worker should act to ensure that all persons have access to the resources, services, and opportunities which they require.

"The social worker should act to expand choice and opportunity for all persons, with special regard for disadvantaged or oppressed groups and persons."[7]

It would seem that you fulfilled these particular responsibilities by seeing to it that the adolescent group was offered to the community on a trial basis. If making a report to the authorities makes it unlikely that any other adolescent groups will be offered to the community in the near future, you have lost much and the code has been served badly.

A$_2$:IV   To inform the authorities is to conform to the law; as an employee, one has a responsibility to not embarrass the agency by illegal professional activity. However, telling the authorities may also result in diminished financial support; the agency may be seen as meddling in the private affairs of families. In turn, this may result in a curtailment of services to the community at large, which goes against the societal responsibilities of the social worker alluded to in the previous paragraph.

A$_2$:V   The purpose of the law concerning child abuse is the protection of children. The hope would be that informing the authorities about Susan's story would be conducive to

Susan's welfare (and that of her mother).

One then goes through the same kind of review for each of the other promising alternatives. Briefly, in the case of A_6, one would be seen to keep one's promises, respect the privacy of individuals, maintain group trust and retain the possibility of serving one's client well, break the law, run the risk of not preventing preventable physical abuse, etc.

It should be noted that there is no fixed order among the five sources of constraint as I conceive them. Clearly, some preferences are more weighty than others. It would not be safe to assume, however, that the preferences of any one of the five would always outweigh the preferences embodied in any of the others. These are five sources of simultaneous constraint and our task is to live creatively within this tension. It may be pictured thus:

Structure 3

This step of the decision-making format makes clearer for us which important preferences each main alternative satisfies and fails to satisfy at the level of instrumental values. It does not tell us which alternative to choose. That is left up to us. It only tells us what it appears we are likely to get in the way of satisfaction if we choose one or the other.

Final Evaluation

The last step in the format is an opportunity to bring our most important preferences to bear on each of the most promising alternatives—our basic needs and our ultimate life goals. These are the least public, the most personal, the most fundamental and comprehensive, and the least accessible of our preferences. Everyone has some conception of what makes a full human life possible and worthwhile; such information is predominantly covert unless one has made an effort to unearth it. In preparation for this final evaluation, then, each of us must become aware to some extent of our vision of life.

On the matter of basic needs, what do you conceive of as the necessary prerequisites to a full human life? One might usefully think about this from the perspective of Maslow's hierarchy of needs[8]:

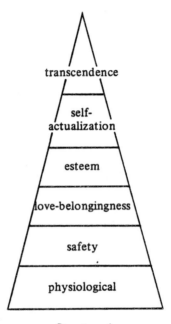

Structure 4

It is clear from the quotation in the chapter introduction that Maslow considered everything up to and including esteem as a basic need. What matters here is what *your* conception of basic needs includes. How far up the hierarchy does "basic" take you? What has Maslow left out in the way of particulars that informs how you think of basic human needs?

On the matter of becoming aware of one's ultimate life goals, Rokeach is helpful. As mentioned, he proposes eighteen terminal values (in alphabetical order):

A comfortable life (a prosperous life)
An exciting life (a stimulating, active life)
A sense of accomplishment (lasting contribution)
A world at peace (free of war and conflict)
A world of beauty (beauty of nature and the arts)
Equality (brotherhood, equal opportunity for all)
Family security (taking care of loved ones)
Freedom (independence, free choice)
Happiness (contentedness)
Inner harmony (freedom from inner conflict)
Mature love (sexual and spiritual intimacy)
National security (protection from attack)
Pleasure (an enjoyable, leisurely life)
Salvation (saved, eternal life)
Self-respect (self-esteem)
Social recognition (respect, admiration)
True friendship (close companionship)
Wisdom (a mature understanding of life)

Rokeach has used this list to ascertain the ultimate life goals of many hundreds of people from diverse socioeconomic and educational backgrounds. The accompanying instruction is simply this: "Your task is to arrange them in order of their importance to *YOU*, as guiding principles in *YOUR* life."[3] To become more aware of one's ultimate goals, I recommend that one spare a few minutes ranking their values. I have found this to be useful in my medical ethics classes. For the purposes of this final evaluation, we may consider the five or six most important values to represent your ultimate life goals.

The task now is to see the extent to which each of the most promising alternatives satisfies or disappoints your basic needs and ultimate life goals:

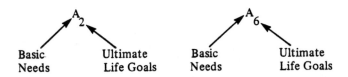

Basic   Ultimate   Basic   Ultimate
Needs   Life Goals   Needs   Life Goals

Structure 5

Steps 1 and 2	Alternatives	Consequences	Consequences of Consequences	Valuing
	A_1 . . . . .(a) . . . .(i)			(+/-)
	(b) . . . .(i)			(+/-)
	.		(ii)	(+/-)
	(n)		.	
			(n)	(+/-)
	A_2			
	.			
	A_n			

Step 3   **Candidate Decisions** The alternatives promising the best overall satisfaction of preferences are selected.
Suppose they are A_2 and A_6.

Step 4   **Instrumental Evaluation** A_2 and A_6 are assessed in light of the five sources of constraint on the social worker.

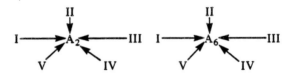

Step 5   **Final Evaluation** The most promising alternatives are assessed in light of basic needs and ultimate life goals.

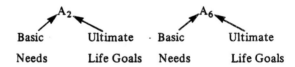

It remains for one to make a decision.

Figure 2-1. Schematic summary of the decision-making format.

As above, the format still does not tell us which alternative to choose. It only clarifies which preferences are likely to be satisfied if one or another choice is made.

This is as far as reason can take us. The outlined decision-making procedures have clarified to a considerable degree what we may expect in the way of satisfaction if we choose one or another alternative. It remains for us to decide what it is that we *want* in the face of all of this. This is a matter for the heart.

CONCLUSION

I have resisted to the very end bringing matters to a close, the closure of a forced decision. Some will find this disconcerting; others will welcome it.

Almost everywhere I turn I witness premature closures. Decisiveness itself has become a highly regarded virtue. We want decisions to be made so that we can get on with it; we are not much open to wonder about what *it* is or where we are getting *to*. The more I reflect on these matters the clearer it becomes that we need both closure and openness. Accordingly, I have emphasized what I think our culture has come to deemphasize, the human capacity for openness.

Step one of the decision-making format (*see* Fig. 2-1) encourages one to remain open to any relevant information about alternatives and consequences. There are natural limits to our knowledge and imagination, as well as on the time and energy we may devote to making any particular decision. We know this and so we must be prepared to act without perfect knowledge. We may regret that we do not know more than we do when a decision must be made; however, if we decide in light of the best of our knowledge at that time, there is no need for guilt for evils springing from innocent ignorance, nor is there any reason for remaining ignorant. We can learn from unfortunate consequences if we will face them. Being decisive on one occasion does not mean that we must be closed-minded concerning new information, information that might make for a more satisfactory decision the next time we face a similar situation.

Step four reminds us that there are very diverse kinds of (instrumental) preferences simultaneously pulling on a social worker. It is unlikely that there would be unanimity on the matter of which kinds of preference outweigh the other kinds. For example, some would hold our legal responsibilities to be paramount. Others would argue that moral responsibilities are overriding. Still others would hold that one's professional responsibility to serve the well-being of the client surpasses moral and legal obligations. Tolerance for diversity on the matter of how to weigh preferences at the instrumental level is called for. I think we should respect fellow decision makers who conscientiously organize themselves at the level of instrumental values in ways that differ from our ways.

At the level of ultimate life goals and basic needs, we may anticipate even greater diversity. The fact is that people have substantially different visions of what makes life possible and worthwhile. This is evident *within* families if one looks carefully; everyone sees it in contrasting ethnic groups and cultures. It is noteworthy that the codes of professional ethics for both the C.A.S.W. and the N.A.S.W. emphasize the following:

(1) the worth, dignity, and uniqueness of all persons,
(2) the importance of maximum self-determination,
(3) an absolute prohibition of discriminatory behavior.

Thus, it is required at the instrumental level that clients with diverse conceptions of basic needs and ultimate life goals be accorded respect. Step five invites the social worker making decisions about clients to pay the same high regard to his/her own views about basic needs and ultimate life goals. In addition, by not laying down specific guidelines for the final evaluation, step five reminds us that we must be prepared to be respectful and tolerant of considerable diversity among fellow decision makers at the level of basic needs and ultimate life goals. There is no basis for dogmatism at the level of the final evaluation.

When one adopts or maintains preferences at the level of basic needs and ultimate life goals, one is choosing what kind of person he/she wants to be and what kind of world or society one wants to live in. It is not that one cannot make mistakes in making such choices. It appears that people do make serious mistakes in these matters: their choices yield them lives with little or no satisfaction. The crux of the matter is that there is almost no room for useful argument about such things.[2,9]

As mentioned in the chapter introduction, basic needs and ultimate life goals constitute the court of highest appeal when justifying decisions: we usually argue from them, not about them. However, when thinking *about* these kinds of preferences we should shift from the metaphor of the court to that of the laboratory: *choosing basic needs and ultimate life goals is more like conducting an experiment with one's life than it is like arguing a case before a judge.* Whether one does it with any consciousness, and whether one chooses or maintains one of the prepackaged visions of life offered by one's culture or one pieces together her/his own way of life from diverse sources, the fact is that one is offering up the resources and possibilities of one's life to that vision, at least for a time. In the face of such an important commitment, a kind of gentle openness and respect is appropriate, not dogmatic criticism.

As mentioned above, this business of models or visions of life is mostly below the surface: most of us choose and maintain our vision of life without much conscious awareness. Those who conduct their experiment with some measure of consciousness and those who are of a mind to carry out several such experiments in the course of their life are especially deserving of our encouragement and thanks: it is from them that we are most likely to learn how to live well. However, such conscious experimentation with life can only flourish in a climate of openness to diversity. My hope is that someday we may come to celebrate our capacity for openness rather than meet it with fear and punishment.

REFERENCES

1. Maslow, A.: *The Farther Reaches of Human Nature.* New York, Penguin Books, 1976, p. 289.
2. Beck, C.: *Ethics.* Toronto, McGraw-Hill Ryerson Ltd., 1972, ch. 4.
3. Rokeach, M.: *The Nature of Human Values.* New York, The Free Press, 1973.
4. Watzlawick, P.: *The Language of Change.* New York, Basic Books, 1978.
5. Laing, R. D.: *The Politics of the Family.* Toronto, Canadian Broadcasting Corporation, 1969.
6. Allen, R.: But the earth abideth forever. In Meyer, J. et al. (Eds.): *Values Education.* Waterloo, Wilfrid Laurier University Press.
7. N.A.S.W. Code of Ethics, section VI, paragraphs 2 and 3.
8. Roberts, T.: Beyond self-actualization. *Re-vision,* 1(1):
9. Hare, R.: *Freedom and Reason.* New York, Oxford University Press, 1963, Ch. 8.

Chapter 3

CLARIFYING "VALUE CONFLICTS" IN SOCIAL WORK PRACTICE

SHANKAR A. YELAJA AND JAMES GOUGH

INTRODUCTION

Values are an integral part of the social work profession. Social work intervention, both implicitly and explicity, is predicated upon values. The goals and objectives of the social work profession are also derived from values. The profession through its code of ethics has committed itself to a set of values that are intrinsically valuable or desirable for the profession. These value statements are addressed to the relative worth, utility, or importance and to the degree of excellence in the value system espoused by members of the profession. However, there are conflicts in the value system. Value conflicts and dilemmas occur in almost every sphere of social work practice. Clarification of these conflicts is a useful and creative exercise. It can, hopefully, result in better understanding of the conflict and lead the way toward resolution.

The focus of this chapter is on value conflicts and dilemmas that social workers experience in their practice. An examination is made of current approaches to value clarification. An alternate approach, called universal ethical standards, is discussed with supporting arguments. The underlying thesis of this paper is that value and ethical conflicts in social work practice are unavoidable; however, clarification of the conflicts is a useful, creative, and growth-producing experience.

VALUE CONFLICTS DEFINED

A conflict, according to Webster's dictionary, is "a disagreement ... (an) emotional tension resulting from incompatible inner needs or desires ... the opposition of persons or forces that give rise to the dramatic action. . . . "[1] A conflict suggests that there are irreconcilable or antagonistic points of view and/or positions resulting in a discord. Conflicts in values occur because of intrinsic differences. They produce a degree of conflict because one is required to choose from a set of alternative points of view.

According to Milton Rokeach, a value "is an enduring belief that a specific mode of conduct or end-state of existence is personally or socially preferable to an opposite or converse mode of conduct or end-state of existence."[2] Furthermore, a value system is " . . . an enduring organization of beliefs concerning preferable modes of conduct or end-states of existence along a continuum of relative importance."[2] It is important to emphasize here that the term preferable is employed as a predicate adjective (and not as a noun), specifying that "something is preferable to something else."[2] There is a choice to be made and the act of choosing and deciding upon that choice inherently invites a process of conflict. After the completion of this process, one makes the decision as to appropriate or preferred values.

FUNCTIONS OF VALUES AND CONFLICT RESOLUTION

What is the function of values? Values serve as standards that guide ongoing activities; value systems serve as general plans employed to resolve conflicts and to make decisions. Milton Rokeach identifies seven functions of values: They (1) lead us to take particular positions on social issues and (2) predispose us to favor one particular ideology over another. They are standards employed (3) to guide presentations of the self to others and (4) to evaluate and judge, to hold promise and fix blame on ourselves and others. (5) Values are central to the study of comparison process; (6) they are standards employed to persuade and influence others; (7) they are standards that inform us how to rationalize, in the psychoanalytic sense, beliefs, attitudes, and actions that would otherwise be personally and socially unacceptable so that we will end up with personal feelings of morality and competence—both indispensable elements for maintaining and enhancing self-esteem.[2] For social workers, then, values embodied in professional ethical codes serve as standards for conflict resolution and decision making.

Social workers are required to make value judgments and

decisions. In any given situation several values are activated, requiring a social worker to choose between alternatives, to resolve conflicts, and to make decisions. The heart of the decision-making process in social work practice, therefore, is the value choices the social worker must make.

Alan Keith-Lucas states that, generally speaking, there are two kinds of situations in which a social worker or a social agency is called upon to consider value conflicts and ethical implications arising out of a given conflict:

> ... the first situation involves a choice between one course of action that has been declared or accepted as good, moral, or correct and another that is of the opposite nature. Here the only ethical problem is to determine whether the action to be taken does in fact have this nature. Once this is clear, the right decision becomes obvious.
>
> Much more difficult and numerous, however, are decisions that have to be made between two courses of action both of which are potentially good, although perhaps in different circumstances. A choice might also lie between two contradictory goods that cannot both be attained. Here one immediately is involved not in distinguishing between good and bad, but between a greater and a lesser good, about which there is likely to be much more disagreement.
>
> The first kind of decision, which might be called "good-bad" is the only kind that can be controlled to any extent by a [professional] code of ethics. And even then, as students of ethical codes have discovered, conflicting values are sometimes present.... [3]

Thus, conflicting values are clearly evident in any decision-making process by a social worker or a social agency. To escape from a value conflict in social work practice is to deny its existence.

SOCIAL WORK RESPONSE TO VALUE CONFLICTS

If value conflicts and dilemmas are inherent in day-to-day practice, how have social workers dealt with them? It is useful to consider the traditional social work response in order to understand why the present approach and response is not very helpful in resolving value conflicts. Traditionally, social workers have approached value conflicts and their resolution in the following three ways: (1) social work values are considered absolutes and therefore moralizing about them (right-wrong etc.) is seen as a useful response to conflict resolution; (2) benevolent manipulation of values occurs in the belief that social work can do no harm;

and, (3) a modeling behavior is presented whereby social workers attempt to personify the values. None of these methods have proved to be satisfactory; quite the contrary, they have polluted the process of value clarifica ion by confusing means and ends.

For a long time social workers have operated on the belief that values are absolutes and that it was their duty to uphold them in practice. Educators taught these values to students; social agency supervisors disseminated them to beginning practitioners, thus continuing the cycle of unquestionable allegiance to social work values. Textbooks on social work stressed the absolute nature of these values. For example, Florence Hollis writes in her social casework text that "from its inception casework has stressed the value of the individual, and for the past forty years, at least, has constantly emphasized the right of each man to live in his own unique way, provided he does not infringe unduly upon the right of others. This emphasis upon the innate worth of the individual is an extremely important, fundamental characteristic of casework "[4] She further states that this value is fundamental in helping to establish relationships, which are so essential for effective treat- ment. From it grow two additional value subsets: acceptance of the client and respect for the client's right to make his own decisions, often referred to as self-determination [4]

These values in casework have remained as principles of good and effective casework practice. The method of communicating them to future practitioners was one of encoding them. However, indoctrination can be a dangerous roadblock to communication. Social workers wishing critically to examine the value base of casework practice need to go beyond the absolutes and explore the situations where absolutes fail. Indoctrination is also confusing. Social workers represent a vast array of differences in their per- sonal and professional values stemming from a variety of sources (we shall be looking at these later). Indoctrina ion, in itself, is not of much help in value conflict resoluti n

Another approach to conflict resolution social workers have used in the past is benevolent manipulation. In situations where they had to impose their own values on clients, they justified this by rationalizing that it was in the client's best interest; or, the clients failed to make use of the alternatives and choices so intervention was justified. In other cases, the choices were either spurious or limited. In fewer cases, clients were manipulated with rewards and/or punishments. The manipulation was always considered as benevolent, for it was not meant to enhance the self-gratification of the social worker. The welfare and best interest of the client were regarded as the primary objective.

Benevolent manipulation, though effective in the short run, does not help social workers in the long run because of its failure to help them acquire a critical, inquiring mind. Social workers have had limited success in developing an approach to value conflicts without necessarily manipulating their clients. Solutions to value conflicts have proved to be temporary. These could not be translated to other practice situations involving value conflicts.

Modeling behavior has also turned out to be of limited value. Social workers attempted to model their own personal behavior on the basis of absolute values the profession espoused. Social workers, especially those in power and authority, have attempted to act as ideal agents whose behavior would exemplify a desirable approach to value clarification. Being human, and thus less than perfect, social workers do not always set the ideal moral example, nor can they, as individuals, be free from value conflicts themselves. Thus, this approach to conflict resolution has not worked. It has brought into sharp focus contradictions, anomalies, and paradoxes in the private and public behavior of social workers.

VALUE CONFLICTS IN SOCIAL WORK PRACTICE

Let us now turn to the types of value conflicts social workers are confronted with in their practice. These are categorized on the basis of personal values; professional values; social agency values legitimated in goals, objectives, and methods of operation; societal values legitimated in public laws; and client values. Thus, value conflicts arise in the process of interaction of one or more of these values. A detailed consideration of the nature of value conflict follows.

Conflict Between Personal Values and Social Agency Values

A conflict between personal and agency values may occur from a number of sources: (1) personal values of the social worker may collide with the values of the agency; (2) personal values may collide with values of the worker's immediate supervisor in the agency; (3) personal values may collide with dominant values of a peer group in the agency; and (4) a personal value conflict may arise because of some peculiar individual circumstances of the social worker beyond his/her control.

The personal values of the social worker are always present. Social workers are not robots; because they are individual human beings with unique value systems of their own, there are bound to be occasions when these will come into conflict with agency values. For example, a female social worker has a strong favorable disposition towards the right of women to make independent decisions concerning abortion, whereas the agency, the Department of Social Services in a hospital, is mandated—before any decision is made—to give ample opportunity for input by others concerned, including the father of the unborn child. The agency policy, then, is to require social workers to involve not only the woman seeking the abortion but also others directly affected by the chosen course of action. A conflict is inevitable as long as the social worker has not reconciled his/her personal values with those of the agency.

Values of the immediate supervisor are just as important as the personal values held by the social worker. Supervisors have both formal and informal authority: formal authority derived from their hierarchical position in the agency and informal authority and/or power legitimated through superior experience, practical wisdom, knowledge, etc. Values held by supervisors may or may not be in concert with agency values. Research studies on managerial values point to the significant conclusion that supervisors holding managerial responsibilities may hold values different from those values legitimized in policies. For example, social agency policy and its implicit value states that social workers should preserve the family unit and only as a last resort, when all other measures fail, remove a child from parental care and custody and place it in the agency's receiving home pending family court action. The agency's value is clear. Family sanctity ought to be maintained, for it is in the best interest of the child. However, there could be disagreement on which approach would serve the best interests of the child. The supervisor responsible for ongoing supervision of the field social worker, if he/she does not accept the policy, may exercise overt as well as covert pressure on the social worker to act according to the values of the supervisor. A social worker, then, may find himself/herself pulled in three directions: the agency values regarding family, the supervisor's value notion and interpretation of the best interests of the child, and personal values, which may differ from both the agency and the immediate supervisor. A conflict in values around the role of the family, the best interests of the child, and societal responsibility toward the child and the family would occur because of varying value interpretations and differences in preferred courses of action to be followed.

A social agency is a living organism of individuals with varying personalities, backgrounds, cultures, and norms. In any organization, peer groups are formed around common interests. Common value preferences are one of the bases of peer group formation. When social workers in a given agency share common values and have established mechanisms for influence, then value conflicts can easily ensue. This phenomenon was clearly evident during the 1960s when peer groups in social agencies were instrumental in exercising influence and even control over their fellow social workers, so much so that those social workers who felt either pressured or intimidated by their peer-group activities often had to decide whether it was worthwhile to continue to fight for their beliefs and commitments, or whether to leave the agency. The tyranny of peer groups in pushing their own values and the ensuing conflict was all too familiar during the 1960s and early seventies. The influence of peer groups on values has not vanished nor has it been lessened. Peer groups do not deliberately polarize conflicts, but when an individual social worker's values differ from those of the peer group, conflict is unavoidable.

An individual social worker might experience value conflicts arising from peculiar, personal circumstances. These may range from profoundly new personal experiences resulting in a new value orientation, critical encounters with one's values, questioning of one's past values, changing life-styles and consequent value implications, value changes and effects resulting from therapeutic experiences, and the loss of significant members of one's family or friends. All of these situations inevitably produce and result in a personal experience that takes a heavy toll in one's own values. Beliefs change, existing values come under intense scrutiny, questioning of long-held values occurs, and commitments to values are examined.

For some social workers, awareness of the value orientation and change occurs through their work with clients in counseling and therapeutic situations. Although social workers may be unconsciously experiencing these value conflicts, they do not become consciously aware of them until they come into contact with similar situations in their work with clients. It is, therefore, possible to argue that a counter-transference phenomenon in values occurs in the lives of social workers, but this is not without a process of conflict. Value conflicts accompany transference and new values are either accepted or rejected.

For still others, a personal value conflict is mirrored in a particular social agency policy. Tacit acceptance of agency values gives way to critical examination when a social worker is undergoing a profound value change in his/her personal life. The agency value serves as a launching pad for value conflicts to surface and take off in a higher direction. Here again, a social worker's personal values or value system might come in collision with the agency's values.

Value Conflicts Arising Out of the Professional Ethical Code

The primary function of the social work ethical code is twofold: (1) to serve as a guide to the everyday conduct of social workers and (2) to serve as a basis for the adjudication of issues in ethics when the conduct of social workers is alleged to deviate from the standards expressed or implied in the code. The code, therefore, represents standards of ethical behavior and a viable means for resolving value conflicts. The social work code of ethics is based on certain fundamental values respected by the profession.

The problem, however, is that various principles in the code in themselves can create value conflicts. This is a rather ironic situation because, on the one hand, the ethical code is created for easing value conflicts and setting standards; on the other hand, there are elements in the code itself that can and do cause conflict. For example, the National Association of Social Workers' current code of ethics emphasizes the social worker's ethical responsibility to society. It, therefore, expects that the social worker should promote the general welfare of society. By the same standards, the code is emphatic with respect to the social worker's ethical responsibility to clients. It requires, therefore, that the social worker "should make every effort to foster maximum self-determination on the part of clients . . . ."5; furthermore, "the social worker should respect the privacy of clients and hold in confidence all information obtained in the course of professional service."5

These two provisions of the code, one dealing with the general welfare of society and the other with rights and prerogatives of clients for self-determination as well as the right to confidentiality and privacy, collide with each other. How can both principles be equally upheld in practice? There may be occasions when clients' rights and prerogatives may have to be supplanted or sacrificed for the sake of promoting general societal welfare. These principles collide with each other on numerous occasions in social work practice. A social worker must inevitably decide which principle should be upheld in a particular situation and context and which principle is expendable and under what mitigating circumstances.

Revisions to the ethical code in the form of commentary and specificity still do not ease or resolve the conflict. Perhaps one way of dealing with this paradox is to rank various principles. Ranking principles in the ethical code would help provide specific guidelines to social workers in making decisions in their daily practice situations. It is inconceivable that, given the current social work diversity, the profession is ready to address these fundamental, complex issues, which touch very deeply at the very core of the objectives and goals of social work. The profession simply is unable to reach a consensus on these issues. Continuing debate on the relative worth of the principles is certainly desirable, but the prospect of arriving at a reasonable consensus appears grim.

In the absence of general rules provided for in the ethical code, social workers are required to make their own decisions as to which principle should or ought to receive priority. These decisions obviously are influenced by the value system or preferences of the individual social worker.

Close scrutiny and examination of current ethical codes adopted by social work associations reveal that the codes do not provide specific rules of guidance concerning the client-therapist relationship. Historically, ethical codes for the therapist were drawn up to protect the profession from regulation by external agencies. Implicit in the official codes, however, is a model for the client-therapist relationship that fosters the goals of mental health. Given the lack of specific rules for decision making, social workers acting as therapists must rely on their individual judgments for the protection of client rights. These rights are an integral part of every therapeutic strategy interaction and plan of treatment pursued by social workers. When client rights are to be protected, decisions such as these must be made: providing clients with information to make informed decisions about theories using contracts in therapy, responding to clients' challenges to therapists' competence, and handling clients' complaints. These decisions often cannot be made without an intense value conflict.

Conflict Between Personal and Professional Values

Conflicts in values arise when there are differences in beliefs and attitudes between what is considered professionally desirable and important and a social worker's opposition to this stance. Advocacy is one such area where the conflict can be readily identified and understood. During the 1960s and seventies, advocacy was accepted by some as a major social work value. It gained professional acceptance because it was widely practiced by social workers. It does, however, raise value conflicts for a social worker who disagrees with its acceptance and use within the profession.

For a long time social work has recognized its obligation to defend the rights of those who are oppressed or dispossessed. Advocacy, by definition, means pleading in support of a cause or interest. An advocate, therefore, espouses and speaks for a case or cause. When others differ and disagree with the reasons put forth by an advocate, an adversary process/procedure might ensue, resulting in a conflict. If it is a simple matter of the denial of a right to one party and the recognition of that denial by the other party, there are no problems. Advocacy in this case is relatively simple. However, when there are conflicting rights or when advocacy of one person or group means treating other people without understanding and human respect or in violent, hostile ways, the right of the social work profession to align itself with selective segments of the population raises ethical questions.[3] Problems also arise when advocacy for one group means denial of the basic rights and privileges of others.

Furthermore, some acts of advocacy may involve a conflict with authority, violation of public laws, dishonest behavior, etc. These means, too, may be rationalized as justified in order to achieve the end dictated by the cause of advocacy.[3] For an individual social worker who is uncertain and wishes to raise ethical questions about the concept of advocacy, there is bound to be a conflict before a decision is reached as to whether or not one should go along with advocacy.

The potential for value conflict may arise when social workers are confronted with discrimination issues in their work. Discrimination can occur on a number of grounds including racial background, ethnic origin, sex, age, religious beliefs, and ideological preference. Legislation to protect the individual's right against discrimination by employers exists in both federal and provincial statutes. New grounds of discrimination are being added constantly. For example, proposed amendments to the Ontario Human Rights Code include provisions for sexual harassment and discrimination on the basis of age. Still, a conflict can arise when a social worker is a victim of discrimination, which may be either subtle or blatant. Blatant acts of discrimination can be brought before the legislative and enforcement bodies for redress. However, acts of subtle discrimination are difficult to prove. In either case the social worker will experience serious conflicts in terms of what action to take. There are costs and benefits to whatever choice one makes in seeking redress for discrimination.

When a social worker suspects that clients of social agencies are discriminated against and has reasonable evidence to take further action, he/she is confronted with yet another value conflict. A choice has to be made from a number of alternatives, each of which has its own consequences and implications. These alternatives may range from doing nothing to acting as advocate on behalf of the client's rights. Past experience has demonstrated, however, that when social workers are acting as advocates for client discrimination issues, an adversary relationship quickly ensues. The motives of each party in the dispute become suspect, hostility develops, and the quality of service is affected. The psychological as well as other tangible costs of advocacy for discrimination must be weighed in terms of benefits. Some social agencies are totally paralyzed when litigation continues, others recover but only after paying heavy costs in personnel changes, and still others are closed down because of a lack of community trust. Value conflicts in acting or not acting on behalf of clients experiencing discrimination have ramifications and consequences that may be beyond the control of a social worker. This makes a clear resolution of the conflict even more difficult.

Conflict Between Personal and Local Community Values

Recent experiences in local community politics have brought a greater awareness of both potential and real areas for conflict when personal values collide with local community values. Social workers are caught between opposing demands. For example, a social worker genuinely believes in contributing to local United Fund drives and has done so for many years. His personal beliefs and, therefore, values come into conflict when it is discovered that a few social agencies receiving financial support from the funds are failing in their attempts to control the quality of service, but the United Fund is unable to take any corrective measures. If the social worker stops contributing and campaigns for others to do likewise, the agencies could be closed, resulting in the denial of service. Some local politicians and social workers have argued that some service is better than no service at all. The social worker, then, must decide whether it is worthwhile to stop contributing to the United Fund or to continue to do so in the hope of future improvement in the quality of service.

Still, a conflict can arise when the social worker and, for that matter, the general public finds out that agencies receiving United Fund money are not fulfilling their mandate for accountability. Stopping financial contributions altogether might force the issue out in the open, but it may also prove perilous in terms of unanticipated or unforeseen consequences for local community social agencies. Furthermore, social workers might find that their own jobs are in jeopardy if such issues are pursued to their ultimate end.

Conflict Between Personal and Societal Values

Societal values are legitimated through public laws. A conflict is certain when social workers are in charge of implementing laws in contradiction with their personal value systems. This value conflict is nowhere more apparent than in work with involuntary clients and in social work practice involving authority and control over clients. Still another occasion when conflicts are severe occurs when social workers are required to act in order to fulfill obligations imposed by legislative and/or bureaucratic mandates.

Value conflicts and dilemmas arising out of social work activities with involuntary clients have received considerable attention in the literature.[6-9] Social work intervention with involuntary clients who either have not asked for social work service or who are unable to give their rational, informed consent has been justified on the grounds that some degree of coercion is inevitable in society and that no right is absolutely given. The social work profession has assumed, albeit not without considerable controversy, the role of performing as an agent of social control for the "deviant" members of society.

There are numerous court decisions in the U.S.A. and Canada that rule on the state's right to assign individuals to involuntary therapy or hospitalization on grounds justifiable under the law. Social workers employed in correctional service agencies, mental health service agencies, child protective services, drug addiction treatment facilities, etc., have justified the use of coercion as a necessary element in the treatment or rehabilitation of their clients. Value conflicts occur, however, when social workers become aware of the abuse, both potential and real, inflicted upon their clients under accepted social norms and conditions. Some therapeutic procedures have led to greater harm than good; some have resulted in inflicting undue pain and stress and even causing irreparable damage in some cases. However, the fact that successful treatment and/or positive gains in rehabilitation have occurred for some clients cannot be denied. The essential problem for social workers dealing with involuntary clients is to gauge and carefully weigh the positive benefits against the risks involved. Social workers often find themselves in a double bind when working with a captive client population.

The social worker's personal values, including those of his own social class, culture, ethnic group, religion, and ideology enter into his professional judgments and decision making in every practice situation and context. The influence of these values occurs in counseling relationships, therapy, community work, social planning, policy analysis, and administration. An artificial separation of facts and values in the past has led to a deemphasis of the influence of values in social work practice. Certainly a mature and experienced social worker has learned to handle the value conflicts in a responsible way. Conscious attempts are made, for instance, at not translating personal values into treatment goals for clients or legitimizing them into social agency policies.

There is some empirical evidence to suggest that value conflicts, if unresolved, may have a deleterious impact on social workers' morale and performance.[10-13] Low morale, lowering of productivity and early burn-out seem to correlate with a continuing state of conflict.[14] Psychological effects of unresolved conflicts also seem to occur in social workers who are experiencing confusion and frustration. Thus, the very effectiveness of professional service is endangered as a result of unresolved conflict situations in practice.

Moral and value conflicts are endemic in social work practice. These cannot be resolved into a single set of principles with enduring application or utility for conflict resolution. What is required is a method of approaching value conflicts so that these can be clarified and better understood. Ethical principles that are capable of providing guidelines can be much more productive as well as effective in clarifying conflicts. We shall now turn our attention to a value clarification approach.

CLARIFYING VALUE/ETHICAL CONFLICTS: AN APPROACH

When faced with deciding what approach to take in resolving ethical conflict situations, the professional social worker's choice is complicated. To make a considered choice, he/she is required to take account of his/her own ethical standards, the ethical standards of the profession, the standards embodied in the group or agency to which he/she is attached, the normative standards in society, the standards embodied in the law of the land, and finally the standards of the client in whose interests the social worker is acting. Obviously, this situation offers several possibilities for conflict between ethical standards. Not every situation will involve a conflict between all of these standards. In some cases, a conflict may arise as the result of a considered appraisal of the standards of the client and the law of the land or between the social worker's own standards and those of the social service agency. It seems necessary to aim for some sort of stability in this potentially chaotic situation. In many cases, the responsibility for arriving at the ultimate decision rests with the social worker.

How a professional social worker confronts and deals with ethical conflict situations is a function of how well he/she has thought through the implications of his/her overall approach to these problems. The N.A.S.W. Code of Ethics sets out some standards of conduct, but these general guidelines are not intended to provide determinate resolutions to particular ethical conflict situations. This guide does not, by itself, provide us with the necessary methods, procedures, or approach for dealing with individual situations. The resolution of individual conflict situations takes place at the personal level between the professional social worker and the client/agency/society/law of the land. Many ethical problems *require* a solution; consequently, any waffling on a determinate resolution of the situation counts against those professionals in a position to effect such a resolution. Abdication of one's responsibility as a professional social worker to make a choice where one is required can sometimes be as bad as making the wrong choice. In most ethical conflict situations, a no comment/no opinion approach is *not* the maintaining of some value-neutrality objective observer position but rather a copping out. **Principle #1:** In most moral conflict situations a considered, determinate resolution of the conflict should be sought by all parties concerned, including the professional social worker.

Obviously, the first problem we encounter is how to go about resolving or attempting to deal with the dispute or conflict.

It is important, from the outset, that we decide upon the best possible strategy or approach for dealing with the problem since an approach that is too superficial will likely yield an indeterminate solution. This is not unlike the problems associated with scientific experimentation. In designing an experiment that encapsulates an approach to the subject area, we seek out means which will best guarantee that the results will not be indeterminate or superficial. We are careful about the constitution of the control group, the control of experimentally relevant variables, etc. The same applies to approaches taken to resolve the ethical conflict situations. **Principle #2:** The best possible way to arrive at a viable resolution to an ethical conflict situation is to select an approach that will best guarantee a determinate and nonsuperficial resolution to the conflict.

In choosing such an approach, it would be more efficient to select one that could conceivably cover the maximum number of possible cases. This would obviously be more efficient and practical, since it would involve more time and effort to attempt to arrive at a different approach to match each new situation. The consistent application of one approach to numerous similar situations seems preferable to a diverse set of approaches to different situations, since the former but not the latter has the asset of adding stability/consistency to our considered position.

This notion of stability is important as a how-do-you-stand indicator for ourselves and others. That is, it is important for others to know how I would go about approaching a new moral/ethical situation in which they are involved. This knowledge of my general approach would aid others in predicting what course of action I might take resolving a conflict situation involving them. Our strategy in dealing with someone's possible objections to our proposal in the committee meeting will be determined partly by an accurate appraisal of what we consider to be that person's univocal (one voice) approach in dealing with such proposals in the past. This is not to deny that each case a professional social worker confronts is not in many important aspects unique, involving a particular set of circumstances not exactly like those of any other case. It is to deny, however, that we ought to let these particular circumstances dictate a unique approach.

Our univocal approach is subject to modification in its application in each new situation. This stability/consistency view is itself consistent with the set of professional standards of social work *per se* that we take to every case. **Principle #3:** The most efficient approach in resolving ethical conflict situations will be a univocal approach that covers the maximum number of cases/situations or ethical problems.

Facts by themselves do not determine value. How could they do so in the areas of either ethics or science? To make use of facts we have to be able to distinguish between those which are relevant and those which are irrelevant. We do this conceptually by the application of something like a meaning grid over the initially indeterminate landscape of facts. The scientific hypothesis I seek to prove or the ethical principle/rule I seek to apply operates as this meaning grid. In evaluating any ethical situation, certain facts are irrelevant and unless we have some way of separating the relevant from the irrelevant, we will be overloaded with useless information. Such overloading could seriously negate the possibility of making any choice at all by clouding what should be a clear perception of the situation. We need a general or universal sorting device. This is both a theoretical and a practical necessity.

Consider the following situation. Someone tells me that I should include information about the practices and beliefs of South American primitives, North American Eskimos, and the ancient Greeks in arriving at my professional decision about whether or not I should condone my client's abortion-on-demand view in opposition to her husband's objections. I ask, frankly puzzled: What relevance does the fact that the ancient Greeks practiced infanticide, North American Eskimos condoned voluntary patricide, and South American natives practiced cannibalism have on the deliberations concerning my decision in this situation or any similar situation? The obvious answer is, "Not very much." It is sometimes interesting to compare cross-cultural values in this way, but comparing them is not the same as assuming that one should assimilate them in a particular decision process or as a major part of the basis for a general rule or principle for dealing with such situations. Each of these three cultural/social facts can only make sense when understood within the context of a particular set or system of beliefs inherent in the culture, a system itself subject to the usual constraints of consistency and coherence. If the system of beliefs is suspect, then surely the extrapolation of one belief from it is initially problematic, especially if one attempts to make use of this isolated belief (from one system) in another system with a different foundational source.

Comparisons such as these get off the ground only on the basis of some universal or consensus standard of measurement. To compare *a* to *b*, it is not only useful but necessary to know on what basis the comparison is being made. Information regarding the disparities or even similarities in ethical norms from culture to culture or society to society requires the postulation of a universal set of ethical standards in order to assess the relevancy of this information and to generate useful comparisons.

Starting from a considered, principled, ethical standard we can proceed to place these anthropologically interesting facts in the ranked order of relevance they deserve; hopefully we can thus arrive at a way of separating customary social practices from ethical norms or standards. If, for example, a social worker was to move from one society to another with a radically different set of both ethical norms and social or customary practices, then it would be important for his/her appraisal of a particular action to know whether or not the practice was considered an ethical norm or a social custom. Certainly, in many cases it is more serious to violate an ethical norm than a customary practice. There are cases when one act falls under both classifications. As well, the social worker enters the new society with the set of ethical norms and social practices from his/her own society. As he/she enters the new society, the first test he/she is likely to face is this: Which members of the set of ethical norms from my previous society have cross cultural/cross societal application in this new society? The need for an appeal to a universal set of ethical standards as a device for comparing acts cross culturally and as a means of appraising whether a particular act is a viable ethical norm or an acceptable social practice thus becomes obvious.

Social reformers and social reform itself would generate no progress in the area of values, nor have any substantial grounds for convincing anyone of the need for change, without some reasonable recourse to such universal ethical standards. As well, there is a consensus view that such standards do exist through the support accorded the United Nations Universal Declaration of Human Rights, the work of Amnesty International, and legal precedents based on the decisions of the Nuremburg War Trials. To suggest that ethical standards are determinately relative to the customary practices or ethical norms of a particular geographical location is uncritically to paper over the distinction between a customary social practice, an ethical norm, and universal ethical standards, as well as to overlook the significant similarities between individuals and the motivation for their actions. Thus, **principle #4:** It is desirable to employ universal ethical standards in the appraisal and attempted resolution of ethical conflict situations. This is an integral part of a univocal approach.

The "Relativist" Approach to Conflict Resolution

Some attempts to resolve ethical conflict situations appeal to a currently popular approach known generally as ethical relativism. This view is generally posed as a viable alternative to an approach based on universal ethical standards; it is now necessary to look critically at the merits and drawbacks of this approach. We support the *universal ethical standards univocal approach,* so the onus is on us to show what is wrong with the relativist's approach.

In response to how ethical conflict situations ought to be resolved, the ethical relativist answers: Look to yourself, your interests, your preferences, your wants, your desires, the special interests of your exclusive group/society, etc. The way to approach each new ethical conflict situation, then, is from "your relative point of view."* What is meant here by "relative" is itself relative. It is relative to some variable. It may be relative to (1) some particular

---

*The scope of this chapter does not allow us to pursue fully the history of ethical relativism from its early Greek beginnings (in the writings of Epicurus and the views expressed by Thrasymachus in the *Republic* of Plato) to later views and arguments expressed by Westermarck[17] and more recently by those advocating the Moral Values Education approach to teaching values education in North American schools. We offer, then, a brief overview of the kind of approach ethical relativists would take and likely support.

individual (me and my interests/preferences), (2) some specific group or class of individual interests (us, the elite, the working class, etc.), (3) some particular society or culture (existing now or sometime in history), or (4) some particular developmental stage of an individual (linked generally to the intellectual/psychological development of individuals).

In each and every case (1 through 4), the relativist strategy seems to be to reduce the area or range of ethical concern to the particular interests of an individual (at a particular developmental stage, according to [4]) or to an exclusive group. The ethical relativist argues that the range of ethical concern is reduced in order to facilitate a more manageable area for ethical decisions.

Clive Beck suggests that individuals ought to consider overriding ethical values in favor of pursuing what he calls an individual's "ultimate life goals," so that "There are many areas of value apart from the moral, and all areas of value are equally subordinate to the ultimate life goals that lie beyond them...moral considerations must be weighed against others—and the overriding consideration is the promotion of ultimate life goals, not the promotion of moral principles."[16] Mr. Beck is a proponent of the Moral Values Education (MVE) approach in Ontario.

As the range of ethical concerns is diminished, a more efficient procedure for making ethical decisions is thought to result. What is right or wrong conduct, according to this view, is relative to what a particular individual, group, or society takes to be right or wrong at a particular time in a particular situation. Since standards of ethical conduct are relative to one of the four variables, there are no *absolute* standards in areas of ethical concern. As Westermarck stated, "I flatter myself with the belief that I have, in no small measure, given additional strength to the main contentions of this book: that the moral consciousness is ultimately based on emotions, that the moral judgment lacks objective validity, that the moral values are not absolute but relative to the emotions they express."[17]

If you were an individual relativist, there would surely be something both self-defeating and odd about anyone else attempting to convince you that you ought to accept his/her attitude toward right conduct or subjective interests. For, according to the individual relativist, right conduct is nothing else but that which is in my subjective interest. Standards of right conduct are subjectively relative to my egoistic interests. But it may clearly be in my interest to engage in what you (from your subjective interest point of view) would characterize as wrong conduct. In other words, one and the same action could be both right and wrong at one and the same time, relative to each individual's subjective interests and evaluation of the situation at the time.

"My moral judgments spring from my own moral consciousness; they judge of the conduct of other men not from their point of view but from mine, not in accordance with their feelings and opinions about right and wrong but according to my own."[17] "No doubt, to say that a certain act is good or bad may be the mere expression of an emotion felt with regard to it, just as to say that the sun is hot or the weather cold may be a mere expression of a sensation of heat or cold produced by the sun or the weather. But such judgments express subjective facts in terms which strictly speaking have a different meaning."[17]

It would seem, then, that right and wrong conduct could be defined in exactly the same way: that which is in my subjective interests. But how can this be possible if right conduct is the opposite of wrong conduct? In this view the distinction between right and wrong conduct has effectively collapsed; we are left with a characterization of right conduct that does not function as either a workable standard or a practical definition. We are thus left with no rational means for discussing, let alone resolving, ethical conflict situations. The individual relativist's reduction of ethical standards to subjective self-interest has wrought havoc on an acceptable definition of ethical conduct. Furthermore, the individual relativist, in lieu of this consequence of his/her position, has created the means for the proliferation of possible ethical conflict situations between individuals and has provided no viable means for resolving such problematic situations. Moreover, this view is in violation of the general set of procedures suggested earlier to arrive at a resolution of any ethical conflict situation (Principle #1 through Principle #4).

There is one strategy by which the individual relativist could maximally enhance his/her self-interests and possibly minimize conflict situations. This strategy we will call the covert double standard (CDS) strategy, for want of a better name. This preferred strategy for the individual relativist aims at successfully convincing everyone else to become not an individual relativist but rather an altruist—someone who works in the interests of others. This relativist would obviously be better off if everyone else was allocating resources and effort towards enhancing his/her self-interests (rather than their own), since this would increase the amount of resources available to him/her and decrease the effort needed on his/her part to satisfy his/her self-interests. This individual is in the peculiar position of accepting a particular ethical stance for himself, namely relativism, while arguing that everyone else should hold the opposite position. The obvious question is, Why would (should) anyone else become an altruist and accept this essentially subservient position? If he were a father, for example, he would have to educate his children to believe that altruism was the right course for them to follow. He would have to tell his daughters: What is right or good for me is what is right or good for me, but what is right or good for you is what is right or good for me. This is like arguing: Don't do what I do, do what I say. It probably would not take too long before his daughters saw through this double standard, so the father has to convince his daughters of the lie that he too is an altruist (perhaps by performing a minimum number of altruistic acts while covertly holding to his relativist stance). He cannot publicize or promote his actual stance since the worst situation for him is one in which everyone is an individual relativist and the best position for him is one in which everyone else is an altruist. His position, then, employs special pleading in the successful execution of a lie in order to use other people to satisfy his interests. The entire strategy is paradigmatically immoral from everyone's point of view.

At this point, the question may be posed: If ethical relativism is defective as an ethical theory, why would any reasonable person support it? To answer this question, it will be useful to look at the merits ethical relativists claim for their theory and its approach to ethical deliberations.

Merits of the Ethical Relativist's Approach

Ethical relativists claim certain merits for the approach. Not all of these claims are explicit; some are implied by the procedures they employ in the attempted resolution of moral/ethical problems. A brief look at these claims will show that each of them falls short of the theorist's expectations. The claims may be summarized as follows.

ER I: Ethical Relativism provides an *accurate descriptive picture* of the way individuals actually deal with ethical situations in a pluralistic society.

OBJECTION: Descriptive approaches may serve as a starting point for ethical deliberations but no more, since ethical theories serve to provide direction as to how people should behave, and no descriptive theory or approach can serve this essential function. Further, no description can serve as an appraisal of the intent, motivation, or ethical purpose of a particular human action. This claim, then, cannot be used to support this or any theory since it falls far short of the objectives or needs of any ethical theory.

ER II: The ethical relativist's approach enhances an individual's *autonomy* by promoting the free development of an individual's self-esteem/self-respect through the self-assessment of what is in that individual's self-interest. It follows that this promotes a self-critical attitude, which serves to make the individual fully responsible for his/her actions. Such an autonomous individual would be free from the coercive restraints of *absolute* social and or religious standards, standards that serve to repress an individual's self-realized growth in a pluralistic society. As Gow has stated,

> Kolberg's Stage-6 person is autonomous, a sovereign being, apparently above the value of society's rules. . . . Yet much of current MVE implies an out-and-out conflict between Authority and what is often seen as its opposite, Individual Autonomy. These two concepts are consistently portrayed as incompatible in the models of Simon, Kohlberg, and Beck. But it is possible that in pitting Autonomy against Authority, we create a false opposition. It is not the existence of authority which dehumanizes children—or any group of people, for that matter—and renders them unable to reason and develop judgment. It is the way in which authority is exercised that can be dehumanizing. By setting up authority per se as the factor which must be eliminated, we take ourselves down a long and

winding road only to discover anarchy at its end.[18]

OBJECTION: We can agree that the enhancement of individual autonomy is a desirable goal in a pluralistic society but disagree with the ethical relativist's approach for realizing this goal. As we saw earlier, the father's use of the CDS ethical relativist's strategy did not promote the realization of his children's individual autonomy but actually had the opposite effect of making them subservient to their father's interests. We could also agree that the mindless adherence to absolute ethical standards, rules, or norms was undesirable, but at the same time we could disagree that all non-relativist ethical standards were *absolute* standards requiring such uncritical obedience. Again quoting Gow, "I believe that critical, analytical scrutiny of values is vital to moral education — provided the age-topic match is appropriate. The objective of moral education should certainly not be to program automatic rule-followers who comply with value pronouncements without thought or question."[18]

Freely chosen and accepted general or universal ethical standards actually serve to enhance individual autonomy in a pluralistic society where cooperation is not only desirable but required in order to realize individual potential. As well, such universal standards are far from being absolute since they are subject to revision and sometimes modified when applied to individual situations and subjected to the authority of consensus support. Thus, there are other more desirable ways of enhancing individual autonomy than the approach offered by the Ethical Relativist.

ER III: Ethical relativism promotes tolerance among individuals in a pluralistic society by making everyone aware of the lack of absolute ethical standards and the subsequent diversity of individual value systems. As Westermarck stated, "Could it be brought home to people that there is no absolute standard in morality, they would perhaps be on the one hand more tolerant and on the other hand more critical in their judgments."[17]

OBJECTION: Again, we can agree that tolerance is a desirable aim of any ethical view but disagree that the ethical relativist has the best answer for promoting this attitude. Do I tolerate you by essentially ignoring you and your interests in the pursuit of my self-interests? If so, then this ethical aim has very limited value. Tolerance seems to involve more than a mere live-and-let-live attitude. It involves, on my part, a comprehensive understanding of your views, a concern for your interests, and (at least the possibility of) my treating you as an equal. The interpretation of tolerance is antithetical to the self-interested approach of the ethical relativist who could only promote tolerance to the limited extent that it directly enhanced his self-interest. More than lip service must be accorded the notion of tolerance before its promotion can have the desirable effect of minimizing discrimination. But how could the ethical relativist's approach minimize discrimination when this view is founded on the notion that I should always discriminate in favor of my self-interests at the inevitable expense of the interests of others? Although trade-offs and compromise *may* be possible, these are always designed in favor of my self-interests at the likely expense of the interests of others. What other grounds could there be for such trade-offs? Thus, it seems that the ethical relativist's approach is unlikely to promote a useful notion of tolerance.

A Viable Approach to Ethical Conflict Situations

Throughout this book you will discover a variety of ethical conflict situations that a social work professional encounters and must deal with in everyday practice. For social workers especially, societal participation involves working in an ethical testing ground, which invaribly creates the conditions necessary for ethical conflict situations. A viable procedure or approach for dealing with these situations is not only useful but necessary. We have seen that the ethical relativist's approach not only fails to provide an adequate means of resolving ethical conflict situations but may also serve to create such situations. We have also seen that the no choice/neutral observer stance can be tantamount to the wrong choice in situations where a determinate resolution is required. We maintain, then, that the only viable and acceptable approach to ethical conflict situations will involve the application of universal ethical standards (UES).

Universal standards of ethical conduct are those that are cross-cultural, not solely determined by the accidental geographical/ historical borders of a particular society and not relative to the subjective preferences of a particular individual. The authoritative appeal to what is right or wrong in ethical conduct or treatment is measured against the fixed, but not inflexible, consensus ethical standard encapsulated in a rule. This rule, then, is universal but not absolute. Unlike the rules that flow from the edicts of religious dogma, there is no absolute, suprahuman authority vesting them with more than consensus support, since these rules do not depend on the prior acceptance of the UES and since it involves the notion of treating everyone equally in similar situations; in other words: Do unto others as you would have them do unto you; or Perform such individual ethical actions or choices that you would, at the same time, will that everyone in a similar situation perform the same action or make the same choice.* This universal princi- ple serves as the backdrop and testing ground for more specific rules, like Do not harm/inflict needless pain/murder; or Always act in such a way as to promote the well-being of the maximum number of individuals. Some of these particular rules cite negative prohibitions against certain acts while others promote a positive appraisal of certain acts.

Some rules tell us to (positively) act in certain ways, while others tell us to refrain from acting in certain ways. Some rules are encapsulated in a set of human rights while others are manifest in a set of moral obligations or duties. In each case, the priority ranking of such rules is determined by the degree to which nonadherence to such particular rules will violate the universal principle. These rules are prescriptive; they tell us what we should do.

Many survival-type, life-and-death situations do not involve the application of UES rules or considerations, since the intersubjective replacement of one individual by another in such situations will not affect the determination of the outcome. A fully determined solution cannot be arrived at in a situation where there is no consensus authority. If six of us were in a lifeboat that could only support five and it was required that one of us be eliminated, then it is as reasonable to flip a coin as it is to appeal to UES considera-

---

*We are suggesting that in order for a principle to be thought acceptable, it must in some relevant sense be capable of being universalized. This, in part, accounts for the authority of the principle.

tions in arriving at which of the six should be eliminated. Supramoral heroic acts may occur but they could not be required in such situations. However, such *unusual* situations should not cause us to retreat from the application of UES rules, since to generalize an approach from an insignificant number of unusual situations to all possible ethical situations seems not only foolish but unwarranted.*

CONCLUSION

Throughout this chapter, we have been arguing that the relativist approach to dealing with ethical conflict situations not only does not contribute to a reasonable dialogue but may even be a complicating factor that contributes to the creation of such situations. The viable alternative approach we have proposed suggests we speak clearly and precisely with *one ethical voice,* that we do not change our approach when we are confronted with each new situation. This *univocal* approach provides us and others with a clear measurement of our intentions and actions in a diverse set of ethical conflict situations. It offers considered stability in place of a simple reflex response or individual calculations based on the ebb and flow of self-interest. It is crucially important for the social worker carefully to consider his/her role in ethical conflict situations, since he/she functions as (1) an individual moral actor required to resolve personal ethical conflicts and (2) a professional counselor required to deal with the ethical conflicts of society and individuals within it.

Given this diverse and important set of functions performed by a social worker, his/her ethical position in society is unique. The multitude of ethical conflict situations calls not for a multitude of approaches but rather for one approach capable of determinately resolving these conflicts. To choose otherwise is both psychologically and ethically dangerous to each and every one of us, as the required stability in our judgments vanishes in the haze produced by the supermarket of values.

---

*Kathleen Gow, in her book, makes numerous references to the use of these kinds of situations in which immature students are asked to envisage themselves making life and death decisions under stressful conditions of scarcity and coercion.

REFERENCES

1. *Webster's New Collegiate Dictionary,* 1980, p. 235.
2. Rokeach, Milton: *The Nature of Human Values.* New York, The Free Press, 1973.
3. Keith-Lucas, Alad: Ethics in social work. In *Encyclopedia of Social Work,* 17th issue, Vol. 1. Washington, D.C., National Association of Social Workers.
4. Hollis, Florence: *Casework: A Psychosocial Therapy,* 2nd ed. New York, Random House, 1972, p. 14.
5. *Code of Ethics of the National Association of Social Workers.* Washington, D.C., National Association of Social Workers, 1980.
6. Yelaja, Shankar A. (Ed.): *Authority and Social Work: Concept and Use.* Toronto, University of Toronto Press, 1971.
7. Wasserman, Harry: The professional social worker in a bureaucracy. *Social Work, 16:*89–95, Jan 1971,
8. Green, A. D.: The professional worker in the bureaucracy. *Social Science Review, 40:*74–83, March 1966.
9. Piven, Merman: The fragmentation of social work. *Social Work, 50:*89–94, Feb 1969.
10. Raths, Louise E., Harmin, Merrill, and Simon, Sidney B.: *Values and Teaching: Working with Values in the Classroom.* Columbus, Ohio, Charles E. Merrill Publishing Company, 1966.
11. Hart, Gordon M.: *Values Clarification for Counselors.* Springfield, Charles C Thomas, Publisher, 1978.
12. Sparrow, Jane: *Diary of a Student Social Worker.* Boston, Routledge & Kegan Paul Ltd., 1978.
13. Bryant, Clifton D.: *Deviant Behavior.* Chicago, Rand McNally, 1974.
14. Patti, Rino J.: Social work practice: Organizational environment. In *Encyclopedia of Social Work,* 17th issue, Vol. 2. Washington, D.C., National Association of Social Workers, 1977, pp. 1534–1541.
15. Westermarck, Edward: *Ethical Relativity.* Totowa, NJ, Littlefield, Adams and Co., 1960.
16. Beck, Clive: *Ethics: An Introduction.* New York, McGraw-Hill Ryerson Limited, 1972, p. 13.
17. Westermarck, Edward: *Ethical Relativity* (The International Library of Psychology, Philosophy and Scientific Method). Littlefield, Adams and Co., 1960.
18. Gow, Kathleen: *Yes Virginia, There is Right and Wrong.* John Wiley and Sons Canada Limited, 1980.

Part III

Values and Ethics in Social Work Practice

Chapter 4

HOMOSEXUAL CLIENTS

HARVEY L. GOCHROS AND WENDELL RICKETTS

The 1970s witnessed the emergence of efforts among social workers to enhance the effectiveness of their practice with sex-related problems. Courses on human sexuality proliferated in schools of social work; associations of social workers and social work educators began to address these problems at their national meetings; and articles on social work practice with sex-related problems appeared for the first time in our professional literature. This attention, at least initially, was focused on the sexual plumbing problems of the "sexual elite"—married, or at least committed, white, middle class, healthy, heterosexual couples—a population our society favors and whose sexual expression is generally sanctioned.[1] Professional interest in restoring, maintaining, or even improving the sexual functioning of the sexual elite has also come to be considered fairly legitimate, and social work efforts in this direction rarely provoke agency or community criticism.

Social workers, in addition, have never been reluctant to follow the leadership of the medical profession, and such models as Masters and Johnson's approach to the treatment of sexual "plumbing" problems have gained considerable support, respectability, and prestige. This observation is not intended to minimize the personal suffering resulting from the sex-related problems of the sexual elite nor to challenge the ethics of those many social workers who have chosen to devote part of their practice to these problems. Social work is committed to dealing with the family unit as a major focus of its interventions, and sexual functioning and related problems often arise within traditional families. It would be unfortunate, however (but not unprecedented), if social workers were to devote the mass of their attention and efforts to these concerns while giving only superficial attention to the problems of the "sexually oppressed" (such as the aged, retarded, institutionalized, ethnic minorities, etc.) who are characterized by some degree of deprivation of sanctions and opportunities to express their sexuality.

As we enter the 1980s, the sex-related problems of these populations are beginning to receive a good deal more attention by the helping professions in general and by social work in particular. Social work, after all, is distinguished by its historic and ethical commitment to serve those whose needs and rights have tended to be violated or ignored by others. This should be no less true in the area of sexuality.

Range of Homosexualities

One of the most sexually oppressed groups is comprised of those men and women who — to a greater or lesser extent — enjoy (or given the opportunity, think they would enjoy) loving relationships and/or erotic activity with others of their own sex. For the sake of this chapter, these people will be collectively referred to as the "homosexually oriented." It is important, however, in discussing these individuals to recognize an appropriate context for homosexuality (or "homosexualities" as Bell and Weinberg call their Kinsey Institute report). Men and women who are attracted to others of their gender have a variety of choices about the expression of their same sex interests. First, they can choose whether or not to act on their impulses. Although sexual behavior is usually concordant with thought and fantasy, this is not always the case. Many men and women who are aware of their homosexual feelings are heterosexually married, and although they may rarely or never go outside their marriages for gay contact, their masturbatory fantasies, wishes, and desires are about their own sex.

Second, they can choose whether or not to accept the labels "homosexual," "gay," or "lesbian." In cases where homosexual experience is minimal, where concern about taking on a "deviant" identity is high, or where the individual does not identify with any of the standard labels, some men and women who have gay sex will prefer to consider themselves heterosexual, or perhaps "bi," or will reject any naming of their sexuality. Rarer, but still of some significance, is the gay woman or man who has been involved in only one ongoing "gay" love relationship and has no sexual or emotional attraction to others of her or his gender.

Third, they can choose to keep their gay feelings more or less hidden from others. The process of "coming out" is more accurately described as moving through a tunnel than as opening a closet door, for once one has accepted a gay or bisexual identity (personal coming out), an infinite number of degrees of openness or covertness about that gay identity or experience may be adopted.

Fourth, they can choose whether or not to align themselves with an active gay community. A major flaw in much "gay" research is that it focuses on gays and lesbians who either frequent homosexual bars, baths, coffee houses, private clubs, and political and social organizations or who otherwise identify with a more or less cohesive gay community. A degree of overtness is required to associate with other gays in these ways, and certain patterns of behavior and of acculturation develop in subgroup settings. We can hardly say, then, that the attitudes and experiences of publicly overt, community-associated gays and lesbians are typical of homosexuals in general.

In addition, crossing these four dimensions of "gay" experience are countless other life-styles and personality factors that make it impossible to identify "typical" homosexuals. The San Francisco gay man who cruises nightly and has 1000 partners in his lifetime is not the same as the gay man in Moberly, Missouri who has lived monogamously with the same lover for twenty years, yet it is extremely common for all gay women and men to be lumped together solely on the basis of their sexual proclivity. The difficulty in understanding and responding to the needs of this population is obviously compounded by the fact that we do not all mean the same thing when we say "gay."

A SOCIAL WORKER'S IMBROGLIO

Tully and Albro[2] rightly call homosexuality a "social worker's imbroglio," and point to the moral dilemma of social workers faced with a sexual revolution including increased acceptance of homosexuality, which appears to conflict significantly with the family values they have traditionally upheld. At the same time, negative attitudes toward the homosexually oriented in our society are widespread and often very strong. One major attitudinal research effort reported these findings: 65 percent of subjects surveyed thought homosexuality was "very much" obscene and vulgar; 74 percent believed homosexuals would try to get sexually involved with children and should therefore not be youth leaders or teachers; 69 percent believed homosexuals "act like the opposite sex"; and 70 percent said that gay sex is "always wrong" even when between two adults who love each other.[3]

In spite of markedly increased visibility for homosexually oriented women and men in the past few years—due in part to the 1977 Anita Bryant campaign, which forced many gays out of their closets rather than back in—and despite widespread educational efforts aimed at ameliorating oppressive stereotypes, we have no reason to believe that any major shift has occurred in the general perception of homosexuals as deviant. A 1980 CBS news report on "Gay Power, Gay Politics" in San Francisco reinforced popular stereotypes by depicting "drag queens, public sex aficionados in Buena Vista Park, and a sado-masochistic 'consultant' who played show and tell with his leather bag of S-M toys...."[4] Clearly, the sensationalistic aspects of gay life make good television, and "yellow press" reportage of homosexual child molestation only contributes to the perception in the minds of most Americans that gays are the people our mothers warned us about.

Although compelling evidence refuting virtually every popular stereotype may be found both in the professional literature and, more importantly, through contact with the gay women and men who are social workers' neighbors, friends, and co-workers, dentists, mail carriers, and perhaps even their parents, children, or spouses, it is interesting that many helping professionals cling so tenaciously to negative attributions of homosexuals, even in the face of evidence to the contrary. Part of the reason for this is that in contrast to other oppressed groups (such as ethnic minorities, the aged, or physically handicapped), the homosexually oriented tend to be invisible; relatively few demonstrate the appearance and behavior typically ascribed to those with a homosexual orientation. Furthermore, a sizable portion of the homosexually oriented choose to avoid using the social services, seeing " ... the helping professions as their worst enemies, as the very agents which act to increase their guilt and shame."[5] Social workers, therefore, may either have no contact with gay clients at all, or will assume that clients who do not reveal their sexual orientations to them are heterosexual. In either case, it is quite possible for social workers to think the homosexually oriented are a small population of little concern to them and to have no opportunity to examine their own negative impressions and attitudes.

In addition to being the product of a society in which homosexuals are at the same time unseen, feared, and disliked, some social workers may also avoid homosexually oriented clients because they fear that showing interest, acceptance, and understanding of gay problems will lead to speculation about their own sexual orientation. *Only a minority of social workers are exclusively homosexual,* and even fewer have "come out" and formally identified with a gay subculture, but a much larger number have at some time or another, for a greater or lesser time, engaged in sexual relationships with people of their sex or have fantasied such relationships. Whether or not these individuals have identified themselves as gay, they may have substantial discomfort with this history.

It is, nonetheless, becoming more difficult to avoid working with the homosexually oriented. As a result of the gay liberation movement and of stands taken by both the Council on Social Work Education and the National Association of Social Workers supporting the "right to be different," we are beginning to address the problems encountered by this population. Not only do the homosexually oriented experience difficulties in adjustment associated with living in a society that still basically condemns homosexuality, but they may also have problems associated with developing and maintaining bonded relationships, especially gay men who have no models for intimacy and noncompetition in their relationships with other men. In addition, there are problems of homosexually oriented people who are heterosexually married, as well as the concerns of their wives, husbands, and children, the many problems associated with "coming out," and the potential problems experienced by the relatives and friends of those who have come out.

In the performance of counseling tasks, as well as of advocacy

and brokerage roles in supporting the legal rights of the homosexually oriented in such matters as housing, employment, and
child custody, the social worker's attitudes toward homosexuality
will inevitably color his or her efforts on behalf of gay clients. The
"moral majority" has used its profamily mission as a rationale for
its antihomosexual policies, and to the extent that social workers
are profamily to the exclusion of atypical life (and family) styles,
one might expect reservations about homosexuality.

Developing an ethical stance on homosexuality is complex,
since it does involve integration of social values, religious beliefs,
legal sanctions, and clinical traditions as well as convictions about
human rights. As this book repeatedly points out, we cannot deny
the influence of our ethics and values on a professional practice,
and the development of an ethical approach to social work practice with homosexually oriented clients must be guided by careful
examination of the common myths and biases that influence social
attitudes toward homosexuals.

One of the most common themes in these attitudes is adherence
to a rigid "sexual dichotomy," that is, insistence on the belief that
one is either gay or straight. This view persists even among sex
educators and counselors, despite Kinsey's elaborate conceptuali-
zation of a continuum of human sexual response, with approximately one-third of the population falling somewhere between
the exclusive heterosexual and exclusive homosexual categories.[6]
This model contributes to a tendency for even the most incidental
same sex experience to be considered evidence of a homosexual
orientation and actively encourages labeling. For those unsure of
their commitment to a homosexual life-style, or who are able to
respond to both men and women, such labeling is inaccurate and
potentially damaging.

Another attitude that commonly pervades traditional approaches
with gay clients is the notion that being gay is, if not sick, at least a
misfortune. Garfinkle and Morin report that clinicians often lack
awareness of the adaptive advantages and potential satisfactions of
gay life-styles, and generally believe that homosexuals are destined to lead difficult lives.[7] Homosexually oriented individuals,
according to this bias, can be helped to cope with their "deviant"
feelings and can even learn to live reasonably happy lives,

but they can never hope to attain the fulfillment heterosexuality might bring.

Donald Brown, in an otherwise helpful article, falls easily into this "heterosexual bias" when he says "Because of the additional problems associated with homosexuality, an individual having complete freedom of choice would probably be better off as a heterosexual."[8] His comment may be appraised on several levels, not the least of which is its implication for any group struggling against an oppressive status quo, but the basic message here regarding homosexuality is that it is second best. It would be completely unsympathetic to dismiss Brown as a "closet homophobic," yet his ambivalence about homosexuality is obvious. Similarly, many workers may feel unsure about the degree to which they want to endorse homosexuality, and where this conflict is manifested in an attitude toward gays that is condescending (although "politically correct"), it may be preferable to have their biases, even their negative ones, out in the open.

A striking example of the manner in which homosexuality is often relegated to "side issue" status is Bernie Zilbergeld's widely acclaimed *Male Sexuality*.[9] By virtually ignoring gay relationships and issues in his book, Zilbergeld implies that male sexuality is essentially synonymous with male *heterosexuality* and reinforces the notion that gay feelings and behavior are somehow outside the range of normal sexual expression. Surely no one ought to be forced to write about gays or to include them in his research, but omissions such as these point glaringly to the bias against full sexual enfranchisement for the homosexually oriented.

THE ISSUE OF CONVERSION THERAPY

In discussing issues related to effective social work practice with the homosexually oriented, it is appropriate to consider the subject of "conversion" or "reorientation" therapy. Although social workers are themselves not generally involved in doing conversion therapy, a discussion of the basic values involved here is crucial to the development of an ethical approach with lesbian and gay clients. As we have said, movement has been made recently toward acceptance of homosexuality as one variation of the needs for love and sexual expression, and the 1973 decision of the

American Psychiatric Association to remove homosexuality per se from the *Diagnostic and Statistical Manual* represented great progress in separating homosexuality from the "illness" model to which it has been linked for so long. However, one survey of behavior therapists published that same year revealed that 13 percent would consider the use of aversive techniques to eliminate homosexuality even in cases where the client did not want to change,[10] and the recent Masters and Johnson report on homosexuality claimed to have effectively reoriented gays in remarkedly short treatment durations.[11] The questions, then, of the efficacy and, indeed, the propriety of conversion therapy are still open to consideration. Relatedly, the relative "sickness" or "adjustment" of gays has traditionally depended on the consensus of associations of behavior therapists, psychologists, and psychiatrists (as it did in 1973), and we would do well to reflect on the implications for a society in which "normalcy" is determined by groups of professionals and where majority opinion is considered scientific evidence.

On the basis of the literature, the types of change therapy may be divided into two broad categories. The first type attempts to eliminate homosexual impulses completely and replace them with heterosexual arousal, while the other seeks simply to increase or enhance heterosexual feelings while not necessarily affecting homosexual ones.

Rather than review techniques or rates of "cure," we will attempt to put the question of conversion directly into the ethical arena; too often only the potential success or failure of such therapies has been discussed, while the political, philosophical, and moral statements made by the very existence of conversion therapy go unexamined. The various ethical problems may perhaps be more clearly demonstrated here by drawing an analogy between blacks and gays. Obviously, blacks do not have the choice to remain invisible as gays do, and for this reason are perhaps subject to more overt discrimination, but the analogy will nonetheless be illustrative.

Suppose we were to begin to establish clinics that could change blacks into whites. These clinics would employ dermatologists and cosmetologists who could prescribe drugs and creams to lighten the skin, hairdressers to straighten and bleach the hair, speech therapists to teach blacks to talk like whites, and psychologists to instill WASP cultural mores and values. No one would be forced to come to these clinics, and no one would have to continue therapy who did not want to. But, since it is still easier to be white than black in most places in America, and since many blacks face discrimination and poverty because of their race, it might seem that such a program would serve a useful and humanitarian purpose.

Obviously, the existence of such clinics would make a clear statement about being black in our culture, and we could say that the bias evinced against the homosexually oriented by the promulgation of change therapies is similar.

Perhaps the most controversial aspect of this issue is that of the "voluntariness" of clients who seek reorientation therapy. Presumably, if a client desires or requests a particular treatment outcome, then he is a "voluntary" client and the counselor or therapist has some obligation to meet his expressed needs. Clearly, however, "therapists constrain themselves in many ways when clients ask for certain kinds of help,"[12] and the argument that therapists are neutral in their accession to voluntary requests is used in the case of homosexuality to justify enforcing a "social morality."[13] What is more, those who advocate repudiation of behavior therapies for homosexuals altogether feel that the "voluntary" conversion client is a myth: "To grow up in a family where the word 'homosexual' was whispered, to play in a playground and hear the words 'faggot' and 'queer', to go to college and hear of 'illness', and finally to the counseling center that promises to 'cure' is hardly to create an environment of freedom and voluntary choice."[13]

The effect of the environment on a client's request for change therapy, though traditionally ignored in most clinical evaluations,[14] is of unparalleled importance here. No one wants to change something about him or herself that is perceived as a positive, satisfying aspect of life. Gay men and, less often, lesbians who ask to be changed have accepted their socially imposed "abnormal" role, usually without any anger or resentment toward society.[13] Davison prompts examination of a client's motivation in this way: "Given the cultural bias against homosexuality, it is problematic to assert that people who ask for change or orientation are expressing a 'free wish.' We have been remiss in examining why people request certain kinds of treatment."[17]

Central to the question of client "voluntariness" is the issue of "subjective distress." If a client's homosexual behavior, thoughts, and desires are grossly upsetting to him, are we obligated first to relieve his suffering, or is this secondary to an evaluation of his overall adjustment, environment, etc., and their influence on his desire to change? Some therapists feel that the criterion of "subjective distress" is the only valid consideration in attempting reorientation[10] and in line with this, the latest *DSM-III*[15] lists only "ego dystonic homosexuality" as a psychopathology. In other words, homosexuality is a mental disorder only if one is unhappy with and wishes to change gay impulses or behavior. This can hardly be considered a reversal of previous psychiatric opinion, since psychiatrists do not see gays and lesbians who are happy with being gay as conversion patients. Homosexuals who are comfortable with their gay feelings and desires do not present for treatment, and this new category successfully manages to ignore the issue of why some homosexually oriented individuals consider their same sex interests unacceptable. John Money faces the issue directly: "The inclusion of this category (ego dystonic homosexuality) must be seen for what it is—a political maneuver to appease the opposition."[16]

Other therapists feel that "subjective distress" is an inexact criterion on which to base a defense of disordered behavior.[17] Especially with homosexuality, one must always consider the effects of current environment, past learning, and access to information on a client's desire to change.[14] Before a client seriously considers the possibility of reorienting, "He should have at least some idea as to the extent to which his current suffering or uneasiness is related to oppressive environmental stress, particularly that stress generated by society's intolerance of homosexuality."[14]

Davison, Begelman, and others advocate completely abandoning reorientation procedures although, as Davison points out, "Some people can be hurt by my proposals. . . ."[12] Situations in which individuals could be hurt by the absence of conversion regimes can arise, such as the case of a convicted homosexual pedophile who is granted a reduced prison sentence in exchange for submitting to reorientation. Unfortunately, the view of much of society, including the courts, is that homosexuality per se is dysfunctional, and social workers should do everything possible to promote the more accurate view: that the behavior of homosexuals (as of heterosexuals) is sometimes maladjusted, compulsive, even criminal, but that in the absence of an analogous "problem of heterosexuality," the concept of the "homosexual problem" ought to be discarded.

We have so far touched only on instances of true "conversion," not of heterosexual enhancement. Where such "enhancement" is a euphemism for reorientation, it should likewise be repudiated, but in cases where a person is heterosexually married, wishes to preserve the marriage, and is unable to function sexually with his or her spouse,[14] or in cases where the client wants the "social package" of heterosexuality,[18] or where the homosexual contact is furtive, compulsive, and unsatisfying and the client desires more fulfilling heterosexual contacts, perhaps these opportunities should not be summarily denied. (Cases involving adolescents evolving homosexually often evoke considerable ethical conflict in social workers and will be discussed later in this chapter.)

To those committed to insuring a better life for the more or less homosexually oriented, it is obvious that much oppression still exists. Gays continue to be stereotyped in situations where similar stereotyping of blacks or women would not be tolerated (anti-gay jokes, for example, are still acceptable television comedy fare). Ignorance of the variability of "homosexualities" and, indeed, of human sexuality, and insistence on a "sickness" or "deviance" model for all sexual/emotional expressions not destined to result in socially approved pregnancies also contribute to an atmosphere of repression for gays. It is understandable then, that sensitivity to this oppression may lead gays and their supporters to question the motivation of those whose biases in work with the homosexually oriented are not clear.

In discussing ethical and moral issues, however, it is easy to lose sight of the client. The adoption of rigid policies regarding the homosexually oriented, even when these policies arise out of a desire to break with the oppressive past, are very likely to result in a loss of freedom and choice for both the client and the counselor. In attempting to curtail the power of psychiatrists and behavior therapists who, with their facade of "scientific neutrality," have made generations of gay patients the victims of their homophobia,

Silverstein, Davison, and others may have oversimplified this complex issue, but the problem with arguments that favor even limited use of behavioral intervention in decreasing homosexual arousal is that they are generally much more conservative in implication than they appear.

Above all, we support the right of the individual to experience his or her own variability and uniqueness, sexual or otherwise, unhindered by fear of society's reprisal against nonconformity. If individuals who request elimination of their homosexual feelings and behavior could be relieved instead of the stigma of such involvement, would they still want to change? We do not know. As long as treatment efforts are focused on changing sexual orientation per se rather than on modifying the dysfunctional aspects of the expression of that orientation, it is reasonable to suspect reorientation procedures of being "yet another element in the causal nexus of oppression . . . even when (these procedures are administered) out of concern for the alleviation of client distress."[17]

ISSUES RELATED TO ADOLESCENT HOMOSEXUALITY

Another sensitive and value-laden area for social workers is that of counseling adolescents with homosexual concerns. In facing the challenge of the adolescent client ethically and effectively, a worker will have to deal with his own feelings about homosexuality, and also with administrators and parents who, in some institutional and school settings, may consider the very discussion of homosexuality with adolescents highly inappropriate. In addition, the question of whether supportive and empathic interventions actually "encourage" homosexuality will be raised by some.

Any work with adolescents is subject to the influence of those concerned with providing "moral absolutes," but adolescents are a "sexually oppressed" group,[1] and the tendency to view them as wild and "impressionable" youth is no doubt one factor in that oppression. The desire of parents to keep their children from influences they consider adverse is understandable and not always unjustified, but the almost conspiratorial avoidance of adolescent sexual needs and concerns provides no basis for healthy, functional adult sexual expression. Predictably, the desire to control the kind of sex information available to adolescents reaches hysterical proportions when it comes to homosexuality. Anita Bryant based her nationwide antigay campaign on the "Save Our Children" theme, and the "Briggs Initiative," presented to California voters in 1978, called for the firing not only of lesbian and gay teachers but also of those who "advocated" homosexuality in the classroom. The belief that adolescents can be seduced into homosexuality—not only by sexual contact with others of their gender but also by hearing homosexuality discussed openly and without condemnation—is strong, and the cold reality of contradictory evidence is often no match for the emotional assaults of anti-gay groups.

Interviews with gays themselves show that few cite examples of unwilling seduction in childhood or adolescence, nor do they report being exposed to adult gays socially or having heard much positive information about homosexuality in growing up.[19] It is almost a universal experience of gay men and lesbians, in fact, that until they "came out" (usually as adults), they were sure they were the "only one." The effect of this information on the fear and hostility of those who subscribe to the seduction theory is certainly minimal, but it is information that should be considered by those who wish to be helpful to adolescents with concerns about homosexuality.

Kinsey found that about 50 percent of all adolescent males had some homosexual experience and, of fourteen to eighteen year olds, approximately 16 percent—or one in six—had half or more of their sexual experiences with other boys. (The figure is about 3% for adolescent females with "some" lesbian experience.[20]) Obviously half the adult male population is not committed to homosexuality, and there is no reason to believe that even more than incidental adolescent homosexual experience is indicative of an adult homosexual preference.

Beyond this argument, however, is another issue that should be addressed, and that is the recurring theme of the gay "apology." Our hurry to reassure adolescents (and ourselves) that their gay experiences are only a "phase" can of itself be oppressive, in that it denies the viability of gayness as an adult life-style. The emphasis on the transience of adolescent gay feelings and experiences implies that the adolescent will "outgrow" them the way he or she might outgrow a speech impediment or a bad case of acne and that it is, in fact, desirable to outgrow them. Many gays report that the trivialization of their adolescent sexual feelings in this way was a bitterly frustrating experience, as it must also be for adolescents who do not continue to evolve homosexually. Social workers must weigh their responsibility not only to adolescents having more or less incidental gay experiences but also to those who will develop a primarily homosexual orientation, for whom adolescence is often a time of loneliness and isolation.

It is not difficult to separate adolescents who have isolated gay experiences (perhaps no more than necking with a close friend) and are upset by it from those who have a greater degree of involvement in gay activities. The emotional aspects of these relationships should also be explored, for as Money points out it is the ability to fall in love with (be "limerent" with) a member of one's own sex that determines gayness and "bilimerence," not sexual response alone.[16] Moreover, it should be remembered that same sex experiences satisfy not only sexual needs but also needs for self-validation, intimacy, and affection. Many gays report, as do many heterosexuals, that they fell in love for the first time in high school, and the positive aspects of any desire to be close to other human beings ought to be emphasized. The development of intimate relationships in adolescence, in addition, is part of the normal process of emancipation from the family.

With the exception of those rare gay and lesbian adolescents who have access to an adult gay community that will support them, or who have close gay friends, the majority of young gays receive virtually no validation for the feelings they are experiencing or for the relationships they may be developing with others of their sex. It is unlikely, furthermore, that gay experiences—sexual or limerent—will lead to any prolonged commitment to a gay or lesbian "life-style" for those not already so inclined. Rather, the sudden attention focused on an adolescent's gay experiences—including ostracism by peers, parental outrage, and institutional punishment—can so overemphasize the significance of these events that the youth's self-identification as a gay may actually solidify.

Because of concerns about masculinity and femininity and increasing pressure, particularly on young males, to "prove" themselves by becoming heterosexually active, adolescents are acutely affected by homophobia. Fear of being labeled homosexual for transgressions of "proper" masculine behavior is high for males, and feminine worth, traditionally measured by attractiveness to men and the degree to which a woman seeks heterosexual pursuit, may similarly be threatened by gay feelings. As a result, for both males and females, low self-esteem often accompanies anxiety about homosexual fantasies or experiences, and the pressure to label oneself is strong. Regardless of what positive associations gayness may have for overt, self-actualized gays, the adolescent has as role models only the strongly negative stereotypes of degeneracy and sickness that our culture reinforces in myriad ways, and it is no wonder that the recognition of gay feelings is often a shocking and traumatic experience.

Since we cannot predict with certainty which individuals having gay experiences in adolescence will develop a more or less permanent adult homosexual preference, the counselor should not be concerned with attempting to second guess the outcome. To be sure, some of these adolescents will be gay and some will not, but for all of them the counselor can provide an environment of support and acceptance, ameliorating the anguish of dealing with feelings society has condemned. What is of paramount importance is how the adolescent feels about him or herself and how he or she relates to family, friends, lovers, and so on.[21]

An approach that combines both the recognition of a client's freedom of choice about the expression of his or her sexuality and active support in whatever areas the client and counselor identify as problematic is probably best, although the extent of "homosexual panic" on the part of the adolescent as well as overreaction on the part of the worker, the parents, and others involved must also be considered.

For adolescents who have sufficient awareness and experience to decide they are gay, and who wish to begin to "come out," the counselor can "use himself by becoming a role model of a caring human being who understands and is nondiscriminatory toward homosexuals,"[22] and can work within families and institutions to foster tolerance and acceptance of human variability and to insure that adolescents with a greater or lesser degree of homosexual involvement are not ostracized by parents, peers, and teachers.[21]

Social workers can reduce labeling and, above all, can preserve and protect their adolescent clients' right to make their own way as they grow to adulthood. Finally, workers may consider as valid treatment goals even such controversial interventions as moving a client away from hostile relatives or an oppressive school environment.[22]

FRAMEWORK FOR ETHICAL PRACTICE

Once social workers have divested themselves of the common myths and stereotypes associated with homosexuality, they can begin to build an ethical framework for practice within which they can provide effective services compatible with the value base of the profession. Such a framework would include a number of elements.

ACCEPTANCE: An ethical approach to homosexual individuals depends on the full acceptance of homosexuality not as pathology nor even as "second best," but as a viable sexual orientation. Individuals who experience stress and discomfort with their sexual orientation do exist, and the strains associated with being a member of any oppressed population affect the homosexually oriented as well. This does not indicate, however, that homosexuality per se is pathological. To feel this way would be to assume that heterosexuality per se is pathological because within a heterosexual context there is often divorce, suicide, sexual dysfunction, child and spouse abuse, rape, incest, and so on. Similarly, acceptance is further manifested by avoiding the assumption that a homosexual orientation is at the root of all problems experienced by gay men and women.

RECOGNITION OF THE NEEDS FOR LOVE AND NURTURANCE: A homosexual orientation is not only a preference for a particular gender for erotic expression, it also involves a focus for one's needs for love, intimacy, and companionship. Society does not support ongoing love relationships between people of the same sex any more than it supports same sex erotic contact, yet this is an area of particular concern among the homosexually oriented. An ethical approach would thus entail a concern for, and an awareness and acceptance of, the *emotional* as well as the erotic needs of the homosexually oriented.

ADVOCACY: An ethical social work approach to needs of the homosexually oriented goes beyond clinical service. As noted earlier, the problems of the homosexually oriented often stem from oppressive legal practices, legislation, religious stands, and social discrimination. Often the social worker will be called upon to assume an advocacy role for the client, particularly where the client's civil rights have been violated (such as in custody decisions or the loss of job or housing because of the revelation of a homosexual orientation), and a knowledge of community resources available to gay clients may be valuable.

SUPPORT FOR SOCIAL POLICY CHANGE: The social worker may also choose to support local or state social action programs to overcome legal discrimination against the homosexually oriented in such areas as employment, housing, and child custody. Closer to home, the social worker may wish to explore discrimination against clients or staff who are homosexually oriented. For example, are homosexually oriented couples accepted for relationship counseling by a family agency? Can openly homosexual individuals adopt or provide foster care for children? Are openly homosexual workers rejected for employment by an agency? Are residents in an institution punished for displaying sexual interest in others of their sex? It is in these areas that workers can be of direct benefit to the gay men and women in their community.

FUTURE DIRECTIONS

Understandably, heterosexuals, including those in the helping professions, may to some extent be distrusted and seen as potential agents of continued oppression. Many gays, in addition, are drawn to homosexual subcultures and even "gay ghettoes" such as Castro Street in San Francisco and Greenwich Village in New York. These areas are not fundamentally different from the ethnic ghettoes in many large cities, and like other minority groups, gays have fled to them to escape discrimination and oppression. Unfortunately, also like other minority groups, ghettoized gays tend to reinforce stereotypical behavior, exploit one another, and heighten their rejection of outsiders.

At the same time, many of the most liberal and concerned heterosexual social workers are majorly influenced by their homophobic society. Doubts about the "mental health" of gays persist despite abundant evidence that the homosexually oriented live satisfying, constructive lives within the context of their sexual orientation.

What can social workers do to bridge this gap? One excellent technique for shattering stereotypes and increasing understanding is to become acquainted with nonclient gay people who are willing to be open about their sexual and emotional preference. Research has shown that exposure to gay men and women in classroom units on homosexuality, for instance, was effective in reducing negative stereotyping[23,24] and that "the freeing of individuals of their homophobic attitudes in the course of professional training (may) allow them to feel better about themselves and better enable them to deal therapeutically with people as people rather than as clinical categories."[24]

Agencies can explore how well their services are made available to homosexually oriented consumers, and can see to it that advertising and public relations emphasize the agency's support of nontraditional life-styles. Staff members who are knowledgeable about homosexual needs and concerns can become resources within the agency, examining policies and services to see that they are responsive to gay people, and may even conduct in-service training to prepare other workers to deal more effectively with problems commonly encountered by the homosexually oriented. Whether or not these staff are themselves homosexually oriented is not as important as their ability to be accepting and sensitive to potential gay clients.

Biases obviously give rise to ethical issues and this chapter's clear bias in favor of the social and sexual enfranchisement of the homosexually oriented may likewise lead to a question of ethics; we have not attempted to be "objective," if such a thing is possible. We feel, however, that the clear challenge of life today is dealing effectively with our increased freedom. The social foment of the 1960s and 1970s resulted in acute changes in social and sexual roles, and we are now faced with more choices than ever. Some respond by trying to limit the options available to us, but the development of a personal ethic that respects choice will probably prove to be the most adaptive course in a fast changing world.

Attitudes toward the homosexually oriented that curtail their access to a life that is happy and satisfying will ultimately be of no consequence, for in the remarkable interdependence of nations and of individuals today is clear evidence that we will not be able to continue to operate in a "some gotta win, some gotta lose" world. Not only with their gay clients but also within their agencies and institutions and with their family and friends, social workers can promote the idea that a nurturing and supportive life is possible for everyone, with no one left out.

REFERENCES

1. Gochros, Harvey, and Gochros, Jean: *The Sexually Oppressed.* New York, Association Press, 1977.
2. Tully, Carol, and Albro, Joyce C.: Homosexuality: A social worker's imbroglio. *Journal of Sociology and Social Welfare, 6(2):* March 1979.
3. Levitt, Eugene, and Klasser, Albert: Public attitudes toward homosexuality. *Journal of Homosexuality, 1:*30–32, 1974.
4. Shilts, Randy: Cleve Jones rising. *Christopher Street,* p. 16, Oct/Nov 1970.
5. Killinger, Raymond: The counselor and gay liberation. *Personnel and Guidance Journal, 49(9):*718, May 1971.
6. Kinsey, Alfred, Pomeroy, Wardell B., and Martin, Clyde E.: *Sexual Behavior in the Human Male.* Philadelphia, W. B. Saunders, Co., 1948.
7. Garfinkle, Ellen M., and Morin, Stephen F.: Psychologists' attitudes toward homosexual psychotherapy clients. *Journal of Social Issues, 34(3):*109, 1978.
8. Brown, Donald: Counseling the youthful homosexual. *The School Counselor,* p. 330, 1975.
9. Zilbergeld, Bernie: *Male Sexuality: A Guide to Sexual Fulfillment.* Boston, Little, Brown, Co., 1978.
10. Davison, Gerald, and Wilson, G. Terence: Attidutes of behavior therapists toward homosexuality. *Behavior Therapy, 4:*690, 1973.
11. Masters, William H., and Johnson, Virginia E.: *Homosexuality in Perspective.* Boston, Little, Brown, Co., 1979.
12. Davison, Gerald C.: Not can but ought: The treatment of homosexuality. *Journal of Consulting and Clinical Psychology, 46(1):*170–171, 1978.
13. Silverstein, Charles: Homosexuality and the ethics of behavioral intervention. *Journal of Homosexuality, 3(3):*206–207, Spring 1977.
14. Halleck, Seymour: Another response to "Homosexuality: The ethical challenge." *Journal of Consulting and Clinical Psychology, 44(2):*168–170, 1976.
15. *Diagnostic and Statistical Manual of Mental Disorders,* 3rd ed. New York, American Psychiatric Association, 1980.
16. Mass, Lawrence: The birds, the bees and John Money. *Christopher Street,* p. 28, Sept. 1980.
17. Begelman, D. A.: Homosexuality and the ethics of behavioral intervention.

*Journal of Homosexuality, 2(3):*215–217, Spring 1977.

18. Davison, Gerald: Homosexuality: The ethical challenge. *Journal of Consulting and Clinical Psychology, 44(2):*161, 1976.

19. Spada, James: *The Spada Report.* New York, Signet Books, 1979.

20. Kinsey, Alfred C., Pomeroy, Wardell, Martin, Clyde E., and Gebhard, Paul: *Sexual Behavior in the Human Female.* Philadelphia, W. B. Saunders, 1953.

21. Gilberg, Arnold: Psychosocial considerations in treating homosexual adolescents. *American Journal of Psychoanalysis, 38:*356–357, 1978.

22. Needham, Russell: Casework intervention with a homosexual adolescent. *Social Casework,* p. 394, July 1977.

23. Greenberg, Jerrold S.: A study of personality change associated with the conducting of a high school unit on homosexuality. *The Journal of School of Health, VLV(7):*394–398, Sept. 1975.

24. Morin, Stephen F.: Educational programs as a means of changing attitudes toward gay people. *Homosexual Counseling Journal, 1(4):*160–165, Oct. 1974.

Additional Reading

Berger, Raymond M.: An advocate model for intervention with homosexuals. *Social Work,* p. 280–3, July, 1977.

Boswell, John: *Christianity, Social Tolerance and Homosexuality.* Chicago, University of Chicago Press, 1980.

Churchill, Wainwright: *Homosexual Behavior Among Males: A Cross Cultural and Cross Species Investigation.* New York, Hawthorn, 1967.

Cory, Donald Webster: *The Homosexual in America.* New York, Greenberg, 1951.

Evans, Arthur: *Witchcraft and the Gay Counterculture.* Boston, Fag Rag Books, 1978.

Gochros, Harvey L.: Counseling gay husbands. *Joy of Sex Education and Therapy, 4(2):*6–10, Winter 1978.

Gochros, Harvey L.: Teaching more or less straight social work students to be helpful to more or less gay people. *Homosexual Counseling Journal, 2(2),* April, 1975.

Hatterer, Myra S.: Problems of women married to male homosexuals. *American Journal of Psychiatry, 131:*275–278, March, 1974.

Hudson, Walter W. and Ricketts, Wendell: A strategy for the measurement of homophobia. *Journal of Homosexuality, 5(4),* Summer 1980.

Kremer, Ellen, et al.: Homosexuality, counseling and the adolescent male. *Personnel and Guidance Journal, 54(2),* 95–99, October, 1975.

Lehne, Gregory: Homophobia among men. In David, Beborah S. and Robert Brannon: *The Forty-Nine Percent Majority.* Massachusetts, Addison-Wesley Publishing Company, 1976.

Ross, Lawrence H.: Modes of adjustment of married homosexuals. *Social Problems, 18:*385–393, Winter 1971.

Szasz, Thomas: *The Manufacture of Madness.* New York, Harper and Row, 1976.

Weinberg, George: *Society and the Healthy Homosexual.* New York, Anchor Books, 1972.

Chapter 5

MISTREATED CHILDREN

JEANNE M. GIOVANNONI

If ethics is considered the establishment of principles by which choices can be made between conflicting values,[10] then there is perhaps no area of social work practice more fraught with ethical issues than that centered on mistreated children. The very concept of child mistreatment derives from choices between two basic societal values: the autonomy of the family and the protection of children. Child mistreatment can be defined as parental care that is deemed sufficiently deviant to warrant intrusion into families' lives by the community and its agents. The parameters of what constitutes such deviant parental behavior are themselves expressions of social values, values that shift and change over time and that, even at any given time, are apt to be controversial rather than universally shared.[3] Situations of child mistreatment thus involve competing values at every stage of their management, from definition and identification to final resolution. These values in turn are reflective of the multiple interests at stake: those of the children, of their parents, and of the community. The relative compatibility of these interests can range widely from situation to situation.

The ethical issues that derive out of the nature of child mistreatment are necessarily complex and involve the individual practitioner, agency administrators and policy makers, and the profession as a whole. It must be noted that child mistreatment is not solely a problem of social work, though social work is one of the professions integrally involved. It is also a legal and a medical problem, involving members of the legal profession, the judiciary, law enforcement, and medicine. For each of these groups, child mistreatment poses ethical issues within the context of their respective ethical codes, some that overlap those of social work. Mandatory reporting of child abuse, for example, conflicts with physicians' ethics regarding the doctor-parent relationship. Perhaps reflecting ethical conflicts within the legal profession, the product of years of effort by the American Bar Association to develop standards for court intrusion into cases of child mistreatment has been rejected, and that organization is presently without any such standards.[5] Thus, while it is possible to distill in this article what some of the key ethical issues posed by situations of child mistreatment for the profession of social work might be, resolution of those issues—principles for setting priorities, in selecting among the competing values—cannot be expected to be without controversy, either within the profession of social work or in relation to the other professions integrally involved.

The Role of Social Work in Child Mistreatment

Social work's involvement with child mistreatment has evolved gradually over the last century. Today it is one of the core professions involved, mandated to perform key functions in the identification, disposition, and amelioration of situations of child mistreatment. At each step of the process in the management of child mistreatment cases, social workers have dual responsibilities. On the one hand, they exercise the authority of the community to interfere in parent-child relationships, and on the other hand, they are expected to contribute to amelioration of the situation through rehabilitation of the parent-child relationship and/or the provision of substitute parental care. Generally speaking these functions are lodged in child welfare agencies and include child protective services, foster care, and adoption. While these are the key social work actors in child mistreatment, social workers in a variety of settings may also play important roles. They may be involved in identification of mistreatment, and in most states now are mandated to report such cases for investigation. They may also be involved as ancillary service renderers in the rehabilitative efforts of the families. Thus, while child welfare workers are central to child protection, as Kahn[7] noted long ago, and Kadushin[6] has reemphasized, "protective" responsibility is lodged in the whole community, and all agencies serving children are, in aggregate, responsible for "protecting children, so as to ensure their rights." We would add that all agencies serving family members who have responsibility for children are also, in aggregate, responsible for ensuring children's rights. Hence, ethical issues inherent in child mistreatment are apt to affect all social workers at some time or another, as individual practitioners, as agency administrators, and as policymakers, and the profession as a whole. We begin our discussion with issues pertaining to the individual practitioner.

ETHICAL ISSUES FOR THE INDIVIDUAL PRACTITIONER

Essentially social work involvement in child mistreatment can be delineated along steps in a process. Depending upon how various systems are organized within child welfare agencies, the following are the essentials. The first function calls for the registering of a complaint of child mistreatment, and the next the responsive investigation of that mistreatment. Next, the complaint will be either dropped without further actions or the validation of the mistreatment itself will be made and action taken to ameliorate the situation. Such action may be maintained within the province of the social service agency and include rehabilitative efforts, or additional action may be taken to involve the courts in making a further disposition. Options available to the courts are simply dropping the matter, allowing the child to stay in his own home with some kind of court supervision and social services, or removing the child from the home in custody and supervision of the social service agency while in a foster home or in an institution. In rare instances, the court could terminate parental custody altogether at the outset or, more commonly, after a longer period of time. As long as the child is in care (whether placed there by the courts or through a voluntary arrangement with the parent), a decision about the child's future lingers: to return home, to remain in care, or to be legally terminated from the parents' custody and placed in adoption. From the standpoint of children and their families this is a single process. It can extend over a few hours, days, months, or years, but from the standpoint of children and their families it is still a single process, one initiated by an accusation of mistreatment, a process that is essentially the societal response to that accusation and its validation.

The issues involved at each step of this process involve identical decisions, identical judgments about the children's relationships to their families. Whether it be investigation of a complaint of child mistreatment, the recommendation that the child be removed, the decision as to whether to return the child, or the decision to terminate parental rights, the same value issues present themselves. Priorities must be assessed among the same competing interests: those of the child, the family, and the community. If the issue were simply the protection of children versus the legal rights of their parents, matters would be difficult enough. However, the current viewpoint and value stance concerns not only the harm to children that might emanate from their parents, but equally important the harm to children that might come to them through separation from their parents and particularly, the harm that can come to them from ambiguous substitute family arrangements. Hence, maintenance of family integrity is seen not simply as a matter of parents' rights but as an integral consideration of children's welfare. Protection of children from their parents must be weighed against protection of children from the harms of family dismemberment. Hence, at every step of the process, how the agencies and their workers relate to parents is integrally involved in the efforts to protect children from the relative harms that might befall them in the alternative courses to be chosen. Indeed, from the moment of recognition of child mistreatment until a family is dismissed from agency purview, reunited, with the child no longer in danger, or until the family is totally dismembered through termination of parental rights, this delicate balance of the child's interests must be sought. Clearly these are matters that present serious issues in professional competence and professional judgment. However, they also give rise to potential ethical issues.[4,15]

The multiplicity of functions presents the most serious ethical issues. Indeed, it is difficult to judge where matters of professional competence leave off, where matters of legal proscription and those of ethical issues begin. At the crux of both the issue of professional competence and of the ethical issue is the high potential for role conflict involved in the proscribed positions in dealing with these issues. Whether it be the child protective worker making an investigation or the foster care worker charged with making a recommendation about return of a child home, the functions are complex and with high potential for conflict. At once the social worker is expected to gather evidence, to perform a surveillance role, and to establish and maintain a productive helping relationship. Within that context how indeed are values on self-determination, respect of privacy, and confidentiality to be upheld?

Studt has most comprehensively developed our understanding of these ensuing, conflicting roles for social workers who are engaged in fields of practice where agencies are involved in carrying out both a social control function and a social support one.[11,12] That both functions should be vested in the same professional is itself controversial.[13] At the root of the controversy lies the notion of coercive action, whether legally sanctioned or not, even when that coercion is benevolent in intent. Some argue that it is morally wrong to engage persons in therapeutic relationships under duress, some that it is impossible, and still others—certainly those in protective services—that it is the only way to help some people. The weight of evidence is actually on the side of the latter, as the entire literature on child protective services is replete with accounts of initially hostile and unwilling parents, who subsequently were able to establish significant and healing relationships with protective workers, whose initial entry into their lives was based on the exercise of authority.[6]

Although much has been written describing the nature of the authority of social workers in situations of child mistreatment, essentially distinguishing between authority that is based on professional competence as opposed to that which is essentially legal in nature, the distinctions in practice are blurred and ambiguous.[2]

Authority to remove children from their parents, even temporarily, must come from the courts if parents are unwilling. Hence, the exercise of professional authority is always reliant on the back-up of legal authority. In day-to-day practice, the nature of such relationships requires an exquisite balance of casework skills and personal integrity. The line between honestly informing a parent of the risks that they are running by not cooperating and simply threatening or even blackmailing them can become a fine one. Sometimes the perception of threat by the client may be beyond the control of the worker, even though not intended. Some parents, for example, may be very fearful of going to court and submit to a suggestion that they voluntarily place their children, even though that is very much against their wishes. A similar kind of situation may exist when workers in carrying out their surveillance role in protecting children make unannounced visits to the home. Such a practice itself is controversial, but some who oppose it do not do so on the basis of an infringement of the parents' right to privacy, but rather that it might interfere with the establishment of the casework relationship.[1]

As noted these kinds of problems are not unique to protective work in child mistreatment but overlap those in other areas where the client is not a voluntary one, and where the worker has the dual roles of helper and social control agent, including correctional work and work with the mentally ill. It is perhaps somewhat more complicated in child mistreatment because of the ambiguity of just who the client is: the child, the parent, or the community? As we have already noted the belief that the child is in fact best served through rehabilitation of the parents, and maintainance or reunification of the family unit, then presumably the only "client" is the entire family unit. The protective function, however, does imply that the child's safety takes precedence over all other possible priorities.

In the early era of child protective work under the Societies for the Prevention of Cruelty to Children, these issues were not so pronounced. These societies performed primarily a law enforcement function, their only role was to protect children, and rehabilitation of the parents and maintenance of the family unit was not their concern. It is with the latter day mingling of the two functions that the issues emerge, and they emerge especially out of ethically adhering to casework principles and values, predicated more on the assumption of an individual client who voluntarily seeks help. Nowhere, for example, does the Code of Ethics of the National Association of Social Workers deal with the use of authority, nor with the fine line between coercion and engagement.[8] Yet these are matters that go to the core of ethical issues in social work's involvement in child mistreatment.

To some extent, willingly or unwillingly, social work has been relieved of coming to resolution of some of these issues, principally those of balancing the rights of parents with the protection of children. Given certain changes in the legal requirements of the conduct of the Juvenile Court, coupled with an aggressive interest in social work's performance by some segments of the legal profession, the authority and the power of social workers in the court's proceedings have been curtailed. The two principal changes involve the appointment of counsel for the parents with a concomitant move toward stricter adherence to the rules of evidence in the court's proceedings. Representation of the child's interest by counsel is becoming more common. Recent legislation setting standards by which federal monies may go to states in dealing with child mistreatment require at least that a guardian *ad litem* be appointed for all children going through court proceedings.[14] What this means is that the previous role of social work in court proceedings involving child mistreatment with respect to protecting the legal rights of any of the parties is being gradually eroded. What this also means is that the dominant ethical code influencing court proceedings, and hence the disposition made in cases of child mistreatment, is that of the legal profession, not that of the social work profession. It can also be expected that such changes in the courts will and are having an influence on social workers' behavior in cases where court involvement is not sought. For example, workers learn what types of mistreatment the court will or will not entertain, what kinds of evidence will or will not be admissible, and in effect must distinguish those situations where their professional authority is in fact backed up by the court's authority and those where this is unlikely. Thus, even in social work intervention that does not concern the courts, it can be expected that professional performance will still be influenced by the ethics of another profession.

To some this is a welcome change, especially to some in the legal profession. To others, including many line workers in protective agencies, this erosion in their power is perceived as a barrier to their adequate protection of children and the effectiveness of their treatment plans with the parents, parents who are unwilling to voluntarily cooperate. For many this indeed raises an ethical dilemma as to what their responsibility is to children who they think are in need of protection, but for whom they are not empowered to administer their protective intervention. At a very basic level, this can concern a child in a home where the parents refuse the social worker entry and where law enforcement does not consider the matter within their purview. On the other hand, it can mean that a foster care worker who thinks that parental visiting is upsetting to the child's adjustment in the foster home is helpless in curtailing the visitation rights of those parents, if the courts will not enforce such curtailment. These painful dilemmas for the child welfare workers perhaps may be contributing factors to the very high turnover rates. The dilemmas stem, however, not only from changes in the courts and legal profession but as much from the ambiguity and confusion that exists in the child welfare worker's role, the confusion between authority and helping, and the confusion between allegiance to two parties, parents and children, when in fact at times these parties are themselves adversaries.[9] Clarification of such role definition cannot be expected to be resolved by individual workers but rather are the responsibility of administrators and policymakers and of the entire profession.

Social workers other than those directly involved in child welfare settings may also have ethical issues in their practice with respect to child mistreatment. What, if any, is the responsibility of social workers whose adult clients may be potentially or actually victimizing their children? To some extent this is already mandated by law in many states, those that specify social workers among those who are mandated to report child mistreatment. For those who work directly with children, who are in a position to observe their state of well-being, this legal mandate is clear. However, what about the implications for those social workers who do not work directly with children, but whose adult clients have children in their care? Where does their responsibility lie? Obviously, one does not report what one does not know about, but what is the responsibility of social workers to find out how well or how poorly their clients are fulfilling the parental role? This is particularly important with respect to those working with clients whose problems can reasonably be expected to affect adversely their parental role performance, including drug and alcohol abuse, some mentally ill parents, and some criminal offenders. Reporting of child mistreatment is not the fundamental issue here. Clearly no suggestion is being made that all social workers take on the function of investigating child mistreatment in their clientele. Rather what is being suggested is that all social workers have a responsibility to their clients and to their client's children to know about and be concerned about this very important relationship in their lives, regardless of what the focal or presenting problem may be in their relationship to the social worker.

To some extent increasing legislation regarding the rights to privacy of various clienteles dictates social workers' behavior. We may, however, have come to the point where the laws themselves conflict. For example, restrictions on releasing information about drug abuse clients can sharply conflict with child abuse reporting laws. Whether the laws absolve one from a basic responsibility to protect children may be more of an ethical concern than a purely legal duty.

Another set of issues concerns social workers who are dealing with the clienteles of protective agencies. Principally these revolve around confidentiality. To what extent should they be expected to share information with the protective agency? To what extent, for example, should their records be available to the protective agency, including liability for court subpoena? These are matters of agency policy and will be dealt with in the next section pertaining to those issues.

ADMINISTRATIVE AND POLICY MAKING ISSUES

Although ethics may indeed be concerned with matters that essentially involve the individual social worker, respect and fulfillment of the ethical obligations often cannot be achieved without administrative structures that enhance such achievement.[16] Further, some goals of social work ethics cannot best be reached by the individual worker, but only by the collective action of agencies and of the profession. With respect to child mistreatment, these kinds of issues center on three points. The first concerns the structuring of the roles of child welfare workers, the kinds of supervisoral supports that are given them, and the expectations that are made of them. A second major area concerns the responsibility of child welfare workers to improve the social conditions that both engender the problems with which they must deal and that hamper the efficacy of their work. Included here, in the nature of all social agencies' relationships to the communities they serve, is an inherent ethical issue in the contract that is made with them, implicitly or explicitly, as to the goals that they can and cannot achieve. We deal with each of these in relation to child mistreatment.

The complexities of the child welfare workers' role, whether it be the child protective worker or the foster care or adoption worker delineated in the last section, clearly calls for administrative consideration of the ethical issues involved in carrying out that role. Although it is possible that the dual function of helping and of surveillance can be successfully carried out by the same individual, it is also possible that at least in some cases more effective performance could be achieved by separating the roles. Such a method has been tried in some local authorities in England. In a given case adjudicative matters are handled by one worker on a case while matters pertaining to therapy and rehabilitation are handled by another, in essence a team approach, with all workers playing one or the other role on all of their cases at a given time.[17] Studt similarly has suggested a team approach deriving out of correctional work.[12] This is an imaginative approach, which should have strong potential for reducing the role strain that the ethical dimemma can produce, as well as a means of insuring more adequate fulfilling of the function in any given case. The potential for the abuse of authority in the helping relationship would seem to be reduced also.

The supervisorial relationship in social work has traditionally been one wherein workers are helped to resolve issues not only involving their professional competence but also to help them meet ethical standards. However, supervisors themselves may be torn in their own allegiances to children or to parents, and shared responsibility, through group supervision, peer consultation, and the like, is a means of infusing multiple viewpoints on a given situation, in the hopes of reaching greater objectivity. These issues, well recognized in child protective work, may become more pronounced with the new legislation and social action to reduce the length of time that children spend in foster care, through either their return home or through termination of their parents' rights and adoption.[15] The present organizational arrangements that prevail in most public child welfare agencies, and certainly in those child welfare systems where responsibilities are shared with private agencies, tend to run counter to these goals. If reunification is to take place, obviously parents of children who are in foster care must be actively involved with the agency and with their children. The issue becomes once again one of allocation of function. Does the same worker maintain responsibility for work with the family, work with the child, and supervision of the foster home placement? Is that same worker also the one who is charged with making the recommendation as to whether reunification should take place, or whether parental rights should be terminated? These may sound like organizational matters unrelated to ethical issues beyond those to promote adequate professional performance. However, at the root of any ethical code there must be honesty. If child welfare workers are to work under a mandate that parents be given an opportunity to bring their parental performance up to expectations, and a child welfare agency accepts responsibility for assisting them in that regard, then that responsibility must be met. If it is not, the danger is twofold. Some parents may be unjustly deprived of their parental right. On the other hand some children may be returned to homes that are unsafe. The latter is especially true because of the current pressure on workers and agencies to respond to case review, case reviews that have as their goal the reduction of the number of children in care. The challenge posed by these mandates can of course be simply met bureaucratically, through the shuffling of papers and the filling out of required forms. If, however, they are to be met professionally, then it would seem that there are grave ethical questions as to how the interests of both parents and children can best receive adequate attention and just treatment. Among these is the question of where responsibility for rehabilitating parents, protecting children, and supervising their care is to be allocated.

A related set of issues, involving the use of agencies and workers outside the protective network, are germane here. It is thought, by some, that all therapeutic and ancillary social services to families who have mistreated their children should be lodged outside of the protective services and placement agencies. Essentially, this would separate the two functions, at least organizationally. Additionally, it is thought that other agencies are better equipped to provide such services. To what extent then is the surveillance function to be simply transferred to or shared with them? Here, agency policies must clearly delineate what the relationship is to be. If some agencies refuse to deal at all with the clients of protective services, then it would seem that they violate free access of their services to them, which is discriminatory. Protective agencies, on the other hand, can contribute to such a situation by insisting on total access to information. These issues are yet to be resolved, but they may become of paramount importance as the use of contractual arrangements in the delivery of social services becomes increasingly common. One possible guideline for resolution might be that agencies and their workers are responsible for acting on matters where they see that children are endangered, which in most cases are already covered through the reporting laws. Beyond that, contracting agencies should be able to follow the conventions of confidentiality in all other matters. In any case, it is imperative that all agencies involved be clear about the sharing and use of information. Otherwise it is impossible for their workers to be clear with their clients as to the nature of their relationship, its limitations and boundaries, and its safeguards and protections. Without such assurances, the workers and clients cannot possibly proceed in a relationship within the usual bounds of social work ethics.

A strongly related issue, with respect to both child protective work in dealing with the initial phases of mistreatment as well as the ultimate disposition of them through reunification or adoption, concerns the matter of available resources. Accumulated experience with situations of child mistreatment gives child welfare agencies knowledge about both the social conditions that contribute to mistreatment and equally important the social conditions, including the lack of community resources, that stymie their own efforts to abate and ameliorate these situations. If one part of the social workers' ethical code includes a commitment to improving social conditions, does it not follow that identification and pursuit of amelioration of these conditions is a responsibility of these agencies? The entanglement of conditions of poverty with all forms of child mistreatment is too well known. These same conditions persist in the lives of these people after they are identified as cases of child mistreatment, and these same conditions have an impact on the efficacy of any social work efforts to ameliorate their situations. While change in these conditions may be well beyond the influence of any individual worker, at the very least it would seem that the administration of child welfare agencies has a responsibility to document those factors which intrude on their efforts to fulfill their responsibilities to the children, the family, and the community.

Issues of racism, as well as poverty, are enmeshed in problems of child mistreatment. While it is clearly impingent on the individual social workers to live up to their own ethical code, not to discriminate against anyone because of race, color, religion, sex, or national ancestry, the kinds of judgements that must be made in situations of child mistreatment are highly vulnerable to such discrimination. Indeed one of the accusations most often made against child protective efforts is that they constitute the imposition of one set of cultural values on groups with different values. Clearly, then, a continuing ethical issue in the management of child mistreatment revolves around the underrepresentation among those managing it of persons from racial, ethnic, and religious groups who are the victims of discrimination in our society. Only through such representation can the ethical standards be met.

ISSUES FOR THE PROFESSION

Some of the ethical dilemmas that confront social workers dealing with child mistreatment can really only be solved by the profession as a total entity. Three issues are paramount. The first concerns the further development of social workers' ethical stance in relation to the involuntary client and in relation to the use of authority. The second is related to the first and that is the value placed by the profession on work with this type of situation and its obligation to the families and the children who are victims of mistreatment. The third and final issue concerns the profession's own responsibility for documentation of its performance in this area.

In the discussion of individual workers' own ethical problems that ensue from the dual obligations of performing both a helping and a social control function, it was noted that nowhere in the

National Association of Social Worker's Ethical Code can one find any mention of ethical guidelines for professional behavior in such situations. While there have been some in the social work profession who have dealt with these issues, the literature is scant. Child protective work, it was noted, is not the only social work endeavor that puts social workers into such a position. Perhaps the most important ethical question facing the profession with respect to child mistreatment is a final coming to grips with the fact that social work as a profession does accept among its societal mandates responsibility for exercising authority and control over certain clientele. Unless the limitations of that authority are more clearly spelled out than they presently are, by the profession itself, not by other professions, that authority is neither professional nor legal—it is unbridled power. We can wait to have the bridle put on by others, as has happened to some extent in the area of child mistreatment, or we can exercise our own ethical responsibility and make intregal to social work practice theory and philosophy how that authority might justly be utilized, and what its abuses are.

A second area of concern of the entire profession, its organizations, and its educational institutions is the relative value within the profession placed on work with child mistreatment. What status and prestige is accorded such work? To what extent have educational institutions attended to the dilemmas that the work presents, and to what extent have they developed methods and techniques not only for resolving the dilemmas but for insuring professional competence among the workers? The best available knowledge indicates that most child welfare workers have not had formal social work education at the bachelors and/or at the master's level.[6] The National Association for Social Workers, for example, has clearly stated that the entry level worker in child protective services should be the B.S.W., yet they are without support from large segments of the profession in achieving implementation of that standard. If it were met, can we truly demonstrate that the profession of social work can produce superior practitioners, practitioners with clear ethical standards about their work?

With respect to the current thinking about the proper handling of child mistreatment, social work bears a special responsibility. Those over the decades who have sought a change in society's orientation to the problem, a change from criminal prosecution to therapy and rehabilitation, have had social workers in their forefront. Unless we, as a profession, are prepared to provide both protection of children and rehabilitation of their families we have placed ourselves in a serious ethical bind. By removal of criminal sanctions from the mistreatment of children by their own family members, sanctions that would apply to strangers committing the same act, we may have made the family a very dangerous place for children unless we are successful in our rehabilitative efforts. Consequently, it is impingent on us to be vigilant in the assessment of the efficacy of our endeavors.

REFERENCES

1. Brombaugh, Olive: Discussion, *Child Welfare, 36* February 1957.
2. De Schweintz, Elizabeth and Karl De Schweinitz: The place of authority in the protective service function of the public welfare agency. *Child Welfare, XLIII:* 286–91, 1964.
3. Giovannoni, Jeanne M. and Rosina M. Becerra: *Defining Child Abuse.* New York, The Free Press, 1979.
4. Goldstein, Joseph, Anna Freud, and Albert J. Solnit: *Beyond the Best Interest of the Child.* New York, The Free Press, 1973.
5. Institute of Judicial Administration and American Bar Association: *Juvenile Justice Standards Project: Standards Relating to Abuse and Neglect.* Cambridge, MA., Balinger Publishing Company, 1977.
6. Kadushin, Alfred: *Child Welfare Services* (3rd Edition). New York, Macmillan Publishing Co., Inc., 1980.
7. Kahn, Alfred: *Planning Community Services for Children in Trouble.* New York, Columbia University Press, 1963.
8. National Association of Social Workers: *Code of Ethics.* New York, National Association of Social Workers, 1978.
9. Rosenfeld, A. and Eli Newberger: Compassion vs. control: Conceptual and practical pitfalls in the broadened definition of child abuse. *Journal of the American Medical Association, 237:* 2086–2088, May 1977.
10. Siporin, Max: *Introduction to Social Work Practise.* New York, Macmillan Publishing Co., Inc., 1975.
11. Studt, Elliot. An outline for study of social authority factors in casework. *Social Casework, XXXV:* 233–43, 1954.
12. Studt, Elliot: *A Report of the Parole Action Study: Survellance and Service on Parole.* Washington, D.C., U.S. Department of Justice, Bureau of Prisons, National Institute of Corrections, 1978.
13. Szasz, Thomas S.: *The Myth of Mental Illness: Foundations of a Theory of Personal Conduct.* New York, Harper and Row, 1961.

14. United States Congress: *Public Law* 93–247.
15. United States Congress: *Public Law* 96–272.
16. Vinter, Robert: Analysis of treatment organizations. In Hazenfeld, Y. and R. English (Eds.): *Human Service Organizations: A Book of Readings.* Ann Arbor, The University of Michigan Press, 1974.
17. Wasserman, Sydney: Personal communication.

Chapter 6

ASIAN MINORITY

RAJU VARGHESE

It is not good conduct in universal terms that makes for ethical
conduct in social work practice; it is behavior that is consonant
with the requisites of the social work situation.
(Levy, 1976; p. 45)

Introduction

Asian immigrants constitute one of the most diverse and least
understood minority groups in North America. Much of the
cultural heritage of the Asian minority in North America is often
based on concepts and principles unique to Eastern societies and
alien to the West (Kim & Condon, 1975). These differences-in-
culture of Asian immigrants, both with their host country as well
as among themselves, can present the social worker with a number
of ethical dilemmas. Social work with Asian minority individuals
and groups requires a sensitivity to the special needs of these
people as well as an appreciation of the cultural and political
conflicts they are likely to experience in the postindustrial societies of Canada and the United States.

Simply considering "ethical issues in the practice of social work
with the Asian minority" in itself involves an ethical dilemma of
sorts. There is value in recognizing the unity and common heritage of Asian settlers in North America, as implied by the title. All
of the immigrants share in common the dream of a better life in
the new country. There also is value in being aware of their real
diversity and individuality (Morales, 1974). The author has been
aware of a tension between these two worthwhile objectives in
writing this chapter. Asian immigrants are a heterogenous group
of people who have come to North America from many different
countries of origin, including Japan, China, Korea, India, the
Indochina peninsula (Vietnam, Cambodia, Laos, Thailand), the

121

Philippines, and Samoa (Kitano, 1980). As a group they are divided by differences in language, religion, educational level, and general socioeconomic background (Schaeffer, 1979). These differences are maintained in the new country and passed down through succeeding generations. Although the Asian minority may come together for political reasons, Chinese immigrants rarely mingle socially with Japanese immigrants, for example, and vice versa. Even though most Asians subscribe to arranged marriage, intermarriages between Asians from different countries of origin, such as a bride from India and a groom from Japan, are seldom completed.

Another characteristic of this diversity is that it is not limited to national differences alone. Often people migrating from only one country seem to be so diverse culturally that there is little in common among them other than their country of origin. For example, in India, northerners feel little kinship with their southern countrymen, and vice versa. Differences in religion, language, and culture separate the two groups.

In a similar manner there may be variation in the loyalty of the immigrants between the host country and their homeland. Some immigrants have come to the West voluntarily, while others have been forced out of their homelands by famine or because of political and religious persecution. The circumstances under which one has made the decision to emigrate can have a considerable impact on the quality of each immigrant's feeling toward the new country.

While the maintenance of certain social and cultural differences among Asians has proven helpful in preserving each group's customs and values in a foreign culture, these same differences can erect barriers around each group, thus preventing a full integration with the host culture as well as among the separate groups themselves. Therefore, caution must be exercised when making generalizations about any group of people as diverse as the Asian minority in North America, as will be done in this paper. Overgeneralizing about a group of individuals can inadvertantly lead to stereotypical thinking. It has been all too easy for many people to characterize Asians as devious, crafty members of a "yellow horde" (California Advisory Committee on Civil Rights, 1975; Kitano, 1980; Lyman, 1974). However, in order to facilitate an understanding of several ethical issues in social work practice with this minority, it has been necessary to focus on the common heritage of Asians and their shared status in North America, to the exclusion of fully outlining their ethnic diversity and individuality. For the purpose of presentation, therefore, the Asian minority in North America will be considered together as a group.

Three Types of Ethical Dilemmas

It should be noted from the outset that many of the ethical conflicts in social work practice with the Asian minority involve decisions that have to be made between two courses of action, both of which are potentially good, although for different reasons. A choice has to be made between two positive yet conflicting goals that cannot both be attained at the same time. The ethical task confronting the social worker is not the simple matter of distinguishing obvious good from obvious wrong (Keith-Lucas, 1977). Instead, the dilemma involves weighing the relative benefits of each of two positive, yet competing, objectives and then choosing between them.

The social worker is confronted with three general types of ethical conflicts in practice with Asian immigrants (see Fig. 6-1). To be sure, there are many important issues in social work practice with the Asian minority. However, the ethical dilemmas that underlie these issues generally fall within three categories. The first dilemma involves handling attitudinal conflicts between the immigrants and their host countries on a number of matters relating to the family and certain sociopolitical issues. The question here is whether the social worker should respect the attitudes of the Asian immigrants at the expense of their assimilation into the dominant culture of their new homeland. The second dilemma refers to the difficulties of mediating the inner value conflicts of each Asian immigrant. For example, many Asian immigrants once settled in this country become acutely aware of a conflict between their desire to retain their old cultural heritage in their new home, on the one hand, and their desire to enjoy financial security and upward mobility in the new culture on the other, giving rise to value conflict. It sometimes appears as though one worthwhile objective must be sacrificed to the other. Finally, the social worker is confronted with ethical dilemmas of a sociopolitical nature, involving the distribution of power and limited resources among Asian settlers versus other interest groups and minorities in Canada and the United States. Each of these dilemmas will be

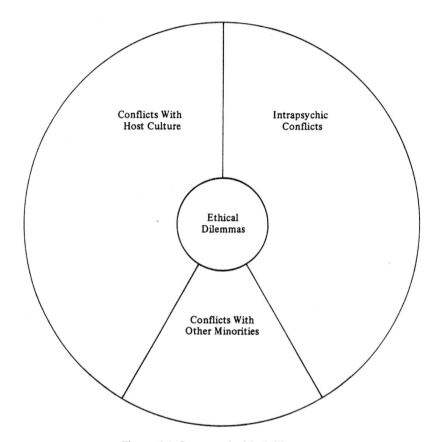

Figure 6-1. Sources of ethical dilemmas.

Asian Attitudes Regarding the Family

analyzed further in succeeding sections.

As previously mentioned the cultural heritage of many Asian immigrants includes certain values and practices antithetical to corresponding norms in the West. Prominent among the differences are those pertaining to the family and the roles of men and women in general. In several Asian countries, for example, women often assume a traditional role of subservience and obedience to men. To the male belongs the authority and prerogatives of family leadership and property ownership (Kitano, 1980). Wives are expected to follow their husbands for the remainder of their days. Even in the Hindu communities of India that follow a matriarchal system in which inheritance is carried down through the females in in a family, the men still exercise the power of governing the household.

Asian couples as well as single men and women who carry these sex roles with them to their new home in the Anglo society are likely to experience conflict with the evolving images of manhood and womanhood prevalent in Western culture. Asian women in particular are likely to feel a tug-and-pull between the safety of old ways and the freedom and challenge of a more "liberated" life-style available to them in the West. Counseling immigrant couples or individuals of either sex is likely to involve the social worker in thorny issues. For example, if a married woman seeking help is encouraged to take advantage of the freedom and opportunity offered women in the West, it may put additional stress on her marriage, possibly destroying or breaking it, and adversely affect her husband's adjustment to the new culture. On the other hand, counseling the wife to remain loyal to her traditional Asian concept of womanhood will almost inevitably lead to a sense of relative deprivation and of being out of step with the times. Either way something is gained and something is lost. The central ethical issue is whether the stability of a marriage built along traditional lines should be jeopardized for the sake of the woman's personal development and her assimilation into Western culture. This issue cannot be sidestepped by simply saying that it is up to the woman to determine what she wants, or through similar appeals to client self-determination. Especially if the woman is a wife and mother, others besides herself will be affected by her decision.

Just as relations between husbands and wives among Asian immigrants are different from most marriages in the West, so too do the relations between parent and child in the Eastern family vary in several respects from those common to the West (Ho, 1976). Asian parents often assume certain rights and expectations over their children that are at variance with most contemporary child care practices in the Anglo society. Children of Asian families living in North America, for example, are often at an early age expected to assume supervision of any younger brothers and sisters for a large part of the day, especially if both the mother and father are employed. Many Asian parents freely apply corporal punishment in response to infractions, and sometimes make use of guilt and shame as effective measures of discipline with their children (Ho, 1976; Kitano, 1980). Laughter, for instance, can be a potent mechanism of control which Japanese parents use in response to their children's misbehavior (Kiefer, 1974). Marriages are still arranged by parents in several of the Asian countries.

The author is aware of two separate incidents that illustrate the control Asian parents often exert over their children. In one case involving a first-generation Chinese family, seventeen-year-old twins were each led to commit suicide in response to the conflict they experienced between the values of their parents and those of their peers. The freedom and opportunity offered them in their new country made a strong impression, but their loyalty and attachment to their parents was so great, and the thought of disappointing them by becoming Americanized so unacceptable, that they concluded suicide was the only way out.

In another, an Indian family living in the United States, an eighteen-year-old woman was sent back to India by her parents as punishment for her elder sister's marriage to a black American. Not only was this interracial marriage unacceptable to the parents, it also preempted their prerogative in selecting a groom for each of their daughters. The punishment inflicted upon the second daughter was intended to set an example for the other children in the family. Parents may view their children's acceptance of Western ways as a personal failure on their part, leading them to exert more pressure on their children to conform to old ways. This action may also be tacitly condoned by the minority community-at-large.

As these two examples illustrate, one ethical conflict in working with Asian families involves weighing the rights of parents versus those of their children. Which should receive greater priority? Should the child's welfare be sacrificed for the sake of allowing the Asian parents to exercise their traditional rights? The second case points to another conflict, this being the one between the norms of the traditional culture and the laws of the adopted country. Clearly the eighteen-year-old woman, being of majority status, had the legal right to remain in the United States. However, from a cultural standpoint her parents were acting within their traditional

Indian rights by sending her back to India. Not only that, this move enabled the parents to save face to some extent among their fellow immigrants.

The worker is confronted with another dilemma. His (her) knowledge of the writings of Erikson (1963) and other personality theorists places him firmly against the parental use of shame and guilt with children. As he is well aware, feelings of guilt and shame can seriously impede a child's psychosocial development. On the other hand, challenging the parents on this issue entails other risks. If the parents should become conflicted between the old and new ways of child rearing and conclude that they are less-than-adequate as parents, the children also are likely to suffer from the anger and anxiety experienced by their parents over this question. The parents are being asked to make a break with one aspect of their cultural tradition, on the one hand, or else remain isolated and in conflict with their new society of peers on this issue. The children will also be confused if one parent decides to accept a more Western pattern of child rearing, while the other parent clings to a more traditional pattern. Thus there are risks involved whatever the social worker's plan, whether it be to assume a hands-off attitude or to guide the parents toward a less authoritarian style of parenting. The second generation of Asian American families has altered considerably this traditional family structure, but the configuration of the traditional parent-child interaction is basically unchanged (Reischauer & Fairbank, 1960). This creates yet another dilemma for social workers who have to deal with more than one generation of Asian minority families.

A similar dilemma involves the issue of the relation of each family member to the family unit itself. Family therapists have pointed to the dangers of an "undifferentiated family ego mass" (Bowen, 1972), or a family in which each member has no real separate identity apart from their membership in the family. When family members are overidentified with each other, the developmental process of achieving greater individuation and ego autonomy is hindered (Abbot, 1970). However, this thinking conflicts with the cultural norms in much of the East. Asians generally believe that when a clash of interests occurs between the family as a whole and one of its members, the individual member should automatically sacrifice his self-interest for the sake of the family (Ho, 1976). If given a choice between caring for needy parents on the one hand, and pursuing a promising career in a distant city on the other, for example, a young man or woman should be expected to stay home and care for his/her parents. Asians stigmatize anyone who abandons his/her familial responsibilities. It can never be determined whether such an action is morally right or wrong; one can only express an opinion about a decision or a preference for a particular decision (Reamer, 1979).

Undoubtedly arrangements and customs of this nature have adaptive values throughout much of Asia, where the extended family is often a more significant source of support and resources to the adult than in the West. It may be less necessary in the West, however, where public social services perform many of the functions served by the Eastern family. The dilemma is this: if the children of Asian immigrants are encouraged to individuate and develop an identity apart from their family—an outcome that may be more adaptive in our culture—the older members of their families, who have learned to depend upon family unity as a source of stability and meaning in their own lives, will be adversely affected. The social control every family exercises over its members serves a useful function to many Asian adults. On the other hand, the children of Asian immigrants will probably feel unnecessarily frustrated and deprived of freedom and an inner control of their lives relative to their peers if they are expected to continue to provide as much life-long loyalty to their families as would have been the case in their country of origin. Regardless of which objective is pursued in social policy and clinical practice, there are risks involved and a price to be paid by one or more segments of the Asian minority. The question is how much maintaining the viability of the family system in the Asian community should take precedence over developing the individual potential of each person in this minority. On a deeper level, the conflict is one between the benefits of personal control versus those of social control. Should social custom, rather than personal aspirations and dreams, be the dictate of personal destiny?

The Stigma of Receiving Outside Help

In still other respects the social worker involved with Asian immigrants is likely to experience a conflict between the need to respect the ethnic identity of his clients, including certain attitudes that may be antithetical to his own, and the need to mobilize whatever resources he feels are necessary for effective helping. Asian immigrants attach a greater stigma than do North Americans to receiving help from public, nonfamily sources (Weaver, 1976). As mentioned earlier, the extended family is the primary source of social and financial support throughout much of the Far East (Kitano, 1980; Schaefer, 1979). This fact can place the social worker in a dilemma. He may be aware of certain public services that are designed to handle specific problems a client may be having, but to get his client involved with one of these problems may be considered by his client to be insulting or demeaning.

In the case of adults this represents somewhat less of a concern since each adult has the right to receive or reject help from a public source after being made aware of its availability. In cases involving families with children, however, there is a real question about whether the child's welfare should be compromised out of a need to respect the parents' reluctance to use those public services that could effectively help their child. On the other hand, the family situation will not be helped if the parents feel humiliated over receiving assistance from an outside source. A similar dilemma may arise when the aged are still living with their adult children. The children may be reluctant to have their parents apply for Medicare or utilize the services of a retirement home or even a local senior citizens drop-in center, even if they are in need. This is done out of a fear of the stigma attached by their community to receiving help outside the family institution.

A corollary dilemma involves cultural confidentiality versus professional sharing. It is a dictum of the Asian culture that "whatever happens in the family stays within the family." The Asian client who seeks professional help may feel pressured to violate this rule and his family loyalty. Thus, while a full understanding of the situation may be a prerequisite to effective service, the social worker may be loathe to ask his client(s) to violate their standards of confidentiality. On at least one occasion this author has been politely reminded by an Asian couple in family counseling that whatever happened between the two of them should remain between them and was none of the worker's business.

Asian Social Philosophy

There are likely to be additional areas of conflict between social workers and Asian immigrants, which can lead to further ethical dilemmas. There is a world of difference between the social philosophies of both groups. Together social workers are committed to the concept of an egalitarian society with a permeable structure affording upward mobility to all citizens (Fink, 1974). Social problems and the dysfunctional behaviors of individual members all are considered to have a social cause in factors such as poverty, injustice, the unequal distribution of goods and services, and other structural considerations. These social problems are all amenable to change through appropriate intervention in the social structure. Life is not simply to be accepted as is; something can and should be done about socioeconomic problems. Finally, in regard to authority, the only legitimate authority is considered to be that which has been *earned* through knowledge, breadth of experience, or achievement. Authority *conferred* upon someone by reason of age, family of origin, or financial status is less worthy of respect (Eitzen, 1978).

This activist, egalitarian philosophy contrasts with the more fatalistic social philosophy of many Asian immigrants living in the United States and Canada. Asians harbor great respect for relative status and are relatively comfortable with the presence of a rigid hierarchy of socioeconomic positions (Kitano, 1980). One is reminded of the caste system in India, for example. Caste in India is passively accepted and endorsed by many Indians on the basis of religious and philosophical explanations (Berreman, 1960). Authority conferred upon someone by reason of age, wealth, or family of origin is often considered as legitimate as rational authority earned through knowledge and achievement.

Asians frequently have a more fatalistic outlook on life: each individual should accept his station in life (Ho, 1976). Social problems, including the unequal distribution of resources, are often seen as being manifestations of a divine mystery. Some even consider material wealth and possessions irrelevant to the primary concerns of life. Those believing in reincarnation, such as the Hindus of India, believe we may have to travel through many different stations of life before reaching "nirvana."* It is therefore considered futile to tamper with the fabric of society with its rich and its poor—what shall be, shall be.

This creates a dilemma for the social worker. On the one hand, he should respect the ethnic identity of this minority, which includes respecting their sometimes fatalistic philosophy of life. On the other hand, he also is expected to work for the betterment of their lives, in part by marshalling social resources in their behalf. This helping process may prove disruptive to the ideology of many Asian immigrants, creating tension between their cultural heritage and their awareness of legitimate efforts being made in their behalf. The social worker's role is that of a helper and an enabler; his practice with Asian minorities, or any other group for that matter, is predicated on the assumption that positive change *is* feasible in most situations. Effective changes are sometimes accomplished by challenging established authorities and dealing directly with the secular, earthly causes of poverty, injustice, poor housing, and high levels of unemployment that the Asians may face. In these tasks the social worker may be successful, but he may achieve success at the expense of disregarding the Weltanschauung of his clients.

In still another respect Asians differ significantly from North Americans in their social outlook. In the East, personal fulfillment can be achieved only through the satisfaction of one's social commitments to family and community. The strength of the individual primarily lies in the strength of his family and community. Displaying conspicuous talents and individual precocity are both frowned upon in Eastern societies (Kiefer, 1974). This position contrasts with the individualism of Western culture, where family and society exist to serve the individual's needs, and not vice versa. The social worker's dilemma is that while the socialism of

---

*A term mentioned in Hinduism and Budhism to denote the "perfect happiness in which the self becomes part of the supreme spirit of the universe."

the Asian immigrant may still be functional in certain respects within each minority community, this outlook may nevertheless be less-than-adaptive in the competitive rush of life in the West.

Inner Conflicts of Asian Immigrants

Just as there are attitudinal conflicts between Asians and North Americans that can create ethical dilemmas for the social worker, so too Asian immigrants are likely to experience conflicts in their own value-system when they settle in North America. These inner conflicts in turn can lead to moral dilemmas for potential helpers. What are some of these conflicts? Basically, they involve the tension between the desire to retain one's ethnic identity and the desire to assimilate oneself into the host culture (Kitano, 1980; Schaefer, 1979). Both are legitimate interests, but the pursuit of one may lead to the sacrifice of the other. One specific conflict frequently experienced involves the desire to achieve economic success and upward mobility in the new culture, but not at the expense of losing contact with one's culture of origin. Unfortunately these two values often conflict; to achieve the comforts and security of a well-paying job in Western society it may be necessary to "fit" into the dominant culture and give up old ways that appear foreign in the host country. To go ahead and make this compromise may prove unsettling to older members of the Asian family. On the other hand, a decision to preserve old ways and customs at the expense of greater assimilation into the host culture may interfere with the adjustment of the children at school and limit their opportunity for later advancement.

A similar conflict involves the choice between having the sense of safety and security afforded by old customs and routines, and the sense of freedom offered by the opportunities for new activities and friendships that will unfold in the new culture. Many Asians, especially those escaping persecution at home, have come to North America in pursuit of a greater choice in determining their destiny; however, the security and familiarity of the more rigidly structured life they left behind may still exert a seductive appeal in the face of the relative normlessness and greater freedom-of-choice open to them in the West. Sometimes it is easier to have decisions regarding career, marriage, and life-style ready-made by the culture and one's family, rather than having to grapple with them alone. This need for security with autonomy, coupled with the absence of a clear social network that supports the immigrant in their pursuits of safety and independence, can lead to what Erikson (1963) refers to as the "crisis of identity." This crisis is experienced in elevated levels of stress and anxiety among many immigrants. As a result of this, hypertension, suicide, and psychiatric disorders are not uncommon among second and third-generation Japanese and Philippino immigrants (Weaver, 1976).

Group Versus Individual Identity

A deeper issue underlies both of these conflicts: the tension between maintaining a group identity versus maintaining an individual identity. To what extent is the Asian immigrant willing to sacrifice opportunities to develop his individual identity in the new country for the sake of maintaining his ties to his family and the Asian community, or vice versa? This same issue must be faced by everyone who is a member of a group, whether it be a family, an ethnic minority, or a group at work or in the community.

As before, this conflict presents a moral dilemma to anyone who is working with this minority. Which goal should guide social work with the Asian minority—maintaining the group integrity of the Asian community, or encouraging each immigrant to pursue his own individual interests and potential as a member of the host culture? Which objective should provide the basis for policies and programs directed to Asian immigrants living in North America? If the maintenance and unity of the ethnic group (including individual families as well as whole communities of Asian immigrants) is pursued as the primary objective, the individuality of each Asian immigrant, with his own special needs and interests and talents, may be severely compromised. Preserving the integrity of the Asian community may perhaps affect the children of Asian immigrants the most, creating greater tension in them between the worlds of home and school (Kim and Condon, 1975). Maintaining the integrity and separateness of the Asian communities in North America will also tend to limit their opportunity or capacity to make use of educational and social resources available to the general populace, and to be fully assimilated into the work force and therefore upwardly mobile. However, pursuing the other objective, the development of each immigrant's uniqueness and his personal potential, will also exact a penalty from certain members of the Asian community. This would include those immigrants, especially older ones, who have been completely socialized into a tightly knit family and community and who stand to lose the most by its gradual dissolution as individual members break away and dissolve their strong identity with the group.

Ethical-Political Conflicts

This last conflict has a political dimension as well. While from a purely psychological standpoint it might be advisable to foster the development of each immigrant's personal identity and his awareness of himself as a separate, inner-directed being, there are political advantages to having the members of this minority, as with any other minority, conceive of themselves largely in terms of their belonging to a particular minority group. This advantage is based on the truism "united we stand, divided we fall." If Asian immigrants act as a group and are perceived as a united bloc of people, their political influence in legislative decision making and policy formation will be far greater than if they act and are perceived as being a collection of separate individuals/groups divided in their interest and needs, with little uniting them.

The problem thus is that while building self-autonomy and individuality is psychologically healthy, at least in this Western culture, it may be counterproductive from a political standpoint. Perceiving each Asian immigrant solely in terms of his membership in a tightly knit group can lead to stereotypical thinking and a general perception of the Asian immigrants as an insular, alien people. However, it can also lead in government to a greater awareness of the potential of the Asian minority to act as a powerful bloc of votes in North American elections. This, in turn, can lead to a greater sensitivity on the part of politicians to the needs and special interests of the Asian minority.

Compared to other minorities such as Blacks and Spanish-Americans, Asian immigrants are sometimes labeled the "model minority" or "the quiet Americans." The media often portray Asians as clean, frugal, and industrious people. Many believe

Asians are free from collective disadvantage and unfulfilled aspirations, because they rarely demonstrate disapproval or dissatisfaction with their social position (Kitano & Sue, 1973). This circumstance points to another political problem for the Asian immigrants. The higher their esteem in the public eye, the less incentive there is for the majority to pay attention to their specific needs and problems (Kim, 1973). It seems as though a minority must become "a problem" to Anglo society before it receives the needed attention of the public. So, the dilemma is that the positive image of Asians in Western culture may actually be counterproductive to the long-term political needs of this group.

Still other political questions raise moral dilemmas for the social worker involved with Asian immigrants. The Asian minority is but one of many minorities in North America, all of which to some extent are competing among themselves for a greater portion of the distribution of goods and services, and better access to opportunities in education and employment. The question is to what extent each minority must achieve these goals at the expense of the other minorities. For example, will special-education programs designed to help the children of Asian immigrants learn the English language and prepare them for admission to the public school system also divert funds needed for other educational programs primarily serving blacks and other minorities? How much will retraining Asian adults for entry into the job market enable them to successfully compete against other minorities for jobs? The recently publicized tensions between blacks and Cuban immigrants in Florida only call attention to the fact that the claims of separate minorities are often perceived as being in conflict with each other. Each group believes it is competing with the others for a limited slice of the pie of socioeconomic opportunity and resources. To the extent that this is true, a balance must be sought between the legitimate needs of Asian immigrants with those of other minorities to arrive at the best distribution of financial and social services among the needy groups. This is not an easy process, and to some extent involves pitting the welfare of one group against that of the others.

Conclusion

There can be no universal formula available to resolve the
ethical conflicts in social work with the Asian minority. Returning
to the quotation at the beginning, each situation must be assessed
on its own merits, with the individual needs and rights of each
involved party being carefully weighed and balanced one with
another. This will be a less-than-satisfactory conclusion for those
looking for a neat, comprehensive solution to the dilemmas considered in this chapter. However, the need to resolve each dilemma
on its own individual terms and within a uniquely personal frame
of reference provides one of the stimulating challenges for social
workers in their practice with the Asian minority.

These ethical dilemmas have important clinical implications.
For one, effective work with Asian immigrants at all levels of
practice entails an awareness of these conflicts and the problems
they are likely to create. It is not necessary that the social worker
himself be Asian to achieve this sensitivity; an awareness of Asian
culture can be developed in non-Asian social workers through
workshops and other appropriate training. Engaging in values
clarification with individual clients may be a necessary prerequisite to their becoming responsive to social work intervention, so as
to help them resolve their inner tensions and overcome conflicts
they are experiencing with the host society. Their adaptation to
the new country will be enhanced if the social worker is able to
find a common ground between the old and new cultures, thus
making the new culture seem less alien and forbidding (Kuramoto,
1971).

Social work with the Asian minority will test the worker's flexibility and his tolerance for values and practices that, while being
antithetical to his own beliefs, nevertheless have a functional
value to many Asians. Applying pressure to force this minority to
conform to Western ways of thought will only force the immigrants to retreat back into their own enclosed communities. Because
of the importance the Asian groups attach to their social and
cultural heritage, the social worker may have to flexibly adapt
himself to the unique contingencies of Asian communities and
rely upon resources in each community that are different from the

public social services he usually draws upon in his work with non-Asian clients.

Asian communities may continue to confront several sociocultural difficulties even if they were fully assimilated into the Anglo society. What we see now is the need to recognize the specific consequences of cultural differences and communalism and take action to deal with them. Moreover, just as many of the social and psychological problems suffered by the Asian minority are distinct, so are the organizational patterns and cultural traits that form the context in which social work practice must take place. These distinctive social patterns are obstacles only to efforts that attempt to deal with Asian groups as a monolithic entity. When this distinctiveness is recognized and community structures understood, social patterns become avenues.

REFERENCES

Abbot, Karen A.: *Harmony and Individuation.* Taipei, Oriental Cultural Service, 1970.

Berreman, Gerald D.: Caste in India and the United States. In Celia S. Heller (Ed.): *Structured Social Inequality.* New York, Macmillan Co., 1969.

Bowen, Murray: Towards the differentiation of self in one's own family. In J. L. Framo (Ed.): *Family Interaction.* New York, Springer, 1972.

California Advisory Committee on Civil Rights: *Asian Americans and Pacific Peoples, a case of mistaken identity.* 1975.

Eitzen, Stanley D.: *In Conflict and Order: Understanding Society.* Boston, Allyn & Bacon, 1978.

Erikson, Erik H.: *Childhood and Society,* 2nd ed. New York, Norton, 1963.

Fink, Arthur E.: *The Field of Social Work,* 6th ed. New York, Holt, Rinehart, 1974.

Ho, Man K.: Social Work with Asian Americans. *Social Case Work, 57(3):* 195–201, 1976.

Keith-Lucas, Alan: Ethics in social work. In *Encyclopedia of Social Work,* Vol. 1. National Association of Social Workers, 1977, pp. 350–355.

Kiefer, Christie W.: *Changing Cultures, Changing Lives.* San Francisco, Jossey-Bass, 1974.

Kim, Bok-Lim C.: Asian minority: no model minority. *Social Work, 18:* 44–53, 1973.

Kim, Bok-Lim C. and Condon, Margaret, E.: A study of Asian Americans in Chicago: Their socio-economic characteristics, problems and service needs. *Interim Report to the National Institute of Mental Health.* Washington, D.C., 1975.

Kitano, Harry H. L.: *Race Relations,* 2nd ed. Englewood Cliffs, N.J., Prentice-Hall, 1980.

Kitano, Harry L. and Sue, Stanley: Asian American: a success story? *Journal of Social Issues, 29:* 1973.

Kuramoto, Ford H.: What do Asians want? an examination of issues in social work education. *Journal of Social Work Education,* 7:3, 1971.

Levy, Charles S.: *Social Work Ethics.* New York, Human Sciences Press, 1976.

Lyman, Stanford M.: *Chinese Americans.* New York, Random House, 1974.

Morales, Royal: *Makibaba.* Los Angeles, Mountain View Publishers, 1974.

Reamer, Frederick G.: Fundamental ethical issues in social work: an essay review. *Social Service Review,* 53(2): 229–243, June 1979.

Reischauer, Edwin O. and Fairbank, John K.: *East Asia: The Great Tradition.* Boston, Houghton Mifflin, 1960.

Schaefer, R. T.: *Racial and Ethnic Groups.* Boston, Little, Brown & Co., 1979.

Weaver, J. L.: *National Health Policy and the Underserved.* Saint Louis, Mosby, 1976.

Chapter 7

OLDER PEOPLE

ABRAHAM MONK AND MARCIA ABRAMSON

THE UTILITARIAN HERITAGE

The attitudes of policy makers and human service professionals toward the care of the aged have traditionally reflected a utilitarian set of values. Questions concerning the sense or purpose of serving the elderly have usually drawn negative answers, which were also couched in the inevitable language of futility: after all, the argument goes, the aged are not going to get any better. It was further rationalized with the phraseology of cost-benefit analysis, which found no "multiplier effect" in service investments for the aged. This is quite in contrast to spending money for the education of the young: the capital may here provide good returns in skills, productivity, and other positive contributions to society. It added that costly health and social welfare services for older persons do not hold the promise of future payoffs, simply because the old may have no future left. Ultimately, the formalized service rendering function for this population cannot be intrinsically justified from a utilitarian perspective: it can only be accepted if it lessens the burden that befalls the relatives of the old.

From a utilitarian perspective, older persons are stereotypically viewed as an undifferentiated population category pretty much alike in the relentless march toward deterioration and helplessness. The frequency, for instance, with which physical and psychological symptoms of aged patients are subsumed under the label of senility led Glassman to define it as a "wastebasket" diagnosis irrevocably pinned to a person without the benefit of medical and sociopsychological assessments (1980).

The fact that mental failure may be triggered by reversible

factors, rather than brain damage, is ignored in the haste and fatalism of the utilitarian practitioners. Regrettably, their mistaken diagnosis of senility, when not questioned, leaves pathology untreated and on the way of becoming a self-fulfilling prophecy of true, irreversible senile dementia.

The utilitarian ethics failed to acknowledge the intrinsic significance of old age and, for that matter, the right of a human being, regardless of age, to complete his or her expectable life cycle. The reasoning of this ethics, when carried to its extreme logical consequences, may find justification to sanction geriatric genocide. The idea, incidentally, has been fictionalized *ad nauseam* in portraits of imaginary societies where skin wrinkles are found offensive and those over thirty are disposed of in joyous festivals.

There is, however, a grim policy reality that transcends the realm of fiction, and it consists of programs that hardly meet the needs of the aged. The corollary of the utilitarian philosophy has, therefore, been the disvaluation of the old in the apportionment of societal resources, as if the equity principle would not apply to them. This is a traumatic realization for new retirees reaching their sixty-fifth birthday and finding that their incomes are suddenly reduced by half or even less.

Many aged complain against the injustice of having the standard of living they enjoyed in their best productive years suddenly denied to them. They do not accept the argument that they can manage with less. As pointed out by Monk (1979), certain expenditures such as health care and home maintenance are particularly higher for this age. Many elderly must hire help for home chores and maintenance they could once do themselves. In addition, many elderly live in homes that require more repairs and have higher heating bills. Elderly people also feel they have the right to enjoy some amenities and take advantage of their leisure years in ways other than the virtual confinement forced on them by the loss of financial resources. The utilitarian ethic values productivity but places little emphasis on rewards for past productivity. Its related principle of distributive justice does not rest on reverence for the past. It is future oriented instead, seeking "multiplier effects," or present centered when advocating that those who work and raise families should get a larger and better share of rewards and benefits.

The utilitarian ethic does not perceive the aged as a repository of social wisdom. It simply considers them an obsolete category of people who outlived their usefulness.

The Anachronism of Utilitarianism

Although it may seem anachronistic, the utilitarian ethic emerged at a time when decreasing fertility and mortality rates have made older Americans more numerous and more visible than ever before in history. The relative representation of the aged will continue to grow in the near future: In 1900 the population 65 and over did not account for more than 4 percent of the total population. It has more than doubled—9.9 percent in 1970—and it will probably climb to 14 percent (one in 7 Americans) by the turn of the century. Given the longer life expectancy, morbidity rates inevitably go up. The number of multi-problem, frail elderly, actually the most intensive consumers of health and social services, is increasing at a faster rate than the overall number of elderly. Between 1975 and 2010, the population 85 and older is projected to increase by over 110 percent, while the expected increase in the 65 to 74 age group is less than 40 percent. Neugarten suggested the aged be dichotomized into an old-old group (75 and older) and a young-old (55 to 74) group because of their distinct generational characteristics and their implications for policy and services (1978). The "old-old" of today constitute the higher risk group. Many were immigrants who had little formal education. Many worked at low skill occupations for most of their lives and probably lost their occupations and meager resources during the Great Depression and did not recoup in the period of prosperity ushered in by the Second World War. Furthermore, they did not build up sizeable equities under the social security program as it developed in the 1940s and 1950s. Most now are no longer vigorous and active but instead require a wide range of supportive and restorative health services. These are the most vulnerable aged group for whom social losses are heaped onto the material losses of age. They are the group for whom, according to Christiansen, the general rule of geriatric ethics (that losses should not be compounded) most applies (1974).

The young-old are a more diversified group. Many are still healthy and vigorous. Distinguished from the middle-aged primarily by the event of retirement, many continue to seek meaningful ways to use their time, either in self-fulfillment or in community participation. Many continue to see their children frequently. Ties of affection and obligation are strong, and the family may continue to be an important part of daily life. Although their economic status is seriously jeopardized by inflation, for the most part they are neither poor nor near poor. Clearly, the ethical issues that confront social workers working with the young-old are of a very different nature than those with the old-old.

While the social work values of primacy of the individual and belief in the dignity and worth of persons applies to all people irrespective of age, issues of equity are a greater preoccupation among the "young-old." Concerns about autonomy, self-determination, and dependence affect, in turn, more directly the "old-old."

EQUITY AND THE YOUNG-OLD

It must be borne in mind, however, that no single-value morality can be adequate for professional practice. Callahan uses law, journalism, and medicine as examples of professional fields where competing values may act as sources of ethical dilemmas (1980). In journalism, the right of citizens to privacy, confidentiality, and respect of their personal reputation have become as important a moral consideration as the right of the public to information. In law, the interests of the client are being counterbalanced with the values of fairness and protection of the system of law. In medicine, finally, issues related to public health, the welfare of the family, and the allocation of scarce resources compete with a patient-centered ethic. It is not different in social work, where the fundamental values of the worth and uniqueness of all persons, as well as their inherent rights and opportunities, are often challenged by equally important values of family and society.

In the case of "the young-old" their right to work is challenged by the expectation of making room for younger generations of workers. It must be recalled that the principle of mandatory retirement was primarily instituted as a means to resolve the ills of unemployment among the young, not to benefit the aged. Today, it is being postponed from age sixty-five to age seventy, and it may be done away altogether because of the uncertain solvency of the social security system. Although structured as a social insurance program, in reality it functions as intergenerational transfer program: today's workers are taxed to support those of yesterday. Given, however, the growing numbers of the old, the readiness or docility of the labor force to pay increasing social security taxes cannot be taken indefinitely for granted. In essence, the aged were once forced out of the labor force to make room for the young. Tomorrow, they may be forced to stay in order to reduce the tax burden of the young. What the aged may wish or consider as their primary benefit is not taken into account as a primary determinant of social policy.

Retired persons find themselves constantly in a double moral jeopardy: they were first forced to leave the labor force without consideration to their wishes and capacity, by a society guided by a work-ethics and the value of productivity. They were subsequently disvalued and denied equitable enjoyment of society's resources precisely because they do not work. The risks of double jeopardy are repeated on a different level for the frail old-old, as discussed in the next section.

CASE MANAGEMENT AND PROTECTIVE SERVICES

An ethical consequence of ill health in the aging, and most specially among the "old-old," is that the crisis is defined as a chronic or definitive condition regardless of its real prognosis. An ill child or young adult, or even a middle aged person, is expected and encouraged to return to his or her premorbid normal functioning as soon as possible. No such anticipations are usually held in the case of the aged. Ordinarily in our society, the provision of health care services presuppose a temporary suspension of responsibilities, a right to care by others, and an imperative to get better. This applies to the elderly in a negative way: if once ill, they never really recover the role of a responsible, independent individual. Once applied, the sick label sticks and follows the aged person for the rest of his or her life. Aging, illness, and dependence thus turn into synonymous terms.

To a large extent this confusion often results from an absence of

adequate diagnostic procedures. The medical and psychosocial
assessment of elderly people requires a thorough familiarization
with the modal and expectable behavioral traits of this age category. Clear baseline criteria of typical functioning in later life are,
however, lacking. The resulting uncertainty coupled with the
attitudinal disinterest about old age among many human service
professionals leads to the therapeutic nihilism formerly alluded
to.

It is the responsibility of the social worker to assume a more
critical participation in the conduct of the medical and psychosocial
evaluation, to stress the need for more responsible treatment plans
and to ultimately advocate for continuity of care through a case
management function that insures periodic reassessments, at
repeated intervals. Regrettably, the social work participation in
multidisciplinary geriatric teams is often reduced to a service
linkage and resource locating function. As case managers, they are
absorbed in the task of facilitating access to a continuum of care
and attempting to provide the opportunity of choice among a set
of service alternatives. They spend their time and energies insuring and negotiating the coordinated delivery of services, to the
detriment of the periodic reassessment of client status and functioning. It thus represents a long-term maintenance task focused
on the mobilization of community resources and on the actual
delivery of health and social services more than on the understanding of the presenting and underlying problems. Case management is a highly individualized relationship. Although ethically consistent with client self-responsibility, the risks of slipping
into a paternalistic stance are constant, most specially when dealing with clients who require protective services.

AUTONOMY AND DEPENDENCE

The moral vision of the authentic existence of man as an autonomous individual is specially tested in the case of the aged. Autonomy depends on self-determination, which social workers foster by
presenting clients with viable alternatives from which to choose,
full information about these alternatives, and the opportunity to
freely choose without undue coercion.

If autonomy is a right, it implies obligations on the part of others who are in control of the opposite necessary means. They are required to provide both the positive means, i.e. give full information, and the negative means, i.e. refrain from unduly influencing or coercing.

What are the implications of autonomy for the elderly person? Take for instance Mrs. B., a seventy-four-year-old woman with diabetes and who is partially blind, who has lived in a nursing home for the past ten years supported by Medicaid payments. She feels secure in the home where she has many friends among patients and staff.

An arbitrary grading system has been established to evaluate skilled nursing patients to determine their suitability for transfer to a lower level of care. Patients are assigned a certain number of points according to ability to dress, feed, clothe, and toilet themselves. When she was evaluated, the patient received more than the designated number of points, indicating that she should be transferred to a health related facility, a lower level of care. In this way, the State can save money by caring for her at the lowest possible cost.

What are the competing values to patient autonomy in this situation? One is the allocation of scarce resources. By reassigning the patient to an institution that will provide adequate care at less cost, money can be saved for other elderly patients or even for younger patients who may need preventive or curative care. Furthermore, the medical and nursing resources of the nursing home can be used for someone who has more need for them.

A second principle concerns beneficence. Although Mrs. B. prefers the known nursing home because of familiarity and comfort, those who are responsible for her care feel that she can benefit from a move to a place that will allow her more independence. Therefore, the nurses and social worker who have been closest to Mrs. B. will attempt to convince her that the move will be in her best interest; she will be in a less restrictive setting where she will have more freedom. Since the access to treatment in the health related setting is also considered a right, by moving Mrs. B., the staff would be enhancing her autonomy. On the other hand, involving the principle of nonmaleficence, *premium non nocere* ("Above all do no harm"), one can question whether a move after ten years could be considered a traumatic transfer and cause more harm than good. Since the duty of nonmaleficence encompasses both intentional and unintentional harm, moving Mrs. B. may be interpreted as a violation of that principle.

In its most general sense, beneficence is a moral duty that consists in enabling others to further their interests. According to Beauchamp (1979) it becomes paternalism when the conception of benefit, harm, and their balance held by the social worker differs from that of the client, but professional judgment takes precedence. Some social workers experience moral and legal trepidations to impose service beyond attempts of gentle persuasion even when the older person may opt for a harmful course of action. They are concerned with civil rights and the fear of meddling injustifiably and taking over other people's lives. Client resistance certainly exerts an intimidating and even paralyzing effect. Other social workers are inclined to protect elderly clients against the consequences of their choices by a more direct form of intervention. In this instance benevolent paternalism conflicts with independence, and it is illustrated in a myriad of treatment situations, such as withholding information, less than full disclosure, and deception in order to increase benefit or at least to prevent further harm. The use of deception is even sanctioned in some forms of psychogeriatric treatment. Goldfarb starts from the premise that the elderly patient develops a misperception that the therapist is a powerful parental authority (1962). Goldfarb encourages the therapist to foster the image that he is in fact a protective parent at the client's service. Third, by granting the patient his demands, the therapist cultivates the illusion that the patient can control and exercise mastery over his parent surrogate and achieve control over this major source of gratification. Deception, like all forms of beneficient paternalism, is controversial, but it underscores the importance of manipulation in the lives of the aged and, for that matter, of any dependent population.

FAMILIES AND THE INSTITUTIONALIZATION DILEMMA

Respect of the autonomy of the elderly remains an important factor in their ability to age with full dignity. In the family situation, this ability often conflicts with the welfare of caretaking relatives. What happens, for instance, when family members feel that the old person is no longer capable of decision making but the elderly person insists that he is? A ninety-six-year-old man was admitted to the hospital for a gastrointestinal work-up by his fifty-nine-year-old daughter because of increasing incontinence. The daughter was also caring for her ninety-three-year-old mother who was dying of cancer of the esophagus. She felt she could no longer manage both parents; since her father in addition to his incontinence was also hard of hearing and uncooperative, she wanted him placed in a nursing home after hospitalization. The patient, who seemed perfectly intact mentally once one could get through the barrier of the hearing loss, did not want to be in the hospital, refused to allow the various medical procedures such as blood drawing, cathertization, or dietary regulations. It turned out that the patient did have a small gastrointestinal bleed, but he was unwilling to consent to surgery so no further treatment was planned. Thus, he remained in an active medical treatment unit where he was essentially receiving custodial care to await a nursing home bed to which he did not want to go.

Social workers are increasingly confronted with cases like the above involving several generations within a family. They tend to become serious when there are two generations of aging people, the younger one in its sixties or even seventies, caring for ailing parents in their eighties and nineties. Despite the ethical imperative that families ought to assume greater responsibilities for their old relatives, research evidence indicates that family responsiveness is adequate in emergency or acute situations but tends to weaken in the case of prolonged, chronic care. Although the majority of elderly persons have living children, the latter often have children of their own to care for. When confronted with the dilemma of responding to needs of those two generations, Streib found that the middle generation will give primacy to their own offspring rather than to their progenitors (1965). With smaller families and increased longevity, mainly of women, the aging cohorts are dominated by widows with fewer children as potential caregivers. Furthermore, many of the traditional caregiving women—daughters—are likely to be enrolled now in the work force. Even when families assume the responsibility to care for ailing older relatives, they may soon develop a burn-out syndrome and reach the limit of their helping capacity. True, there are instances in which relatives will not consider any plan other than the elderly patient's return home, no matter how great the hardships it will cause. In others, the relatives, while willing to take the older person in, are fearful for his or her safety—particularly if all members of the household are out of the home for most of the day. Still others—actually a growing majority—will resist encroachment on their time, energies, and emotions.

The result is that many of these aged persons end up in institutions. There are a number of complicating factors in selecting an institution suitable for an elderly patient who is medically ready for discharge from a hospital. These include the trend in psychiatric hospitals to exclude the elderly patient, the mix of young and old in some nursing homes, the mix of the mentally intact and the mentally infirm in others, the limits on time and scope of services written into the provisions of Medicare, the complex requirements for transferring elderly patients from hospitals to other facilities, the fragmentation and discontinuities in services and the uncertainties regarding payment for services that result from lack of coordination of Medicare, Medicaid, and voluntary health insurance programs.

The availability of suitable placements for an elderly patient changes constantly. Finding a vacancy at the time the patient is medically ready for discharge is complicated by unpredictable changes in institutional and reimbursement policies. As a result, patients are sent to institutions that provide a higher or lower level of care than is needed with little regard for preference or accessibility. Furthermore, the shortage of home health care facilities means that many elderly are sent to institutions when they could be maintained at home with adequate supportive home-care services.

Studies show consistently that, when given the choice, the elderly prefer home to institution (Shanas, 1968). In addition, studies have documented rapid functional deterioration of the institutionalized population while persons supported by homemakers and day care centers had higher levels of contentment, mental functioning, and social activity as well as lower mobidity and mortality (Yawney and Slover, 1973).

The nursing home, as an all-purpose solution to the health problems of the elderly, has created a set of iatrogenic problems: increased dependency, depression, and social isolation among the aged. Nursing homes in the United States imply some form of supervised care for medical and medically related problems; the term embraces those facilities that offer skilled nursing care, those that are personal care homes, and those with intermediate levels of care. The nursing home has become a last resort for a variety of problems from the terminally ill individual who requires intensive care, to recuperating patients who need brief convalescence time, and the less ill but infirm aged who lack the social resources to be able to remain in the community.

Nursing home residents vary along a continuum of physical impairment and mental disorientation. The deinstitutionalization in the 1960s of long-term elderly patients from state mental hospitals to nursing homes has resulted in a substantial number of nursing home residents with primary psychiatric disorders other than senility. Little social planning takes place to minimize the effects of mixing the mentally alert with the mentally frail.

Much of the recent debate over nursing homes has been concerned with poor quality of care and fiscal fraud. This emphasis has in many ways obscured the quality of life issues that arise from an inherent conflict of interest between a bureaucratic institution and the interest of the individual patient. For example, patients often wish to vary their meal times, come and go as they please, have visitors at different hours, and retain personal belongings and privacy, while the home's interests may be focused on administrative order. As Glasser points out, "When such conflict of interest arise, the nearly parental powers of the nursing home can quickly suffocate the basic rights of individual patients" (1978, p. 109).

As a result, many nursing home patients find themselves stripped of power and dignity. Although most of them are presumed competent in the eyes of the law, they realize that the institution has almost total control of their lives. The elderly person is dependent upon the institution for food, clothing, recreation, companionship, medical care—in short, for all the physical and emotional elements of survival. The reach of the institution extends to the most personal almost intimate aspects of one's life.

The institutional alternative cannot, however, be avoided in those instances when the elderly patient requires care and supervision around the clock and has no viable or reliable primary support systems. Social workers must consider it as an avenue of last resort and avoid the well-meaning temptation to overprotect an older person by institutionalizing him or her prematurely. In all instances, social workers have to balance the rights and needs of the aging patient with those of the family, as well as the obligations of each to one another. Issues of autonomy and benevolence must be considered and weighted.

The social work skill rests mostly on the holistic assessment of these factors. The first consideration has to do with the patient's ability to make rational choices about his care. More than an issue of competency, this question is concerned with intellectual ability as well. A second factor is whether the decision is consonant with his previous behavior and values. A third has to do with the nature of the illness, particularly whether it can be diagnosed and what its prognosis is. Fourth, the attitudes and values of the attending physicians, nurses, and other health workers must be taken into account. Fifth, the nature of the clinical setting is an important factor in the situation. Finally, the role of the family, their relationship with and knowledge of the patient, as well as their wishes concerning the patient's wishes must be taken into account.

RIGHTS VERSUS NEEDS

The 1970s saw the evolution of a new rights language as a new mode of ethical discourse in the helping professions. The emphasis on rights rather than benefits or harms signaled, among other changes, a shift toward greater public involvement and patient participation in decisions concerning their lives.

At the heart of the consumer movement in social and health services is the recognition that individual rights are not abdicated simply because of entrance to a hospital or a nursing home. This resulted in a growing public demand for the return or affirmation of prerogatives such as the right to the whole truth, the right to privacy, the right to personal dignity, the right to refuse any test, procedure, or treatment, and the right of access to their medical and social records.

The right to personal dignity requires social workers to avoid compounding the humiliation of dependence. Physical loss does not warrant inflicting social penalties such as infantilization, loss of privacy, and affront to modesty. Social loss should not in turn provoke physical confinement and isolation. Mental deterioration does not justify treating patients as if they have lost their personal identity, turned into vegetables, and are no longer capable of social participation.

The transfer of information is one of the indices of equality between individuals. Lack of sharing or doctoring of information can be seen as an indication of paternalism.

In surrendering to the recommendations of the physician or other human service professionals, the older person like any patient gives up a certain autonomy in hopes that some impaired capability for action will be restored; that is the trust. If that capability is not recovered, there is still some expectation of full disclosure of information so that the remaining power of decision can still be exercised. There are those who feel that withholding information from elderly patients is yet another insult to their dignity and autonomy. There are those, however, who believe equally fervently that, in some situations, withholding information is kind and protective. The right to information implies an obligation on the part of others to tell the truth. When professionals decide to withhold truthful information because they believe such knowledge will cause psychological harm to the individual hearing it, as in the case of a terminally ill elderly patient, they are acting upon a conflicting ethical principle, that of beneficence. In honoring one moral principle they violate another.

A seventy-six-year-old woman developed cancer of the kidney, which quickly metastasized to the lung, liver, and brain. Because of earlier psychiatric difficulties resulting in hospitalization for depression, the family asked the physician not to tell her that she had incurable cancer, and he agreed. The social worker in her conversation with the patient sensed, however, that she was not only aware of her rapidly deteriorating condition but that she felt isolated and alone. The social worker questioned whether it was really ethical to deny this person the opportunity to make her peace with her family and her God, to settle her own affairs, and to control her style of dying much as she controlled her style of living. She wondered whether the family or the physician had the right to withhold such information. Furthermore, she asked whose decision it ought to be to disclose the information, when to disclose it, and in what manner.

One of the most vulnerable groups are the terminally ill elderly, and a major dilemma for social workers with this group is whether to advocate for autonomy or paternalism.

The situation of the dying person introduces significant moral dilemmas for that person, his family, and all involved health and social care providers. These issues are most apparent when dealing with competent conscious adults for whom death is seen as an inevitable fate or a release. In that situation a moral distinction is often made between taking an action that will hasten the death (active euthanasia) or omitting an intervention that will prolong the life of the person (passive euthanasia). Another way of framing it is the distinction between prolonging the dying and prolonging the living. Must social workers advocate the preservation of life at all costs as physicians do? A third concern is that legitimizing the active termination of the suffering of dying patients might serve as a wedge to justify other forms of killing, i.e. the mentally ill or persons who are considered to be undesirable or useless.

The question of death with dignity is one in which one can more easily appreciate the differences between autonomy and paternalism.

One solution to moral ethical dilemmas is to establish categorical rules that obviate the necessity of making agonizing choices in difficult situations. Robert Veatch, in his writings, has consistently emphasized autonomy as the highest moral principle (1976). For him, the commitment to individual freedom and self-determination and the concomitant need to limit the power and authority of the medical profession is clear. Veatch believes that any adult may refuse any treatment as long as he is competent (a decision to be determined by the courts, not the physician).

Casell, in turn, maintains that the physician has a responsibility to treat that cannot be relieved by the patient's refusal to accept treatment. Furthermore, the patient is morally constrained not to prevent the physician from carrying out his responsibilities to treat him (1977).

Neither of these approaches take into account the context and consequences of the particular situation. Although Veatch recognizes incompetency as a mitigating factor in his emphasis on autonomy, and Cassell is particularly concerned with acute conditions when the physician does not have sufficient time to assess the patient's motives for not wishing treatment, neither adequately deal with the medical and social factors that actually govern decision making in such situations.

There are those who believe that paternalistic interventions in health care are justified only when the patient lacks the conditions of autonomy because of incompetency, ignorance, false beliefs, or a compulsion or when the exercise of autonomy will result in great harm to the patient. Since the health professional is the one who determines whether these conditions are met, autonomy becomes a discretionary right determined by the professional who makes the determinations of competency, ignorance, false beliefs, compulsion, or harm. For example, a patient with what is considered to be a curable cancer who says "I do not want any more operations; I want to die" may only be protesting fate, a loss of control, and depersonalized care. He may be depressed, ambivalent, and fear that treatment will be withheld or stopped. Sometimes staff assume that a patient will react as they would in a similar situation.

In order to ascertain what the patient really wishes, the social worker must spend time and be sensitive to nuances. Temporary paternalism is sometimes necessary to gain the time necessary to determine what is likely to result of various courses of action and whether the person is competent to make a decision.

If social workers emphasize respect for autonomy, they must be careful that antipaternalistic policies do not come to signify lack of compassion and care. Lack of intervention in a situation in which someone expresses a wish to die may appear to be insensitive and noncaring.

EPILOGUE

This chapter alluded to the problems of disvaluation, double ethical jeopardy, and inequitable treatment of the aged. It was pointed out that they result, for the most part, from the influence of an utilitarian approach to life and societal transactions. Utilitarianism remains, however, deeply ingrained in the mores and attitudes of American society, and it is to the credit of the social work profession to have relentlessly opposed it, while advocating in the case of the aged for their right to self-determination and a better quality of life. There is apparently no conceptual ambiguity or ambivalence concerning those rights, but in practice social workers, no matter how well meaning, often slip into overprotectiveness and paternalistic interventions, thus negating the very autonomy of the old they intended to uphold. No foolproof antidote can be offered to these service liabilities, particularly when working with most vulnerable and frail categories of old people. The risks can be reduced, however, when social workers are equipped with a better understanding of the phenomena and meaning of aging.

It is truistic to state that there is a knowledge explosion in the field of aging. Assessment and intervention skills are growing in richness and complexity. Generic service principles, while useful, no longer suffice. Social workers must avail themselves of the new cognitive resources and skills before beginning to work with the aged. Failing to do so, out of overconfidence or recklessness, will further expose the aged to greater risks of dependence and discriminatory disvaluation.

REFERENCES

1. Beauchamp, T., Childress, J. F.: *Principles of Biomedical Ethics.* New York, Oxford University Press, 1979.
2. Callahan, Daniel: Contemporary biomedical ethics. *New England Journal of Medicine, 302(22):*1228–1233, May 29, 1980.
3. Case #558, "Forced Transfer to Custodial Care", *Hastings Center Report,* June, 1979, pp. 19–20. Reprinted with permission of the Hastings Center, Institute of Society and The Life Sciences, 360 Broadway, Hastings-On-Hudson, New York 10706.
4. Cassell, Eric: The function of medicine. *Hastings Center Report, 7(6):*16–19,

December, 1977.

5. Christianson, Drew: Dignity in aging. *Hastings Center Report, 4(1):*6–8, February, 1974.

6. Glasser, Ira: Prisoners of benevolence. *Doing Good.* New York, Pantheon Books, 1978, pp. 97–170.

7. Glassman, Marjorie: Misdiagnosis of senile dementia: Denial of care to the elderly. *Social Work, 25(4):*288–292, July, 1980.

8. Goldfarb, Alvin I.: The psychotherapy of elderly patients. In Blumenthal, H.T. (Ed.): *Medical and Clinical Aspects of Aging.* New York, Columbia University Press, 1962, pp. 106–114.

9. Monk, Abraham: Family supports in old age. *Social Work, 24(6):*533–539, November, 1979.

10. Neugarten, Bernice L.: Social implications of aging. In Reich, Warren J. (Ed.): *Encyclopedia of Bioethics.* New York, The Free Press, 1978, pp. 54–58.

11. Shanas, Ethel, et al.: *Old People in the Industrial Societies.* New York, Atherton Press, 1968.

12. Streib, Gordon, F.: Intergenerational relations: Perspectives of the two generation family on the older parent. *Journal of Marriage and the Family, 27:*469–476, November, 1965.

13. Veatch, Robert: *Death, Dying and the Biological Revolution.* New Haven, Conn., Yale University Press, 1976.

14. Yawney, Beverly, A., and Slover, Darrell, L.: Relocation of the Elderly. *Social Work, 18(3):*86–95, 1973.

Chapter 8

DEVELOPMENTALLY DISABLED INDIVIDUALS

J. DALE MUNRO

Recently revised federal legislation in the United States[1] defines the term "developmental disability" as a severe, chronic disability attributable to mental or physical impairment, which is manifested before the person reaches age twenty-two. Developmental disabilities (DD) include mental retardation, cerebral palsy, epilepsy, autism, and other neurological disorders closely related to mental retardation.

Historically, the social work profession demonstrated little concern for the DD field. Only a small number of committed social work pioneers dedicated their careers to work with developmentally disabled persons.[2] As recently as a decade ago, the medical and nursing professions almost completely dominated the field. However, during the last few years the "medical model" has been replaced by a "psychosocial model" for working with developmentally disabled individuals. As a result, the number of social workers involved in the field has grown enormously. At the same time, social workers have been afforded tremendous authority and opportunity to show their specialized skills as clinicians, community organizers, administrators, and researchers.

This growing authority and involvement with developmentally disabled people makes it imperative that social work professionals become more cognizant of pertinent ethical issues. Analysis of ethical considerations is particularly important since clients who fall under the DD umbrella are among the most inarticulate and easily exploited of any practice population. Severe cognitive, intellectual, physical, and/or emotional deficits leave many developmentally disabled persons particularly vulnerable to professional activities that are negligent, abusive, or unethical.

The purpose of this chapter is to highlight some of the salient ethical issues and questions relevant to social work involvement with developmentally disabled people. In addition, some suggestions that may help ensure more ethical practices will be discussed.

CLIENT SELF-DETERMINATION: AN UBIQUITOUS ISSUE

Can developmentally disabled persons be trusted to make reasonable decisions for themselves? The social work profession has always highly valued the notion of client self-determination.[3-7] Yet, does this principle really make sense in the case of developmentally disabled clients? Are they an exception to the rule? Many well-meaning observers might conclude that since this particular client group experiences severe deficits in intellect and judgment, other "more intelligent" persons should play an executive role in making all important decisions for them. With these concerns in mind, decision-making responsibilities of most developmentally disabled persons, to date, have been delegated to family members or professionals.

Yet, there is a danger in simply dismissing the concept of self-determination when applying it to developmentally disabled clients. Social workers have been cautioned against being overly zealous in jumping in to advocate and make decisions for clients.[5,8,9] As well, contemporary "normalization" philosophy suggests that the right to self-determination involves allowing all client groups—including developmentally disabled persons—the dignity of taking risks and even making "bad" decisions.[10-12]

Nevertheless, trying to weigh the relative value of self-determination against reality factors, which may include severely limited decision-making capacity, presents an ethical dilemma that haunts social workers involved in the DD field. As the reader will find, grappling with *the issue of client self-determination is an ubiquitous thread* that weaves its way through almost all the other issues (e.g. marriage, parenting, choosing among residential placement alternatives, obtaining informed consent for treatment and research, etc.) to be discussed in this chapter.

INSTITUTIONAL AND COMMUNITY ISSUES

Historically, developmentally disabled persons have been perceived in many derogatory or patronizing ways—ranging from subhuman creatures to be pitied or feared, to holy innocents, burdens of charity, and eternal children.[13] Worse still was the fact that these disabled individuals were stripped of their human and civil rights[14] and segregated in large custodial institutions. Institutional placement was considered a final solution to the problems of the disabled person, the person's family, and society. The ethics of this practice were seldom questioned.

Within the last ten years, however, something of a revolution has occurred. Professional advocacy, an outraged public, and enlightened court rulings have created a climate in which great effort has been made to guarantee the rights of disabled individuals. Developmentally disabled *citizens* now are recognized as being entitled to rights such as a minimum wage for institutional work,[15] the right to vote,[16] and free access to "mainstreamed" public education.[17] Yet, without a doubt, the most dramatic event has been the movement of thousands of persons from institutions into community-based residential settings, such as supervised residences, group homes, and completely independent living situations. Populations of many large institutions have been reduced by more than one-half during this period.

Financially, legislators and taxpayers have been attracted to deinstitutionalization since it appears to be much less expensive for disabled people to live in the community.[18] As well, there have been two major theoretical justifications for this emphasis on deinstitutionalization: first, a widespread belief that all people deserve to live in "the least restrictive alternative" possible[19]; second, popular support for "the normalization principle," which has been explained as making available to disabled people "patterns and conditions of everyday life which are as close as possible to the norms and patterns of the mainstream of society."[20]

This deinstitutionalization thrust has been a boon to the social work "business." The role of social workers trained in community organization, social policy, discharge and placement planning, and administrative systems has grown accordingly. Yet, certain questions remain that raise ethical concerns for social workers, and other professionals, involved in the DD field.

Is Deinstitutionalization a Panacea?

Wolfensberger has presented cogent evidence that large institutions have had a long history of treating developmentally disabled persons in an impersonal and dehumanizing manner. He observes that institutions have usually been located in rather isolated, semirural locations. This made it inconvenient for families to visit and tended to attract professionals who were "deviants" themselves. Unlicensed physicians, frequently unable to communicate in English, were notorious, as were professionals who were alcoholics, drug addicted, or otherwise unstable.[13] After hearing such horror stories about institutions, many might quite naturally conclude that the contemporary movement to depopulate institutions is the only ethical alternative for helping developmentally disabled persons. Still, nagging questions are repeatedly raised. Is community living really the best alternative for *every* person? Is deinstitutionalization really a panacea for all the problems in the DD field?

People would generally agree that community placement has certainly assisted many formerly institutionalized residents, especially mildly disabled individuals, achieve a more normal and independent life-style.[21] In fact, research suggests that many institutionalized persons have long dreamed of the opportunity to be placed in some type of community-based setting.[22] However, within the last three or four years a powerful backlash to the deinstitutionalization movement has appeared. Some observers have begun to question whether community living should be relied on as "the total answer."

Growing disillusionment with mass deinstitutionalization is based on several concerns. For instance, readmission rates to institutions are sometimes high; quality of life studies often find little difference between community and institutional facilities; staff working in community settings frequently are poorly trained; community support services are extremely limited in many regions; and since regulations regarding involuntary incarcerations have relaxed, some former "involuntary patients" have signed themselves out of institutions only to end up implicated in violent or criminal acts. Complicating the deinstitutionalization picture further is that parents sometimes vehemently disagree with plans to place their

developmentally disabled child in community settings; neighbor-
hood groups have violently opposed establishment of community
residences in their district (some group homes have been "mys-
teriously" firebombed); and unions representing institutional
employees have become potent forces for demanding that politicians "stop dumping" institutionalized people into what are
described as unsanitary, lonely, or hostile community settings.[23-25]

These concerns raise severe ethical dilemmas for social work
professionals. Institutional social workers are often almost totally
responsible for coordinating community discharge and placement
plans. At the same time, the taxpaying public expects social workers
to move disabled people from institutions with per diem rates of as
much as 65 dollars to community settings that operate for possibly
one-third of this amount. What should workers do when a community vacancy exists, but an otherwise suitable institutionalized
candidate refuses "to fill the bed?" In the interest of saving tax
dollars, should social workers subtly coerce ambivalent clients
into accepting community placements? The following case example helps to illustrate the dilemma.

CASE 1: Mary, age 52, is mildly retarded. She was admitted to the institution 33
years ago because she experienced severe grand mal seizures. The seizures are
now well controlled. Mary's family has no contact with her. She seldom shows
behavior problems and reports "I love working as a lead hand in the laundry."
Recently, Mary's name came to the attention of the unit social worker. Mary was
described as "an ideal candidate" for placement in a new community-based residence located about fifty miles from the institution. When the social worker
arranges a trial visit for her at the residence, Mary is hesitant about going, but
does finally agree to "give it a try." After the trial visit, the residence staff state
Mary did very well and will be accepted to live there. However, on the day Mary is
scheduled to leave the institution for the community placement, she becomes
uncharacteristically aggressive. She slaps a staff helping her pack her suitcase and
screams "I'm not going to that goddamned hole! They need me at work and my
boyfriend will miss me too much!"

Should the social worker load Mary into a car and force her to
move into the residence? Should attempts be made to coax her to
go at a later date? Should Mary's right to self-determination be
respected by allowing her to stay at the institution?

A recent article[26] asks: Does deinstitutionalization represent an
enlightened revolution or an abdication of responsibility? It is
probably too early for a definitive judgment, but if deinstitution-

alization programs are to succeed in the future, two things must be done. First, since the people still residing in institutions tend to be severely disturbed or multi-handicapped, greater attention than in the past must be paid to preparing them for the realities and responsibilities inherent in community living. Second, comprehensive community services—residential, vocational, financial, religious, medical, counselling, family support, etc.—must be further developed in order to augment the rather inadequate efforts to date by public and private groups to provide these services. Social workers have an important role to play in identifying areas of need and advocating for improvements in existing community resources.

What Should Be the Future of Institutions?

Across North America, over 200,000 developmentally disabled persons still live in institutions. Most of these people suffer from severe handicaps of a behavioral, intellectual, or physical nature that have made it difficult for them to be placed in community residential settings. Yet, the current trend suggests that disabled citizens should live in the community, not in institutions. What, then, should be the future of institutions and the people who still reside in them? Should institutions be torn down? Have they worn out their usefulness? Is it ethical to continue to admit persons to such facilities? These questions demand answers.

A convincing argument can be made that the deinstitutionalization concept—suggesting institutions should be closed or placements of last resort—simply cuts too wide a swath. Thorne[27] suggests that the popular distinction between "institution" versus "community" is a false one; that a human community is composed of people and their institutions; and that even small community-based residential facilities, such as group homes, are actually institutions, as is the household of the conventional nuclear family. Therefore, the issue is not really institutionalization versus deinstitutionalization or noninstitutionalization. The real issue is what kinds of institutions best serve everyone, disabled or able alike.

At the same time, to assume that the large, publicly supported institutions for the developmentally disabled are well on their way to being "phased out" completely is unrealistic. Even some of the harshest critics[28] of large publicly run facilities admit that institutions "will take a long time dying" (p. 36). In fact, whatever reservations people might have about institutions, these large facilities deserve credit for taking great strides in the last decade to "clean up their act." They no longer can be simplistically stereotyped as dehumanizing "snake pits." Institutions have accepted the reality that to survive, they must evolve into helping agencies that provide highly specialized services the community cannot offer to particularly needy residents.[29, 30]

Since senior social workers usually act as admission officers for institutional facilities, they often face questions that can leave them in an ethical quandary. Is this institution really the best placement alternative for this person? The administrator knows we have a vacancy; should we fill the bed as soon as possible? Recent court decisions have greatly assisted admission officers in relation to these questions by providing useful admission criteria. On the basis of the celebrated *Wyatt v. Stickney*[31] case, as well as other court decisions such as *Welsch v. Likens*,[32] it is now understood that borderline or mildly retarded persons should never be admitted to an institution unless they suffer from severe psychiatric or emotional disorders and that persons should not be institutionalized until other less restrictive residential alternatives have been explored.

In the future, large institutions will play an important role in providing three types of services. First, institutions will provide specialized assistance to people who require constant medical supervision and sophisticated behavioral programming. Second, institutions will satisfy the ever-increasing need to provide treatment programs for developmentally disabled persons with special needs—"emotionally disturbed," elderly, hearing and visually impaired—who cannot cope successfully in community facilities. Third, because institutions have the highest concentration of highly trained professionals, they will continue to offer families, private agencies, and other community groups expert consultation concerning research methods, diagnostic and treatment services, and genetic counselling.[33]

Now more than ever before, institutions are aware of their

ethical responsibilities for providing services to developmentally disabled persons, their families, and the community at large. Legal requirements now guarantee institutionalized persons the right to privacy, to individualized treatment programs, to protection from abuse, and to the least restrictive living arrangement.[34] Social workers, in conjunction with other professionals, need to constantly scrutinize methods of providing institutional service, government funding policies, along with admission and discharge criteria, so that institutions can never again become society's "dumping grounds."

CLINICAL ISSUES

Social work sophistication when clinically intervening with developmentally disabled persons has progressed markedly from a simple reliance, a few short years ago, on ego psychology based casework. Because of the profession's relatively late start in the DD field, workers have only recently developed pragmatic approaches, sometimes adapted from related professions, for treating clients manifesting such severe forms of cognitive, intellectual, and communicative handicap. Only recently have professionals begun to put to rest the myth that developmentally disabled individuals do not have the same emotional needs and problems as the rest of us.[35]

Today, social workers are recognized as important members of multi-discipline teams providing treatment and training services to a variety of DD settings.[36] Social workers are beginning to distinguish themselves as "experts" in a wide variety of clinical endeavors, including consultation, family and group counselling, milieu therapy, and behavior modification. Let us now consider some of the key ethical issues and questions relevant to clinical social work involvement in the DD field.

Who is the Client?

Although it is generally accepted that a social worker's primary obligation is to the client, the problem of determining to whom workers owe primary allegiance has always plagued the profession.[37] For example, what if a disabled person's welfare or desire for self-determination conflicts with the needs and aspirations of other significant persons? Nowhere is this dilemma more apparent than in the DD field. The following case illustration helps to illustrate this problem of competing ethical demands.

CASE 2: John, age 38, is moderately retarded and suffers from cerebral palsy. He was referred to the admissions worker of a large mental retardation facility by his brother. The brother frantically reported that John had functioned quite well in his parents' home until the death of his father two years ago. After that, John appeared depressed, broke windows, and put his fist through several doors in the house. Recently, his elderly mother had to be hospitalized after a physical altercation with John. Both the mother and brother are now adamant about the need for John to be immediately admitted to the facility. In exploring the possibility of other less restrictive residential alternatives, the worker learns that no community-based residential settings will accept John because of the severity of his behavior problems. Yet, John says he would "rather die" than be admitted to the institution. He promises "to be good" and pleads with the worker not to admit him.

To whom is the social worker responsible? Who is the real client—the disabled person or the family members? It would be easy to avoid the predicament by simplistically stating that the social worker's primary obligation is to assure self-determination for the disabled individual, but unlike other professions whose principal duty is to individual persons, responsibility to third parties such as family members is essential to upholding social work's professional identity.[38] There are circumstances, such as in cases where families of disabled persons are at risk, when social workers feel primarily responsible to these third parties while still providing service to the originally identified disabled client.

How Much Authority Over Programs Should Families Have?

Social work and family work are often considered synonymous. This is certainly true in the DD field where much of the profession's attention has focused on providing services to the parents and siblings of disabled persons. Numerous approaches have been employed to support families including crisis intervention,[39] group therapy for parents,[40-42] teaching behavior management and training techniques to parents,[43] and family counselling.[44-48]

Yet, how much decision-making authority should families have over program planning for disabled persons? Parents, who themselves often experience confused judgment because of deep-seated feelings of guilt, hostility, and disappointment, have been accused of exercising "a godlike absolute power" over major decisions in the lives of their disabled children.[14] However, recently it has been recognized that family members frequently are powerful resources in the habilitation process. Families usually are important sources of emotional support to disabled persons and have proven helpful as active participants in infant stimulation and preschool programs. Recent American standards now even require not only disabled individuals but their families to participate in the development of individual habilitation and education programs.[2,17] Is it appropriate to allow families such influence over treatment and training programs?

Families of developmentally disabled persons reportedly fall into two general groups: first, families who immediately consent to everything professinals want, trusting that the "experts" must know what they are doing; second, those who automatically oppose anything that might help the progress of their disabled relative.[49] Both extremes provide reason for alarm, although the latter group is of more immediate concern to professionals. Multi-problem families are often encountered by social workers—destructive families who sometimes neglect, abuse, overprotect, infantilize, or have no contact at all with their disabled relative. How much authority should these dysfunctional families have over the lives of disabled people? Should families take part in program planning even if they appear intent on sabotaging constructive efforts on the part of professionals? Are there occasions when professionals should suspend or limit family involvement with disabled individuals? When can disabled persons veto family decisions concerning program matters? The social work profession's long history of experience in the area of family intervention is indispensable in helping to unravel these ethical quandaries.

Is Planned Behavior Change Ethical?

When social workers first were exposed to the principles of learning theory and behavior modification, many were disgusted to say the least. Critics of the behavioral approach condemned the method as being simplistic, manipulative, mechanistic, and not dealing with the "whole person."[50] Important questions were raised. Who is controlling and modifying behavior and for what purpose? How can aversive procedures be justified? Another concern was that the term "behavior modification" often got lumped together inappropriately with other rather drastic but unrelated biomedical modalities such as E.C.T., chemotherapy, and psychosurgery.[51] Social workers who did show interest in this "dreaded" behavioral school of thought were often soundly ostracized by their colleagues. Dogmatic proselytizing by early proponents about the miracles of "behavior engineering" only helped to polarize professional opinion.

Today, however, utilization of behavioral strategies is an accepted form of clinical practice and no longer solely in the domain of psychologists. Other professionals, including social workers, have developed expertise as applied behavior analysts. In fact, most clinicians now consider behavior modification the intervention of choice for helping developmentally disabled persons, many of whom have difficulties participating in more traditional verbal therapies. In addition, specific guidelines, created in reaction to scandalous abuses of behavioral procedures in state facilities in Florida and Minnesota, now make behavior modification a tightly controlled and ethical intervention.[52,53] These guidelines, among other things, require facilities always to attempt the use of positive behavioral approaches (e.g. positive and differential reinforcement), before resorting to aversive and punishing techniques (e.g. positive punishment, time out, response cost, or overcorrection).

With this in mind, it is encouraging to note that schools of social work are moving toward the teaching of behavioral technology and that numerous texts have been prepared for social workers by social workers.[54-56] The value of the social worker's role in the DD field will certainly expand in the future if more social workers become trained in applied behavior analysis.[2] In fact, social workers have been warned that if they do not possess or evolve these relevant clinical skills, they will be called upon less frequently for assistance until their role in DD facilities becomes obsolete.[57]

Yet, it can be argued that in recent years there has been an overdependence in the DD field on behavior modification technology. Is it ethical for social workers, or any other professionals for that matter, to rely so heavily on one mode of intervention? Levy[38] cautions that "excessive identification with a practice philosophy or school of thought may prove a possible deprivation to a client if the social worker's commitment to it results in a failure to avail the client of the benefits of another mode or regimen of service" (p. 36). At a minimum, it seems important that clinicians recognize that to supplement behavioral approaches, the social work profession has a body of knowledge and wealth of experience in applying other treatment modalities. Family therapy, as well as group counselling,[58-66] nondirective therapy, transactional analysis, and concepts from psychodynamically based models, can prove useful with some developmentally disabled clients.

What Should Be Done if Abusive Treatment is Suspected?

Widespread mass media coverage has recently focused attention on the fact that staff from seemingly well-administered community or institutional facilities sometimes subject developmentally disabled persons to abusive treatment. Such abuse may take one of at least five forms. First, psychotropic drugs have been shown to have been used extensively for long periods of time, and at high doses, to control maladaptive behavior.[67] Second, respect for the confidentiality of private information concerning clients is often ignored. Third, professionals frequently misdiagnose the type or severity of disability, thereby leading to improper treatment or placements.[68-71] Fourth, developmentally disabled persons are too often referred to unsuitable programs, denied specialized psychiatric services, or left neglected in sterile community and institutional facilities.

A fifth form of abuse is probably the most widely publicized. This involves staff physically assaulting developmentally disabled individuals. Consider this shocking newspaper story.

> PERTH—A former counsellor at the Rideau Regional Centre for the Mentally Retarded in Smiths Falls was sentenced Tuesday to three months in jail for striking a retarded patient in the groin. . . .
> Judge D. C. Smith found that Anthony Girimonti, 26, had kicked or pressed down with his foot on the patient's penis so hard on the corner of a table that it bled. . . . [72]

Other highly publicized cases of staff abusing disabled persons have involved sexual intercourse, cigarette burns to the skin, provoking disabled residents to fight among themselves, and kicking disabled individuals in the head.

What should social workers do if they suspect or witness such abuse? How does one prove to authorities that disabled persons are receiving abusive medical or psychosocial treatment? Staff have been dismissed, encouraged to report fellow staff who abuse, or reclassified to jobs involving no client contact; and government task forces have been established to deal with the problem of abusive treatment in residential facilities.[73,74] Yet, no easy solutions exist for this difficult ethical problem.

SEXUALITY ISSUES

Throughout history, western society has been rather brutish in dealing with the sexual needs of handicapped persons. No people have been more drastically oppressed because of the mere fact they are sexual than those who are developmentally disabled.[75,76] Myths concerning "the disabled" have ranged from an erroneous belief that disabled people are asexual to fears they are oversexed fiends with uncontrollable urges.[77] Fortunately, professionals and laypersons are gradually becoming more aware of the socio-sexual needs of disabled persons.[78] Yet, while professionals expound platitudes about meeting the sexual needs of disabled citizens, little pragmatic assistance is provided to clients.

Social work, however, is one discipline that has attempted to provide developmentally disabled persons with practical assistance in dealing with sexuality problems, e.g. initiating sex education and counselling services in DD facilities. The profession's unique psychosocial perspective has also helped to clarify sexuality issues that deserve particular attention. Three important questions are considered in this section.

Should Sexual Expression be Encouraged or Discouraged?

What philosophy regarding the sexuality of developmentally handicapped persons should social workers espouse? There are at least three identifiable philosophies from which to choose.[79] The first and most traditional philosophy emphasizes that parents and professionals should attempt to eliminate, repress, or rigidly control sexual interest and expression by disabled people. Adherents to this view believe legitimate sexual expression should be confined to procreative enterprise within marriage. Thus, sexual options such as masturbation, homosexual relationships, and premarital "sex" are frowned upon. The bottom line seems to be that disabled individuals represent enough problems without introducing this business of sexual expression.

According to a second philosophy, sexual behavior and interest by disabled persons should be tolerated, even accommodated. Therefore, developmentally disabled individuals should be helped to express their natural sexual interest in an enjoyable and socially appropriate manner. However, during the last few years, a third even more "radical" philosophy has been revealed. It states that the sexuality of disabled people should actually be cultivated. This view can hardly be said to exist officially. Yet, some developmentally disabled persons—usually with the help of like-minded friends, relatives, or professionals—have put this philosophy into practice in their lives. Contemporary examples of this third philosophy include a school for retarded boys in Latin America which pays approved prostitutes to teach the boys sexual behavior[75] and efforts by third parties such as parents or facility staff to directly assist disabled persons with sexual practices (e.g. setting aside a private "love room," actually masturbating people who have limited use of their hands, prescribing masturbation in program plans as a form of tension release, and making explicit sexuality education part of residential training programs).

Choosing one sexuality philosophy for all developmentally disabled persons is a difficult task. No two clients share exactly the same degree or type of handicap, and today's society provides few ethical or moral absolutes that can act as guidelines for professionals.[80] At the same time, legitimate questions need to be answered. How far should professionals go in encouraging sexual expression in developmentally disabled persons? Is the philosophy that advocates cultivating sexuality simply a fad? Does sexuality instruction actually encourage sexual acting out? What constitutes sexual exploitation of intellectually or physically deficient persons? What qualifications or training should sexuality educators possess?

Should Developmentally Disabled People Parent Children?

Recently, the following Associated Press story appeared in newspapers across North America.

LISBON, Portugal—Isabel Queresma, who spent eight of her nine years in a chicken coop, squeals instead of talks and flaps her arms like wings.... She had a cataract that may have been caused by a hen pecking her eyes.... Her father is dead and her mentally retarded mother fed her food usually fed to the chickens.[81]

This disturbing report is of interest to social workers because of the profession's long history of involvement in child protection work. At the same time, this newspaper account raises oft-repeated questions, questions that are among the most controversial in the whole DD field. Can developmentally disabled persons handle the responsibilities of parenthood? To what extent are disabilities transmitted genetically? Should developmentally disabled persons be involuntarily sterilized?

It is rather easy to argue that sexual intimacy between consenting adults should be a private matter, but when one or both partners are developmentally disabled, the possibility that children might result should be of concern for three reasons. First, because of massive deinstitutionalization, more developmentally disabled persons than ever before are being exposed to the permissive community standards of sexual conduct, therefore creating a greater risk that they will become parents. Second, scientific evidence points to the fact that heredity is a factor in *some* forms of disability. Third, despite deep affection for their children, many developmentally disabled individuals are simply unable to cope, either financially or emotionally, with the demanding responsibilities of parenthood.[82]

Many well-meaning parents and professionals have long argued that developmentally disabled individuals should be involuntarily sterilized. In fact, during the period of "eugenic alarm" (circa 1890–1920), many feared that "deviates," such as epileptic and mentally retarded persons, might reproduce until they eventually outbred the rest of the population. At the same time, thousands of developmentally disabled persons were institutionalized to prevent "promiscuity," and involuntarily sterilized in the hope of preventing the transmission of defective genes.[78,83,84] More recently, the ethics of these practices have been questioned. Disturbing stories have surfaced about marginally retarded *children* being involuntarily sterilized simply on the consent of parents and physicians; of parents coercing unsuspecting disabled persons into sterilization surgery ("We're going to take you to the hospital to have your tonsils out"); and of hysterectomies being performed on disabled women ostensibly to improve menstrual hygiene but really to prevent births.

Involuntary sterilizations have declined dramatically in the last twenty years largely because of improved contraceptive alternatives, revised genetic theories indicating "deviates" will not be taking over the world, and problems regarding who can legally consent to medical procedures on developmentally disabled persons. As well, professionals are now slowly abandoning blanket decisions concerning whether these disabled individuals should or should not bear children. The real issue is whether or not particular parents—able or disabled—can adequately care for their children.[79,85,86]

It is now considered legally indefensible to sterilize people involuntarily simply on consent from parents and physicians.[87,88] Legal and administrative bodies have begun to outline rules for sterilizing developmentally disabled persons. In general, no one under the legal age of consent may be sterilized except for medical necessity; other less drastic methods of birth control must have first been considered; there must be written consent from the client; and if the client is not competent to give consent, there must be a review committee and a court decision to prove sterilization is in the best interest of the person.[89]

The topics of parenthood and involuntary sterilization of developmentally disabled persons involve enormous social implications and present seemingly imponderable questions, which many jurisdictions are currently debating. Is it right to deprive the perceived "abnormal" of the ordinary happiness the "normal" ascribe to parenting and family life? What objective criteria differentiate responsible from inadequate parents? Should genetic counselling be mandatory for all disabled persons? What kind of home environment do children deserve to be born into? Discussion of these delicate matters cannot simply be left to medical and legal authorities. Social workers, with their first-hand knowledge of family systems and adequate parenting practices, must play a role in influencing decisions concerning these important issues.

Should Developmentally Disabled Persons Marry?

Our society is geared towards marriage, not only as the major expression of our sexual roles as men and women but also as the only fully accepted vehicle for sexual expression.[90] Therefore, it is not surprising that social workers frequently are confronted by developmentally disabled persons eager to marry. Should the worker encourage or discourage the marital plans? What should be done if it seems certain the impending marriage will fail?

Traditionally, laws have been made to prohibit "mental defectives" from marrying. However, these laws have seldom been stringently enforced. As it now stands, most developmentally disabled individuals who wish to marry are doing so.[84] Parents and professionals sometimes argue that these disabled persons should not marry because they unrealistically romanticize wedlock as a relationship panacea for combating loneliness. Yet, in this respect, the disabled persons are probably no different from many impulsive, unrealistic "normal" individuals who enter into disastrous marriages.[91,92]

Interestingly enough, many developmentally disabled persons have demonstrated they can meet the demands of married life and benefit from the relationship.[93-95] There is even evidence to show the marital success rate for developmentally disabled individuals may be comparable to, if not better than, that of the general population.[96] However, numerous writers indicate that marriage can be particularly difficult if the couple become parents.[79,97,98] Follow-up studies of previously institutionalized individuals report that their marriages often meet with obstacles such as limited incomes, an absence of family models or extended family support, and an intense struggle to exist on a day-to-day basis.[99]

Developmentally disabled couples who decide to forego a marriage ceremony and "live together" may find the arrangement satisfying, but can also run into problems. Consider the following newspaper story:

> EDMONTON—The Alberta government has ordered two retarded adults who live together in a government-sponsored apartment project to be separated for fear that public criticism could lead to the project's cancellation. . . .

> Rob, 31, and Bea, 32, told program administrators they hug and kiss but don't "sleep together". They take turns cooking, and go shopping and to Church together.
> Both have been sterilized. . . . [100]

Obviously, many problems can crop up when developmentally disabled persons decide to marry or live together. What obligations might social workers have in helping these couples? At a minimum, these couples probably deserve access to special counselling to help them prepare for their life together. It is encouraging to note that social workers have already shown leadership in this area.[101] Such counselling sessions should include practical discussions concerning money management, running a household, sex education and contraception, possible genetic consequences of bearing children, how to make social contacts and enjoy leisure time, ways to utilize available community support services, how to deal with interfering in-laws, and other relevant topics.

ENSURING ETHICAL PRACTICE

Ensuring ethical social work practice in the DD field is no mean feat. Yet, there are several ways social workers can attempt to do so.

First, as a starting point, it is imperative that social workers clarify their own value dilemmas and the extent to which their personal beliefs influence their ability to work with clients, colleagues and the community ("Know Thyself—Nosce Te Ipsum"). Effective social work intervention demands that practitioners clearly understand the ethical framework that shapes their own words and actions. Unfortunately, social workers often set ethical standards for themselves that are truly beyond their grasp. Social workers must be cautioned against setting impossible ethical expectations for their work. To resolve this dilemma, social workers must begin to recognize that their value system is both a source of expectations and a set of unreachable goals, that there is always a constant tension between workers' feeling of obligation on the one hand and their inability to live up to these obligations on the other.[102]

Second, social workers must attempt to model ethical behavior in their everyday practice. Like it or not, practitioners should remember that at all times they are demonstrators of how ethics and values are actually applied in the DD field.[37] Students and inexperienced workers will gradually learn to conduct themselves in an appropriate, "professional" manner, if positive ethical behavior is exhibited by the more experienced practitioners.

Third, schools of social work need to increase greatly the amount of emphasis they place on practice with developmentally disabled people. Few schools even provide optional courses dealing with the needs of developmentally disabled persons. As a result, many workers become involved in the DD field almost by accident as a poor second choice after being unable to secure suitable employment in more prestigious fields, e.g. psychiatric social work. This situation is indeed regrettable since many social workers enter the DD field virtually unprepared to deal with the particular clinical, administrative, and ethical problems that await them.

Fourth, social workers from the DD field should become more actively involved in professional associations, e.g. The National Association of Social Workers, The American Association on Mental Deficiency, or The American Association of Marital and Family Therapy, in order to give the needs of developmentally disabled citizens a higher profile in the eyes of the professional community at large. As well, attention should be given to developing ethical standards for social work practice specific to the DD field, not to replace but to supplement existing "Code of Ethics" statements by established professional associations. These DD ethical standards should confront ethical dilemmas common in work with developmentally disabled individuals, as well as procedures for reporting, adjudicating, and imposing sanctions on social workers who exhibit unethical conduct.

Fifth, social workers should become members of human rights committees, ethical review boards, and peer review groups that now have been established for most DD facilities.[103] These formal mechanisms have been developed to protect basic human rights and to encourage ethical treatment of developmentally disabled persons. Fortunately, these "ethics committees" have well-accepted statements that can be referred to regarding the rights of disabled persons,[104-106] as well as ethical guidelines for applying behavior modification procedures[52,53] and for conducting research.[107]

Sixth, social workers should recognize the tremendous possibilities that exist for conducting both "pure" and "applied" research in the DD field. To date, the profession has not made a significant impact on empirical work in the field. In fact, many social scientists have been hesitant to do research because of the difficulty in obtaining informed consent from developmentally disabled subjects.[108] However, important decisions regarding such issues as deinstitutionalization, the efficacy of clinical interventions, marriage, and parenting concerns should not be determined solely on the basis of intuition or good intentions. Objective data should be collected to help guarantee that ethical decisions are made.

Seventh, social workers must intensify their traditional commitment to act as advocates. Ambitious plans in the past few years to pair every disabled individual with an untrained "citizen advocate"[109] — who fills the role of friend and legal adviser — have met with only limited success. Therefore, social work professionals still have two important advocacy functions to perform.[106] One function involves directly assisting developmentally disabled persons to live more independently by facilitating the delivery of social, legal, and medical services. A second function stresses social action and social reform. Here the social worker actively participates in public education about the problems and needs of disabled people, while simultaneously "fighting" for change in inadequate social and administrative policy.

Finally, the social work profession should support all efforts by disabled persons to advocate for themselves. We can no longer stereotype all developmentally disabled persons as dull, naive, childlike creatures who possess little ability to think or act for themselves, especially since some developmentally disabled persons (e.g. those with epilepsy, borderline retardation, cerebral palsy) suffer little or no intellectual deficiency. It is becoming more apparent that developmentally disabled persons should speak for themselves; what they say should be listened to and acted upon; and they should take a more active role in developing their own programs. Self-help organizations such as People First, Disabled in Action, and The American Coalition of Citizens with Disability attest to the fact that self-determination can become a practical reality for many disabled people.[110, 111]

CONCLUSION

The future integrity and identity of our profession in the DD field demands that attention should be paid now to the important issues analyzed in this chapter. More than ever before, the taxpaying public, legislators, courts, and consumers are carefully scrutinizing the quality and ethical nature of social services. Therefore, social workers must be more aware of the ethical consequences of their practice than ever before.

Absolute solutions to ethical problems in the DD field, most noticeably concerning client self-determination, seldom exist. Often more questions are raised than answered when attempting to tackle these dilemmas. In fact, discussing ethical issues may result only in clinging to one's beliefs more intensely, or in understanding both sides of a debate more clearly. In the end, however, *social workers who care enough to struggle daily with the ethical quandaries inherent in the field can proudly call themselves professionals.* It is indeed impardonable to ignore these issues, which have such significant implications in the day-to-day lives of untold numbers of developmentally disabled people.

REFERENCES

1. Public Law 95-602: October 13, 1978.
2. Horejsi, C. R.: Developmental disabilities: Opportunities for social workers. *Social Work, 24:*40–43, 1979.
3. Richmond, M.: *What is Social Case Work?* New York, Russel Sage Foundation, 1922.
4. Hamilton, G.: *Theory and Practice of Social Case Work.* New York, Columbia University Press, 1951.
5. Biestek, F. P.: The principle of client self-determination. *Social Casework, 32:*369–375, 1951.
6. Perlman, H. H.: *Social Casework.* Chicago, The University of Chicago Press, 1957.
7. Bernstein, S.: Self-determination: King or citizen in the realm of values? *Social Work, 5:*3–8, 1960.
8. Salzberger, R. P.: Casework and a client's right to self-determination. *Social Work, 24:*398–400, 1979.
9. Gilbert, N.; and Specht, H.: Advocacy and professional ethics. *Social Work, 21:*288-293, 1976.
10. Soyer, D.: The right to fail. *Social Work, 8:*72–78, 1963.
11. Perske, R.: The dignity of risk and the mentally retarded. *Mental Retarda-*

*tion, 10:*24–26, 1972.

12. Nirje, B.: The right to self-determination. In W. Wolfensberger (Ed.): *Normalization: The Principle of Normalization in Human Services.* Toronto, National Institute on Mental Retardation, 1972, pp. 176–193.

13. Wolfensberger, W.: *The Origin and Nature of Our Institutional Models.* Syracuse, Human Policy Press, 1975.

14. Skarnulis, E.: Noncitizen: Plight of the mentally retarded. *Social Work, 19:*56–62, 1974.

15. Souder v. Brennan, 367 F. Supp. 808 (D.C. 1973).

16. Cleland, C. C.; Swartz, J. D.; McGaven, M. L.; and Bell, K. F.: Voting behavior of institutionalized mentally retarded. *Mental Retardation, 11:*31–34, 1973.

17. Katz-Garris, L.: The right to education. In J. Wortis (Ed.): *Mental Retardation and Developmental Disabilities: An Annual Review (Volume X).* New York, Brunner/Mazel, 1978, pp. 1–22.

18. Intagliata, J. C.; Willer, B. S.; and Cooley, F. B.: *Cost Comparison of Institutional and Community Based Alternatives for Mentally Retarded Persons.* Buffalo, State University of New York, 1978.

19. Switzky, H. N.; and Miller, T. L.: The least restrictive alternative. *Mental Retardation, 16:*52–54, 1978.

20. Nirje, B.: The normalization principle: Implications and comments. *Journal of Mental Subnormality, 16:*62–70, 1970.

21. McDevitt, S. C.; Smith, P. M.; Schmidt, D. W.; and Rosen, M.: The deinstitutionalized citizen: Adjustment and quality of life. *Mental Retardation, 16:*22–24, 1978.

22. Munro, J. D.: Attitudes of adult institutionalized retardates toward living in the community. *The Social Worker/Le Travailleur Social, 45:*130–136, 1977.

23. Crawford, J. L.; Aiello, J. R.; and Thompson, D. E.: Deinstitutionalization and community placement: Clinical and environmental factors. *Mental Retardation, 17:*59–63, 1979.

24. Huey, K.: Placing the mentally retarded: Where shall they live? *Hospital & Community Psychiatry, 29:*596–602, 1978.

25. Neufeld, G. R.: Deinstitutionalization procedures. In R. Wiegerink and J. W. Pelosi (Eds.): *Developmental Disabilities: The DD Movement.* Baltimore, Paul H. Brookes, 1979, pp. 115–126.

26. Bassuk, E. L.; and Gerson, S.: Deinstitutionalization and mental health services. *Scientific American, 238:*46–53, 1978.

27. Thorne, J. M.: Deinstitutionalization: Too wide a swath. *Mental Retardation, 17:*171–175, 1979.

28. Wolfensberger, W.: Will there always be an institution? II: The impact of new service models. *Mental Retardation, 9:*31–38, 1971.

29. Roos, P.: Changing roles of the residential institutions. *Mental Retardation, 4:*4–6, 1966.

30. Rowland, G. T.; and Patterson, E. G.: The developmental institution: A proposed reconceptualization. *Mental Retardation, 10:*36–38, 1972.

31. Wyatt v. Stickney, Civil Action No. 3195-N., U.S. District Court, Middle District of Alabama, North Division, 1972.

32. Welsch v. Likens, Civil Action No. 415, U.S. District Court, District of Minnesota, Fourth Division, 1974.

33. Willer, B.; Scheerenberger, R. C.; and Intagliata, J.: Deinstitutionalization and mentally retarded persons: A review of the recent literature. *Community Mental Health Review, 3:*1–12, 1978.

34. Repp, A. C.: On the ethical responsibilities of institutions providing services for mentally retarded people. *Mental Retardation, 16:*153–156, 1978.

35. Walker, P. W.: Recognizing the mental health needs of developmentally disabled people. *Social Work, 25:*293–297, 1980.

36. Balthazar, E. E.; and Stevens, H. A.: Social work and emotional disturbance in mental retardation. In *The Emotionally Disturbed, Mentally Retarded: A Historical and Contemporary Perspective.* Englewood Cliffs, Prentice-Hall, 1975, pp. 167–171.

37. Pumphrey, M. W.: Transmitting values and ethics through social work practice. *Social Work, 6:*68–75, 1961.

38. Levy, C. S.: *Social Work Ethics.* New York, Human Sciences Press, 1976.

39. Giannini, M. J.; and Goodman, L.: Counseling families during the crisis reaction to mongolism. *American Journal of Mental Deficiency, 67:*740–777, 1963.

40. Murphy, A.; Pueschel, S. M.; and Schneider, J.: Group work with parents of children with Down's syndrome. *Social Casework, 54:*114–119, 1972.

41. Sugar, M.: Premature withdrawal from group therapy: Parents of intellectually retarded girls. *Group Process, 4:*60–72, 1971.

42. Appell, M. J.; Williams, C. M.; and Fishell, K. N.: Changes in attitudes of parents of retarded children effected through group counselling. *American Journal of Mental Deficiency, 68:*807–812, 1964.

43. Lance, W. D.; and Koch, A. C.: Parents as teachers: Self-help skills for young handicapped children. *Mental Retardation, 11:*3–4, 1973.

44. Begab, M. J.: Counselling parents of retarded children. *Canada's Mental Health, 12:*2–5, 1964.

45. Solomons, G.: Counseling parents of the Retarded: The interpretation interview. In F. J. Menolascino (Ed.): *Psychiatric Approaches to Mental Retardation.* New York, Basic Books, 1970, pp. 455–475.

46. MacKinnon, M. C.; and Frederick, B. S.: *A Shift of Emphasis for Psychiatric Social Work in Mental Retardation.* In F.J. Menolascino *(Ed.): Psychiatric Approaches to Mental Retardation.* New York, Basic Books, 1970, pp. 493–503.

47. Noland, R. L. (Ed.): *Counselling Parents of the Mentally Retarded.* Springfield, Thomas, 1970.

48. Schild, S.: Counseling with parents of retarded children living at home. *Social Work, 9:*86–91, 1964.

49. Repp, A. C.; and Deitz, D. E. D.: Ethical responsibilities in reductive programs for the retarded. In M. S. Berkler et al. (Eds.): *Current Trends*

for the Developmentally Disabled Baltimore, University Park Press, 1978, pp. 67–90.

50. Bruck, M.: Behavior modification theory and practice: A critical review. *Social Work, 13:*43–55, 1968.

51. Begelman, D. A.: Ethical issues for the developmentally disabled. In M. S. Berkler et al. (Eds.): *Current Trends for the Developmentally Disabled* Baltimore, University Park Press, 1978, pp. 41–66.

52. May, J. G.; Twardosz, S.; Friedman, P.; Bijou, S.; Wexler, D.; et al.: *Guidelines for the Use of Behavioral Procedures in State Programs for Retarded Persons.* Arlington (Texas), National Association for Retarded Citizens, 1975.

53. Thompson, T.; and Grabowski, J.: Ethical and legal guidelines for behavior modification. In T. Thompson and J. Grabowski (Eds.): *Behavior Modification of the Mentally Retarded* (2nd Edition). New York, Oxford University Press, 1977, pp. 495–523.

54. Jehu, D.; Hardiker, P.; Yelloly, M.; and Shaw, M.: *Behaviour Modification in Social Work.* London, John Wiley, 1972.

55. Schwartz, A.; and Goldiamond, I.: *Social Casework: A Behavioral Approach.* New York, Columbia University Press, 1975.

56. Fischer, J.; and Gochros, H. L.: *Planned Behavior Change: Behavior Modification in Social Work.* New York, the Free Press, 1975.

57. Fuller, E. H.; and Keith, K. D.: The social work role in institutions: A critical assessment. *Mental Retardation, 12:*60–62, 1974.

58. Kaufman, M. E.: Group psychotherapy in preparation for the return of mental defectives from institutions to community. *Mental Retardation, 1:*276–280, 1963.

59. Scheer, R. M.; and Sharpe, W. M.: Group work as a treatment. *Mental Retardation, 3:*23–25, 1965.

60. Mowatt, M. H.: Group approaches to treating retarded adolescents. In F. J. Menolascino (Ed.): *Psychiatric Approaches to Mental Retardation.* New York, Basic Books, 1970, pp. 435–453.

61. Nitzberg, J.: Group work with mentally retarded adolescents and young adults in a vocational habilitation center. *Group Process, 4:*18–31, 1971.

62. Payne, J. E.; and William, M.: Practical aspects of group work with the mentally retarded. *Group Process, 4:*8–17, 1971.

63. Richards, L. D.; and Lee, K. A.: Group process in social habilitation of the retarded. *Social Casework, 53:*30–37, 1972.

64. Lee, J. A.: Group work with mentally retarded foster adolescents. *Social Casework, 58:*164–173, 1977.

65. Davis, K. R.; and Shapiro, L. J.: Exploring group process as a means of reaching the mentally retarded. *Social Casework, 60:*330–337, 1979.

66. Adams, M.: *Mental Retardation and its Social Dimensions.* New York, Columbia University Press, 1971.

67. Sprague, R. L.; and Baxley, G. B.: Drugs for behavior management, with comment on some legal aspects. In J. Wortis (Ed.): *Mental Retardation*

and *Developmental Disabilities: An Annual Review (Volume X).* New York, Brunner/Mazel, 1978, pp. 92–129.

68. Bogdan, R.; and Taylor, S.: The judged, not the judges: An insider's view of mental retardation. *American Psychologist, 31:*47–52, 1976.

69. Braginsky, B. M.; and Braginsky, D. D.: The mentally retarded: Society's Hansels and Gretels. *Psychology Today, 7:*18–30, 1974.

70. Finch, R. H.: *The Six-Hour Retarded Child.* Washington, The President's Committee on Mental Retardation, 1970.

71. Sarason, S. B.; and Doris, J.: The use and misuse of labels. In Psychological Problems in Mental Deficiency (4th Edition). New York, Harper & Row, 1969, 18–35.

72. Canadian Press Wire Service, August 30th, 1978.

73. Michigan M.H. department trying to eliminate abuse in mental retardation facilities. *Hospital & Community Psychiatry, 29:*621–624, 1978.

74. Freedman, J.: Encouraging staff members to report cases of abuse. *Hospital & Community Psychiatry, 30:*636, 1979.

75. Perske, R.: About sexual development: An attempt to be human with the mentally retarded. *Mental Retardation, 11:*6–8, 1973.

76. Kempton, W.: The mentally retarded person. In H. L. Gochros and J. S. Gochros (Ed.): *The Sexually Oppressed.* New York, Association Press, 1977, pp. 239–256.

77. Chipouras, S.; Cornelius, D.; Daniels, S. M.; and Makas, E.: *Who Cares? A Handbook on Sex Education and Counselling Services for Disabled People.* Washington, George Washington University, 1979.

78. Wolfensberger, W.: Meeting the socio-sexual needs of severely impaired adults. In W. Wolfensberger: *the Origin and Nature of Our Institutional Models.* Syracuse, Human Policy Press, 1975, pp. 164–174.

79. Johnson, W. R.: *Sex Education and Counseling of Special Groups: The Mentally and Physically Handicapped, Ill and Elderly.* Springfield, Thomas, 1975.

80. Narot, J. R.: The moral and ethical implication of human sexuality as they relate to the retarded. In F. de la Cruz and G. LaVeck (Eds.): *Human Sexuality and the Mentally Retarded.* New York, Brunner/Mazel, 1973, pp. 195–214.

81. Associated Press Service, July 1st, 1980.

82. Green, B.; and Paul, R.: Parenthood and the mentally retarded. *University of Toronto Law Journal, 24:*117–125, 1974.

83. Neville, R.: Sterilization of the retarded: In whose interest? The philosophical arguments. *Hastings Center Report, 8:*33–36, 1978.

84. Swadron, B. B.: *Mental Retardation — The Law — Guardianship.* Toronto, National Institute on Mental Retardation, 1972, 77–100.

85. Robinault, I. P.: *Sex, Society and the Disabled: A Developmental Inquiry into Roles, Reactions and Responsibilities.* New York, Harper & Row, 1978.

86. Hale, G.: *The Source Book for the Disabled.* New York, Paddington Press, 1979, pp. 162–179.

87. Gostin, L. O.: Consent to involuntary and non-medically indicated sterili-

zation of mentally retarded adults and children. *Déficience Mentale/Mental Retardation, 29:*10–17, 1979.

88. Allen, R. C.: Law and the mentally retarded. In F. J. Menolascino (Ed.): *Psychiatric Approaches to Mental Retardation.* New York, Basic Books, 1970, pp. 585–611.

89. Martin, R.: Legal regulation of services to the developmentally disabled. In M. S. Berkler et al. (Eds.): *Current Trends for the Developmentally Disabled.* Baltimore, University Park Press, 1978, pp. 5–40.

90. Bidgood, F. E.: Sexuality and the handicapped. *The Journal for Special Educators of the Mentally Retarded, 11:*199–203; 1975.

91. Wikler, D.: Paternalism and the mildly retarded. *Philosophy & Public Affairs, 8:*377–392, 1979.

92. Mattinson, J.: Marriage and mental handicap. In F. de la Cruz and G. LaVeck (Eds.): *Human Sexuality and the Mentally Retarded.* New York, Brunner/Mazel, 1973, pp. 169–185.

93. Abbott, J. M.; and Ladd, G. M.: Any reason why this mentally retarded couple should not be joined together? *Mental Retardation, 11:*31–34, 1973.

94. Andron, L.; and Sturm, M. L.: Is 'I Do' in the repertoire of the retarded? *Mental Retardation, 11:*31–34, 1973.

95. *Like Other People.* A 38 minute film produced by Kestrel Films about the satisfying relationship of a severely disabled couple suffering from cerebral palsy. Released in Canada by City Films, Willowdale, 1972.

96. Craft, A.; and Craft, M.: Partnership and marriage for the subnormal? *Déficience Mentale/Mental Retardation, 26:*18–19, 1976.

97. Pallister, P. D.; and Perry, R. M.: Reflections on marriage for the retarded: The case for voluntary sterilization. *Hospital & Community Psychiatry, 24:*172–174, 1973.

98. Bass, M. S.: Marriage for the mentally deficient. *Mental Retardation, 2:*199–202, 1964.

99. Floor, L.; Baxter, D.; Rosen M.; and Zisfein, L.: A survey of marriages among previously institutionalized retardates. *Mental Retardation, 13:*33–37, 1975.

100. Hartman, S. S.; and Hynes, J.: Marriage education for mentally retarded adults. *Social Casework, 56:*280–204, 1975.

102. Pilsecker, C.: Values: A problem for everyone. *Social Work, 23:*54–57, 1978.

103. Treadway, J. T.; and Rossi, R. B.: An ethical review board: Its structure, function and province. *Mental Retardation, 15:*28–29, 1977.

104. Rights of Mentally Retarded Persons. In *Position Papers of the American Association on Mental Deficiency.* Washington, A.A.M.D., 1973–1975, 1–3.

105. *Declaration of General and Special Rights of the Mentally Retarded.* The International League of Societies for the Mentally Handicapped, October 24, 1968.

106. Diamond, S.: Developmentally Disabled Persons: Their Rights and Their Needs for Services. In R. Wiegerink and J. W. Pelosi (Eds.): *Developmental Disabilities: The DD Movement.* Baltimore, Paul H. Brooks, 1979, pp.

15–25.

107. *Ethical Principles in the Conduct of Research with Human Participants.* Washington, American Psychological Association, 1973.

108. Tymchuk, A. J.: A perspective on ethics in mental retardation. *Mental Retardation, 14*:44–47, 1976.

109. Wolfensberger, W.; and Zauha, H. (Eds.): *Citizen Advocacy and Protective Services for the Impaired and Handicapped.* Toronto: National Institute on Mental Retardation, 1973.

110. Heath, D. L.; Schaaf, V.; and Talkington, L. W.: People first: Evolution toward self advocacy. *Déficience Mentale/Mental Retardation, 28*:3–8, 1978.

111. Varela, R. A.: Self-advocacy and changing attitudes. In R. Wiergerink and J. W. Pelosi (Eds.): *Developmental Disabilities: The DD Movement.* Baltimore, Paul H. Brookes, 1979, pp. 77–82.

Chapter 9

TERMINALLY ILL PATIENTS

DAVID L. W. ADAMS

INTRODUCTION

For years, the health system has generated a myth that all professions will act in the best interests of patients. Recently, however, there has been growing recognition that the rights of patients
and their kin are not necessarily protected in contact with any
professional group in the health system.[3, 10, 12, 23, 42] Social work is
no exception, although it is recognized that the philosophy and
skills of social workers can complement those of the traditional
health disciplines. Social workers are not devoid of the suspicions
and problems that face other professions. In practice, they are
often caught between conflicting loyalties that involve patients,
relatives, other professionals, and employing institutions.[12] The
complexities of differing value systems and interests of all parties
give rise to many serious ethical issues that are amplified in work
with dying patients. The assumption of power in making life and
death decisions and the overwhelming personal strain created by
death combine to provoke ethical dilemmas that severely affect
what social workers do to help the patient and his family. This
chapter focuses upon their interaction with colleagues from other
disciplines and the importance of professional values and beliefs
in practice. It examines major ethical issues arising from questions, such as "Who should survive?", "How should people die?",
"When should they die?", and "Where should they be allowed to
die?" Some thought-provoking questions and guidelines for practice based on experiences of the writer and his colleagues are
integrated into each section.

Social Work Interaction with Interdisciplinary Teams

In the health system social workers interact most frequently
with physicians and nurses. These disciplines, like professional

social work, focus on promoting life, maintaining physical and mental health, preventing suffering, and easing death. However, medicine and nursing may operate from a different set of values than those of social work.[11,13,39,26,36] Physicians, as traditional healers and agents of cure, and nurses, as sources of comfort, value patient compliance and recovery.[42] Their goals tend to be based on removing the cause of discomfort, or effecting relief from disease. Each discipline has been traditionally task-oriented—patients accept prescribed treatment, are expected to improve, and ideally, should reduce contact with medical personnel.

Social workers, on the other hand, operate more from a value system based on belief in the patients or clients' rights to self-determination. Patients are expected to share in developing treatment goals and proceed at an individual pace.[2,42] Patients should be allowed to express feelings openly and freely and receive, as a basic human right, all pertinent information related to their case. The social worker's tendency to place a lower value on compliance and a higher value on personal growth and learning than physician or nurse colleagues is one area that creates the potential for conflict between disciplines. Role expectations imposed by other disciplines and by organizational policies add to this potential.[29,42]

Susan Watt, in her study of the social workers' relationship with physicians and nurses in hospital settings, pointed out that these professionals conflicted with social workers when they defined social workers as agents of control and compliance. Social workers were valued for their intervention with patients who deviate from expectations of doctors and nurses, and those who must be helped to exit from the system. Physicians viewed the social workers as capable of dealing with instrumental and organizational issues particularly pertaining to the poor and the disadvantaged. They saw the social workers' role as a means of making their own role easier. Nurses sought social workers as allies when families were in conflict with nursing staff. Interestingly, social workers were also seen by nurses as being less subject to the dominance and authority that physicians imposed on them by reason of expertise. In contrast, social workers tended to view themselves as experts in treating psychological problems. They worried greatly about the physician's power in controlling referrals and the right to provide therapy to patients.[42] Watt's findings lead us to question how much social workers were concerned with the ethics of countermanding the role expectations of the physician as "boss" as opposed to the ethics of ensuring that the rights of patients to receive social work treatment were protected.

When work with dying patients is combined with the conflicts described above, interactional problems increase along with the role strain and the inevitable ethical issues that accompany dying patients.[1] Despite the fact that palliative care programs have oriented some physicians and nurses to focus on comfort and acceptance of death by patient, family, and staff, many still view death as a personal defeat.[1,37,38,39] They find death difficult to face, to talk about, and to accept. Death upsets medical and nursing staff; it conflicts with their values, generates feelings of failure, and threatens them personally by bringing the reality of their own death closer.[1,4,14,23,37,38] It often causes some of them to treat the dying patient differently, even to the point of near neglect.[11,23,25] The dying patient is a constant reminder of what one wishes to forget. Dying patients may not heal, or comply physically or behaviorally with the prescribed treatment, and will likely not improve or reduce the burden on the physician or nursing staff.

The dying patient is seldom the ideal or "good" patient. Consequently, professional and personal conflicts may be resolved at the expense of the patient. Social work role strain may increase, and as a profession it must confront three problems. First, social workers must assess who is serving and who is using the dying patient and/or his family. Second, they must set priorities. Should they act as patient advocates or struggle to maintain harmony in professional relationships? Are these behaviors mutually exclusive? Since their major concern is for the patient, should they attempt to change staff attitudes slowly by working within the professional structure, or should they use their concern about staff behavior toward a particular patient to confront colleagues directly in hopes of effecting immediate change? Third, social workers must discern how much the dying process is affecting themselves personally and professionally.

Social Work Values and Beliefs

Social workers are liable to the same threats to the self as any other professionals. The death of others makes one's own death and vulnerability very real and close. Like most other professionals, social workers have had to learn to face death through life experiences and work with dying people rather than through academic experiences. However, one element in their formal learning — awareness of how social workers use themselves in the casework process — has attuned them to the need to recognize and work through their own feelings. This is a strength other disciplines may not utilize. Social workers tend to be identified with patients who deviate from the normal expectations of staff, e.g. patients who withdraw, are depressed, refuse medicines, threaten to leave, disobey medical orders, act out physically, or are seen as being self-destructive. Thus, they are likely to be requested to work with the dying patient.[42] Since families are usually part of the process, the family will also be included.

In principle, because social workers value the rights of patients to self-determination, they should be able to accept patients' needs to experience strong emotions and to play a major role in determining what should happen to them. Since, as Levy points out, social workers believe in honesty and candor, they recognize that dying patients must be advised about what is happening to them.[18] As advocates and believers in loyalty and devotion to the patient, social workers are expected to defend the rights of the dying patient and protect confidentiality in the process. In so doing, they must see that his cultural and religious beliefs are respected. Since death is inevitable and since social workers believe in proceeding at the patient's pace, they should be prepared to facilitate the setting of goals that may differ from those of other clients and recognize the short-term nature of the process of terminal care.

Ideally, most social workers would agree with these principles. Circumstances, however, frequently complicate the application of principles. For example, if the dying patient deteriorates into unconsciousness, who determines what is right for the patient? Does the family become the patient? Does the social worker then serve the family? If the family and physician are in conflict, where does the social worker fit? Do social workers ally themselves with one or the other, because they know what the patient wants? The following sections address some of the ethical dilemmas that must be faced in day-to-day practice.

WHO SURVIVES AND WHO DECIDES WHO WILL SURVIVE?

CASE 1: Baby Jason, born after a very stressful pregnancy, weighed less than 1,500 grams at birth. He had numerous congenital anomalies including hydrophalus, a severe heart defect, and respiratory insufficiency. He was placed on a respirator in Intensive Care. His parents were extremely distressed by his sickly appearance, by the monitoring equipment, and the Intensive Care Unit. They were anticipating the birth of a healthy baby, despite warnings that their first child might have both physical and mental difficulties. The physicians were guarded about the baby's prognosis and after ten weeks, agreed that Jason would probably not survive major heart and neurological operations. Because of his poor condition, physicians were prepared to reduce nutrition and shut off the respirator. His mother had been trying, with difficulty, to develop an attachment to him, and together, the parents had shared their concern about their child's future with the social worker. They were anxious and upset and had difficulty coping with the demands of the paternal grandparents that Jason be moved to another hospital as the grandparents believed his life must be saved at any cost.

The social worker became involved because the nursing staff were concerned about Jason's parents. The parents became the social worker's clients or patients, and introduced to the situation a new and different obligation from that already in existence for the physician. Although physicians are charged with the responsibility of taking into account all aspects of care for any given patient, in reality it is often agreed that their primary obligations are to the child—to treat and cure, if possible. The parents must be consulted and their abilities and deficits understood, but they are secondary.[19, 20, 40, 41] As a result physicians are granted considerable power in respect to the nature and quality of medical care the child receives initially. The impact of this power is further enhanced by the fact that physicians can, as Lorber notes, predict the minimum amount of disability the child must face in the future.[19, 20] How physicians use this power and how much is relinquished to others, particularly to the parents, becomes a major ethical concern. This concern increases when, as Smith points out, physicians may not be experts on whether or not life is worth living, and values and the setting of priorities are not necessarily the area of the physicians' expertise.[41]

With the parents as patients, the social worker takes an interest in their well-being and their role in sharing the child's care. Since they are responsible for the child, they have a right to be part of the decision making about their child's health and life direction. They cannot, however, make life and death decisions in isolation. Society expects them not to neglect or abandon their child. In exchange, there is an expectation that their beliefs about what is right for their child and for themselves should not be overruled. Ethical questions are bound up in medical/legal decisions negating parental decisions, as in child abuse, transfusion, and the nature of treatment. Parental authority, vis-à-vis parental rights to make decisions, in dying and death, as in life, involves serious social and ethical considerations.

As part of the process, professional ethics indicate that social workers cannot be direct participants in deciding whether baby Jason should live. They do not have the medical expertise and should not attempt to give medical advice. They do, however, have expertise in family dynamics and human interaction and can enter meaningfully into the process leading to the decision. The parents can be helped to sort out their thoughts and feelings and facilitate the use of their relationship and past experience to decide how much to integrate the beliefs of other family members into their own decision-making behavior.

Most important of all, social workers can help medical and nursing staff, parents, and other important persons the parents may select to communicate honestly and openly thus ensuring that life and death decision making can be shared with all parties. The social worker can make certain that there is an understanding of what can be participated in and pursued. In accordance with professional values and norms, social workers believe that families must know what is happening to their child and must be given the time to proceed at their own pace in the decision making process free of constraints and coercion. Attempting to facilitate this raises additional concerns for social workers.

Since much of professional social work activity focuses on families, social workers are frequently involved in conflicts, and hence ethical problems, arising from the differences of vested interests between patient and family. This is particularly true with infants or patients who are confused or are unconscious. These conflicts frequently lead to "taking of sides" and force social workers to question whom they should represent.[12,23] Do they always take the side of society and the legal point of view implied or dictated by societal concern, regardless of the situation?

If a decision is reached to turn off the respirator and allow the patient to die, and if social workers are part of the decision making, are they personally supporting euthanasia? Ramsey points out that ceasing care is a decision about which kinds of care should be given.[35] Lorber indicates that babies who can be helped medically should be treated.[21] If a cure is impossible, or if the cure is more painful to the patient and indirectly to the family than not to treat and try to cure, then many practitioners would choose to withdraw life support systems and allow the infant to die.[24,30,33] Would this hold true for social work as well? Can social workers really divorce themselves from personal values, beliefs, and prejudices that conflict with decisions to end life? Do they behave differently toward participants when such emotionally laden conflicts surface?

Professional social work is built upon the practitioners' awareness of self and recognition of how personal values and feelings affect the process of interaction with the client or patient. In no other area of social work are principles and control of biases and prejudices more apt to be eroded than in work with the dying. Therefore, if the social worker is fully cognizant of untenable conflicts with personal values, prejudices, and beliefs, recognition of these at the outset should lead to voluntary withdrawal from the situation and substitution by a less biased colleague. In some situations, however, a therapeutic relationship has already begun and the social worker, like other health professionals, is prone to experiencing feelings of anger, anxiety, and sadness much like those experienced by patient and family. If these feelings become so intense that they are unmanageable, jeopardize the therapeutic relationship, and lead to loss of objectivity, the social worker may find it necessary to seek the aid of peers. Their opinions may lead to withdrawal from the case and substitution of another colleague who can renew the helping relationship.

HOW SHOULD THE PATIENT DIE?

For years the dying patient has been plagued by problems inflicted by the system of care. Often dying patients are treated less well than their relatives. They have had problems obtaining honest answers about their medical condition and have been avoided or neglected.[1,3,5] Dying patients are faced with loss of control, self-esteem, and their place in social systems.[9,31,32] Aries suggests that the prevailing societal attitude is that the dying should not bother the living.[5] Cassel points out that more attention is given to the disease than to the person. Families have relinquished at least some of their responsibilities in favor of technical measures and public services. Because of the emphasis placed on the knowledge of disease, in a situation where disease is poorly understood, death is also poorly understood, and people tend to become depersonalized.[7] May notes that loss of control is a major concern for the dying and that physical illness complete with weakness, pain, sleeplessness, and emaciation erodes intimacy, reverses roles, and makes the dying patient become a stranger. Thus, physicians become parents and family surrogates; as authority figures they are charged with the responsibility of relieving suffering and deferring death.[24]

Social workers in the health care system are constantly confronted with the issues of how a person should die. The closeness of relationships established with patients and their families often places social workers in a unique position to help the physician, patient, and family cope with some of the many issues delineated by these writers, particularly the question of "conspiracy of silence," the patient's right to self-determination, and the issue of "death with dignity."

The "Conspiracy of Silence"

When the family pressures the physician not to tell the patient that he or she is dying, several concerns arise. First, the patient loses the right to be treated as a competent person. Patients are no longer deemed capable of making decisions about treatment, and responsibility is assumed by other persons regardless of whether or not the patient suspects that he may die.[3,7,11] When entering the health care system, patients entrust care-givers with their lives and enter into a covenant relationship with physicians and their associates. A contract is established, and duties related to diagnosis and treatment are delineated along with rules of conduct.[13,21,25,42] When deviation from this relationship occurs, such as when information is withheld from patients, social workers must ask whether or not the behavior is acceptable. In principle, the answer is "no." Social workers are obligated to be honest and must support the patient's right to know about and participate in decisions about their lives. However, patients may wish to keep information confidential to themselves, their physicians, and their associates, and this may include social workers. Maintenance of rigid rules of confidentiality could be required unless physicians negotiate otherwise or patients wish family or friends to know that they will die. It can be asked, then, what happens if patients do not want to know or deny what is happening to them? What if physicians refuse or neglect to provide patients with information about their condition? Where do social workers stand if patients refuse to tell spouses or children what is happening?

It can be argued that when patients do not wish to know that they will die, the right not to be told the truth should be respected.[9,11] This leads to several questions. Do patients already know but not want to discuss it? At what point in the process of the examination and diagnosis have patients made their wishes known? How do patients express these wishes? Too often, professionals assume that they know what patients want and use their own feelings to govern their actions. In the writer's experience, patients usually want to know they are dying, and failure to inform them is frequently due to the reluctance of medical staff to spell out the finality. An even more frequent occurrence is the patient's wish to deny the reality of impending death.[38] Assimilation of life-threatening information is extremely difficult, and patients and families will require the information to be repeated several times, because they are shocked and personally threatened.[1] This is particularly true when patients have not been exposed to prolonged chronicity leading to death. Social workers can help facilitate careful repetition of information by colleagues, especially since patient emotions and receptivity to information shift frequently, even from hour to hour.

However, when physicians refuse to tell patients, social workers face a major problem. How can they be the patient's advocate? If they pressure physicians, they will not make the job of medical staff any easier and the physicians may retaliate. How vulnerable are social workers? How vulnerable are patients and families? Will the organization support the social worker's stance that patients should be told or will it decide that this is strictly a medical prerogative? It seems that to be fair to patients and medical colleagues, social workers need to understand not only the rationale for decision making but also whether or not patients suspect that they are dying and what relatives believe should happen. Most of all they can use their skill to facilitate a bringing together of patient, family, and physician so that the rights of the patient are upheld even at the expense of personal conflict with colleagues. If this is so, can social workers also suggest that it is wrong for patients to keep information about impending death from families? Where do their beliefs about what is right come into play? Can or should they breach the confidence of patients who wish to face death alone? Is it ethical to use their influence to make patients decide to tell families? Clearly, social workers cannot tell patients how to behave or decide what is right. However, in principle, they are obligated to help patients explore the implications of decisions.

For example, after a lengthy discussion with a social worker, Mr. C., a forty-five year-old with leukemia, decided that his wife should share in his decision about not wanting heroic measures, and this enabled her to offer emotional support until he died. In most instances, inhibitions about telling other persons are founded on fear of the unknown and the desire to protect them. Patients do not wish to be a burden and often feel guilty because they believe that they are letting their families down by dying. Hospital staff often protect patients for the same reason. Underneath, they have feelings of failure and guilt. This can lead to misunderstandings and communication problems.[21] The social worker in Mr. C.'s case helped the staff on the ward understand both the reasoning and feelings for Mr. C.'s decision, and they were very helpful and supportive to him and his wife. Social workers' knowledge of human behavior and skill in facilitating the sharing of ideas and feelings can help all parties. Based on social work principles and current codes of professional ethics, it is highly unlikely that any social worker would betray the confidence of patients who are conscious and capable of making self-directive decisions unless compelled to do so by law.[6,27,28]

The Right to Self-Determination

The pain and discomfort to patient, family, staff, and social worker play on everyone's emotions and may overwhelm the inclination to follow professional and ethical guidelines. The ethics of collusion or confrontation are complex and, therefore, require careful consideration. For instance, if social workers really believe in the right to self-determination, then how do they cope with a situation such as the following:

CASE 2: Mrs. S., a seventy-one year-old widow, was admitted with abdominal pain and was found to have pancreatitis and chronic lung disease. After a respiratory arrest, the family asked that the ventilator be stopped, but the request was refused in light of the excellence of the patient's previous health and the fact that she might improve. When she developed further complications, it was agreed that no resuscitation for cardiac arrest would be instituted and as she deteriorated further, the ventilator was turned down. When she died, the family was relieved that the ordeal was over.

Do social workers believe that hospital staff should base their decisions on how family members think she would have liked to die? Should the family be allowed to request cessation of the ventilator against the advice of medical staff? Should the medical staff overrule the family, because they believe the patient would have wanted to live?

In this case the social worker's concerns hinge partially on the timing of intervention. Did the social worker really know Mrs. S. prior to her respiratory arrest? Did the family have a chance to discuss her condition and her concerns with her? Has the social worker anything to contribute that can help the family and physician know what she wished to have happen regarding her life? If the social worker only became involved with the family, is their well-being the primary concern? Are they asking that the respirator be turned off because of emotional stress or because they have reviewed in detail their mother's life, knew her beliefs, and can bring them to bear on the situation? Can the social worker facilitate the family's understanding of the medical position and help them to recognize the nature of the implicit contract between their mother and the physicians regarding medical care? Did the medical and nursing staff have a chance to discuss with Mrs. S. the implications of the hospital's "No Resuscitation Policy" at the time of admission to the Intensive Care Unit? Was this overlooked because of her age, condition, or the hope that she would live? All of these factors must be examined.

Social workers must confront several ethical concerns. Are the wishes of the patient being respected even though she is no longer able to choose how or when she might die? Has the process given her the best medical care available so that she has not been arbitrarily forced to live in pain or in a permanent state of unconsciousness? Now that she is no longer competent to make decisions, can the concerns of her kin and the contract between herself and the physicians be jointly discussed so that suitable goals for treatment or lack of it can be reached? Social work beliefs dictate that a patient's personal worth, wishes, and the need for dignity should be recognized and respected. Are they?

In the case of Mrs. J., a sixty-six year-old cancer patient, the situation was quite different. On admission she wanted to die because she had suffered intensely. She refused chemotherapy and surgery and was very involved in choosing her own destiny. Elements of defeat, conflict with personal values, and societal expectations all influenced how she was viewed by family and hospital staff. Inevitably, questions arose about mental competence: was she mentally ill? Even though there were no legal grounds for psychiatric consultants to declare her to be mentally incompetent, the staff behaved as though she was. For them, it was wrong and unreasonable to want to die.

Since social work values support her right to make decisions, surely this must include her right to choose to die? If so, would the social worker be prepared to be her advocate, interpret her decision to family and staff, and help to protect her rights to govern her own future?

CASE 3: In another case, Mrs. M., a forty-two year-old mother of three teenagers, had suffered from progressive renal disease for fifteen years. She was on dialysis for five years, and physicians had been reluctant to recommend transplantation due to her poor prognosis. Now, because she was deteriorating, they recommended immediate transplantation to prolong her life for a few months. She felt sick and fatigued and refused the operation. The hospital staff was upset because they felt she was ending her life too soon, whereas she and her family felt that she had suffered enough.

If Mrs. M. dies, she will deprive her children of a mother; is she just being selfish? No one can deny that choosing a course that leads to death when life may be prolonged, even briefly, is extremely stressful for everyone. When patients will not comply with treatments, social workers are caught between the questions and biases of staff and the pleas of a person who can no longer endure the stress of treatment.[11,12,23,37] It is a challenge to help the staff understand the needs of the patient, but should it be reversed? Perhaps the patient must understand the staff? Can social workers condone the patient's choice to die? It seems reasonable to suggest that it is worse for the patient to have added pain and suffering than to have pain controlled and be allowed to die peacefully. This is particularly true when the decision not to treat the patient further can be reached with the full support of those who must survive and who can comfort the patient through the course of dying. When Mrs. J. did not want the operation, surely ethical concerns would lead social workers to support her? Social workers do not condone coercion, and she was not prepared to assign power over her body to the medical staff. In addition, it would be reasonable to expect the social worker to be prepared to be her advocate. This would help her to protect her rights and help family and staff to understand the rationale for her decision. In the case of Mrs. M., the issues may be less clear. Are the patient and family using sound judgment based on knowledge and understanding rather than response to the patient's anxiety? Can the social worker support her emotionally so that she can set goals that will enable her to be content with her decision and provide the means to care for her survivors? Can the social worker help family and staff to reach the point where they no longer chastise her, even obliquely, for what she has chosen?

To Die with "Dignity"

Choice in how one dies leads to concern about how patients can be assured of death with dignity. Because of its popularity in the early 1970s, this phrase may have become much overused. This does not, however, change the significance of the concept.[38] Philosophers have spent a great deal of time defining the meaning of dignity and its place in the process of death.[16,24,34] For example, Kass believed that death with dignity involves not just the absence of indignity but the creation of a situation worthy of a human being, allowing for honor, realization of human potential, and opportunities for excellence. Death may offer new hope and an end to monotony and, in so doing, may enable the greatest display of human dignity.[15,16]

As an applied discipline, social work is concerned that patients are comforted and respected during dying. Social workers would support those who believe that patients who have a choice in how they die, with or without artificial life support systems, have a better chance to ensure that death will come more peacefully. In recent years, palliative, hospice, and home care programs have begun to take into account the need for care-givers to accept the inevitability of death and to honor the person's right to die in familiar surroundings, or at least in the presence of familiar objects and family.[25] Reduced concern about addiction to pain medication, and a change away from meeting institution and staff needs towards helping patients to be loved and cared for, fits in with social work belief in human worth and dignity.

Unfortunately, in acute care settings where active treatment is a priority, it is difficult for hospital staff to change their goals from curing patients to simply keeping them comfortable and ensuring that death comes as a natural process. Often busy, acute care staff are frustrated and find that the goals of controlling symptoms and relieving physical and emotional stress are alien and fall short of their expectations about what they should be doing. The feeling that they have given up is frustrating, and the tasks of simply communicating and providing minimal physical care make medical and nursing staff feel uncomfortable.

When these staff members are frustrated, they may unwittingly fail to respect patients' wishes or meet patients' needs for emotional support. Sometimes they become too busy to spend time with dying patients or become callous or critical towards them or towards other staff. In extreme situations, they may fail to respect the patient's wishes and meet their own needs instead. An example of this may be found when terminally ill cancer patients are given large doses of chemotherapy in situations where recovery is impossible and patients suffer severe side effects. Another example arises when some staff members insist upon carrying out painful procedures or tests when it is known that the information will do nothing to add to either the length or quality of the patient's life.

For the social worker, concern about human worth and dignity may mean conflict with professional staff from other disciplines. Therapeutic sessions involving the social worker, patient, and family may lead to their willingness to question and, where appropriate, confront staff who fail to consider the patient's needs and rights. In some instances where the patient is unable to speak out and the family is unable to lend support, the social worker, because of human concern and social work principles, may be placed in the role of adversary to hospital staff. Being an adversary and being the patient's advocate can be uncomfortable. The social worker's ability to negotiate on the patient's behalf is challenged to the extreme. Loyalties and accountabilities to patient and family and to staff and hospital are all part of the equation. In most instances the negotiating process and the resulting increased awareness of other disciplines about the impact of their behavior will lead to positive change. If compromise is not reached, however, the social worker's obligation is to the patient; occasionally social workers find themselves in the unenviable position of being the patient's only supporter.

Further Questions

Consideration of how persons should die leaves social workers with continuing ethical questions. How do they deal with the reluctance of colleagues to discuss "No Resuscitation" policies with patients and families? How do they cope with family, societal, institutional, and staff resistance to choices about how patients should die when such resistance is based on religious principles, legal qualms, inability to let go, and personal discomfort? Where does the line between suicide and the right to choose how and when to die occur? Who should broach the question of diagnostic autopsy, organ donation, etc.? When, and to whom?

WHEN SHOULD THE PATIENT DIE?

In each case presented so far, the issue of when the patient should die or be allowed to die has played a major role in determining patient, family, and physician behavior. Although most patients cannot control the exact moment of death, some can limit their suffering or prolong their lives by consenting to additional treatment, heroic measures, or simply by being determined to live. For baby Jason and Mrs. S., the timing of death follows rapidly on the cessation of life support systems; for Mrs. J., death will probably come more quickly without surgery or chemotherapy. When patients can help make decisions, they may exercise some element of control over the time of death. Mr. C., for example, was able to ensure that he was not revived and that his suffering was not prolonged. Mrs. M. was able to govern the timing of her death by shortening her life, while at the same time reducing intolerable pain and suffering.

Hospital staff are intensely concerned about the timing of death.[11,38] Often behavior of staff members from other disciplines generates ethical problems for social workers. This can be especially obtrusive when the subjective value systems of staff members influence their behavior toward dying patients—most noticeably the elderly, severely disabled, or disagreeable patients. Glaser and Strauss discuss the "dying trajectory."[11] They describe how nurses, in particular, map out a course leading to death from their very first encounter with the dying patient. Such expectations involve the certainty and uncertainty of death as well as the issue of time. Staff behavior is guided by the attending physician, and signs of the progress of illness are read and interpreted. Expectations about whether or not a person will die quickly or linger on, will go home again, or will be readmitted frequently are all estimated with varying degrees of accuracy depending upon the ability of staff to communicate, to interpret, and to judge what is happening.[11]

Schneidman points out that this evolving expectation about the course of death dictates patient behavior. In order to be a "good patient," it is expected that a person will die according to staff schedule. When a patient dies too early or lingers on too long, staff tend to be embarrassed. Lingering also inflicts additional pain on relatives who have premourned and who have anticipated that relief of their burdens through the patient's death will ensue at a specified time.[38]

When social workers encounter such staff behavior, should they intervene? Should they explain staff behavior to the patient in order to promote understanding, or "cover-up," deny what is happening? Should they agree with the patient's sensitivities and confront colleagues? Should they attempt to bring patient and staff together to discuss the implied need to "be good"? It has been suggested that the response to dying patients differs as to their appearance, age, family role, community status, willingness to talk about death, and with the staff's assessment that patients are sufficiently strong to face death.[11,38] Consequently, when patients are dying they are subjected to normal biases and prejudices, amplified by the age, culture, belief structure, and attitudes of staff. The predictability of the time of death, the patient's awareness that they are dying, and the behavior of key persons in their lives further complicate the picture. The ability to assess patients and perceive feelings help social workers recognize that dying patients are apprehensive, lack control of their destiny, and are vulnerable to having the behavior molded by the expectations of staff.[9,11,22,38]

However, it can be asked whether staff behavior can direct a patient to die on schedule? How much can staff behavior affect whether a patient fights, surrenders, despairs, or denies in the face of death? Most important for social workers is the issue of whether or not they are bound to the dying trajectory projected by colleagues or whether they can be objective enough to determine how staff behavior is influencing patients and consequently help patients determine what is right for them. Along with this concern must come the need to be certain that the patient and relatives are fully cognizant of the progress of the illness. As Glaser and Strauss point out, the degree of awareness about dying influences the patient's personal goals, particularly in relation to the tidying up of "unfinished business."[11]

The need to ensure that patients deal with the issue of the dying trajectory can be facilitated through the approach social workers advocate in the casework process and the values upheld in practice. Although social work practice is greatly influenced by medical conditions, social workers can engage patients in interpreting what is happening and help them work through and express feelings of guilt and bitterness that others may not readily accept, and facilitate access to systems that can support them until the time of death and their family beyond it. This process enables patients to move at their own pace and protects their right to seek solace and refuge. Gearing social work intervention to the needs and the pace of dying patients can allow social workers to be sufficiently free from the constraints of the medical system and its requirements for compliance to be cognizant of patient needs and to act responsibly. This allows social workers to bring objectivity to the health team and helps to increase the awareness of colleagues from other disciplines of their impact on patient and family. To think ahead to when a patient will die can be helpful and healthy for everyone concerned. It is how social workers participate in the process that counts.

In another context, the timing of death can be influenced by the tragedy of human circumstances, which place social workers in ethical dilemmas resulting from uncontrollable limitations on their effectiveness.

CASE 4: For example, eighty-two-year-old Mrs. H. was admitted to the Chronic Ward with chronic obstructive lung disease. She wanted to return to her house but she and her family had no resources to provide adequate companionship and care. She had been a responsible, self-governing woman since her husband's death twenty-five years earlier. She wanted to pass some antiques on to her grandchildren and loved the comfort of her own home. Financial problems dictated that her house be sold, so she would have to disperse her valuables among the family. To do this threatened her security, as she was worried that they would stop visiting. The social worker was concerned not only about the practical issues of Mrs. H.'s housing and management of her resources but also about her feelings concerning her family's attitude and her loss of place and possessions. In the sorting out process with patient and family, no other alternatives could be found. The social worker could only make certain that the patient's concerns were known and understood by the family. Shortly after her home was sold, Mrs. H. seemed to give up on life, her condition worsened, and she died several months earlier than anticipated.

Unfortunately, the impact of change for the elderly and the resultant demise that can ensue from societal dictates and circumstances is too common. Levy suggests that social work should know its limitations, and at times social workers are limited by systems that go against values and beliefs of patient, profession, and self.[18] For Mrs. H., once her purpose in life was relinquished, she was no longer motivated to struggle to survive and died earlier than staff expected. She rejected approaches by the social worker, family, and others to help her adapt after the sale of her home, and in a sense, she chose to die. It can be asked if she had the right to select death? Could she have chosen to have returned to her home and die more quickly from there? Whose reality should the social worker recognize? Is the social work role to facilitate compromise between all parties concerned? Should the social worker find solace in the fact that instead of choosing to reorganize her life or adjust to a chronic care ward, or to continue to cope with her illness, Mrs. H. selected death as the most suitable alternative?

WHERE SHOULD THE PATIENT DIE?

The case of Mrs. H. leads us to consider the question of where dying persons should end their lives. The mobility of society, the emphasis on nuclear families and one-family dwellings, and the reliance on institutions to care for the elderly, sick, and dying have all moved the focus away from death at home and care by relatives and friends.[7] Formal Home Care services have helped some elderly patients, but total care for dying patients requires attendance both day and night, and thus, the elderly may be deprived of an opportunity to die at home. Frequently, elderly patients die in hospitals or extended care facilities. Staff can be put in an adversary position in which they may take the side of the patient against the family and vice-versa.

Social factors such as age disparity, unresolved role relationships, and individual value systems affect the staff's choice. For instance, when young hospital staff encounter elderly dying patients, they are tempted to identify with the needs of the patient's sons or daughters, rather than those of their patient. Staff frequently force elderly patients to lose dignity by using their first names or overlooking their opinions when decisions are made about care.

When social workers encounter the elderly dying patient, they are faced with several ethical dilemmas. With whom do they identify, the dying patient or the family? Can they honestly ensure that the patient's rights are protected? Do social workers believe in the value of death at home as opposed to death in the institution? If so, can they behave nonjudgmentally towards relatives who could but will not care for patients because they do not want their lives disrupted?

Death at home provides the comfort of familiar surroundings, accessibility to neighbors and family, and often means the presence of pets that patients treasure. For the elderly, the stability of the surroundings, their roles as respected senior members of families, their need for independence, and their difficulty in adapting to change may dictate that death at home would be desirable. The social work role seems clear; social workers should help the elderly person remain at home and die there, thus facilitating their need to control their destiny. However, other factors cloud the issue. Is it safe for the person to be at home? Is the person capable of being alone with only periodic attendance of others? Can medical or nursing care be provided regularly enough? Can the patient be maintained without being overwhelmed by fear? What are reasonable expectations for relatives and friends? Is it what the patient wants? When it is considered that many families are more highly organized in their activities than ever before, imposed change is often resented.[5,22] Is it fair to expect a son or daughter to visit two or three times a day, to ensure that nursing care is given, and to make certain that their parent is fed, bathed, clothed?[4] What should it cost for a person to die at home in terms of the strain on friends or loved ones?

Ethically, where do social workers stand in allowing nuclear families to control their own destiny? Are they really concerned about the power issue created when younger, active offspring control what happens to father or mother? How does social work intervene? Is the social worker the elderly person's advocate? Do social workers facilitate the process of negotiating? Are compromises that may be worked out acceptable? If care at home is not possible, then one compromise might be to have elderly persons cared for in the homes of sons or daughters. If so, is the impact on the nuclear family less disruptive? Are families prepared to have the patient die at home? Many people are frightened by death; many parents protect their children from death—should they have the right to refuse an elderly patient's need to die with the family? What about the patient—is death at a son's or daughter's home an acceptable second choice? Perhaps it is more uncomfortable to die there than in the hospital or even in the nursing home. Maybe patients believe that they are a nuisance and feel guilty. If they believe in social work values, should social workers advocate that, within sensible limits, the elderly person who is dying should remain in familiar surroundings as long as possible?

Factors such as time, degree of illness, and type of living situation all influence decisions about what will be acceptable to all concerned. Where patients are already living with a nuclear family, care at home may be more acceptable. Ethically, the emotional needs of patient and family must always be considered as part of the equation leading to a decision. Mental and physical strain on both patient and family, and the potential for progressively increasing demands, must be considered. For social workers the ethically determined decision requires attention to the length of time anticipated and the need versus strength quotient of all persons involved. Increasingly, families who are able to face the realities of the situation are willing to have members die at home. This is particularly true for children. When children die at home, it has been suggested that families are able to cope with the actual death and bereavement better than when patients die in a hospital.[8] When major fears of death by hemorrhage or air hunger can be overcome, home can offer accessibility to peers, the outdoors, and a more relaxed style of living, free of the medical procedures and bodily intrusion present in the hospital.[8]

In some instances, social work with the dying child involves similar ethical dilemmas as work with the elderly dying patient. For example, what happens when the parents want children to die at home and the child insists on coming to the hospital, or when adolescents want to be in their own bedroom but the family cannot endure the strain of seeing their teenager die at home? In many ways social work obligations are similar to other cases that concern any patient and a third party. Families become part of the patient care system because of the parental responsibility for what happens to the child.[1,17] When children come to the hospital because it offers greater security than at home, where parents are frightened, children feel the need to protect parents and reduce the strain of caring for them night and day.

When Tommy, age nine, began to deteriorate from metastases following two years of treatment for a solid tumor, his mother, a divorcee, became fatigued and irritable. His brothers began to misbehave in order to seek attention. Tommy asked to come to the hospital and seemed to be content there, as if relieved. Attempts by the social worker to intervene with the whole family prior to hospitalization were blocked by the mother's anxiety about discussing Tommy's impending death. Was death in the hospital depriving Tommy, or was it in his best interest? Was hospitalization best for the family? Should Tommy be allowed to decide upon hospitalization? Should his mother have been forced to tell him he was dying? If so, would that have affected his choice or did he really know but just would not discuss death with anyone? When mother seemed content and Tommy seemed relieved, was it right for the social worker to believe that a satisfactory decision had been reached?

In another case, Susan, seventeen, was dying of cancer and wanted to be at home but felt her family could not cope. She went home for short stays but felt that the best place for her was in the hospital. When Susan refused to allow the social worker to help her discuss her feelings with the family, she was fighting for control and independence. Susan had a warm and positive relationship with them and decided that where she died was less important than having them close to her and feeling reassured that everything possible was being done. For the social worker, letting Susan have control over her death complete with recognition of the consequences of her decision and realization that the family's needs were being met raised several questions. Were the feelings that governed Susan's decision working against reason? Were her family being allowed to share responsibility? At what age are people capable of making such decisions? What criteria should the social worker use to evaluate the implications of what the social work role should have been? Should the social worker be satisfied that Susan died peacefully?

IN CONCLUSION

In each situation described in the preceding pages, the dying person brings to light the need for social workers to reexamine their beliefs and reassess methods of practice. They can never fully divorce themselves from their personalities, biases, and beliefs, but awareness of how they influence behavior is never more important than in work with the dying. The key to social work behavior lies in the basic beliefs and values that are not only part of upbringing but are instilled in the process of professional social work education. As medical technology advances and more choices are available for dying patients, the patient's right to self-determination will become even more significant. The importance of social workers as communicators, educators, interpreters of behavior, negotiators, facilitators, and patient advocates will increase. The social work function in helping all parties concerned (physicians, nurses, patients, and families) become aware of the need to examine thoughts and feelings, explore all of the available options, and consider the ethical implications will become even more valuable. Both the present and the future challenge social workers to pay greater attention to the ethical dimensions of practice and to the provision of settings, which prepare our new practitioners to face not only the issues and problems of life and living, but of death and dying as well.

REFERENCES

1. Adams, D. W.: *Childhood Malignancy: The Psychosocial Care of the Child and His Family.* Springfield, Thomas, 1979, pp. 40, 55–60, 135–150.
2. Adams, D. W., and Soifer, A.: Social work: An holistic approach to helping disabled persons and their families. In J. A. Browne, B. A. Kirlin, and S. Watt (Eds.): *Rehabilitation Services and the Social Work Role: Challenge for Change.* Baltimore, Williams and Wilkins, (in press).
3. Annas, G. J.: Rights of the terminally ill patient. In J. Thomas (Ed.): *Matters of Life and Death.* Toronto, Samuel Stevens, 1978, pp. 105–115.
4. Assell, R. A.: If you were dying. In R. G. Caughill (Ed.): *The Dying Patient: A Supportive Approach.* Boston, Little, Brown, 1976, pp. 47–71.
5. Aries, P.: Death inside out. In P. Steinfels and R. Veatch (Eds.): *Death Inside Out.* New York, Harper and Row, 1974, pp. 9–21.
6. Canadian Association of Social Workers, *C.A.S.W. Code of Ethics.* Ottawa, Ontario, 1977.
7. Cassell, E. J.: Dying in a technological society. In P. Steinfels and R. Veatch

(Eds.): *Death Inside Out.* New York, Harper and Row, 1974, pp. 43–48.

8. de Veber, L. L.: Families, children and death, lessons we have Learned. *U West Ont Med J, 48*:18–20, 1978.

9. Du Brey, R. J., and Terrill, L. A.: The loneliness of the dying person: An exploratory study. *Omega, 6 (4)*:357–371, 1975.

10. Friedson, E.: *Professional Dominance: The Social Structure of Medical Care.* Chicago, Aldine, 1970, pp. 120, 145–151.

11. Glaser, B. G., and Strauss, A. L.: *Awareness of Dying.* Chicago, Aldine, 1965, pp. 1–25, 204–256.

12. Holden, M. O.: Dialysis or death: The ethical alternatives. *Hlth Soc Wk, 5 (2)*:18–21, 1980.

13. Hopkins, C.: The right to die with dignity. In R. E. Caughill (Ed.): *The Dying Patient: A Supportive Approach.* Boston, Little, Brown, 1976, pp. 73–93.

14. Jones, R. B.: Life threatening illness in families. In C. A. Garfield (Ed.): *Stress and Survival. The emotional realities of life threatening illness.* St. Louis, C. V. Mosby, 1979, pp. 353–362.

15. Kass, L. R.: Death as an event. In P. Steinfels and R. Veatch (Eds.): *Death Inside Out.* New York, Harper and Row, 1974, pp. 71–78.

16. Kass, L. R.: Averting one's eyes or facing the music?—On dignity and death. In P. Steinfels and R. Veatch (Eds.): *Death Inside Out.* New York, Harper and Row, 1974, pp. 101–109.

17. Lansky, S. B.: Tribhawan, V., and Cairns, N. U.: Refusal of treatment: A new dilemma for oncologists. *Am J Ped Hem/Oncol, 1 (3)*:277–281, 1979.

18. Levy, C. S.: *Social Work Ethics.* New York, Human Sciences, 1976, pp. 108–143.

19. Lorber, M. D.: Results of treatment of myelomeningocele. *Dev Med Child Neur, 13*:290–300, 1971.

20. Lorber, M. D.: Early results of selected treatment of spina bifida cystica. *Br Med J, 4*:204, 1973.

21. McIntosh, J.: Processes of communication, information seeking and control associated with cancer: A selected review of the literature. *Soc Sci Med, 8*:166–180, 1974.

22. May, W.: The metaphysical plight of the family. In P. Steinfels and R. Veatch (Eds.): *Death Inside Out.* New York, Harper and Row, 1974, pp. 53–59.

23. Milner, C. J.: Compassionate care for the dying person. *Hlth Soc Wk, 5(2)*:5–10, 1980.

24. Morison, R. S.: The dignity of the inevitable and necessary. In P. Steinfels and R. Veatch (Eds.): *Death Inside Out.* New York, Harper and Row, 1974, pp. 97–100.

25. Mount, B. M.: The problem of caring for the dying in a general hospital; The palliative care unit as a possible solution. *Can Med Assn J, 115*:119–121, 1976.

26. Mueller, C. B.: Medical morals, medical ethics and Medicare. *Surg Gyn Obs, 132*:700–703, 1971.

27. National Association of Social Workers: *N.A.S.W. Code of Ethics*, Washington, D.C., 1979.
28. N.A.S.W. social workers leans on ethics code in recent court case, *N.A.S.W. News, 26, (2)*, February 1, 1981.
29. Olsen, K. M., and Olsen, M. E.: Role education and perceptions for social workers in medical settings. *Soc Wk, 12(3):*70–78, 1967.
30. Paulson, G. W.: Who shall live? *Geriatrics, 28:*132–136, 1973.
31. Pattison, E. M.: The experience of dying. In E. M. Pattison (Ed.): *The Experience of Dying.* Englewood-Cliffs, N.J., Prentice-Hall, 1977, pp. 43–59.
32. Pattison, E. M.: The will to live and the expectation of death. In E. M. Pattison (Ed.): *The Experience of Dying.* Englewood Cliffs, N.J., Prentice-Hall, 1977, pp. 62–73.
33. Rachels, J.: Active and passive euthanasia. In J. Thomas (Ed.): *Matters of Life and Death.* Toronto, Samuel Stevens, 1978, pp. 90–97.
34. Ramsey, P.: The indignity of death with dignity. In P. Steinfels and R. Veatch (Eds.): *Death Inside Out.* New York, Harper and Row, 1974, pp. 81–96.
35. Ramsey, P.: *The Patient as a Person.* New Haven, Yale University Press, 1971, pp. 144–153.
36. Riley, C. J.: A doctor's moral obligation to his patient. In N. Schnaper et al.: *Management of the Dying Patient and His Family* (collected papers). New York, M.S.S. Information Corporation, 1974, pp. 137–142.
37. Rothenberg, M. B.: Problems posed for staff who care for the dying child. In L. Burton (Ed.): *Care of the Child Facing Death.* London, Routledge and Kegan Paul, 1974, pp. 39–46.
38. Schneidman, E. S.: Some aspects of psychotherapy with dying persons. In C. A. Garfield (Ed.): *Psychosocial Care of the Dying Patient.* New York, McGraw Hill, 1978, pp. 201–214.
39. Schnaper, N.: Management of the dying patient. In N. Schnaper et al.: *Management of the Dying Patient and His Family* (collected papers). New York, M.S.S. Information Corporation, 1974, pp. 9–22.
40. Shaw, A.: Dilemmas of informed consent in children. *N Eng J Med, 17:*885–890, 1973.
41. Smith, D. H.: On letting some babies die. In P. Steinfels and R. Veatch (Eds.): *Death Inside Out.* New York, Harper and Row, 1974, pp. 129–138.
42. Watt, M. S.: *Therapeutic Facilitator: The Role of the Social Worker in Acute Treatment Hospitals in Ontario.* Los Angeles, University of California, 1977, pp. 101–110. (doctoral dissertation).

Chapter 10

WOMEN SEEKING ABORTION

JOHN L. E. THOMAS

I n the last couple of decades no issue has triggered more vigorous debate than the abortion issue. We have witnessed a pendu-
lum swing in opinion from the extreme conservative position
expressing as much concern for the "rights" of the fetus as for the
rights of the pregnant woman, to the extreme liberal position in
which the fetus' rights, if any, are nullified by the pregnant woman's overriding right to exercise control over her own body. Mod-
erates have tried, though not very successfully, to strike a balance
between these two extremes. The abortion issue has produced a
spate of literature, countless talk shows, lectures, panels, and dem-
onstrations. Emotions run high over gory film presentations of
mutilated fetuses answered by equally barbaric films of do-it-
yourself and back-room abortions.

Perhaps the most effective way to introduce the abortion issue is
by means of an example. Mary is the mother of three children
who are now old enough to be partially independent of the need
for mothering. This degree of freedom has enabled her to enroll
in part-time studies at a local university. Mary is one-third of the
way through an enriching and challenging program when she
discovers, in spite of a conscientious employment of contraceptives, she is pregnant for the fourth time. When the pregnancy is
confirmed, Mary seeks a therapeutic abortion on the grounds that
she has three children already and that a fourth would effectively
terminate her chances to complete a much desired program of
education.

I could have chosen a more dramatic example to introduce the
abortion issue, like a case of rape, in which the decision would be
more clear cut. Mary's case, however, focuses on the conflict between
the "rights" of the fetus and the "rights" of the mother. The rape

case would have tipped the balances in favor of the pregnant woman—few would deny an abortion to a victim of rape. By contrast, Mary's case is sufficiently problematic to make us think twice whether fetal life may be subordinated to the wishes of the pregnant woman.

THE LEGAL STATUS OF ABORTION

The Canadian Experience

Twenty years ago, in Canada, if Mary had wanted an abortion she would have been driven to seek the services of a back room abortionist. Since, in her case, the fetus posed no threat to her life or health, no "abortion committee" would have approved the termination of her pregnancy. How would Mary's petition for an abortion fare in Canada today? What is the present state of the law? The amendment to the Criminal Code, Section 251 (1969) stipulated that abortions must be approved in writing by a Therapeutic Abortion Committee. According to that amendment, abortion is warranted when in the opinion of this committee the continuation of the pregnancy constitutes a threat to the woman's life or health, including her mental health. So *if one were to follow the letter of the law* in Mary's case, since neither of these conditions apply, she would be refused an abortion.

There are relatively few cases in which the woman's life or mental health are seriously threatened by pregnancy. Therefore, the 1969 Amendment to the Criminal Code, strictly interpreted, did not significantly enlarge the grounds for legal abortions. Even so both the demand and the supply of therapeutic abortions have exceeded the limits of the law. This has been made possible only by a courageous although flagrant disregard for the legal regulatory machinery by practicing physicians and psychiatrists. As one American psychiatrist confessed when the legal position in the United States corresponded closely to the present situation in Canada: "I write letters recommending abortion that are frankly fraudulent, because I am satisfied to be used so that someone may obtain what our society would otherwise deny to her."[1] Letters of that kind are being written every day in Canada. The President's Commission on Law Enforcement and Administration of Justice in 1967 made a comment about the situation in the U.S. then, relevant to the situation in Canada today: "A considerable number of the most serious and persistent kinds of unethical conduct are connected with failure to enforce laws that are not in accord with community norms."[2]

Not infrequently, circumvention of the 1969 Amendment resulting in freer abortion practice is justified by an appeal to the World Health Organization's (WHO's) definition of "health": "Health is a state of complete physical, mental and social well-being. . . ."[3] Under this rubric both elective and therapeutic abortions have been accommodated. The upshot of this is that while, *in theory*, abortions are permitted only for the most serious of medical reasons, *in practice* in Canada, they are virtually available on demand.

The claim, just made, that abortions are available virtually on demand in Canada creates a false impression of liberality. Whatever liberality has been achieved in the practice of abortion since the 1969 Amendment is not so much attributable to that Amendment itself as to the readiness of doctors and psychiatrists to put themselves at risk of legal action by breaking the law.

In her paper *Therapeutic Abortion and the Law*, Dr. May Cohen draws attention to the deficiencies of the 1969 Amendment: "The law did not require any hospital to appoint a Therapeutic Abortion Committee. Nor did it prevent a variety of provincial regulations governing the establishment of Hospital Therapeutic Abortion Committees. Nor did it prohibit diverse interpretation of the indications for this procedure by hospital boards and the medical profession."[4] Given these legal loopholes it is not surprising that the Badgley Committee, appointed to study the operation of the abortion law in 1975, identified "inequities in the operation of the abortion law and sharp disparities in how therapeutic abortions were obtained by women within various cities, regions or provinces."[4]

These disparities and inequities can be brought out as follows. Suppose Mary in our example had lived in a large city like Toronto, Hamilton, or Vancouver. The chances are that the formalities could be conducted in time to permit abortion in the first trimester of pregnancy by a relatively simple procedure that would ensure, judging from past experience, a much better recovery measured in terms of physical safety and reduced guilt, depression, and regret. If Mary lived, however, at some distance from such cities, the delays incurred necessitated by referral could hold up the abortion until the second trimester, increasing the risk of complications, and necessitating a more painful and traumatic procedure. Problems multiply if Mary happened to reside in a rural area. The likelihood of such a hospital having an Abortion Committee is slim (only 20% of general hospitals in Canada have such committees[4]). This necessitates referral to a larger city possessing such a facility. We now run into delays in setting appointments with the three members of the Therapeutic Abortion Committee. When that is over a further delay may be encountered because of demands on the hospital's facilities and resources. Mary may find her name on a waiting list for hospital admission. From these considerations, the abortion option for women living in rural or remote areas is almost certain to be a second trimester procedure. Commenting further on Canadian practice Dr. Cohen writes:

> There was an average eight week delay from the time that a woman suspected she was pregnant until the actual abortion was performed. Indeed, India and Canada share the dubious honour of having the highest rate of second trimester abortions (after the thirteenth week of pregnancy) in the world. Christopher Tietze in his report, "Induced Abortion", states that whereas in India this is due to poor access to medical care, in Canada it is due to the fact that of all western countries, Canada has the most restrictive law and the most cumbersome authorization procedures. The impact of this on the health of Canadian women is extremely serious since the risk of complications increases significantly in the second trimester with each week that abortion is delayed.[4]

The American Experience

Legally, the present restrictions in Canada closely resemble those in vogue in the United States until the *Roe v. Wade* decision of 1973[5] made abortion available on demand during the first trimester of pregnancy. During the case, attention was focused on the tension between the woman's right to privacy and the state's interest in protecting fetal life. The compromise decision reached incurred subsuming the woman's right to control her own reproductive capacity under the woman's right to privacy. In turn, the right to privacy was linked with the "Fourteenth Amendment's concept of personal liberty and restrictions upon state action. . . ."⁵ This is a roundabout way of liberalizing abortion policy.

The woman's right to privacy, however, is neither unqualified nor absolute. Rather, it is to be exercised in a way consistent with the state's interest in protecting prenatal life. The compromise reached was to allow the woman's right to privacy absolute sway during the first trimester of pregnancy. During this period abortion is available on demand for reasons of "convenience, family planning, economics, dislike of children, the embarassment of illegitimacy, etc."⁵ This ruling clearly enlarges the grounds for abortion as compared with the Canadian statute, which, *in principle*, restricts abortions to pregnancies posing a threat to the physical or mental well-being of the woman during all three trimesters. In practice, however, as noted above, abortions are *virtually* available on demand in Canada. This raises the questions: (1) Who would be refused an abortion under present Canadian law who could obtain one under American law in the *Roe v Wade* era? and (2) What difference, if any, in practice has the *Roe v Wade* decision facilitated?

It is doubtful if anyone would be refused a therapeutic abortion in Canada nowadays, although, if what has been said earlier is borne in mind, the woman may be inconvenienced by delays and put at greater risk by postponement of abortion until the second trimester. I do not mean to minimize either the inconvenience or the increased hazards but simply point out that it is unlikely that a woman would be refused an abortion in Canada, the restrictiveness of the 1969 Amendment notwithstanding.

While present Canadian law does not significantly block therapeutic abortions, thanks to the practitioners who are prepared to put themselves at risk, this does not mean that no gains would follow from a legislative framework akin to the one provided by *Roe v Wade*. That decision created a less restrictive context in which therapeutic abortions may be performed and consequently modified the practice of abortion. One welcome side effect of such legislation is that more liberally minded physicians and psychiatrists do not need to write fraudulent letters in support of women

who wish an abortion. Thus our U.S. counterparts in the therapeutic abortion drama are no longer legally vulnerable because of
their disregard for the law. The legal roadblocks to elective abortions have been removed. Consequently, the inequities that exist
under the present Canadian regulations have been remedied, insuring fairer treatment of pregnant women. Furthermore, health care
professionals may function unafraid within more precisely defined
legal limits. During the first trimester "the attending physician, in
consultation with his patient, is free to determine, without regulation by the State, that in his medical judgment the pregnancy
should be terminated."[5]

It is interesting to note the scope of this provision. While it
eliminates the need for an abortion committee, the grounds for
abortion are still medical grounds; thus, the liberalization of abortion will be achieved by one person committing perjury rather
than three as under present Canadian law. This would indeed have
reflected the situation accurately but for two considerations—the
definition of health adopted by the contributors to the court's
decision and the women's rights thrust of the whole proceedings.

The definition of "health" with which the formulators of the
Roe v Wade decision were operating becomes clear from the list of
detrimental consequences stemming from a refused abortion:

> Specific and direct harm medically diagnosable even in early pregnancy
> may be involved. Maternity or additional offspring, may force upon the
> woman a distressful life and future. Psychological harm may be imminent.
> Mental and physical health may be taxed by child care. There is also the
> distress, for all concerned, associated with the unwanted child, and there is
> the problem of bringing a child into a family already unable, psychologically
> and otherwise, to care for it. In other cases . . . the additional difficulties
> and continuing stigma of unwed motherhood may be involved. All these
> are factors the woman and her responsible physician necessarily will
> consider in consultation.[5]

These, then, are the conditions a physician must take into account
when helping a woman to decide whether she should terminate
her pregnancy. The notion of "health" underlying the court's
decision is clearly compatible with the World Health Organization's definition cited earlier.

The women's rights thrust of the *Roe v Wade* decision emerges
in the agonizing over whether the state has any compelling inter-

est in protecting the fetus. The answer to that question for the first trimester is clearly and unequivocally negative. What of the second and third trimesters? *Roe u Wade's* language on that issue is a model of caution. The state "may regulate the abortion procedure [after the first trimester] to the extent that the regulation reasonably relates to the preservation and protection of maternal health."[5] Note that the intervention, if it should take place, is made in the interests of maternal health and not out of deference to the degree of fetal development. This confirms the "rights" thrust of the court's decision.

The point at which the state may be expected to intervene protectively on behalf of the fetus is at the point of viability — that point in fetal development when the fetus can survive outside of the womb with or without support systems. Since viability may be placed as early as the twenty-fourth week of pregnancy, it is clear that *Roe u Wade* permits abortion on demand up to the end of the second trimester. This leaves the third trimester as the period during which the state may be counted on, if at all, to protect the fetus. Here again, however, the language of *Roe u Wade* is hedged with caution: "*If* the State is interested in protecting fetal life after viability, it *may* go as far as to proscribe abortion during that period except when it is necessary to preserve the life and health of the mother."[5] The modifiers "if" and "may" confirm the women's rights thrust of *Roe u Wade*.

The failure of *Roe u Wade* to provide protection for the fetus led Mr. Justice White to observe "The court apparently values the convenience of the pregnant mother more than the continued existence and development of the life or potential life which she carries."[15] The word "convenience" is likely to trigger a negative response even from those with a more liberal view of abortion than Mr. Justice White's. If one takes seriously the list of detrimental consequences associated with refused abortions just referred to, the appropriateness of the term "convenience" is called into question. If Mr. Justice White had used the less inflammatory term "interests" rather than convenience it would have reflected more accurately the spirit and content of the *Roe u Wade* decision.

THE MORAL CONTROVERSY OVER ABORTION

Wisely or otherwise, *Roe u Wade* avoided the difficult question of when life begins: "When those trained in the respective disciplines of medicine, philosophy and theology are unable to arrive at any consensus, the judiciary . . . is not in a position to speculate as to the answer."[5] Philosophers, however, are wont to rush in where lawyers fear to tread. The moral issue needs to be addressed, even if not resolved, since it is frequently a factor to be taken into account when counselling pregnant women contemplating an abortion.

The moral dilemma arises over a dispute over the status of the fetus and a disagreement over the woman's right to control her own reproductive processes. I propose to discuss the status of the fetus and the rights of the pregnant woman from three perspectives: liberal, conservative, and moderate.

The Liberal View

In the liberal view, the fetus has no legal or moral claim on the woman or society, hence it may be disposed of at will. If we inquire into the reasons for this position, we are likely to be told that a woman has the right to exercise control over her own body including her reproductive processes. One would be hard pressed to deny this, but in itself, it is hardly sufficient grounds for disposing of the fetus at will. Even if we have the right to exercise control over our own bodies, that right does not entitle us to ride roughshod over the rights of others. Therein lies the problem, however, for in the view we are considering, since the fetus is not human, it has no rights. This is not to deny that the fetus is biologically human — that is, human rather than feline or bovine; but, that admission carries no moral clout. A doctrine of human rights designed to protect the fetus *in utero* must establish the humanity of the fetus in a stronger sense than the biological sense. Two lines of justification are usually offered in support of the "no rights" view. First, it is claimed that the fetus is *not* a person. To be a person entails being a social being capable of interacting with other human beings. Life *in utero* precludes this possibility. Until viable (capable of existence outside of the womb) the fetus cannot meet the social criterion, which is advanced as a necessary condition for personhood. Therefore, the decision to abort a fetus prior to viability is not the moral equivalent of killing an infant. Since our legal and moral commitments extend only to persons, abortion up to the point of viability is permissible. Second, the no rights view is sometimes grounded in the tissue theory, according to which the embryo/fetus is likened to a group of cells in the woman's body. If this view is tenable, then abortion becomes the moral equivalent of the removal of a wart or polyp. The important point for our present purpose is that either the social criterion of person or the tissue theory affords maximum freedom to the pregnant woman and no protection for the fetus while *in utero*.

Acknowledgement of the social criterion, however, should not blind us to the fact that the newly delivered fetus is no more a social being than the fetus *in utero*. The socializing process takes time. "Social being" as applied to a newborn infant only has the status of a promissory note. While this is true, it does not undermine the social criterion of personhood. The newborn infant is able to relate to other humans in a way that is not possible for the fetus *in utero*.

What of the tissue theory? Those who object to the tissue theory tend to do so on the grounds of the significant difference between a single cell zygote as compared with other bodily tissue. The single cell zygote is the focus of the full complement of genetic information from both parents. As Paul Ramsey expresses it: " ... modern genetics ... teaches that there are 'formal causes,' immanent principles, or constitutive elements long before there is any shape or motion or discernible size. These minute formal elements are already determining the organic life to be the uniquely individual human being it is to be."[6] Ramsey's point is well taken. The possession of the DNA blueprint sets the fertilized ovum apart from any other bodily tissue.

There is another sense in which the tissue theory fails to be discriminating enough. If the tissue theory has any force it would be in the very earliest stages of pregnancy. As the fetus develops it becomes less and less defensible to equate it with other bodily tissue.

The quotation from Ramsey and the remarks on the tissue theory provide a convenient bridge to the conservative view on abortion.

The Conservative View

The conservative is prepared to apply the label "human" in the honorific sense of that term to the conceptus from fertilization. Life tends to be viewed as a continuum. Since the various stages from fertilization to birth (and indeed beyond birth) form a continuum, without being arbitrary, it is impossible to pinpoint with accuracy one stage in the process rather than another at which the conceptus may be dubbed "human." Whatever stage one chooses, quickening, measurable brain waves, or viability, it is always pertinent to ask "But what of the stage immediately preceding that one?" Since this question admits of no satisfactory answer, advocates of the conservative view regress along the life continuum to fertilization as the only nonarbitrary stopping place for intervening to protect the conceptus. At conception a new entity comes into existence; lacking strong reasons to the contrary, e.g. to save the mother's life, the conceptus should be allowed to actualize its potential. Frequently the continuum thesis is linked with a religious position or a doctrine of natural rights. The fetus, like the pregnant woman, enjoys the right to life. This right is unalienable, that is, it is grounded in God's will or nature, depending on the viewpoint, and is therefore nonnegotiable. If it were a right accorded by society, a matter of convention, it would be negotiable; because it is a natural or spiritual right it is nonnegotiable.

The dispute between liberals and conservatives reduces to a contest between the woman's right to control her own body and the fetus' right to life, with a slight bias in favor of the woman. This bias is most clearly in evidence where the continuation of the pregnancy poses a threat to the life of the pregnant woman. If it is a case of the woman's life versus the life of the fetus, then the fetus' life may be sacrificed without compunction. If it is the fetus' life versus the woman's convenience or quality of life, the conservative would find it difficult to permit an abortion. The convenience and quality of life are negotiable while life itself is not.

The equal-rights view has the force of offering maximum protection to the fetus and minimum flexibility to the pregnant woman. The conditions under which abortion would be permitted are few — to save the life or insure the mental well-being of the mother, with stringent regulation of abortions permitted on the grounds of mental health.

Critics of the equal-rights view have been quick to point out that only persons are bearers of rights. Since fetuses are not persons, they have no rights. At most, fetuses are potential persons, and it is a mistake to accord rights to potential persons. To do so would involve invoking the dubious assumption that "something is what it *will be;* that is, since the fetus will be a human person, it already is one" [italics added].[7] Certainly the fetus has no legal status; hence those who seek to protect it *in utero* do so on *moral* rather than legal grounds.

The Moderate View

Those who adopt the moderate view seek to discover a view of fetal status that is less permissive than the social criterion of the liberal and less restrictive than the biological criterion (DNA blueprint) of the conservative. Since there are a number of such criteria, it is misleading to speak of *the* moderate view. There are a number of moderate positions. What they have in common is that at some point considerably later than fertilization the fetus is disposable. Once it reaches that point, however, it must be protected unless there are good reasons to the contrary. Criteria include quickening (the point in pregnancy at which the woman perceives movement in the fetus) and measurable brain activity. On either of these views, no moral significance is attached to abortion prior to quickening in the one case, or measurable brain waves in the other. The *Roe v. Wade* decision is also a moderate view of sorts, permitting abortions on demand up to the end of the first trimester, thus modifying the overly stringent biological criterion of the conservative view. Thus, discussions of the status of the fetus during the first trimester were successfully circumvented. The moderate views assure greater flexibility to the pregnant woman in the early stages of pregnancy and greater protection to the fetus in later stages. It is a moot point whether the *Roe v. Wade* decision affords any protection to the fetus at all. It certainly does not in the early stages of its development and promises only minimum protection, if any, in the later stages of pregnancy. Nevertheless, in attempting to forge a public policy on abortion, the formulators of the *Roe u Wade* decision were probably wise to avoid getting embroiled in the question of when life begins.

Summary

Consideration of the liberal, conservative, and moderate views has endowed us with an embarrassment of riches. We have been provided with not one but several criteria to aid or inhibit us in arriving at a decision whether or not to have a therapeutic abortion on the grounds of fetal status. One wishes that the abortion issue could be settled by an appeal to the facts. Differences in moral viewpoints, however, stem from a different reading of the facts. Whether one plumps for viability, quickening, fertilization, or measurable brain waves, one's view can correctly be claimed to be grounded in the facts of experience. All three positions — liberal, conservative, and moderate — begin from facts that "entail" a moral conclusion. From the facts the proponents of their respective views move imperceptibly to value judgments. The possession of the DNA blueprint is a fact; that we ought to protect the zygote is a value judgment. Viability is empirically verifiable; that we ought to protect the fetus at the point of viability, rather than some other, is not. The same is true of measureable brain waves.

The presence of a plurality of factual bases that may be appealed to in answering the question "When does human life begin?" precludes the possibility of achieving agreement on the answer. Clearly, the question whether therapeutic abortions can be permitted in our society as a matter of public policy cannot wait for a resolution of the conceptual-cum-moral dispute. Because this is so, I register a plea for peaceful coexistence, or detente. This would allow for a more flexible policy in permitting abortions for those who desire them while allowing those who feel protective towards fetal life to eschew abortion.

Law is most effective where there is consensus among a nation's citizens. Since we lack such a consensus on the rightness or wrongness of abortion in our society, recourse to legal means to resolve our moral differences is a *cul-de-sac*. Since women are going to have abortions anyway, prohibitive laws will not eliminate them. Indeed it is not even clear that prohibitive laws will diminish abortions. Rather, they are more likely to drive women in desperation to the back room abortionist. Regulative legislation holds greater promise of success. It proceeds in the spirit that, since abortions are going to be performed anyway, we should legislate the conditions under and the manner in which they are to be done.

In a pluralistic society like ours, the most satisfactory solution would allow for those who want an abortion to have them, and those who do not to refuse them. This amounts to an acknowledgment that public policy must make concessions to practicality that individual morality need not, and cannot.

In a recent paper Richard McCormick offers a feasibility criterion as a test of public policy. When we ask if a policy is feasible, we are not merely asking whether it is possible, but also whether it is "practicable, adaptable, depending on the circumstances, cultural ways, attitudes, traditions of a people."[8] Feasibility, therefore, raises questions such as — Will the policy by obeyed? Is it enforceable? Is it prudent to undertake this or that ban in view of possibly harmful effects to other sectors of social life? Can control be achieved short of coercive measures?[8]

Apropos of the abortion issue we have to inquire whether a ban on therapeutic abortions is feasible in the present social climate. Indeed, it may not even be possible for a conservative to pull moral rank on the liberal or moderate. In a pluralistic society, it is wrong for one to impose one's conscience on others whether one happens to be in the majority or the minority. Even if a society boasts a liberal abortion policy, this does not prevent those who oppose abortion on moral grounds from trying to influence others by precept and example, but both of those techniques are also open to those who hold the opposing viewpoint. Coercive measures, however, are denied to supporters of both sides. A liberal abortion policy still leaves open the option for women who oppose abortion to testify to their attitude towards embryonic and fetal life by behavior that is protective of those forms of life. Perhaps we have now passed the point where laws prohibiting abortion can ever hope to be reinstated. Those who feel protective of fetal life will be required to operate at a level of behavior the law cannot demand. When that happens we have passed from the realm of legality to the realm of unenforceable obligation.

FACTORS IN COUNSELLING WOMEN SEEKING ABORTION

The task of counselling a pregnant woman seeking an abortion calls for a blend of good judgment and sensitivity. When one's advice is sought on so painful and controversial a prospect as abortion, one may be at a loss whether to acquiesce in the woman's desires, help her clarify the issues involved, engage in an exchange of viewpoints, or offer advice. Sartre was of the opinion that people invariably seek the counsel of those who agree with them. If one accepts that sentiment, then the accord between counsellor and counsellee is guaranteed in advance by a shared viewpoint. The counsellor merely inks in a pencilled sketch handed to him by the counsellee. Mere acquiescence in the woman's desires, on the other hand, requires no such previously shared viewpoint but only agreeableness on the part of the counsellor. By contrast with the preestablished harmony of the first stance and the *post hoc* accord of the second, engaging in an exchange of opinions injects the helpful element of reciprocity into the relationship. However, mere exchange of opinions hardly qualifies as counselling in a sense likely to benefit the pregnant woman. One can exchange notes without sharing ideas, although one may always hope that issues will be clarified in such exchanges. Offering advice is different again and may be as one-sided from the counsellor's point of view as seeking confirmation of personal prejudices may be from the counsellee's perspective. There is something missing from these various approaches preserved by the etymology of "counselling." The word "counsel" comes from the Latin "consilium" *via* the French "conseil." "Consilium" meant "considering together." *That* places the emphasis in the right place. The pregnant woman and her counsellor *consider together* the ethical values and issues relevant to the decision whether to abort or not. The term "consider" focuses on the factor of judgment and "together" on sharing. If one takes such a view of counselling seriously, then its primary object is not to club the pregnant woman into submission but to explore the best course of action open to her, given her alternatives.

It would be difficult to counsel women seeking an abortion in an intelligent fashion without being *au fait* with the legal parameters, explored in the first part of this paper, within which the decision to have an abortion must be made. Neither can a counsellor play the ostrich over the moral problems posed by abortion. If abortion is a moral problem for the woman, the counsellor is obliged to recognize that as a factor in the decision-making process. Even if abortion poses no moral problems for the counsellor, he/she dare not assume that these matters are settled for the counsellee. Should abortion pose moral problems for the counsellor, but not for the pregnant woman, referral to another counsellor may be advisable. In the second part of the chapter, the difficulties encountered in pinpointing the origins of fetal life were explored and it was concluded that the adoption of a flexible abortion policy cannot await resolution of the moral issue. While public policy may, even must, be hammered out in spite of opposition from those who consider abortion to be wrong, it is desirable that that policy be sensitive to those who oppose abortion on conscientious grounds. Society may be robust enough to tolerate pluralism; an individual, by contrast, may experience grave difficulties in making a decision when personal morality is out of step with public policy. This amounts to an acknowledgment that there may be a mismatch between the pluralism society can tolerate without disintegration and the degree of inner turmoil an individual can tolerate without a serious breakdown.

Our treatment of the abortion question in the second part of this chapter was more successful in making a plea for a compromise for the greater good of society than in resolving deep personal conflicts. Greater good is likely to be achieved in a society that allows women who desire an abortion to have them than in a society that has a restrictive abortion policy. *A fortiori* this is true when one considers that no attempt is made to coerce women to have an abortion who believe abortion to be immoral. A flexible abortion policy assures us of "the best of both worlds." If it has taken society so long to sort out the interests of conflicting groups, we must not be surprised if the pregnant woman experiences great difficulty in "getting her act together." Hence, there is need for great sensitivity in counselling. The individual counsellor may have achieved a high degree of integration between his own feelings and society's norms. The liberal counsellor is clearly at an advantage if he/she is confident that abortion is not immoral and society's policy towards abortion is "enlightened." In that situation, personal morality and public policy are closely correlated. It need not follow, however, that this fortunate match is duplicated in the counsellor's client. The client may believe abortion to be wrong and, hence, *not* share the high degree of integration between personal feelings or convictions and society's norms achieved by the counsellor. Of course, it could go the other way, too, if society's norms happened to be conservative while the individual held liberal views. My point is that those who counsel pregnant women must be on the lookout for such mismatches because they have a profound effect on the quality and outcome of the counselling. The success of counselling depends upon its quality, and its quality depends, in no small measure, on the competence and sensitivity of the counsellor to all features of the situation—particularly to mismatches of the kind discussed here.

Unfortunately, even under optimum conditions, abortion counselling must take place within a very restrictive time frame. By the time the pregnancy is confirmed and a counselling schedule of two or three visits set up, the woman could well be approaching the end of the first trimester.

First trimester abortions are preferable not only because they are less difficult for the pregnant woman but also because they are less traumatic for the hospital staff, who must tend the woman through twelve to thirty-six hours of pseudo pregnancy. Dilation and evacuation in the first trimester is a much more "antiseptic" procedure than abortions induced by a saline solution in the second trimester. Quite apart from the increase in physical suffering posed by induced abortions, there is the trauma of delivering a dead fetus with recognizable features.

First trimester abortions are preferable for a less frequently acknowledged reason. Second trimester abortions take place after quickening, that is, after the infant-to-be becomes a reality to the pregnant woman. "Destroying that being now has vastly different emotional consequences from removing an embryo that she does not yet consider a real being."[9]

Abortion counselling that is likely to be most beneficial to the woman and to those affected by her decision requires that she be allowed to explore her own feelings in some depth. It is important that the decision be her own decision. This is not tantamount to claiming that the woman's decision takes place in a social vacuum. The conscious and unconscious feelings of the boyfriend or father of the baby, the attitude of the parents of an unmarried teenager, and the spoken and unspoken sentiments of the attending physician have a profound effect on the pregnant woman, who is frequently rendered vulnerable by her condition. If the woman feels pressured by boyfriend, husband, mother, physician, or minister, she may resent this and "may later suffer grief and depression or hate those who push her to seek what in her inner motivation she opposes."[9] The value of patient, understanding, and nonjudgmental counselling cannot be overrated in helping a woman to work through her problem with insight.

Just as external pressure from boyfriend, husband, or family may have a deleterious effect on the quality of the decision whether to abort, so support from these same quarters can improve the quality of the decision and the success of the outcome. The need for family support is especially relevant in the case of the pregnant teenager. Frank G. Bolton Jr. underscores the need for providing the pregnant girl with an atmosphere in which self-esteem is fostered and development and creative fulfilment are encouraged.[10]

While the spouse's involvement may not be viewed as a right, nevertheless, according to Dr. Fleck, "sound clinical practice" frequently demands his participation. Dr. Fleck continues: "we must learn to deal with couples not only with one partner."[11] This is crucial in the case of married couples where "the primary conflict" resides in the spouse.

Where indicated, it is also essential that the support base be broadened. Again I cite Dr. Fleck: "Because pregnancy is an emotionally charged event not only for the woman but also for her partner and possibly other family members, a greater social field must be considered along with the individual personal features of the pregnant woman."[11] The locution "emotionally charged event" focuses on one of the crucial reasons for the poor dynamics characterizing the interactions between the pregnant woman, her spouse or boyfriend, and her family. It is at this point that the collaboration not only of a psychiatrist be sought but also of "a competent social worker or nurse-clinician."[11] Together these may function, if only temporarily, as members of the extended family of the pregnant woman, bringing to the situation insights and perspectives often lost sight of by those who are too close to the problem.

Contemplated abortions for which counselling is indicated may be divided into two groups: (1) abortions for the fetus' own sake, and (2) abortions for the sake of the pregnant woman. Let us look at each of these in turn.

Abortions contemplated for the fetus' own sake usually fall within the province of screening for genetic diseases. It is a well-known fact that women over thirty-five years of age are at a greater risk for giving birth to a child with Down's syndrome than women in the younger age bracket. Until the development of amniocentesis, Down's syndrome could not be detected until the time of birth. Now it is possible to insert a needle into the woman's abdomen and withdraw cells from the amniotic fluid surrounding the fetus. These cells are cultured and the presence of Down's syndrome confirmed or disconfirmed. The pregnant woman is then offered the option of an abortion to avoid giving birth to a defective child.

With the introduction of ultra sound and fetoscopy the fetus may be observed *in utero*. Ultra sound is particularly effective in diagnosing neural tube defects like spina bifida (improper enclosure of the spinal cord), microcephaly (abnormally small head with associated mental retardation), and anencephaly (virtually lacking a brain). Anencephalic newborns usually die within a short time period after birth, so whether the fetus is aborted when diagnosed to have this defect or allowed to come to term the outcome is the same.

Like the anencephalic newborn, the Tay-Sachs baby is also born destined to die. This hereditary disease that afflicts Ashkenazi Jews is characterized by muscle weakness, progressive helplessness, and blindness. Unlike the anencephalic infant, at birth the Tay-Sachs baby is like any other baby. With the onset of symptoms, however, the disease is irreversible and death is inevitable.

Contrast these two cases with that of a victim of Down's syndrome, who is not immediately or irreversibly dying. Indeed, with supportive care, sufferers from Down's syndrome may look for-

ward to a reasonably happy life within the limits of their handicap. We now enter the domain of quality-of-life considerations.
Should amniocentesis reveal that the woman is carrying a fetus
with Down's syndrome, the decision to abort will be made on
different grounds than in the case of anencephaly or Tay-Sachs
disease, in which the fetus if allowed to come to term is foredoomed
to die.

It should be clear to the reader that the classification we are
presently considering—abortion for the fetus' own sake—is by no
means a watertight one. Obviously, these decisions are for the
pregnant woman or parents rather than the fetus. Within the
context of preventive medicine, however, the claim could be made
that one way to deal with serious genetic diseases is to prevent
children with such defects from being born. While a drastic measure, abortion insures that a child will *not* have to live with a
crippling defect. In the case of anencephalic and Tay-Sachs victims, that seems to be a sound judgment. For severe and irreparable genetic defects, screening with an abortion back-up is com-
mendable. Once sophisticated diagnostic procedures are available,
however, it may prove impossible to restrict abortions to irreparable defects. The same devices that reveal irreparable defects may
also reveal reparable ones like cleft palate or hare lip. At a recent
conference in Montreal, pediatricians and obstetricians expressed
grave concern about the increasing low tolerance on the part of
would-be parents towards accepting children with reparable defects.

Whether we intend it or not, defective children are being
downgraded. Increasingly, parents approach the physician seeking genetic approval for their potential offspring. We are rapidly
elevating to an absolute value a woman's right to have a normal
child by any means.

Add to the reluctance of would-be parents to accept children
diagnosed *in utero* to have reparable genetic defects the possible
use of amniocentesis for sex determination. As early as 1972, the
Journal of the American Medical Association reported a case of a
thirty year-old mother requesting amniocentesis ostensibly to rule
out Down's syndrome.[12] The results of the test revealed the fetus to
be normal but female. Since the couple already had one boy and
two girls, they sought a therapeutic abortion. At that time they

admitted they sought amniocentesis as a means of determining the sex of their child. Initially the opposition to amniocentesis for sex determination was concerted and strong. Already, however, that strong opposition shows signs of weakening.[13]

These examples will suffice to indicate the changing climate in which the counselling of pregnant women takes place. Since, at least initially, such pregnancies fall into the class of wanted pregnancies, the decision to abort is usually a traumatic one. Furthermore, the decision is frequently accompanied by guilt, resentment, and grief. Parents may feel guilty for passing on the deleterious gene to their potential offspring. Resentment may be due to the feeling that God or fate has been unkind. Such bitterness often finds expression in the question "why us?" Grief occurs because the defective child-to-be creates a sense of loss—the loss of the normal child this couple desperately wanted and expected and to whose birth they were looking forward with eager anticipation. Dealing with such matters taxes the ingenuity, patience, understanding, and empathy of the counsellor.

Now we will consider situations in which the contemplated therapeutic abortion is for the sake of the pregnant woman. Sometimes the fetus poses a threat to the woman's life. Of cases where the continuation of the pregnancy puts the woman at serious physical risk two come to mind: (1) ectopic pregnancies that involve the implantation of the embryo outside of the uterus and (2) pregnancies associated with heart and/or kidney malfunction. In a small number of cases the threat of suicide is a genuine and serious one. Serious threat to the woman's life from these sources, however, compose a numerically small class. When they do provide support for a therapeutic abortion, that support clearly and rightly favors the woman.

Such grounds, however, provide too slender a base to sustain the volume of therapeutic abortions performed today, hence, the emphasis in the literature on the emotional and traumatic sequelae of "compulsory parenthood." Writes Dr. Stephen Fleck: "The traumatic consequences of abortion are discernible through painstaking psychotherapeutic investigation but are of no gross clinical significance compared with 9 months of unwanted pregnancy and a lifetime of unwanted motherhood, possibly unwelcome fatherhood, and jeopardized life for the child to be."[13]

This statement dramatizes a deep difference of opinion over whether the woman suffers more from having a therapeutic abortion than from having an unwanted child. Let us examine the evidence on both sides.

On the basis of her own practice, Dr. Eloise Jones cites the case of a woman who after an abortion experienced depression, physical symptoms such as stomach pains and nausea, a growing hatred for her husband, and sexual frigidity.[14] This woman was so preoccupied with her loss that she cried every time she saw a baby. Another woman was "very frightened lest her teen-age daughter discover what she had done."[14] Following the abortion she became "increasingly tearful, hostile and unresponsive to her husband."[14] From these cases and others like them Dr. Jones concludes (1) that an abortion has not helped the self image of any woman she has dealt with, and (2) that post-abortion neuroses and psychosomatic disorder are more common than is often realized.[14]

Although this is disturbing testimony, it needs to be viewed in a wider context, since Dr. Jones' experience does not coincide with that of other psychiatrists, nor is it corroborated by recognized studies conducted to explore the sequelae of therapeutic abortions. Dr. N. Shainess insists that the mental and physical dangers of therapeutic abortions "have been greatly exaggerated and are more often the consequences of self-induced or illegal abortions."[15] Writes Dr. Robert W. Laidlaw: "In thirty years of experience, I have never seen any significant psychiatric aftermath of an abortion arranged in a therapeutic setting."[16] In the same vein Dr. Emily H. Hudd comments: "In general, followup studies show that a small percentage of patients, including those whose pregnancies were concluded in the second trimester by methods other than suction, showed continued emotional or psychiatric disturbances."[17]

There may be a temptation to dismiss appeals to the experience of individual psychiatrists as anecdotal. Hence, let us examine the findings of the World Health Organization: "There is now a substantial body of data reported from many countries after careful and objective follow-up, suggesting frequent psychological benefit and a low incidence of adverse psychological sequelae; moreover, when post-abortion depression does occur, it is often apparently due to stresses other than abortion."[18]

The attribution of the detrimental psychological sequelae of abortion to other causes than abortion itself has been emphasized by Dr. Hudd: "When such [post abortion] disturbances were evident, the data do not determine with any surety whether these women might not have been equally disturbed if they had not become pregnant or if, having become pregnant, a live birth had ensued."[17]

The WHO findings may be further corroborated by studies conducted in Scotland and Sweden[18] when the legal situation closely paralleled present Canadian law in permitting abortions when the woman's life or health is endangered by the continuation of the pregnancy. Dr. Wendell Watters points out that under such legal constraints "by and large, 'sick' women got legal abortions and 'healthy' women were refused. Hence, in comparing outcomes . . . the refused abortion groups were healthier (or 'better adjusted' and so on) to start with than were the granted abortion group."[18]

In the light of these considerations, Dr. Jones' generalizations about the deleterious effects of therapeutic abortions may (a) be based on too small a sample of cases and (b) be due to other factors than the abortion itself.

The foregoing evidence should not blind us to the fact that a decision to terminate the pregnancy often does produce feelings of guilt, regret, or loss in some women. In such cases the decision whether to have an abortion must be weighed against the suffering incurred by alternative solutions like forced marriages, bearing an out of wedlock child, giving up a child for adoption or adding an unwanted child to an already strained marital situation."[19] The psychological problems and traumatic experiences such alternatives trigger for the woman, the child, the family, and society should be explored in counselling sessions with the pregnant woman. These undesirable sequelae, so mounting evidence tends to confirm, attach to the refusal of a therapeutic abortion when the pregnant woman sincerely believes it to be in her own best interests.

From the foregoing remarks on fetal status and the intricacies of counselling women seeking an abortion, it should be clear that there is no easy answer to the question "Should I, or should I not, have an abortion?" Dr. Tomas Silber observed that the prospect of abortion arouses "contradictory feelings."[20] As one involved in working with the fetus' closest relative—the newborn premature baby—and who struggles to save such children, he is painfully and acutely aware of the paradox posed by counselling women to have an abortion. Repugnance at the destruction of fetal life is mitigated by the suffering caused by unwanted pregnancies not only for the pregnant woman but also for the children, who frequently show up in child abuse clinics. Abortion, it turns out, is tragic in the Hegelian sense that once we have looked at the issue from both sides, we cannot ever again be comfortable viewing it from a single perspective.

REFERENCES

1. Eisenberg, Leon: Abortion and psychiatry. In Hall, Robert E.: *Abortion in a Changing World.* New York, Columbia University Press, 1970, vol. 2, p. 62.

2. Schur, Edwin M.: A sociologist's view. In Hall, Robert E.: *Abortion in a Changing World.* New York, Columbia University Press, 1970, vol. 1, p. 203.

3. Beauchamp, Tom L.; and Walters, LeRoy (Eds.): *Contemporary Issues in Bioethics.* California, Wadsworth, 1978, p. 89.

4. Cohen, May: Therapeutic abortion and the law, *Canadian Women's Studies* (forthcoming).

5. 410 United States Reports 113, Decided Jan. 22, 1973. Cited in Wasserstrom, Richard: *Todays Moral Problems.* New York, MacMillan, 1975, pp. 65–83.

6. Ramsey, Paul: The morality of abortion. In Abelson R.; and Friquegnon, M. L. (Eds.): *Ethics For Modern Life.* New York, St. Martins Press, 1975, p. 65.

7. Engelhardt Jr., H. Tristam: The ontology of abortion. In Gorovitz, S. et al (Eds.): *Moral Problems in Medicine.* Englewood Cliffs, Prentice-Hall, 1976, p. 324.

8. McCormick, Richard A.: Fetal research, morality & public policy. *Hastings Center Report, 5(3):* 26, June 1975.

9. White, Robert B.: Abortion and psychiatry. In Hall, Robert E.: *Abortion in a Changing World.* New York, Columbia University Press, 1970, vol. 2, p. 57.

10. Bolton, Jr., Frank G.: *Problems of Premature Parenthood.* Beverly Hills, Sage Publications, 1980, p. 201.

11. Fleck, Stephen: A psychiatrist's view on abortion. In Walbert, David F.; and Butler, J. Douglas (Eds.): *Abortion, Society and the Law.* Cleveland, Case Reserve University Press, 1973, p. 186, 187.

12. *Journal of the American Medical Association,* July 24, 1972.
13. Fletcher, John C.: Ethics and amniocentesis for fetal sex identification. *Hastings Center Report, 10.1:* 15–17, February 1980.
14. Thomas, John E. (Ed.): *Matters of Life and Death.* Toronto, Samuel Stevens, 1978, p. 61.
15. Shainess, N.: Abortion and psychiatry. In Hall, Robert E.: *Abortion in a Changing World.* New York, Columbia University Press, 1970, vol. 1, p. 58.
16. Laidlaw, Robert W.: Abortion and psychiatry. In Hall, Robert E.: *Abortion in a Changing World.* New York, Columbia University Press, 1970, vol. 1, p. 62.
17. Hudd, Emily H.: Thoughts on the sociological and psychological aspects of abortion. In Osofsky, Howard J.; and Osofsky, Joy D.: *The Abortion Experience.* New York, Harper & Row, 1973, p. 544.
18. Watters, W. W.: Mental health consequences of abortion and refused abortion. *Canadian Journal of Psychiatry,* 69, February 1980.
19. David, Henry P. et al (Eds.): *Abortion in Psychosocial Perspective: Trends in Transitional Research.* New York, Springer, 1978, p. 84.
20. Silber, Tomas: Abortion in adolescence: The ethical dimension. *Adolescence, XV (58):*461–2, Summer 1980.

Chapter 11

BEHAVIOR MODIFICATION PROGRAMS

RAY L. J. THOMLISON

> To my mind, the most serious threat posed by the technology
> of behavior modification is the power this technology gives
> one man to impose his views and values on another. In our
> democratic society, values such as political and religious pref-
> erences are expressly left to individual choices. If our society is
> to remain free, one man must not be empowered to change
> another man's personality and dictate the values, thoughts and
> feelings of another.[42]

This expression of concern so clearly articulated by Senator
Ervin is representative both of the public's misunderstanding
and anxiety regarding behavior modification.* Certainly the public has reason to view behavior modification with suspicion. Behavior modifiers have generally not been effective communicators.[45, 46]
For that matter, the concepts employed in the behavioral literature have tended to frighten some interested observers away, leaving, perhaps, only a select group of the truly committed practitioners. This lack of knowledge and understanding has resulted in
a type of mysticism surrounding behavior modification. Not surprisingly, a public aware of growing infringement on the individual by a technological twentieth century has quite readily accepted
films such as *A Clockwork Orange* as an accurate portrayal of the
technology and the potency of behavior modification.

The failure to clearly communicate about behavior modification as a means of helping people with problems has allowed the
term to be used by the media in its broadest, literal sense to

---

*The concept of behavior modification will be used synonymously with that of
behavior therapy. While some have argued that behavior modification refers to
approaches based on operant conditioning theory and behavior therapy refers to
approaches based on respondent conditioning, the distinction is far from clear.

include any action on the part of one person (usually one in a position of power) to control or alter the behavior of another. To compound the confusion, newspapers such as the *New York Times* have associated techniques such as brainwashing, psychosurgery, and Chinese water torture with articles on behavior modification.[39]

Dramatic reports have appeared periodically in other newspapers reporting on offensive efforts by individuals who claim to be utilizing behavior modification. For example, a recent report of this nature alleged that in an effort to modify one child's bed wetting behavior the child was required to "sleep in his own urine," while another child displaying an eating disorder was required "to eat dog food laced with hot pepper sauce."[7]

A report of this nature serves to confirm the worst fears of a concerned public. Any approach that attempts to alter children's behavior through such unwarranted punitive measures is highly undesirable and unethical. The public should not be expected to pause and thoughtfully inquire as to whether such tactics are acceptable behavior modification practice. On the contrary, they are more likely to accept "the reprehensible case as the general practice."[2]

All in all, it is little wonder that when the ethics of planned intervention are under consideration among professionals, behavior modification emerges as a focus of attention. For example, the present volume on *Social Work Ethics* has included only one specific social work interventive approach for an examination of ethical issues and dilemmas. It is not by accident that this choice was the approach known as behavior modification.

BEHAVIOR MODIFICATION IN SOCIAL WORK PRACTICE

The acceptance of behavior modification by social workers has been comparatively slow and not without controversy.[4,5,24,38]

However, since the mid-1970s behavior modification has been recognized as a social work method, as evidenced by the inclusion of articles on behavior modification in books on social work practice.[40] Further, recent publications[29,47] have demonstrated the applicability of behavior modification to social work.

The fact that the approach has achieved some degree of respectability within social work, however, makes it no less suspect as a powerful, potentially negative, control of human behavior. For that matter, some have argued that a technology of such supposed potency is potentially more harmful for society in the hands of social workers, given their prominence in positions as controllers of the social order. While this position may presume more power for both social work and behavior modification than they deserve, it does have a familiar tone. Can the social work profession, a profession with long-standing commitment to ethical standards of practice and values such as self-determination and individual rights, accept an approach that has distressed many observers? In order to explore this question in respect to the ethical issues for the social work practitioner, it is essential to outline some of the more salient characteristics of the behavioral approach. In other words, in order to understand the ethics of the approach, some common understanding of the characteristic elements of behavior modification must be achieved.

The Elements of Behavior Modification

It is difficult to arrive at a clear, all-encompassing definition that would do justice to all aspects of behavior modification. In fact, a review of the literature in this area indicates that there are differences among writers as to what aspects should be included in a simple definition. For the purposes of analyzing ethical issues, it is most advantageous to consider the more important elements identified in various statements on the approaches to behavior modification.

(1) Behavior modification practice is based on one or a combination of three learning theories: respondent, operant, and imitative learning. Each of these learning theories have their foundations in the experimental analysis of behavior.

(2) Behavior is learned as the result of an interaction between the individual and his/her environment. This learning process follows certain natural laws, whereby certain behavioral occurrences are increased and others are decreased, dependent upon the nature of environmental events that occur both before and after the behavioral occurrence.

(3) Since behavior is viewed as the product of a natural learning

process, behaviors labelled deviant are acquired in accordance with the same rules governing acquisition of behavior labelled normal.

(4) Normal and deviant behaviors are acquired as adaptive to the environment in which the learning has taken place. In other words, behavior of an undesirable nature is not considered psychopathological, but rather adaptive to the situation within which the learning took place.

(5) As the concept suggests, the behavior modification approach focuses on behavioral change. Behaviors labelled as deviant are altered by identifying, through an assessment procedure, the environmental conditions that maintain these behaviors. Alternative behaviors, considered by the client to be desirable, are selected to replace the deviant behaviors. New environmental conditions are identified in accord with established learning principles. These environmental conditions are then altered to reinforce the learning of the new desired behaviors.

For the most part, behavior modification assessment focuses on the specification of who does what to whom, under what conditions (context), and how often (frequency). Implementation of a behavior modification program, therefore, focuses on alteration of these factors designed to enhance the learning of new behaviors for all members of the interactional field.

(6) With the focus on specific behavioral change, behavior modification emphasizes the need to increase the frequency of desired behavior and decrease the frequency of undesired behaviors. This requires some form of observation or monitoring of the behavioral changes and in so doing the behavioral approach has a "built in" evaluative component.

(7) Behavior modification programs are designed to demonstrate, through experience, the client's role in behavioral change. Through the use of negotiated behavioral contracts, the identification of agreed upon realistically chosen behavioral objectives and mutually agreed procedures, the client is a full participant in the change process.

(8) Behavior modification is viewed by many of its adherents as an educational process wherein the client learns the impact of the behavior of others on his/her own behavior. The client learns

self-control or self-management skills in coping with environmental demands and asserting his/her own rights to self-determination. The ultimate objective is to create the foundation for self-managed behavioral development.

(9) Behavior modification programs are adaptable to all types of human problems where behavioral change is specified as the objective. The professional literature on behavior modification evidences the application of behavioral approaches to a multiplicity of different problems ranging from the simple modification of exercise behavior, through the complex modification of family and marital behavior, to the alleviation of phobic states that have incapacitated the individual.

(10) Behavior modification is not a single approach to change. As might be expected, behavior modification includes a variety of different methods. In some instances the methods are differentially applied in response to the nature of the client's presenting problem. For example, phobias are most often modified by using the method of systematic desensitization or one of its related methods. Parent-child interactional modifications are most often based on a social learning paradigm with a heavy emphasis on changing the level of positive consequences given to the child(ren) by the parents. This approach usually involves the use of a token economy system to assist the parents in the provision of positive reinforcement at a high level during the initial stages of the program.

A number of "specializations" appear to be emerging within the field of behavior modification, with two main themes differentiating the approaches. One group continues to emphasize the theme of environmental change to facilitate individual change. The other group emphasizes the theme of cognitive mediation of the individual's "self-statements" in the role of facilitating changes.

The elements outlined here are in no way intended to be exhaustive but rather are intended to highlight the areas of consensus among the researchers and practitioners in the field. The interested reader is directed to some of the excellent books that describe various techniques of behavior modification within social work practice.[10]

In concluding this section on the nature of behavior modification, it is essential to briefly remind the reader of what is definitely not behavior modification. Behavior modification is not psycho-surgery. It is not electroconvulsive therapy. It is not strapping or hitting children as punishment in order to correct their behavior. For that matter, the place of any physical aversiveness in behavior modification practice is highly suspect regardless of whether it be with children or adults. In this writer's opinion, aversive meas-ures, more often than not, reflect a lack of creativity on the part of the therapist rather than a requirement for behavior change.

In the final analysis, all interventive approaches are essentially the practitioner's ability to interpret and skillfully act on the principles of the approach. In this respect, in examining the ethics of behavior modification, it is useful to keep in mind the words of Albert Bandura: " . . . behavioral principles do not dictate the manner in which they are applied."[2] Competent practice is a requisite to ethical behavioral practice.

A PERSPECTIVE ON ETHICS IN SOCIAL WORK

There is a tendency to believe that the study of ethics is the study of an absolute. Perhaps this stems from our childhood learn-ing experiences where behaviors were easily labelled right versus wrong. Even in later life, for that matter, there is a certain security in being able to clearly delineate between the "rightness and wrongness" of certain behavior. However, regardless of the com-fort that might be derived from an absolute ethic, social workers are faced with a multiplicity of complex factors in deciding what is ethical behavior.[19] In the final analysis, the study of ethics is normative and culturally defined. "It is concerned with principles that ought to govern human conduct rather than with those that do govern it."[43]

Further, ethics is not determined by the individual. Like all behavior, ethical behavior is the product of an interactional proc-ess between the individual, the client (in the case of the professional), and the social systems within which they both function.

Within this perspective, then, social work ethics will never be static. They must be dynamic, impacting upon and reacting to the context within which social work is practiced. A code of ethics will serve only to remind us of our belief in essential human rights in our community, but they cannot be intended to deal with the specifics of the multiple issues arising daily as the social worker intervenes in the lives of a varied client population. Social work is action, and this reality demands that its ethics deal with the consequences of action versus nonaction and the issue of control versus freedom. That is, social work ethics deal with the consequences of intervention and the technology (skills) inherent in that method of intervention.

Perry London, in one of the most valued explorations of the impact of twentieth century behavior control, articulates a clear perspective on absolute ethics versus the need for relative ethics:

> The rigidity of absolute ethics guarantees not only that they will be unjustly harsh or lax, but that they will soon be obsolete as well, especially as the progress of technology accelerates. The ethical questions of technology must largely follow the machinery, as justice must largely follow power. As new machinery brings new impact on people's lives and new need to probe the ethical formulations which preceded it, it will be clear that some old rules have become patently impractical guides for conduct. New ethics, in turn, may seem absolutely valuable in their time, until new realities once again require that newer rules be formed to cope with them.[20]

It is this process social work has gone through, and for that matter, continues to go through, in its deliberations on the ethics of behavior modification.[4] To be certain, it will be seen in the further exploration of the ethics of behavior modification that behavior modifiers themselves have had to formulate and reformulate their ethics in response to community reaction and their own assessment of the impact of behavioral technology.

Ethical Issues in Behavior Modification

The previous, brief enumeration of the central elements of behavior modification indicated an approach that advanced both a theoretical view of individual behavior as well as an accompanying technology or set of operations to alter behavior. This view of human behavior has in some instances served as a philosophy of humankind.[31, 32]

For some, this philosophy has provided the base for disputing the ethics of behavior modification. These concerns have usually focused on the issue of individual freedom, self-determination, and responsibility.

On the other hand, and in many cases resultant from the debate on philosophy, are the ethical issues that emerge from the technology of the behavioral approach. Here, the issue usually focuses on the use of negative, punitive, or aversive methods in altering the behavior of institutionalized individuals. While the division of these two areas of ethical concern is somewhat artificial, it is important to separate the philosophical ideals from the practical issues of action because there are differences between what a worker might believe and what s/he might do.

The Issues of Freedom, Self-Determination, and Individual Responsibility

Behavior is determined on the basis of certain laws of human exchange with the environment. "All behavior is inevitably controlled, and the operation of psychological laws cannot be suspended by romantic conceptions of human behavior, any more than indignant rejection of the law of gravity as antihumanistic can stop people from falling."[1]

At first, this deterministic view might appear to be incongruent with the social work values of individual freedom, self-determination, and individual responsibility that would result in an attitudinal ethical dilemma.

If social work ethics propose that the individual should and does have total freedom of choice, and that the person can choose to behave independently of past experiences and contemporary conditions, then the two positions are irreconcilable. Alternatively, if individual freedom is taken to mean that persons have choices available but the number of choices vary among individuals based on previous learning experiences and existing environmental conditions, then the ethical issue becomes one of how best to elaborate the choices within these constraints.

A common misconception regarding the behavioral approach concerns the degree to which the individual is free to determine his/her own destiny. The individual is portrayed as a passive reactor to stimuli from the environment, vulnerable to behavioral control by anyone who might identify the appropriate stimulus-response connection. "The popular belief that humans can be conditioned automatically and reflexively is largely a myth . . . The notion that one can create automatic internal inhibitors by imposed aversive conditioning, as graphically portrayed in *A Clockwork Orange,* may be captivating drama but it is faulty psychology."[2] The individual must be a participant in the determination of what is to be changed, how, and by whom.

Inextricably related to the issues of freedom and self-determination is that of responsibility. As London points out, "there has always been a dynamic tension between the concepts of freedom and responsibility; they are antagonistic modes of conduct. If a person acts as he pleases, he may be set on a collision course with others, who call themselves society.... But if he acts responsibly toward others, he may not be free to satisfy himself. Individuality always courts social deviance, and social responsibility never promotes it."[20]

The individual bears responsibility ultimately for the choice of change versus no change in a behavior modification program. The degree of responsibility s/he takes for others and the degree of individual freedom that is given up is not determined by the behavior modifier. It is, however, subject to the restrictions of the environment within which the individual initiates the change process.

In the final analysis, ethics deals with action, and it is how these philosophical views are translated into operation that will serve as the basis of ethical scrutiny.

The Issues of Behavioral Control in Behavior Modification

Behavior modification is a change-oriented, goal-directed approach to helping people. The implications of this goal directedness are three-fold. First, the worker activity is at a high level. Second, the approach requires that the worker focus on behavior, either that reported by the client or that observed by others. Third, the approach is more technological compared with other methods. This technique-oriented, high-activity-level approach has resulted in the worker assuming more responsibility for the client change than other models of intervention.

It is likely that these three factors contribute to the behavioral approach being perceived as a method that strives for control over its clientele. This notion of control has a negative connotation and it emerges as the predominant ethical issue in behavior modification. In terms of overall purpose, however, the behavioral approach does not differ from other approaches. Control is a reality and it is the objective of all types of therapeutic intervention.[11] Generally, this control strategy is an attempt to influence clients toward change objectives consistent with the cultural values within which the therapy takes place.[2]

The position of the behavior modifier, therefore, is not whether the individual's behavior is controlled; that is taken as given. The issues are, rather, who is the controller, how does the controller set about to control, and what is the context within which control is being exercised.

The question of who the controller is, within the spectrum of behavioral theory, must theoretically include all people. However, for purposes of planned, systematic behavioral change, it must be a person with knowledge and experience in the field of behavior modification and one who has demonstrated practice competence. Usually this will be a professional helping person who has been trained in behavior modification, in addition to other professional training, and who subscribes to the ethical code of behavior for that profession, such as *The Code of Ethics* of the Canadian Association of Social Workers.

The issues of how and within what context a behavior modification program is implemented are of critical concern from the standpoint of ethics.

The issues arising from the how or the means by which behavior modification is implemented may be separated for discussion purposes into the categories of aversive control and positive control. As these two aspects of behavioral control are being explored, it will be helpful to keep in mind that a behavior modifier operates within two types or categories of context. Some programs are designed and carried out within an institutional setting. Others are designed and implemented outside of an institutional setting or within the natural environment. The principles of behavior modification remain constant across the settings, but most importantly, the conditions for control and, therefore, the behavior modification procedures may vary greatly.

The Ethics of Aversive Behavioral Control in Behavior Modification

Many, if not all, of the more horrific stories reported on behavior modification have taken place within institutional settings such as prisons, residential treatment settings, homes for the retarded, and mental health facilities. The institutional setting, by its very purpose, must provide care for persons who have, for the most part, exhibited behavior that has been unacceptable to the community. Within these relatively closed systems the means by which behavioral control may be exercised are essentially in the hands of those who have been given the mandate by the community to care for the persons within the setting. The concept of care carries with it the explicit or implicit objective to alter the behavior(s) for which the person was institutionalized in the first place. This objective is variously referred to, but most commonly it is labelled treatment or rehabilitation.

One very common approach to altering behavior in the community at large and, therefore, within institutional settings is that commonly referred to as punishment. Most individuals have encountered punishment of some type, particularly as children when their parents attempted to modify or "correct" an unacceptable behavior. While the meaning of punishment may vary from individual to individual, it does have a general connotation of administering something unpleasant, verbally or otherwise, to the individual or withholding pleasure, for example, taking away privileges.

While other approaches to helping have incorporated forms of punishment, such as sanctions against the client for violations of the therapeutic contract, none have so clearly identified and labelled the different aspects of aversive control as have the behavior modifiers. Further, no other approach has so systematically employed aversive control and assessed its relative merits in altering human behavior. This has been both a plus and a minus in terms of ethics. On the one hand, it has resulted in some flagrant abuses of aversive control, some of which were cited at the outset of this discussion. Such instances have clearly violated the norms of the community and have justly been criticized as violating the ethics of the helping disciplines. On the other hand, much of the inquiry into aversive control has resulted in the discovery of its place within a successful behavioral program. The result has been an increased restrictive use of aversive control, one which favors the use of aversive measures with problems so far not amenable to change through positive means.

An ethical dilemma remains, however. Aversive control does continue to be one aspect of behavior modification. For example, some behaviors are injurious to the individual, as is severe head banging by an autistic child. Furthermore, the high frequency of occurrence of a behavior such as head banging makes it nearly impossible to employ positive methods of control.[21] The issue then becomes one of whether it is ethically appropriate to use an aversive approach (punish) to arrest the head banging behavior in order to both prevent further injury as well as facilitate a wider program of intervention.

At issue here is that an aversive technique requires the deliberate and consistent use of some unpleasant or hurtful event, provided by a care-taking individual. Stated in its simplest form, is it ethical for a helping person to administer pain in order to facilitate change in the individual?

In reflecting back to the separately considered questions of what is behavior modification and what is social work ethics, two elements must be drawn out in order to answer this question. First, behavior modification identifies appropriate behavioral change objectives to be those that increase desirable behaviors. Therefore, a program of behavior modification, if it is to be true to its principles, cannot depend solely upon punishment to facilitate change. Second, ethics is viewed here as being the result of a process between the individual, the worker, and the community. The worker must be satisfied that s/he is unable to bring about change in any other manner than by the use of an aversive technique. If aversive control is to be employed based on the best professional knowledge available, it must be of a nature that is well within the standards of community acceptability. This is of particular importance when the program is carried out within an institutional setting, where the care-takers can more easily punish and take away privileges exclusive of community scrutiny.

It was stated earlier that actions on the part of any of the helping disciplines should be constantly appraised both for efficacy and ethics. Many authors[2] have drawn attention to the results of aversive conditioning and its limited effectiveness, which should act to more clearly set limits on aversive control. While effectiveness is not necessarily a sufficient condition for the ethical use of a technique, surely ineffectiveness should be an important consideration in the determination of unethical use.

The Ethics of Positive Behavioral Control in Behavior Modification

The most common manner in which to modify an individual's behavior is to use praise and to "reward" the individual for his/her behavioral achievements in the desired direction. Within the behavior modification approach, this process is referred to as positive reinforcement. In many ways it is very acceptable to a public that values kindness, warmth, support, encouragement, and rewards of various kinds as a means of enhancing the self. Positive control techniques *appear* to have none of the ethical problems that surround the aversive control strategies.

Such is not the case, however. Positive control carries with it some of the inherent ethical issues of control generally. The fact remains that the worker systematically provides positive reinforcers only for those behaviors that worker and client have agreed to increase in frequency. The first ethical issue to be identified in this approach to behavior modification is that of manipulation of the individual. Some argue that a worker's praise and encouragement should be given unconditionally and should not be held contingent on the occurrence of specific behavior. To do otherwise carries the negative connotation of worker manipulation of the client. The practitioner of behavior modification takes the position, however, that worker behaviors such as praise can, under the natural laws of behavior, increase the frequency of those behaviors desired by worker and client.

The question remains, however, as to which aspects of a client's environment may be withheld until an appropriate behavior occurs. Many of the behavior modification programs that depend on the use of positive reinforcement require a procedure known as a "token economy." For example, a patient in a mental hospital might be provided with a predetermined number of points or tokens for each occurrence of a selected set of target behaviors. Selection of behaviors may range from simple behaviors such as brushing teeth, hair, etc. (morning hygiene) to social interactional behaviors such as making eye contact, communication of affect, or socially assertive communication. In a token economy the tokens act as "generalized reinforcers" and may be traded in for any number of prearranged items from a menu of activities or consumer goods, e.g. extra ground privileges or extra purchases from the hospital canteen.

The possible ethical dilemma stems from the realization that some level of deprivation must exist on the part of the individual in order to facilitate the token economy. In other words, the events held contingent on the occurrence of the desired target behavior must not be generally available to the patient. The question of what events or goods may be ethically withheld from an individual is an ethical issue, particularly within institutional settings. Alternatively, this question has given rise to many inquiries as to just what basic rights an individual has within an institutional setting.[42]

The following description of an early token economy program surely demonstrates a violation of ethical standards:

> This group sleeps in a relatively unattractive dormitory set by the state department of mental hygiene. There are no draperies at the windows or spreads on the beds, and the beds themselves are of the simplest kind. In the dining room the patient sits with many other patients at a long table, crowded in somewhat uncomfortably. . . . He may not have permission for off-the-ground visits, and the number of visitors who can see him is restricted.
>
> During this time, the patient learns that his meals, his bed, his toilet articles and his clothes no longer are freely given him. He must pay for these with tokens. These tokens pay for all those things normally furnished and often taken for granted. In the orientation group most of the things the patient wants are cheap; for example, it costs one token to be permitted to go to bed, one token for a meal. Patients find it easy enough to earn the few tokens necessary for bare subsistence.[44]

The issue here of course is not the ease with which a patient might earn his subsistence, but rather whether these aspects of his life should be held on contingency in the first place. There is no doubt that this program was developed on a basic behavioral principle, but without regard to the basic human rights of the patient group. No individual, particularly one within a treatment institution, should have to earn human rights such as food, clothing, and basic privileges. In fact, a program dependent on such deprivation may be cause for the total rejection of a token economy.

It is possible and desirable for a token economy to be set up with the cooperation of the patient and for the economy to be based upon the earning of extra privileges and extra goods, well beyond those considered essential. For example, consider the brief illustration of a program carried out in a family setting where the children were identified as having behavioral problems.

CASE 1: The S. family was referred to the family agency by the family doctor for counselling around the behavior of John, age eleven years. Reports from the school indicated that John was disruptive in the classroom, interrupted the teachers, and repeatedly fought with fellow students. At home, John was described as belligerent, would not do his assigned tasks, and fought with both his siblings and his parents.

The social worker's assessment indicated that the parents, Mr. S., aged thirty-four, and Mrs. S., aged thirty-two, were expressing similar complaints about Sally, aged ten years. The only difference was that Sally was not displaying the problems in school evidenced by John. A younger sister, Rachael, aged six, was reported to be very demanding, stealing from other children, bed wetting, and refusing to dress herself in the mornings.

After a complete behavioral assessment the social worker and all family members agreed to target a total of six behaviors for change. A behavioral contract was drawn up and signed by the parents and all children. In essence the program was a positive control token economy behavior modification. The two oldest children received three tokens and parental praise for each of the completed behaviors of making their beds; clearing the supper table after the evening meal; getting ready for school on time; going to bed on time; and cooperative sibling play. In addition, Rachael, received three tokens and parental praise for dressing herself.

The economy or "trade off" was set at a level that the older children could earn approximately $1.50 per week for complete compliance with the program. Rachael had a potential earning capacity of 75¢ for the same seven day period. This money was earned in addition to each child's weekly allowance (75¢ per week for the eldest and 50¢ per week for the youngest).

The program and the token economy lasted nine weeks, during which time the target behaviors increased in frequency and the problem behaviors diminished. At the end of fourteen weeks, service to the family was terminated. It should be noted that the family began to withdraw the token economy at the end of the ninth week, depending on parental praise and recognition as the behavioral reinforcers for maintaining the successful changes in the children.

Three aspects of this program should be highlighted because of their relevance for the discussion of positive and aversive control. First, while the main emphasis was on the provision of positive reinforcers for desired behaviors, tokens were deducted when the children chose not to engage in a target behavior. Second, the parents were required to communicate a specific message of praise and acknowledgement when a particular target behavior was concluded. The intent of the program is to increase the frequency with which the parents demonstrate these "natural reinforcers." Third, the items available for which the tokens might be traded were considered by all family members to be beyond the guaranteed rights of the individuals in the family. In fact, these extra privileges may well have provided the base for all members to demonstrate their desire and commitment for change, as many "trade offs" involved family activities.

Any program that employs techniques of positive control does run the risk of giving the appearance of what has been referred to as "bribery." Some argue that good behavior should be intrinsically self-satisfying and, thus, not in need of external reinforcement. From the behavioral standpoint, behavior is strongly influenced by its consequences, and in many instances these consequences may be natural or less contrived than a token economy may appear. However, when a behavior modifier has the task of facilitating the acquisition of a new set of behavior(s) which in most cases occur at a low frequency, some device is needed to acknowledge easily and inexpensively each behavioral occurrence. This is even more important if the behavior to be acquired is one chosen to replace an undesirable behavior that has been highly reinforced, e.g. delinquent behavior. The behavior modifier would argue that the choice of behavior for change is one which is valued by the community and the client. The procedure for positive reinforcement is simply to restructure the environment in such a manner as to cause the new behavior(s) to receive positive consequences at a higher rate and intensity than the undesirable behaviors. Once acquired, the desired behaviors need not be reinforced at the rate characteristic of a beginning program of behavior modification. Bribery, however, as a method of behavioral influence connotes the payment of tangibles for illicit behavior. The intention of bribery in human affairs is usually to influence individuals to behave in violation of community ethics, and is quite the opposite of the intention of behavior modification.

At the beginning of this exploration of the ethics of behavioral control, the issue of context was identified as a potential determinant of behavioral procedures. The intent of distinguishing between institutional programs of behavior modification versus those conducted in the natural environment was to highlight the high potential for behavioral control within the institution.

There is, however, one further consideration for the behavior modifier to be aware of and that is the issue of who controls his/her behavior in working with people.

Most social workers are employed by either private or public agencies, each of which is mandated to fulfill certain community objectives. Van Hoose and Kottler point to the all too familiar social worker dilemma when they observe that "there is often a conflict among a therapist's loyalties to his clients, the employing institution and the larger society. The state allows therapists to exist, social institutions employ them, and society encourages their activities. Because of these sanctions and supports therapists are expected to help people 'adjust' to their environments."[43]

It is not news to a social work practitioner that his/her behavior is under the control of the agency who employs him/her. Most practitioners have encountered the difficulties of working toward goals different from their employing agency. The ethics of behavioral control in these situations is not too dissimilar from those of the institutionalized client. Like the client, the social worker must retain dignity and freedom of choice. In the social worker's case, however, the choice is clear. The client needs must emerge above those of any other system, regardless of the attempts of the organization to influence the worker toward furthering incompatible agency goals.

The Ethics of Contracted Behavioral Change and the Right to Refuse Intervention

Much energy has gone into exploring the ethical issues of control in behavior modification, perhaps to the exclusion of understanding that this approach requires the social worker to do a complete assessment of the client's behavioral problems and the controlling conditions for these behaviors. While it is possible to embark upon a program of behavioral change without the client's agreement or awareness, this is neither desirable nor ethical. Rather, the requirements of a competently developed program demand that the client be aware of all the salient behavioral problems, their maintaining conditions, and the proposed means to alter these behaviors. Most often the behaviors chosen to be the "targets" for change are not those specifically identified as problems. In these cases the social worker must demonstrate the reason for the selection of these target behavioral choices.

Once the behavioral objectives have been identified and agreed to, the client and worker must work out a clear agreement or contract as to what is going to occur when the desired behaviors are engaged in and what sanctions are going to be brought to bear if the behavior(s) does not occur. Referred to as a contingency contract, all members of the change process are required to agree to those aspects of the program that involve them. In the final analysis, all members of a behavior modification program must have complete understanding of each behavioral goal, the rationale for its choice, and the means by which the change is to take place. At any point in this process any member of the change agreement may express an unwillingness to proceed and/or request a renegotiation of the contract. Without doubt and with very few exclusions, all clients must be assured the right to refuse change. The only proviso that the behavior modifier would want to place on this right to refuse change is that the client must be aware of the consequences of no change. For example, when the delinquent adolescent refuses to enter into a contract for behavioral change, the behavior modifier's responsibility becomes one of exploring and enumerating the consequences of no change, e.g. longer jail sentences, further conflict with the police, etc.

In order to better illustrate the overall process of behavioral targetting and contracting, and the right to refuse service, examine the case of Dick and Susan.

CASE 2: Dick, aged thirty-eight years, had been married to Susan, aged thirty-six years, for seventeen years. Dick was referred to the author because of his inability to stay away from home overnight. This problem was not only of concern to Dick because it symbolized an inability to control himself, but it was also costing his business in "unwarranted" air fares. Dick owned his own business, the nature of which required numerous trips per month. In order to accommodate his behavioral problem, Dick would take an early morning flight to his business meetings and return on a late evening flight. Unfortunately, many meetings went on for two or three days. When his presence was required for such meetings, Dick would fly to and from the meetings on a daily basis.

The behavioral assessment indicated a number of behavioral problems, two of the major ones being a high anxiety level and a severe and long standing marital problem. In addition to these key elements of Dick's problems were an identified fear of death, an inability to interact with people in social situations unless he was drunk, and a perceived inability to assert himself with his wife.

Due to the apparent involvement of Susan in Dick's problems, the worker requested and was granted a meeting with the couple together. During two interviews, Susan insisted that Dick's problems were his own doing and they were related to his drinking. When confronted by Dick with his feelings that she was part of the problem because she was always telling him what to do, Susan announced that she did not want to be a part of the behavior modification sessions.

The worker demonstrated the interrelatedness of their respective complaints and pointed out that while some aspects of Dick's problems could be worked on independent of Susan's participation, other aspects concerned the marital relationship. For example, Dick expressed the desire to be more assertive in his communication with his wife. Such assertive behavior could become a target for change by Dick. Desirably, this behavioral target should involve the full participation of Susan. The consequence of her noninvolvement would likely be confusion and frustration in response to Dick's behavioral change.

Susan maintained that she did not want to participate in any program of marital change and exercised her right to refuse involvement. Intervention proceeded with Dick and focused on the reduction of his anxiety in respect to four different environmental themes, such as death and social interactional situations. Further, behaviors were identified and rehearsed to facilitate Dick's assertive communication with Susan.

Within six weeks of implementation of the program, Dick was able to approach and successfully cope with certain aspects of the environment that precipitated his anxieties. For example, he had been able to visit a friend in the hospital, something he had successfully avoided because of its perceived connection to dying. He had decided to approach all social situations without drinking and was succeeding in handling such situations.

Marital conflict, however, was increasing. Predictably, as Dick asserted his own feelings, Susan attempted to suppress this assertion with a higher level of aversiveness. At the end of the seventh week of involvement with Dick, Susan telephoned the worker requesting that she become involved with Dick in the marital change.

The program switched, by mutual agreement, to a dyadic interactional modification, which lasted an additional eighteen weeks. During this time Dick's individual program carried on, finally succeeding on all counts. The staying out overnight problem began to change initially by staying overnight only about 100 miles away from home. This distance was gradually increased until Dick's business trips were successfully completed as overnight stays.

The marital program necessitated joint behavioral change targets with reciprocal positive reinforcement for change in each behavior. As a result of this program the couple reported a more satisfactory marital relationship at termination and at a one year follow-up.

This case illustrates a behavior modification approach that targetted, initially, some individual changes. One member of the dyad exercised her right not to be involved, and intervention proceeded with a focus on those behavioral changes identified and contracted by one person. Ethically, it might be questioned as to whether any behaviors concerning the dyadic problem should have been targetted for change. It is to be noted that while the target of assertive behavior involved Susan, she chose not to be directly involved in the behavior modification. Further, while the behavior of assertion would ultimately impact Susan, Dick did have a right to work toward the individual goal of increased expressiveness within his marital relationship. Of importance here, although it is not always the case, is that Susan reappraised her refusal to become involved. Interestingly, she cited (as her reasons) her awareness of the changes in Dick and his repeated requests that she attend the sessions.

There are occasions when the right to refuse behavior modification is far more complex than that illustrated here, for example, when a person's behavior is obviously self-injurious. In these situations the question of individual rights in refusing behavioral intervention must be tempered by an assessment as to whether the individual is competent to appraise the consequences of nonchange. Further, the community must have some say in terms of the cost to the whole of behavior that ultimately inhibits an individual maximizing his/her potential.

The issue of the participation or the right to refuse behavior modification has been dealt with by some practitioners by ensuring that all programs of behavior modification make provision for client informed consent. Informed consent has a number of implications for behavior modification in social work and therefore will be examined as a final ethical issue.

The Ethics of Informed Consent in Behavior Modification

In discussions of practice ethics it has become increasingly popular to present the notion of "informed consent" almost as a panacea for dealing with much of the criticism and anxiety related to behavioral modification. A number of legal decisions relating to certain treatment approaches have held that patients have a right to consent to or reject the procedures used in the treatment program. On the surface, there are many appealing factors in having a client fully informed about the interventive approach prior to securing his/her consent for program implementation. However, the issue of informed consent is more complex than it initially appears, particularly for social work practitioners.

Specifically, informed consent includes the three elements of knowledge, client competency, and voluntary participation. "The term knowledge refers to the information describing the program and its goals, explaining that individuals may refuse to participate in the program before it begins or at any time during the program, and offering alternative programs. The term voluntariness refers to the absence of coercion or duress when the decision to consent is made. The term competency reflects an assessment that the clients can understand the information that has been given to them and make a judgment about it."[33]

As the distressed patient in the accompanying cartoon has found, knowledge about the procedures to be employed does not necessarily enlighten one as to the risks involved, especially if one is unaware of alternative approaches. This is particularly true when the stress caused by the problem is such that help of any kind is wanted, and wanted immediately, e.g. the client in crisis.

Competency in understanding and decision making regarding the behavioral program should be a relatively clear cut judgment

"What we propose to do is remove your head, have a look inside your neck, and then close you up again. It is a brand-new technique and it would be less than candid of me to pretend that it does not involve certain dangers. The question is: How badly do you want to get rid of that cough?"

Figure 11-1. From the *Toronto Sun*. Reprinted with permission of Canada Wide syndicate.

in the case of most clients. However, for many of those in institutional settings, the program of intervention is designed to increase their level of awareness, understanding, and functioning, and it is quite improbable that they could be considered competent in judging the merits of intervention, e.g. institutionalized retarded, schizophrenic individuals, etc.

Finally, the issue of whether a client is in any position to volunteer for a program of behavior modification has been the subject of some debate. There are many subtle and not so subtle coercive techniques that may be employed to involve a client in behavior modification. For example, as Stolz notes, "institutionalized residents are dependent on the goodwill of the staff for release from the institution and also are subject to more subtle forms of coercion related to the privileges that an involuntary detained resident may be allowed to exercise within the institution. . . ."[33]

The arguments identified here against the use of informed consent procedures are intended to demonstrate that informed consent is probably most applicable to those clients who bring to the client-worker encounter sufficient awareness, understanding, and competence to enter into a mutually negotiated and agreed upon behavioral change contract of the nature to render informed consent, at the least, redundant. At the worst, procedures designed to secure informed consent are perceived to be outside the context of the helping process, and as Schwitzgebel has observed they imply that the behavior modifier is doing something harmful or wrong to the client.[30]

The issues that have given rise to the procedure of informed consent are valid ethical concerns. However, they might better be dealt with by enhancing the existing therapeutic behavioral contract procedures that are an integral component of the process of behavior modification. For those who, for whatever reasons, are unable to understand and/or voluntarily participate in a change contract, client advocates or client advisory committees should be utilized. Such individuals and/or groups would represent the interests of the client in scrutinizing and monitoring the behavior modification program.[12] Where the monitoring of a behavioral program evidences violation of ethics, the social worker can be held accountable to explain discrepancies in the behavioral contract. Such a monitoring program not only meets the objectives of informed consent by necessitating the approval of the program by a client advocate, but it exceeds the objectives by evaluating the progress of the behavioral program over time.

CONCLUSION

This inquiry into the ethics of behavior modification in social work practice has taken the position that behavior modification has as its primary objective the improvement of a client's well-being and community functioning by developing and enhancing the client's repertoire of behavioral skills. The choice of behaviors and the means by which the modification takes place remain the prerogative of the client, excepting those situations where client competence is in question.

Central to the discussion has been the use of control and its accompanying ethical dilemmas. Control, as it has been viewed here, is an element of all forms of therapy and it is without question an aspect in all forms of the behavior modification approach. Accepting control as a reality of human functioning, the behavior modifier must deal with the questions of who is the controller, how is control (modification) exercised, and what is the nature of the environment that maintains behavior. The behavior modification approach demonstrates to the individual that s/he is not a passive recepient of the behaviors of others but rather is in a position to acquire behaviors that broaden his/her scope of available behavioral alternatives with which to act on the environment.

With this emphasis on increasing an individual's repertoire of behavioral skills, it is argued that the behavior modification approach fosters increased power in the hands of the client whose behavior has been modified. This behavioral objective is perceived to be well within the social work values of client self-determination, freedom, and responsibility. This position on the ethics of behavior modification is akin to that articulated by Perry London, who argues that —

> In order to defend individual freedom, it is necessary to enhance the power of individuals. If behavior technology endangers freedom by giving refined power to controllers, then the antidote which promotes freedom is to give more refined power over their own behavior to those who are endangered. Since everyone is endangered, this means facilitating self-control in everyone. And self-control does not mean simply the ability to inhibit impulses, but the general mastery of one's own behavior.[20]

To ensure that behavior modification strives toward this value, systems of education,[41] internal controls,[15] and monitoring of practice procedures and practitioner competence[3] must be developed. While effectiveness of intervention is not the sole criterion of ethical practice, it must certainly be a priority, particularly in a society in which over 130 different therapeutic methods are presently available.[25] The proponents of behavior modification have consistently demanded that procedures be subjected to empirical investigation. It is fair to say that they have produced a strong empirical base upon which to appraise the positives and negatives of their approach, empirical evaluation of the means by which it will be possible to rise above what has been referred to as the "prevalence of Madison Avenue messiahs"[43] and ensure the best possible practice. Is that not the ultimate objective of ethical social work practice?

Behavior modifiers as a group have invested a great deal of energy in the exploration of ethical issues in behavior modification. In 1977, the Association for Advancement of Behavior Therapy adopted a statement of ethical issues in the form of eight questions with accompanying subquestions of elaboration designed to guide practice. Because of the clarity of these questions and their relevance for consideration by social workers practicing behavior modification, they are quoted in their entirety.[8]

A. Have the goals of treatment been adequately considered?
    1. To insure that the goals are explicit, are they written?
    2. Has the client's understanding of the goals been assured by having the client restate them orally or in writing?
    3. Have the therapist and client agreed on the goals of therapy?
    4. Will serving the client's interests be contrary to the interests of other persons?
    5. Will serving the client's immediate interests be contrary to the client's long term interest?

B. Has the choice of treatment methods been adequately considered?
    1. Does the published literature show the procedure to be the best one available for that problem?
    2. If no literature exists regarding the treatment method, is the method consistent with generally accepted practice?
    3. Has the client been told of alternative procedures that might be preferred by the client on the basis of significant differences in discomfort, treatment time, cost, or degree of demonstrated effectiveness?
    4. If a treatment procedure is publicly, legally, or professionally controversial, has formal professional consultation been obtained, has the reaction of the affected segment of the public been adequately considered, and have the alternative treatment methods been more closely reexamined and reconsidered?

C. Is the client's participation voluntary?

1. Have possible sources of coercion on the client's participation been considered?
2. If treatment is legally mandated, has the available range of treatments and therapists been offered?
3. Can the client withdraw from treatment without a penalty or financial loss that exceeds actual clinical costs?

D. When another person or an agency is empowered to arrange for therapy, have the interests of the subordinated client been sufficiently considered?
  1. Has the subordinated client been informed of the treatment objectives and participated in the choice of treatment procedures?
  2. Where the subordinated client's competence to decide is limited, have the client as well as the guardian participated in the treatment discussions to the extent that the client's abilities permit?
  3. If the interests of the subordinated person and the superordinate persons or agency conflict, have attempts been made to reduce the conflict by dealing with both interests?

E. Has the adequacy of treatment been evaluated?
  1. Have quantitative measures of the problem and its progress been obtained?
  2. Have the measures of the problem and its progress been made available to the client during treatment?

F. Has the confidentiality of the treatment relationship been protected?
  1. Has the client been told who has access to the records?
  2. Are records available only to authorized persons?

G. Does the therapist refer the clients to other therapists when necessary?
  1. If treatment is unsuccessful, is the client referred to other therapists?
  2. Has the client been told that if dissatisfied with the treatment, referral will be made?

H. Is the therapist qualified to provide treatment?
  1. Has the therapist had training or experience in treating problems like the client's?
  2. If deficits exist in the therapist's qualifications, has the client been informed?
  3. If the therapist is not adequately qualified, is the client referred to other therapists, or has supervision by a qualified therapist been provided? Is the client informed of the supervisory relation?
  4. If the treatment is administered by mediators, have the mediators been adequately supervised by a qualified therapist?

In conclusion, the anxieties of Senator Ervin and others who have feared that behavior modification is a powerful means of control capable of altering personality and dictating individual values should take comfort in the realization that behavior modification, while effective, does not possess the almost mystical potency ascribed to it by some observers.[18]

BIBLIOGRAPHY

1. Bandura, A.: *Principles of Behavior Modification.* Toronto, Holt, Rinehart & Winston, Inc., 1969.
2. Bandura, A.: The ethics and social purposes of behavior modification. In Franks, C. M. and Wilson, G. T. (Eds.): *Annual Review of Behavior Therapy and Theory,* Vol. 3. New York, Brunner/Mazel, 1975:13–20.
3. Braun, S.: Ethical issues in behavior modification. *Behavior Therapy* (6) 1975:51–62.
4. Bruck, M.: Behavior modification theory and practice: A critical review. *Social Work* (13) 1968: 43–55.
5. Carter, R. and Stuart, R.: Behavior modification theory and practice: A reply. *Social Work* (15) 1970: 37–50.
6. Declaration of Hawaii. Ethical issues. *Psychiatric News,* Oct. 7, 1977.
7. *The Edmonton Journal,* Saturday, March 8, 1980, p. 1.
8. Ethical issues for human services. *Behavior Therapy* (8) 1977: v–vi.
9. Eysenck, H.: Behavior therapy and the philosophers. *Behavior Research and Therapy* (17) 1979: 511–514.
10. Fischer, J.: *Effective Casework Practice: An Eclectic Approach.* Toronto, McGraw Hill, 1978.
11. Franks, C. M. and Wilson, G. T. (Eds.): *Annual Review of Behavior Therapy, Theory and Practice,* Vol. 3. New York, Brunner/Mazel, 1975.
12. Friedman, P.: Legal regulation of applied behavior analysis in mental institutions and prisons. *Arizona Law Review* (17) 1975: 39–104.
13. Griffith, R.: An administrative perspective on guidelines for behavior modification: The creation of a legally safe environment. *The Behavior Therapist* (3) 1980: 5–7.
14. Group for the Advancement of Psychiatry: *The Field of Family Therapy.* Report No. VII, March 1970. Chapter 7, "Ethical Issues in Family Treatment," pp. 594–603.
15. Halleck, S.: Legal and ethical aspects of behavior control. *American Journal of Psychiatry* (131) 1974: 381–385.
16. Hartshorn, M.: Comments on the Szasz-Wolpe exchange. *Journal of Behavior Therapy and Experimental Psychiatry* (9) 1978: 211–213.
17. Kassirer, L.: The right to treatment and the right to refuse treatment — recent case law. *Journal of Psychiatry and Law* (2) 1974: 455–470.
18. Kazdin, A.: Fictions, factions and functions of behavior therapy. *Behavior Therapy* (10) 1979: 629–654.
19. Levy, C.: *Social Work Ethics.* New York, Human Sciences Press, 1976.
20. London, P.: *Behavior Control.* New York, Harper & Row, 1971.
21. Lovaas, O.: A behavior therapy approach to the treatment of childhood schizophrenia. In Hill, J. (Ed.): *Minnesota Symposia on Child Psychology,*

Vol. 1. Minneapolis, University of Minnesota Press, 1967.

22. Martin, R.: *Legal Challenges to Behavior Modification.* Champaign, Ill., Research Press, 1975.

23. Martin, R.: The right to receive or refuse treatment. *The Behavior Therapist* (3) 1980:8.

24. Morrow, W. and Gochros, H.: Misconceptions regarding behavior modification. *Social Service Review* (44) 1970: 293–307.

25. Parloff, M. Shopping for the right therapy. *Saturday Review,* Feb. 21, 1976: 14–20.

26. Risley, T. and Sheldon-Wildgen, J.: Suggested procedures for human rights committees of potentially controversial treatment programs. *The Behavior Therapist* (3) 1980: 9–10.

27. Roos, P.: Human rights and behavior modification. *Mental Retardation* (12) 1974: 3–6.

28. Roth, L., Meisel, A., and Lidz, C.: Tests of competency to consent to treatment. *American Journal of Psychiatry* (134) 1977: 279–284.

29. Schwartz, A. and Goldiamond, I.: *Social Casework: A Behavioral Approach.* New York, Columbia University Press, 1975.

30. Schwitzgebel, R.: A contractual model for the protection of the rights of institutionalized mental patients. *American Psychologist* (30) 1975: 815–820.

31. Skinner, B. F.: *Walden Two.* New York, MacMillan Co., 1968.

32. Skinner, B. F.: *Beyond Freedom and Dignity.* New York, Bantam Books, 1971.

33. Stolz, S. et al.: *Ethical Issues in Behavior Modification.* San Francisco, Jossey-Bass, 1978.

34. Stolz, S.: A legally safe environment is not necessarily an ethical one. *The Behavior Therapist* (3) 1980: 7–8.

35. Stuart, R.: Protection of the right to informed consent to participate in research. *Behavior Therapy* (9) 1978: 73–82.

36. Szasz, T.: *The Myth of Mental Illness.* New York, Dell Pub., 1961.

37. Szasz, T.: Behavior therapy: A critical review of the moral dimensions of behavior modification. *Journal of Behavior Therapy and Experimental Psychiatry* (9) 1978: 199–203.

38. Thomas, E.: Selected socio-behavioral techniques and principles: An approach to interpersonal helping. *Social Work* (13) 1968: 12–26.

39. Turkat, I. D., Harris, F. C. and Forehand, R.: An assessment of the public reaction to behavior modification. *Journal of Behavior Therapy and Experimental Psychiatry* (10) 1979: 101–103.

40. Turner, F.: *Social Work Treatment.* New York, Free Press, 1974.

41. Ulrich, R.: Behavior control and public concern. *Psychological Record* (17) 1967: 229–234.

42. U.S. Congress, Senate, Committee on the Judiciary, Subcommittee on Constitutional Rights: *Individual Rights and the Federal Role in Behavior Modification.* 93rd Congress, 2nd session, November, 1974. Washington, D.C., U.S. Government Printing Office, 1974.

43. Van Hoose, W. and Kottler, J.: *Ethical and Legal Issues in Counselling and*

Psychotherapy. San Francisco, Jossey-Bass, 1977.

44. Wexler, D.: Token and taboo: Behavior modification, token economies, and the law. *California Law Review* (61) 1973: 81–109.

45. Willis, J. and Giles, D.: Behaviorism in the twentieth century: What we have here is a failure to communicate. *Behavior Therapy* (9) 1978: 15–27.

46. Wilson, G. T.: On the much discussed nature of the term 'behavior therapy'. *Behavior Therapy* (9) 1978: 89–98.

47. Wodarski, J. and Bagarozzi, D.: *Behavioral Social Work.* New York Human Sciences Press, 1979.

48. Wolpe, J.: The humanity of behavior therapy. *Journal of Behavior Therapy and Experimental Psychiatry* (9) 1978: 205–209.

Chapter 12

GENETIC COUNSELING

CONRAD BRUNK

BACKGROUND OF GENETIC COUNSELING

The idea of genetic counseling as a means of exercising control over the human reproductive process is not new. Soon after Gregor Mendel published his research on the basic laws of heredity in the midnineteenth century, Francis Galton, a cousin of Charles Darwin, became a strong advocate of counseling and other social programs to help prevent the "degradation of human nature" and "produce a highly gifted race of men by judicious marriages during several consecutive generations."[1]

Galton's ideas became especially influential in the United States during the first three decades of the twentieth century. They were popularized by writers like Madison Grant, who promoted massive sterilization programs for "an ever widening circle of social discords, beginning always with the criminal, the diseased, and the insane, and extending gradually to types which may be called weaklings rather than defectives and perhaps ultimately to worthless race types."[2] Ideas like these led to a rash of sterilization laws and mass sterilizations of the mentally retarded in the U.S., the legality of which initially was upheld by the Supreme Court. In the landmark case of Carrie Buck, a mentally retarded black girl who was sterilized by the State of Virginia despite her religious objections as a Roman Catholic, Justice Oliver Wendell Holmes Jr. affirmed the state's right to take measures that would "prevent our being swamped with incompetence."[3]

Following the atrocities of the Nazi eugenic programs, the eugenics movement of the early twentieth century fell into general disrepute in North America. The early genetic counseling centers, such as the Dight Institute for Human Betterment at the

University of Minnesota, dropped their emphasis upon social betterment and "genetic-hygiene" in favor of less eugenically oriented aims. The term "genetic counseling" was coined by Sheldon Reed, the second director of the Dight Institute, precisely to avoid the connotations of the eugenics movement and to describe a process he thought of as a kind of "genetic social work."[4]

This shift in the philosophy of genetic counseling reflects a movement within the entire science of applied genetics from its early grounding in the eugenics social movement to an alliance with clinical medicine and its traditional emphasis upon the prevention and cure of disease.[5] The rapid growth in genetic counseling as a professional social service in recent years has taken place in this context of clinical concern for the alleviation of the consequences of genetic disease. Major factors contributing to this growth include (1) the recent advancements in the science of genetics, (2) an increased awareness of the prevalence of genetic disease, (3) the development of new techniques for the diagnosis of genetic anomalies, and (4) the increased availability of techniques for the control of genetic disorders (e.g., contraception and abortion).

By the mid 1970s geneticists had identified more than 2,300 genetically related diseases.[6] Statistics show that an increasing percentage of deaths are attributable to genetic disease, including over 40 percent of all childhood deaths,[4] that 1 in every 50 babies born has some single-gene disorder, and that 1 in every 10 persons is afflicted with a behavioral or central nervous system disorder.[7] Many health professionals worry that care of persons with genetic disease consumes a steadily increasing share of health-care resources. Some attribute this to a spread of defective genes through the population, caused in part by our practice of medically sustaining the lives of affected persons and allowing them to pass their defects on to their children.

New diagnostic procedures have made possible the early detection not only of those who have a genetic disease but also of the "carriers" of many recessive conditions such as sickle-cell anemia who may pass the disease on to their children. Probably the single most significant impetus to genetic counseling has been the development of prenatal diagnosis technologies such as amniocentesis, which make possible the detection of genetic defects in the fetus *in utero.* Combined with new, highly reliable contraceptives and liberalized abortion laws, these diagnostic procedures have given unprecedented control over the genetic profile of our children and, indeed, of the human species itself.

With control comes responsibility. The new genetic technologies thrust upon parents and policy makers require decisions that never before had to be faced. These decisions involve complex variables: statistical probabilities of a child's risk of genetic defect, uncertain diagnoses of disease, uncertain prognoses of severity and life expectancy, and subjective assessments of social and familial costs. They involve moral and religious principles that run deep in human experience—the "right to privacy," the "duty to tell the truth," the "right to life," the "right to procreate," the "duty to do no harm and minimize suffering"—principles often in conflict in concrete situations. They also involve intense psychological components—the shame of discovering one's genes to be "defective," the guilt of having "caused" illness in one's baby, and the fear of rearing a severely afflicted child. The person who, due to the birth of a genetically defective child in the extended family or a positive genetic screening test, must suddenly face these decisions requires extensive counsel from someone who can help them come to a clear understanding of the facts and the alternative courses of action open to them. It is not surprising that the genetic counselor, whose role this is, has become an essential participant in modern health care delivery. It is also not surprising that medical social workers, skilled in counseling, communication, and the rendering of personal services, have become integral components of the genetic counseling process.

Most definitions of genetic counseling pinpoint two basic functions: (1) the communication of information concerning causes, risks, prognosis, and options for dealing with genetic disease, and (2) assisting in the choice among options for dealing with genetic disease, in carrying out this choice, and in adjusting to the disease or to the means of dealing with it. The medical social worker's role focuses primarily on the second function—helping the client come to terms personally with the genetic defect or its possibility.[8] This means that the social worker is involved in just that stage of genetic counseling at which the ethical questions are likely to be faced most acutely. These questions are many, and they involve issues of social as well as personal morality. Under what circumstances, if any, can abortion be ethically justified? Ought we to tamper with the genetic shape of the human species? To what extent and to what ends? Whose rights should prevail when rights come into conflict?

These ethical choices are not easy ones. Scientific, ethical, and religious experts disagree about what courses of action are proper. Their disagreements stem in part from different basic ethical principles, for example, the principle that we ought to do whatever produces the greatest social benefit (a utilitarian view) versus the principle that we ought not to do harm or violate the dignity of persons (a Kantian view). They also stem in part from different beliefs about the facts. For example, there is wide difference of opinion among geneticists about whether the human gene pool is deteriorating, or even whether genetic counseling will lead to greater or lesser incidence of genetic defects in the population. Productive argument about ethical issues in genetic counseling requires both expertise in genetic science and clarity about the differing basic value commitments that people hold.

PRENATAL DIAGNOSIS

Recent developments in techniques of fetal monitoring and *in utero* diagnosis have given genetic counselors and their clients access to information that greatly increases the accuracy of reproductive decisions. The most widespread and significant of these is amniocentesis, a process of draining a portion of the amniotic fluid from the amniotic cavity and examining the chromosomes of the fetal cells it contains. Nearly all chromosomal abnormalities (e.g., Downs Syndrome, XYY, Trisomy 18), can be detected as well as many other genetic disorders. This procedure is now in common use with pregnant women who are known to have an abnormal risk of carrying a genetically defective child. If amniocentesis reveals a genetic abnormality, the prospective parents can elect to terminate the pregnancy with an abortion or adjust themselves to the prospect of bearing and raising a diseased or "abnormal" child.

The advantage of prenatal genetic screening is that it provides relatively accurate information about the presence or absence of a genetic defect in a specific child. Parents who previously would not have been willing to take a 25 percent or even much lower risk of bearing a child afflicted with a genetic defect no longer have to remain childless but can conceive children and select those who are free of the defect.

Not surprisingly, however, this procedure has stirred a vigorous and continuing debate. Since only a few of the genetic defects diagnosable *in utero* can be treated or alleviated in any way, the primary alternative available upon a positive test result is abortion of the affected fetus. As Aubrey Milunsky, a leading medical geneticist puts it, "the fundamental aim and philosophy of prenatal diagnosis is to provide reassurance to parents at risk for having defective offspring that they may selectively have unaffected children."[9] This means, of course, selectively aborting affected children. Many genetic counseling clinics, in fact, require parents who request amniocentesis to state in advance their willingness to abort if the test is positive, on the grounds that the minimal risks of the procedure are not justified if parents will not abort an affected fetus anyway.

Consequently, as prenatal diagnosis comes into increasing use as a tool in genetic counseling, the genetic counselor becomes more deeply involved in the ethics of abortion. A counselor who is generally opposed to abortion, or at least to abortion of a fetus for the purpose of preventing its postnatal genetic illness, will likely find his or her own participation in prenatal diagnostic procedures to be morally compromising as well. Many people would see a deep inconsistency in opposing "therapeutic" abortions for genetic reasons on the one hand, while on the other hand, participating in a diagnostic and counseling process that assumes the ethical legitimacy of such abortions. Others, those who have a greater faith in the "nondirective" role of the genetic counselor, may not see this as an inconsistency.

In any event, the social worker who counsels women undergoing prenatal diagnosis will be involved deeply in ethical values and principles with respect to abortion. Normally the clients in this situation find the decision to abort an agonizing one, created by the dilemma of wanting to have healthy children but also feeling a great deal of moral shame and perhaps guilt about the prospect of aborting their newly conceived child. They depend heavily upon the manner in which the counselor presents the pros and cons of abortion, as well as upon the counselor's own opinion and moral support for their decision. It is important for a genetic counselor to be able to discern the primary moral commitments of the clients and help them reach a decision that is commensurate with those commitments. For this reason the counselor should know the range of ethical arguments that are made on all sides of the abortion-for-genetic-disease question and the assumptions behind them.

The abortion question is made especially difficult in the case of prenatal diagnosis by the fact that amniocentesis cannot be safely and accurately performed until relatively late in the term of pregnancy (16–20 weeks), so that abortion of an affected fetus can be carried out only after it has developed almost to the stage of viability. This fact makes the question of the "personhood" of the fetus and its rights as a member of the human community much more critical than it might be if abortion were carried out at an earlier stage. Many people who would not find elective (non-therapeutic) abortion of an early-term fetus morally problematic would find abortion of a nearly viable late-term fetus of a wholly different moral character, because the personhood of the fetus is much harder to deny. There is also evidence that the traumatic effects of abortion at this stage upon the mother are much more severe than at earlier stages, possibly due to these same considerations.[10]

Proposed Justifications For Abortion of the Genetically Diseased

Even though many will agree that postamniocentesis abortion of a fetus requires high order moral justifications, if justified at all, there is wide disagreement about what the justifying conditions are. Genetic counselors and ethicists continue to wrestle with questions about what kinds of genetic defects, and what degree of severity of genetic illness, can justify abortion. For example, is the relatively mild defect of Down's syndrome (Mongolism) sufficient? If it is ethically questionable to withhold life-saving treatment from such a baby after its birth, a practice which has stirred widespread public controversy, is it less questionable to abort a late-term Down's syndrome fetus? What about the diagnosis of XYY syndrome (the so-called "supermale")? What about the increasingly prevalent cases of parents using prenatal diagnosis for the purpose of selecting the sex of their baby by aborting "normal" fetuses of the wrong sex? Is it justifiable to abort fetuses who are "carriers" of genetic defects but will not themselves have the disease?

The kinds of answers given to these questions, as to many questions of medical ethics, depends to a high degree upon the view one has about *whose interests* should be given priority in the decision whether or not to abort. That is, whose good should be served and whose can be subjugated to it? An analysis of the debate among ethicists over the question of genetic abortion would suggest that the basic disagreement boils down to the priority given to three different sets of interests: the genetically affected individual, the parents and family, or the society.

Abortion For the Benefit of The Fetus

A common argument in support of aborting genetically diseased fetuses is that it is better for the fetus never to be born than to endure the suffering and pain of a genetic defect as a child or adult. This argument is most compelling in cases of severe genetic disease like Tay-Sachs and spina bifida, which usually result in an early childhood death after a period of severe suffering. Under such conditions many people would prefer death to life and, thus, would choose the same for the fetus, which cannot choose for itself.

This argument carries most weight with those who believe that our primary ethical responsibility is to respect the dignity and worth of individual persons and not to use them for the benefit of others. The case for abortion here is not made on the grounds that others will be better off (e.g. the family or future generations) but in the name of the fetus (or the future child), for whom we are choosing "the course it would choose for itself." There is no appeal here to "improving the human gene pool," or to lowering the incidence of genetic disease in society, but only to the best interest of the fetus. The obverse of this argument is also important—if the fetus itself would be "better off" living with the genetic defect, it would be morally wrong to abort it merely because the family or society would prefer not to carry the burden of another defective person. This argument, it should be noted, is compatible with belief in the full personhood of the fetus, and maintains that abortion may be the best means of respecting that personhood.

The "good of the fetus" argument for genetic abortion is also highly persuasive in the medical community because it comports well with the medical professionals' primary commitment to the prevention and cure of disease in the patient, to whom the physician is primarily loyal. Abortion of the genetically defective fetus is thought of as "therapy" for the sick patient himself/herself. However, many critics of this argument have pointed out that this is a misuse of the term "therapy," which normally means the prevention or cure of a *disease* in an existing individual, for the betterment of that individual's existence. Abortion, which is the termination of an individual's existence rather than of his illness, is not "therapeutic" for that individual, whatever else it may be, say these critics.[11]

Other critics of this position point to the highly paternalistic character of the argument, with its assumption that parents, counselors, or physicians know what kind of life is "worth living" for another. How can anyone know whether a Tay-Sachs child would prefer not having been born to having the few years of life he or she may experience? Says one critic, "Whenever a strong group argues on behalf of a weaker group that their removal would be better than their survival, we should not be duly impressed."[12]

Abortion for Parental and Familial Good

A second group of ethicists emphasize the interests of the family, especially the parents, of a potentially genetically defective child. This view focuses upon such considerations as the "right" of parents to make their own procreative decisions or the psychological and financial burdens that the birth and rearing of a diseased or deformed child often imposes upon family members. The author of one influential study of genetic counseling practices, John Fletcher, argues that the postamniocentesis abortion decision is usually based on the reasoning that "it is more just and causes least suffering to the parents to proceed to other options in child-bearing without the burden of one or more than one defective child."[12] Fletcher thinks this is as it should be although he does not agree that just any genetic anomaly is sufficient to meet the test of family burden. Additional factors to be considered should include the severity of the disease, the availability of treatments for the disease, and the family situation itself (e.g., other children or other obligations that might be adversely affected).[12]

This position is attractive to genetic counselors because of its emphasis upon the interests and autonomy of the party whom they perceive generally as their primary client—the parents. It is also consistent with the view held by many ethicists that the primary ethical responsibility, at least in the area of genetics and medicine, is to minimize the suffering and pain of those who are most directly and immediately affected by one's actions. In saying that those most directly affected are the parents and family, the center of moral concern is shifted away from the fetus.

Ethicists who place the interests of parents and family upper-most in the genetic abortion decision often are most concerned to reject justifications based purely on general social interests. Central to the parental/familial interest view is the conviction that if the parents and family want to have a child despite its affliction with genetic disease, it is their moral right to do so. Considerations of social costs for the care of a defective child, public health concerns for the reduction of genetic disease, or eugenic concerns for the preservation or improvement of the human gene pool ought not to be significant factors in reproductive decision making—at least they ought not take precedence over parental/familial considerations.

Of course, the parental/familial interest argument concerning genetic abortion is open to criticism from both the "fetal interest" side and the utilitarian or "social interest" side of the debate. The former finds the depreciation of the moral status of the fetus ethically indefensible. To them it appears that the fetus is being treated purely as a means to the happiness and well-being of others. There is nothing inherent in the "parental/familial inter-est" position to exclude abortions for such ethically frivolous reasons as sex preference, to say nothing of other "mild" genetic abnormalities such as mild retardation or cleft palate. John Fletcher's qualifications on genetic abortion, noted earlier, reflect a concession to this argument and a concern for the moral worth of the fetus.

Abortion for the Social Good (Utilitarian Argument)

The third type of argument in the debate over prenatal diagnosis and abortion gives priority to the sum total of social goods and interests that are affected by the abortion or birth of a genetically "abnormal" child. In this view, both of the first two positions focus their moral concern too narrowly—the first on the fetus or future child and the second on the family—to the exclusion of the interests of the rest of society and of future generations. Joseph Fletcher, a strong proponent of utilitarian ethics, objects vociferously to the "reproductive roulette" of letting nature decide randomly which children will be born and which genes will be passed on. If we are overly scrupulous about the rights of defective fetuses or the rights of parents to reproduce their deleterious genes this is just what we are doing, according to Fletcher, at the expense of future generations of genetically diseased children and of others in society who will have to pay for their care.[13]

The utilitarian argument takes a variety of forms, depending upon which social "good" is highlighted. Some emphasize the financial cost-benefit ratio of prenatal screening and abortion against the costs and benefits of bearing and caring for defective children. Others emphasize other, nonfinancial benefits that society stands to gain from an improved gene pool, i.e. higher average intelligence, greater creativity, and less social dependency of those who are "selected for." The common theme in these different emphases is that since genetic technology gives us control over the genetic fitness of our children, it would be foolish and morally irresponsible to waste precious social resources on caring for the "unfit," the unproductive, or those who will cost society more than they benefit it. As Joseph Fletcher puts the point, "It is cruel and insane to deprive normal but disadvantaged children of the care we could give them with the $1,500,000,000 we spend in public costs for preventable retardates."[13]

Many ethicists find this utilitarian argument for genetic abortion a morally dangerous one. Too often, they argue, the social costs and benefits that go into the decision are reduced to purely financial ones. Can human lives be valued in such terms, or even in terms of any kind of "value to society"? Who is to say that the contribution of the average inmate of a home for the retarded is less, or the drain on society's resources greater, than that of the average Harvard graduate, asks one critic.[14] The fear reflected in these questions is that our concept of individual personal worth is seriously eroded by the "social good" calculus of determining who shall be born and who shall not.

The Case Against Prenatal Diagnosis

Another group of geneticists and ethicists believe that none of the above arguments successfully justify prenatal diagnosis and abortion of the genetically defective. These critics question why anyone should condone abortion of even the seriously diseased fetus when they would not consider infanticide in the same circumstances. This point, of course, assumes that there is no morally significant difference between a late-term fetus and the newborn baby.

Paul Ramsey, a protestant theologian, has been one of the most influential opponents of intrauterine screening. While he favors preconception screening of parents for genetic defects so that they can exercise "responsible parenthood," he opposes postconception screening of the fetus for several reasons. First, the procedure itself imposes some risks of harm to the fetus, to which it cannot give its express or implied consent. Second, Ramsey argues that there is always the danger of the diagnostic test producing "false positives" of genetic defect, which could lead to damaging treatments or "therapeutic abortion" of a normal fetus.

This is just one instance of the "statistical morality" involved in prenatal screening to which Ramsey objects. In the case of many diseases, such as X-linked diseases like hemophilia, amniocentesis can establish only a statistical probability of the fetus being affected, say 25 or 50 percent. The parents are then faced with a decision whether to take the risk of having a child affected with the disease or the risk of aborting a normal, unaffected fetus. Ramsey believes there can be no moral justification for knowingly aborting one or more normal fetuses in order to avoid the evil of genetic disease in another. Since there is always some risk, however minimal, of amniocentesis leading to the abortion of healthy fetuses, he rejects the procedure altogether.

Third, Ramsey worries about the import of widespread prenatal screening upon society's concept of "normality." "Intra-uterine screening seems destined to degrade society's willingness to accept and care for abnormal children, and at the same time, to enlarge the category of unacceptable abnormality, while narrowing the range of acceptable normality."[15]

GENETIC INFORMATION: THE RIGHT TO PRIVACY AND THE RIGHT TO KNOW

> The social worker should respect the privacy of clients and hold in confidence all information obtained in the course of professional service.[20]

The principle of confidentiality and the right to privacy has become well-established in professional codes, including that of the National Association of Social Workers. While the general principle is widely embraced, the extent and conditions of its application to specific situations are not agreed upon. The NASW Code itself appends to the above statement the qualifier that "The social worker should share with others confidences revealed by clients, without their consent, *only for compelling professional reasons*" (emphasis added).[16] The crucial question for the genetic counselor, of course, is what sorts of reasons are both "professional" and "compelling."

The issue of confidentiality has a special significance in genetic counseling. The oft-cited claim that with the cracking of the DNA code scientists had "unlocked the secret of human life" and, indeed, of human nature is not mere hyperbole. There is something about the structure of each individual's genetic makeup that is very basic to the kind of person he or she is. While the debate rages on about the extent to which individual personality and behavior is a function of genetic endowment rather than the environment, the fact remains that to a very significant extent a person is that set of predispositions, potentials, and limitations that inheres in one's genes. How much of our life is governed by them is not as important as the fact that, whatever portion it is, it is a crucial part of our personal identity. To know one's genetic endowment is to know something about his or her innermost being. Hence, if persons have any right to protect the privacy of their lives at all, it must surely include the privacy of their genes. For this reason many people would argue that the discovery without consent of genetic facts about a person, especially facts about genetic defects, is an invasion of that person's privacy, *regardless of the uses to which that knowledge is put.*

Even if knowledge of genetic endowment or defects is not intrinsically invasive of privacy, as the above argument claims, there remains a concern about the potential for misuse of genetic information in ways harmful to the subject. The practice of genetic screening of children has raised a variety of such concerns.

One of the most controversial cases has been the diagnosis of the XYY syndrome, sometimes called the "supermale syndrome" because of the presence of an extra Y, or male, chromosome. Some early studies of this abnormality indicated that it might be associated with abnormally violent or aggressive behavior, since the incidence of the syndrome among inmates of penal and mental institutions was somewhat higher than among the general population. An attempt in Boston in the early 1970s to undertake a careful study of behavior development in children with the XYY genotype was scuttled by a public concern about the uses that could be made of the information about the children. The study involved regular follow-up reports on children found to have XYY, including interviews with parents and teachers. Critics feared that if parents and others knew that the children were XYY, they might tend to overreact to normal aggressive behavior, possibly even reinforcing it and, hence, creating the "self-fulfilling prophecy" effect. Some worried about the possibility of the information falling into the hands of police and other public agencies where it could be used to discriminate against the persons in various ways. For example, they might become prime suspects in every crime of violence in the community. Proponents of the research project, on the other hand, argued that there was no other way to discover whether the XYY syndrome actually did affect personality or behavior, or to develop therapies if they were needed.[17]

Case Example A at the end of this chapter raises the question whether a genetic counselor should inform the mother who has undergone amniocentesis for Down's syndrome that her fetus is XYY. Some ethicists would argue that the baby in this case has a right to privacy that would be violated if the mother were told of this particular genetic anomaly. Since the information is likely to be used only in ways detrimental to the child, e.g. abortion, and cannot at present be used for his benefit, it ought to be withheld. Others would maintain that the mother has a right to this information, regardless of the uses she may make of it. Often, in cases like this one, the counselor has to decide whether or not the information is of such a nature as to be significant. A plausible argument in this case might be that since the significance of the XYY genotype is unknown, or at least uncertain, there is no reason to reveal it to the mother.

Often the genetic counselor is faced with a dilemma created by the fact that the "right to privacy" of one party comes into conflict with the "right to know" of another party. Typically the dilemma arises when genetic screening of parents or their child reveals an inherited genetic defect that is therefore likely to be present in the siblings of one parent, making them at risk for having genetically diseased children. A parent who discovers that he or she is affected with, or carries, the gene for a serious genetic disease will often, out of shame or embarrassment, refuse to give the counselor or physician consent to inform relatives of their risks. The counselor is caught between respecting the client's right to privacy of this genetic information on the one hand, and the right of relatives to be informed of the risk they face of having or carrying a genetic disease on the other. Case Example B is an illustration of this dilemma. Although the usual practice of genetic counselors in this dilemma is to respect the privacy of the client and hope that relatives at risk discover the problem some other way, there is some concern that this is socially irresponsible. Why, many would ask, do we recognize the right of society to expose information about communicable diseases, e.g. venereal diseases, and take steps to control it through quarantine or other measures, but do not recognize this right or responsibility in the case of genetic disease? Opponents of this view appeal to the idea suggested earlier, that there is something uniquely private about genetic defects that strengthens the case for respecting the confidence of the genetically abnormal person.

Another common dilemma faced by genetic counselors involves the revelation via genetic screening of a child that the husband of the child's mother is not the father. In this case the mother is not interested primarily in protecting the privacy of her genetic endowment nor even that of her child, but rather the privacy of her own personal behavior, which the genetic code of her child discloses. If this information is kept from the father he may conclude that he carries the genetic defect suffered by the child when in fact he does not. He cannot then participate intelligently in the reproductive decisions concerning this child and future possible children. Indeed, he may decide to take steps, possibly irreversible, to prevent future offspring, on the false assumption that he carries the genetic defect. The genetic counselor also has to take into account the harm that might be done to the marriage if the fact of nonpaternity is disclosed to the husband, and, on the other side, the counselor's obligation to be truthful. Often the ethical decision comes down to a matter of the moral weight one gives to each of these values. It may also come down to a decision about who is the primary client of the counselor in the prenatal diagnosis situations. Is it only the mother, or both husband and wife together, the fetus, who suffers the disease, who is the subject of the counselor's primary loyalty?

Problems in the use of genetic information in most instances come down to a question of what the primary goal of the genetic counselor is or should be. In Case Example B, for example, the counselor must decide if his or her primary goal is the facilitation of client autonomy (the right to control use of their genetic information as they choose) or the protection of others in society from genetic disease (the children of Mrs. Edison's sisters). The NASW Code of Ethics affirms the social worker's responsibility to promote the general welfare (Article VI) as well as the autonomy of the client (Article II), but which responsibility should take precedence when the two conflict?

Most genetic counselors place greater moral weight on the duty to respect client autonomy, a value respected by social workers. Some believe that it should prevail in all circumstances, regardless of the consequences of withholding information from others or giving information (such as the XYY information in Case Example A) to the client.

One influential writer on this subject, George Annas, argues for *complete* and *accurate* disclosure of all information to clients in genetic counseling, no matter how insignificant it may seem to the counselor, what effect it may have, or what use they might make of the information (e.g. abortion merely for sex selection). He argues also for *complete* privacy and confidentiality of genetic information, regardless of the consequences this may have for others. Annas bases his view upon a definition of genetic counseling as a service to families with genetic problems who need accurate information to maximize their reproductive autonomy.[18] As we shall see in the next section, others think this definition of genetic counseling and its goals are too narrow.

THE GOALS OF GENETIC COUNSELING

The preceding discussion illustrates the truth that genetic counseling is not a "value free" enterprise. Not only is the counselor involved in moral choices of his or her own as well as those of clients, but the entire function of genetic counseling and the genetic control that it makes possible have far-reaching social consequences with serious ethical implications. It is evident that the way a genetic counselor responds to an ethical issue or dilemma will be significantly influenced by his or her view of the social function of genetic counseling and the aims of genetic control. This action explores some of the broader social questions raised by the whole process of genetic intervention and the manner in which they influence the role of the genetic counselor.

Goal Orientations of Genetic Counselors

The discussion of prenatal diagnosis and genetic abortion pointed out three different ethical approaches to the questions involved. These are reflective of three basic goal orientations that characterize most genetic counselors: the first emphasizes the interests and needs of the individual suffering from a genetic disease; the second emphasizes the interests of parents, especially their interest in reproductive autonomy; and the third emphasizes general social benefits.

These three goal orientations can also be seen to be at work in the differences of opinion over the uses of genetic information that have been considered. For those who adopt the first or second of these orientations, the right to privacy of the child or the parents, as the case may be, takes precedence over the interests others may have in protecting themselves and their children from genetic defects. For those who adopt the third orientation the opposite conclusion appears more plausible. George Annas' defense of absolute confidentiality and full disclosure of genetic information to parents is based, as he himself asserts, on the second orientation.

Marc Lappé has argued that the goal orientation of genetic counselors is significantly influenced by their particular professional training.[19] Counselors who come from a background in the biological sciences tend to be oriented toward social goals, such as protecting the gene pool from deterioration, maintaining genetic diversity, ensuring biological adaptivity, etc. Counselors with backgrounds and training in social work and counseling are oriented strongly toward client, i.e. parent-family, autonomy. Counselors from clinical medical backgrounds are likely to be less concerned with client autonomy and more concerned either with therapy for the affected "patient" or the prevention of genetic disease.

Whose Values Control?

Given the variety of goal orientations that characterize genetic counselors as well as clients in genetic counseling, the question arises as to whose values ought to control the counseling process. To what extent, if any, is it legitimate for the genetic counselor to impose his or her goals upon the client? To what extent is society justified in putting coercive or other pressures upon parents to control the genetic shape of their progeny? To what extent should counselors allow themselves to serve as agents of society's interest in minimizing the cost of genetic defects or in "improving" the gene pool. Genetic intervention is a form of great power—it is the power to shape and reshape human nature itself. Hence, it is important for society to decide who ought to control this power, and to what ends.

The eugenic policies of Nazi Germany serve as a graphic

reminder of how genetic controls can be turned to monstrous political ends. The "Brave New World" scenarios in science fiction present serious questions about what kind of society we are capable of becoming and desire to become. If people are permitted to use amniocentesis, abortion, and other technologies for the purpose of selecting the sex of their children, will this result in a disproportionate number of males or females? What checks should be used to prevent sexist attitudes from producing such a result? Should parents be prohibited by law from overselecting one sex? Should counselors attempt to dissuade their clients from doing so?

Many ethicists are worried about the social implications of genetic screening programs that are being urged in many states as a control on genetic disease. For example, in the early 1970s many regions in the U.S. instituted massive programs to screen prospective parents for sickle-cell anemia, a fatal disease occurring almost exclusively among blacks. Persons who were found to be "carriers" of the sickle-cell trait could be alerted either to avoid marriage with other "carriers" of the recessive gene or to seek genetic counseling before bearing children. While these screening programs for sickle-cell trait at first received the support of the black community in the U.S., serious questions began to be raised in this community about the genocidal implications of a program that screened only blacks and urged only black couples to prevent conception and birth of children. Similar questions have been raised about screening programs for Tay-Sachs disease, a fatal nervous system disorder of infants that occurs mainly among Jews of Eastern European descent.

The most troublesome aspect of genetic screening programs is the political pressure from some sectors of the community, including in many instances the medical community, to make them mandatory for the racial groups affected, as they have become in several states. Many critics are concerned that compulsory genetic screening is only one short step from compulsory sterilization for carriers of these genetic defects, or mandatory amniocentesis and abortion of affected fetuses.

Even if sterilization or abortion are not legally required in cases of genetic disease, the question remains about the extra-legal pressures that are brought to bear upon couples by programs of compulsory screening. Who decides which genetic defects should be chosen for compulsory screening? If screening is compulsory, what is the role of the genetic counselor in helping a couple assimilate the information that they are at risk for a diseased child? Surely a counselor would have a difficult time convincing the couple that whether or not they go ahead with the conception or birth of a diseased child is entirely a matter of their own preferences. Why, they might legitimately ask, is the screening for the disease mandatory if there is no recommended course of action? On the other hand, if the counselor recommends that the couple refrain from conceiving a child or bringing a fetus to term, this pressure, in conjunction with the pressure of the mandatory screening itself, would be difficult for most couples to withstand. Their reproductive decision would hardly be "free" in the fullest sense of that term.

Most genetic counselors find themselves on the horns of a dilemma created by their allegiance as *counselors* to the autonomy of the client and their conflicting allegiance as *medical geneticists* to reducing the number of children who suffer from severe genetic disease. If the counselor maintains complete neutrality in the decision making, he or she might be contributing to an increase in the number of children born with genetic defects, but if the counselor takes an active, directive role in the client's decision making this may infringe upon the autonomy of parents to make their own reproductive decisions.

This dual allegiance expresses itself in the genetic counseling literature. For example, Margery Shaw cites a report of the World Health Organization Expert Committee on Human Genetics, which states that "the counselor should not pursue any genetic program designed to benefit future generations . . . [but] should be as neutral as possible. . . . " Later, the same report states that "Follow-up investigators . . . are to be encouraged . . . to determine how far the advice has been followed, and in what manner." As Shaw remarks, how can we be admonished not to give advice and then be asked to determine if our advice has been followed?[20]

F. Clarke Fraser, an eminent Montreal genetic counselor, suggests that counselors can never be entirely nondirective in their counseling, but neither ought they coerce clients to do what the counselor prefers:

> I disagree with those who say that counseling includes only giving an
> estimate of . . . the recurrence risk, and that is where it stops. I also avoid
> telling anyone explicitly that they should or should not have further
> children. . . . If they push me about what I think they should do . . . I say
> that I cannot really put myself in their situation because I am not them. If
> I try to, as best I can, then I tell them I think I would not have a baby, or
> have one, as the case may be.[21]

Margery Shaw argues that the best situation is one in which
different counselors adopt their own strategies of counseling—
some being highly directive and others trying to be nondirective.
Shaw bases this view on the assumption that greater pluralism of
values will be beneficial both socially and genetically in the long
run. The worst situation in Shaw's view would be one in which
there was total uniformity of viewpoint on the goals of genetic
intervention.[22]

Eugenics and the Future of Humanity

Eugenics is defined as the study and control of various possible
influences as a means of improving the hereditary characteristics
of a race.[23] This "improvement" can be understood as the re-
designing of man to adapt his biology to his social and political
goals, as in Huxley's *Brave New World,* or more modestly as the
prevention or reduction of debilitating genetic diseases. Some
writers speak of "negative eugenics" by which they refer not to the
improving of human heredity from its present state ("positive
eugenics") but to the preventing of its further deterioration, or the
spread of genetic defects through the gene pool.

As is evident throughout this discussion, there is disagreement
among geneticists, counselors, and ethicists about which eugenic
ideals, if any, are legitimate aims of genetic intervention. Some
argue that the counselor's only concern should be for the immediate effects of genetic disease upon the client family or the individual who stands to suffer from the disease. Others argue forcefully
for the realization of the social benefits that would accrue from
eugenic goals. Says one such counselor, Robert Morison, "There is
a limited number of slots that human beings can occupy, and there
do seem to be both social and family reasons to see that those

increasingly rare slots are occupied by people with the greatest potential for themselves and for others."[24] Morison's statement can be interpreted as supporting "positive" eugenic goals in the fullest sense—that of maximizing human genetic potential.

Many geneticists are critical of even the more modest eugenic goal of eliminating or lowering the incidence of genetic defects. Attempts to do so may turn out to have just the opposite effect—the spread of genetic disease—or the moral cost of achieving the goal may be far too great. For example, with recessive diseases (i.e. where both parents must be carriers of the defective gene), the selective abortion of *all* fetuses with the disease (having received the defect from both parents) would not change the frequency of the defective gene in the population at all, because most affected individuals do not reproduce anyway. In fact, many parents will try a second time for a normal child, having aborted the first one and knowing that they can abort again if prenatal diagnosis is positive. Since subsequent children are likely to be carriers of the disease, the abortion of an affected fetus is likely to result in the birth of more carriers, hence *raising* the frequency of the defective gene in the population.

This consequence can be avoided only if *all unaffected carriers* of recessive genetic diseases are aborted along with affected fetuses or are prevented from reproducing. Such goals would require massive, universal screening programs, along with compulsory abortions or sterilizations that would be hard to implement, let alone justify on ethical grounds. These measures are all the more sobering in view of the fact that virtually all of us carry several deleterious or even lethal recessive genes.

Some geneticists, like Marc Lappé, have questioned whether screening programs ought even to adopt the "negative eugenic" goal of preventing the further spread of deleterious genes. Lappé thinks we do not know for sure whether the human gene pool is worsening or whether the genetic "load" has stabilized, neither do we know much about how socioeconomic factors influence the coincidence of genetic deformities. It could be, he argues, that a far greater reduction in defective births could be achieved by the reduction of chemical pollutants in the environment than by a massive program of genetic screening.[25] Lappé himself sees the counselor's primary responsibility as helping to reduce the suffering of the individuals to whom one is most directly responsible—those who are or stand to be affected by genetic disease.[26]

New genetic technologies are continuing to emerge that will only intensify the ethical problems we have cited. *In vitrio* fertilizations (test-tube babies) have opened up the possibilities for much greater control of the genetic shape of children. Sperm banks and egg banks now make it possible for prospective "parents" to pick not only the sex of their children but many other characteristics as well, from eye color to native intelligence levels. As the area of genetic control expands, the need to decide where we should set the limits becomes even more critical.

Daniel Callahan, an ethicist at the Hastings Institute of Society, Ethics, and the Life Sciences, has written that our increasing ability to prevent genetic disease imposes responsibilities that we might not be able to bear without great moral cost. When genetic disease is preventable (via abortion or birth control) how do we view those who act "irresponsibly" by having diseased children? The blame society may heap upon them may make a mockery of our claims that genetic counseling enhances freedom of reproductive choice. Further, Callahan worries about how we will view ourselves and our children, especially those who are not up to the standards of our image of the perfect genetic specimen. Will our cost-benefit analyses lead us to "put a price on everyone's head" according to how much they contribute to, or drain, our precious resources? What will happen to our appreciation of human diversity and our commitment to equal rights when we become dominated by an image of the perfect human being who is the pattern for our genetic interventions? Callahan suggests that we need to work at conquering genetic disease, but at the same time we must learn to live with it, to accept fully those among us who have genetic disease, and work to soften the individual suffering brought on by it. Callahan concludes,

> Our communal task, I believe, is to find a way of combining both logics. That will not be easy, if only because most people find it easier to cope with one idea than with two at the same time. It will mean, for instance, simultaneously working to improve the societal treatment and respect accorded those born with defects, and working to extend our genetic

knowledge and applying it to genetic counseling. It will mean taking the idea of free choice seriously, allowing parents to make their own choice.... Part of the very meaning of human community, I would contend, entails a willingness of society to bear the social costs of individual freedom.[27]

CASE EXAMPLES

CASE A: Mrs. Brock, a thirty-five-year-old mother of two normal children, became unexpectedly pregnant. She came into the Genetics Unit of the hospital to request amniocentesis for the purpose of satisfying herself that her baby would not have Downs syndrome (Mongolism). Because the physician agreed that the risks of this chromosome anomaly were significantly high in pregnancies at Mrs. Brock's age, she was scheduled for the intrauterine tap.

Several weeks later Mrs. Brock was called back to the Genetics Unit to be told the results. Mrs. MacDonald, the genetic counselor who met Mrs. Brock, was in a quandary about what to tell her. The test results from the lab showed that Mrs. Brock's baby boy was free of Downs syndrome. However, the tap revealed that the baby had an extra Y chromosome, or the XYY syndrome. Mrs. MacDonald knew that this anomaly was thought by some researchers to be associated with extraordinarily aggressive behavior, although this had never been established. No other deleterious effects of the XYY syndrome were known.

Mrs. MacDonald was unsure whether to mention the XYY finding to Mrs. Brock. She feared that Mrs. Brock might decide to abort her fetus, which MacDonald did not think was warranted. She also worried about the possible effects on the child later if his parents knew this genetic information. On the other hand, Mrs. MacDonald believed strongly in the principle of parental autonomy. She gave Mrs. Brock the good news that her baby did not have Down's syndrome and sent her on her way.

CASE B: Mr. and Mrs. Edison brought their three-month-old son, Jamie, into the hemophilia clinic with severe bleeding. A diagnosis of hemophilia A was established immediately. Hemophilia A is an X-linked disease, which means that it is carried on the female X chromosome but manifests itself only in males. Hence it is usually passed through the mother to her children, 50 percent of whom will be either carriers (daughters) or affected with the disease (sons).

Mr. and Mrs. Edison were shocked at the news and rejected the doctor's explanation of the inherited nature of the disease. The genetic counselor, Mr. Gerard, requested the Edisons' consent to permit him to contact relatives, especially Mrs. Edison's two sisters, each of whose sons had a significant risk (25 percent) of having hemophilia A. The couple refused consent, even when it was explained that the information might help these relatives ensure the birth of nonhemophilic children in future pregnancies.

Mr. Gerard was upset. He could not believe that the Edisons were so ashamed of their "sickness" that they were willing to allow their relatives to unknowingly risk the birth of other children with hemophilia A. Mr. Gerard believed he had some obligation as a medical social worker to these relatives and their future children.

He also knew that the NASW *Code of Ethics* permitted breaches of confidentiality only for "compelling professional reasons." He wondered if this was such a case.

REFERENCES

1. Galton, Francis: *Hereditary Genetics.* London, Macmillan, 1869.
2. Grant, Madison: *The Passing of the Great Race.* New York, Charles Scribner's, 1916. [Quoted in Reilly, Philip: *Genetics, Law, and Social Policy.* Cambridge, Harvard U Press, 1977.]
3. Buck v. Bell, 274 U.S. 200 (1927).
4. Reilly, Philip: *Genetics, Law, and Social Policy.* Cambridge, Harvard U Press, 1977.
5. Sorenson, James R.: From social movement to clinical medicine—the role of law and the medical profession in regulating applied human genetics. In Milunsky, A. and Annas, G. J.: *Genetics and the Law.* New York, Plenum Press, 1976.
6. McKusick, Victor A.: *Mendelian Inheritance in Man,* 4th ed. Baltimore, Johns Hopkins U Press, 1975.
7. Lubs, Herbert A.: Frequency of genetic disease. In Lubs, H. A. and de la Cruz, F.: *Genetic Counseling.* New York, Raven Press, 1977.
8. Weiss, Joan: Social work and genetic counseling. *Social Work in Health Care,* 2:6, Fall 1976.
9. Milunsky, Aubrey: Prenatal genetic diagnosis: Risks and needs. In Lubs, H. A. and de la Cruz, F.: *Genetic Counseling.* New York, Raven Press, 1977.
10. Powledge, Tabitha M.: From experimental procedure to accepted practice. *Hastings Center Report,* 6:6–7, Feb. 1976.
11. Ramsey, Paul: *Fabricated Man.* New Haven, Yale U Press, 1970.
12. Fletcher, John: Parents in genetic counseling: The moral shape of decision-making. In Hilton, Bruce and Callahan, D. (Eds.): *Ethical Issues in Human Genetics.* New York, Plenum Press, 1973.
13. Fletcher, Joseph: *The Ethics of Genetic Control.* Garden City, Doubleday, 1974.
14. Kass, Leon: Implications of prenatal diagnosis for the human right to life. In Hilton, Bruce and Callahan, D. (Eds.): *Ethical Issues in Human Genetics.* New York, Plenum Press, 1973.
15. Ramsey, Paul: Screening: An ethicist's view. In Hilton, Bruce and Callahan, D. (Eds.): *Ethical Issues in Human Genetics.* New York, Plenum Press, 1973.
16. NASW: *Code of Ethics.* Washington, D.C., National Association of Social Workers, 1979.
17. Roblin, Richard: The Boston XYY case. *Hastings Center Report,* 5:5–8, August 1975.
18. Annas, George J.: Problems of informed consent and confidentiality in genetic counseling. In Milunsky, A. and Annas, G.: *Genetics and the Law.* New York, Plenum Press, 1976.

19. Lappé, Marc: Allegiances of human geneticists: A preliminary typology. *Hastings Center Studies, 1(2)*:63–78, 1973.

20. Shaw, Margery W.: Review of published studies of genetic counseling: A critique. In Lubs, H. A. and de la Cruz, F.: *Genetic Counseling.* New York, Raven Press, 1977.

21. Fraser, F. Clarke: Survey of counseling practices. In Hilton, Bruce and Callahan, D. (Eds.): *Ethical Issues in Human Genetics.* New York, Plenum Press, 1973.

22. Shaw, Margery: Genetic counseling. *Science, 184*:751, May 1974.

23. In Hilton, Bruce and Callahan, D. (Eds.): *Ethical Issues in Human Genetics.* New York, Plenum Press, 1973.

24. Morison, Robert S.: Implications of prenatal diagnosis for the quality of, and right to, human life: Society as a standard. In Hilton, Bruce and Callahan, D. (Eds.): *Ethical Issues in Human Genetics.* New York, Plenum Press, 1973.

25. Lappé, Marc: Can eugenic policy be just? In Milunsky, A. (Ed.): *The Prevention of Genetic Disease, and Mental Retardation.* Philadelphia, W. B. Saunders, 1975.

26. Lappé, Marc: The genetic counselor: Responsible to whom? *Hastings Center Report, 1(2)*:6–8, Sept. 1971.

27. Callahan, Daniel: The meaning and significance of genetic disease: Philisophical perspectives. In Hilton, Bruce and Callahan, D. (Eds.): *Ethical Issues in Human Genetics.* New York, Plenum Press, 1973.

Chapter 13

INVOLUNTARY COMMITMENT OF
THE MENTALLY ILL

CONRAD BRUNK

Several years ago Mrs. Catharine Lake petitioned a court for release from a mental hospital, to which she had been committed after she was found wandering aimlessly about the streets of a large city. She was found to suffer from chronic brain syndrome with arteriosclerosis, which produced periods of confusion and memory loss interspersed with periods of mental alertness and apparent rationality. The psychiatrists were concerned about the risks of harm coming to her if she were allowed to remain unsupervised, although she posed no danger to others and showed no tendency to harm herself intentionally.

At her court hearing Mrs. Lake appeared fully rational and competent. She seemed to understand fully the risks she would be taking if released to live her own life in her own way, but stated that she preferred the risks to the continuing enforced stay at the mental hospital. A psychiatrist testified, however, that she was unable to remember when her husband and other close relatives had died and that she had paranoid tendencies, believing that the government had taken away her pension. Her family claimed that they lacked the means to give her the necessary supervision, and that she was a danger to herself in that she wandered about the streets and was incompetent to care for herself. The court upheld her commitment, which had been based on a statute providing for commitment of a person who "is mentally ill, and because of that illness, is likely to injure himself or others if allowed to remain at liberty."[1,2]

This case of involuntary commitment is not atypical. Yet, it raises a series of questions that lie at the heart of the justification

286

of this practice. Had Mrs. Lake been committed to a mental hospital for her own well-being, as the psychiatrist testified, or for the well-being or convenience of her family? Was she, perhaps, a "nuisance" in the community that neighbors and police preferred not to deal with? Was she incompetent to decide how she could best live her life as the psychiatrist alleged? Was Mrs. Lake really a "danger to herself" in a manner that justifies the deprivation of her liberty? Was she really better off in the mental hospital than she would have been had she been left alone? Were there other community resources that could serve Mrs. Lake better than commitment to a mental hospital? A Court of Appeals to which Mrs. Lake appealed her case asked some of these questions as well, and directed the lower court to reconsider its decision to hospitalize her. The judge ordered that "every effort should be made to find a course of treatment which [Mrs. Lake] might be willing to accept."[1]

The appellate judge's ruling in this case represents a growing concern in our society about the practice of involuntary hospitalization on grounds of mental illness—a concern for its necessity as well as its ethical justifiability. More people are deprived of their liberty in the United States and Canada each year through involuntary mental hospitalization than are sentenced to prison following a criminal conviction.[3] It is probably the most significant deprivation of personal liberty practiced by our society today, certainly the most significant outside of the criminal justice system. Society has for the most part been willing to grant an unparalleled power to mental health professionals to effect this deprivation of liberty. Even where society has attempted to place limits upon this discretionary power with legal requirements of judicial or lay review of psychiatric recommendations for civil commitment, the courts and review committees tend to rely heavily upon the "expert opinion" of the professionals.

Hence, the practice of civil commitment raises fundamental questions of social ethics and political philosophy. What are the conditions under which society can legitimately deprive persons, who may have committed no crimes, of their most basic rights to free movement, association, and bodily integrity? What are the procedures and safeguards that are minimally required to protect all of us from the arbitrary and capricious deprivation of our rights and liberties? How far does the right to be socially deviant extend? Is there a clear distinction between merely being deviant and being mentally sick? Why should the former be permitted to choose his or her own course of life while the latter is not?

These questions involve other even more basic philosophical issues concerning the nature of human freedom and the concepts of health and disease. Are the mentally ill, unlike the physically ill, unable to make autonomous choices concerning their treatment or care? Why should this be assumed? Is mental illness an "illness" at all, or is it merely a medical label for socially deviant behavior? The recent debates about the practice of involuntary commitment have revolved in large part around these questions.

Social workers, especially psychiatric social workers, find themselves integrally involved in the processes of decision making that often culminate in involuntary hospitalization of emotionally disturbed or deviant individuals, as well as in the release-detention decision following such hospitalization. The social worker's reports on the background of the individual, his relationship to family, community, and the laws, and sources of assistance available to him in the community carry a great deal of weight in the psychiatric diagnosis and prognosis upon which the commitment decision rests. Consequently, the social worker has ethical questions of his or her own to answer. Among the most important of these is the question of who, in the final analysis, is the social worker's primary client. Whose interests is it the social worker's responsibility to represent or protect—the interests of the "patient" who sees no need for treatment of any illness and vigorously protests the deprivation of his liberty or the interests of the exasperated spouse or family no longer able to cope with his annoying and bizarre behavior? The individual social worker's answer to this question will be influenced to a great extent by the viewpoint taken on the more general question of how the whole social practice of involuntary commitment to mental hospitals itself can be justified.

It is surprising that despite the central role social workers play in the civil commitment process, and despite the widespread debate about the practice among psychiatrists, lawyers, ethicists, and legislators in recent years, there has been very little discussion of the ethics of civil commitment in the social work literature. Two of the leading medical social work journals, one North American and the other British, have neither had one article on the subject. This may be due to a widespread assumption among medical social workers that civil commitment policy is largely settled in advance by those who write the civil commitment laws and establish the certification and review procedures, rather than a matter of moral choice by the individual social worker or even the psychiatrists. While this may be true, in part, it is still important for those who participate in institutional practices like that of involuntary commitment to reflect upon the ethical justifiability of the practice itself. Such reflection can also serve to clarify the proper role of the individual, in this case the psychiatric social worker, within the practice.

Insofar as the civil commitment of an individual generally involves the confinement of the person within the space of an often highly unpleasant institution in which nearly every aspect of his or her life is monitored and rigidly controlled, it is little less onerous than the typical form of criminal punishment in our society—imprisonment. Indeed, in some ways it can be even more burdensome than criminal imprisonment. The "sentence" to a mental hospital is indeterminate, often lasting a lifetime, a rarity in criminal sentences. In addition, the involuntarily committed mental patient can be subjected to a wide variety of highly intrusive "therapies" seldom, if ever, permitted in penal institutions. Among these are electroconvulsive shock therapy (ECT), aversive therapy, behavior modification, chemical control of behavior, and even psychosurgery. Like the released criminal, who carries the stigma of "ex-con" throughout his life, the mental patient fortunate enough to be released from the hospital carries the stigma of having once been committed to the "looney bin." In addition, he may well carry with him an even more stigmatizing set of psychiatric labels, ranging all the way from "neurotic" and "schizophrenic" to "psychopathic" and "insane."

The involuntary imposition of such onerous deprivations and burdens upon an individual requires justification of the very highest order. In the case of criminal punishment, the justification usually refers to society's right to protect the social order and the security of the individual by establishing a system of sanctions for criminal acts, designed to deter individuals from those acts. The deprivation of personal liberty, whether through incarceration or other sanctions, must be consequent upon a conviction for a criminal act. "No punishment where there has been no crime" is an axiomatic principle of most civilized legal systems. It excludes, among other things, the incarceration or other punishment of a person in order to *prevent* him from committing a criminal act not yet committed—so-called "preventive detention." Further, it extends to those persons accused of crime broad protection of due process designed to prevent conviction and punishment of the innocent. Among these protections are strict rules of evidence, the right to confront and cross-examine witnesses, the right to be tried by one's peers, the right to counsel, and the right to appeal.

Involuntary civil commitment of persons considered to be mentally ill, on the other hand, can be carried out with few, if any, of these protections present. Persons can be, and often are, committed when they are not accused of committing any crime and when they pose no danger to society. Few of the protections of due process present in a criminal proceeding are granted to the subject of a civil commitment, even under the recent, more restrictive, commitment laws of most states and provinces. Rarely does the subject have the opportunity to cross-examine the psychiatrists, social workers, or relatives who may be "witnesses" against him, or to present counter-evidence in his defense. In many areas there is no right to legal counsel, to trial by jury, or to the exclusion of "hearsay" evidence. To a very great extent one's fate as a potential involuntary mental patient hangs upon the discretion of one or two mental health professionals, whose primary criteria of judgment are "medical" rather than legal.

The process of civil commitment is not considered a form of criminal punishment, at least it is clearly distinguished from the processes of criminal punishment and from the criterion of criminal guilt. Since, at least ostensibly, the burden of civil commitment can be as great as, or greater than, those of criminal punishment, it requires ethical justifications of equal or greater force, though of a different kind. If the justifications of civil commitment are not those of criminal punishment, what are they? As might be expected, there is wide difference of opinion among mental health professionals, ethicists, and others about what these justifications are, if, indeed, there is any justification at all. In the following sections we shall examine the two views most commonly put forward for involuntary commitment of the mentally ill, as well as a third view which denies its justifiability altogether. ·

CIVIL COMMITMENT AS THERAPY

Prior to the nineteenth century, society responded to the "mad," the "lunatics," the "demon possessed" in what would seem to us today as highly punitive ways. They were often left to wander aimlessly from town to town or were ostracized completely from society by being placed on board "ships of fools" to be deposited at some distant port. After the sixteenth century they were generally locked up in asylums along with the poor, the homeless, the unemployed, and the criminal.

Today, it is generally considered to have been a great stride forward in civilization when the deviant, the mad, and the simple-minded came to be looked upon as "sick" rather than merely deviant or bad. To look upon persons as "sick" is to look upon them in a very special way. It is to look upon them from the perspective of what is often called the "medical model." Within this model the individual is seen as the victim, usually innocent, of an attack by an invader—the disease. Disease is seen as a dysfunction of some kind, which can be organic (e.g. viral infections, kidney failure), mental (e.g. schizophrenia, manic depression), or even social (e.g. criminality), depending upon how broadly one is willing to extend the concept of disease. Second, because the sick person is the *victim* of the disease (it was not chosen freely), it is not his responsibility. Therefore, it is not proper to condemn, blame, or punish the sick person for his disease, but rather to provide him with special attention and care to relieve his suffering and hopefully cure the disease. In the medical model, treatment of the disease can be carried out most effectively by one who is expert in the causes, control, and cure of the disease in question, the physician.

The application of this medical model to the insane, the simple-minded, and the nonconformist radically changed social attitudes toward their proper treatment. If these people were "mentally ill," they were the innocent victims of diseases of the mind, which could be cured. They should not be treated as criminals who had chosen their misdeeds but as patients who deserve special attention and care, who need therapy rather than punishment, cure rather than condemnation. The emergence of psychology as a science in the late nineteenth century contributed a great deal to establishing the idea of emotional and behavioral abnormalities as mental diseases. Sigmund Freud did much to promote the idea of deterministic processes in the "mind" that dictate human behavior, just as such physical processes dictate health and illness in the body.

How does all of this justify the forcible treatment of a mentally ill person against his will, as is done with involuntary commitment? In the case of physical illness it has come to be commonly recognized that medical professionals do not have the right to treat diseases suffered by persons unless they have given their free, informed consent to the treatment. Treatment without consent of the patient is a form of assault or "unlawful touching" of the patient's body. If informed consent is required for treatment of physical illness, why not for mental illness as well?

The commonly recognized exception to the informed consent requirement in the treatment of physical illness provides a key to understanding the medical model's justification of involuntary commitment. The exception is made in so-called "emergency medical situations" where a person is in grave danger of suffering irreversible injury or loss of life if immediate medical aid is not administered, and the patient is incompetent to give a free, informed consent due to loss of consciousness, extreme shock, or other duress. In these emergency situations treatment is rendered without consent on the grounds that the patient *would* consent to it if he were in a position to make a free choice. The consent of the patient to the treatment is *presumed* because most people (at least "reasonable" people) in similar circumstances would wish to be given emergency treatment. Treatment, especially life-saving treatment, is presumed to be a good that, in fact, would be wrong to withhold from a person who needs it but cannot request it.

The therapeutic argument for civil commitment takes this idea one step further. The diagnosis of a *mental* illness in a person, unlike a physical illness, itself becomes a basis for assuming that the person is incompetent to freely choose or reject psychiatric treatment. Mental illnesses are, by definition, diseases of the mind—of the very organ of the body that thinks, values, weighs alternatives, and ultimately chooses a course of action. To suffer from mental illness is to suffer a loss of one's ability to choose rationally, to choose even those things necessary for one's own good. Hence, even the adamant refusal of a person to submit to psychiatric treatment of his mental illness can be seen as yet another unfortunate symptom of the mental illness, and a confirmation of it. Further, just as the unconscious victim of an automobile accident can be presumed to want medical aid despite her inability to consent to it, so is the "psychotic" presumed to want psychiatric treatment despite her most vociferous denials and violent resistance. Indeed, to respect the *apparent* desires of the "psychotic" and to withhold treatment would be to act against her *real* desires as well as against her best interests.

The medical model is at the heart of the therapeutic argument for involuntary commitment. The good of commitment in this view, and the sole justification for it, is the treatment of the mental disease suffered by the "patient." Commitment is therapeutic for the patient, whether he recognizes it or not, and if it does not prove to be therapeutic there are no further grounds for continued restraint on the patient's liberties. By the same token, if there is no mental illness present, there is nothing to be cured, and no grounds for commitment. Dangerousness to self or to others is not by itself sufficient to justify civil commitment in the therapeutic view; neither are the interests of family, friends, or community in ridding themselves of a problem with the deviant or difficult individual.

The therapeutic argument for involuntary commitment can be summarized in the following basic points:

1. Many behavioral and emotional disturbances are caused by identifiable diseases of the mind, or "mental illness."
2. These mental diseases can be treated, their symptoms alleviated, and often they can be cured, enabling the affected individual to function more normally.
3. Because these diseases affect the mind, which is the center of

free choice, sufferers are rendered incompetent to make free, informed choices concerning the conduct of their lives, including especially the course of treatment or nontreatment of their mental illness.

4. Because treatment of disease is a good, desired by most rational persons, it can be presumed that the sufferers of mental illness also desire treatment and would choose it if they could choose freely.

5. The involuntary commitment of deviant persons can be justified only if their deviance is a product of, or caused by, a mental disease, and the purpose of that commitment is the alleviation or cure of that disease.

The major thrust of the therapeutic argument for involuntary commitment of the mentally ill is that it is essential for the good of the individuals themselves, even if they are incapable of recognizing that it is a good. In this respect the therapeutic argument rests upon the assumption that paternalistic coercion of individuals in society is sometimes justified.

While the Western liberal democratic political tradition has always frowned upon paternalistic interventions in the lives of individuals by government or other social institutions, it also has recognized that society rightfully has certain powers of *parens patriae* (a term derived from the English concept of the King's role as father of the country). Under the doctrine of *parens patriae*, Western societies have taken certain responsibilities for the sick, the disabled, and the impecunious. The modern welfare state is an example of the expansion of this doctrine, as is the shift from treating the mentally ill as criminals to treating them therapeutically. Nevertheless, our society has always sought to limit the paternalistic powers of the state on the grounds that persons have a right to determine their own way of life according to their own conceptions of what is good for them.

One can distinguish between two types of paternalism.[4] The first type, often called *strong paternalism*, involves the restriction of an individual's freedom to engage in activities that others believe to be self-harmful, even though it is admitted that he is competently and thus freely choosing the self-harmful behavior. *Strong paternalism* restricts the rights of individuals to freely choose activities harmful to themselves. Drug laws, the purpose of which is to prevent the use of narcotics and hallucinogens thought to be harmful, are examples of strong paternalism.

The therapeutic argument for involuntary commitment of the mentally ill under the *parens patriae* power of the state is not made on such grounds, however. It is a form of what is often called *weak paternalism*. Paternalism of this variety intervenes in the behavior of individuals to protect them from self-harm, but only because the individuals are not *freely* choosing the self-harmful behavior. Since they are not acting freely, paternalistic intervention of this variety is not viewed as a restriction upon their freedom, but rather as an enhancement of it. The intervention is not only for their benefit, it is in the name of their real wishes, which due to their incompetence or duress they are unable to actualize.

Insofar as the therapeutic argument for involuntary commitment assumes the mental incompetence of the patient to choose freely what is clearly judged by the health professionals to be a benefit or a prevention of further self-harm, it is paternalism of the "weak" variety. Consequently, it is a logical extension of the therapeutic view to include as a justifying condition for commitment the fact that the patient would otherwise be harmful to himself. If commitment is able to prevent or minimize this harm, it is justified on the therapeutic view even though there may be little or no prospect of curing the mental disease. The case of Mrs. Lake is an example of a civil commitment justified on these grounds. The lower court's rejection of her appeal explicitly relies upon this rationale. It accepted the testimony of the psychiatrist that she was mentally incompetent to prevent harm to herself if left at liberty, and viewed this as ample reason for the deprivation of her liberty. There was no suggestion that she might be harmful to others, hence, the rationale was solely a paternalistic one (of the "weak" variety).

Not surprisingly, the therapeutic argument for civil commitment is most popular among those who view themselves primarily as therapists—the mental health professionals. It also has a great appeal to the psychiatric social worker, for several reasons. First, the self-image of social workers is that of the professional "helper" whose primary responsibility is promoting the welfare of their clients. This self-image tends very easily towards the paternalistic stance that the decision whether or not to hospitalize involuntarily is made on the basis of an assessment of what is best for the client. Social workers prefer not to see themselves as representing the interests of the relatives, the community, or the police in having the client "taken care of." When such pressures are brought to bear upon the social worker, the decision to commit is more palatable if it is seen to be in the client's best interest. In addition, psychiatric social workers tend to view themselves as essential components of the "therapeutic team" within the psychiatric institution. Hence, it is not surprising that they tend to share the assumptions of the therapeutic argument for involuntary commitment.

THE SOCIAL PROTECTION ARGUMENT

The therapeutic argument for involuntary commitment of those diagnosed as "mentally ill" has held sway through the last century and a half, especially within the professional mental health community. However, in recent years it has come under increasing criticism from a variety of quarters. These criticisms have derived from a growing uneasiness about the assumptions underlying the therapeutic view, or at least about the applicability of these assumptions in many instances of civil commitment.

Civil libertarians began to suggest that the civil liberties of many citizens were being deprived by mental health professionals where these citizens were neither mentally ill nor incompetent to choose freely the conduct of their lives but were merely nonconformists whom society and friends found difficult to tolerate. Even psychiatrists, like Thomas Szasz (whose viewpoint will be considered in detail later), began to question the whole concept of mental illness itself as well as the appropriateness of the medical model in dealing with deviant behavior. Neuroses and psychoses are often, if not always, merely medical labels for socially deviant behavior that become thinly veiled rationales for controlling the behavior in the name of therapy and cure, these critics alleged.[5-7]

A great number of studies tended to confirm the charges of the civil libertarian critics. These studies showed that psychiatric diagnoses of similar cases could differ widely among different psychiatrists, calling into question the scientific basis of these diagnoses.[8] Further, newspapers, journals, and other media were filled with reports of the crowded and inhumane conditions that existed in many psychiatric institutions, belying the claim that the inmates or "patients" were being treated for disease, to say nothing of being cured. Mental hospitals, many charged, were merely detention centers for the unwanted and unloved of society. Other studies indicated that most diagnoses were made on the basis of extremely cursory psychiatric interviews and that the understaffing of the institutions meant that patients received very little observation or care by professional psychiatrists or psychologists. It was easy to be committed but next to impossible to be released from a mental hospital.[9]

As a result of public concern about the possible widespread abuse of psychiatric diagnoses and subsequent deprivation of liberty of many people who were merely nonconformist or unwanted by families and community, states and provinces began a process of tightening up their legal provisions governing the criteria and procedures for civil commitment. In most cases these statutory changes have moved away from the therapeutic view, with its "medical model" assumptions, towards a quite different basis for civil commitment, the "social protection" view.

The social protection argument rests on the basic premise that the only justification society has for depriving individual members of their liberties is to protect society from the direct harms they threaten against its members. It takes as its credo the view of John Stuart Mill, "that the only purpose for which power can be rightfully exercised over any member of a civilized community, against his will, is to prevent harm to others. His own good, either physical or moral, is not a sufficient warrant."[10] Following Mill, the social protection view rejects the therapeutic rationale for involuntary commitment that it is for the person's own good to be hospitalized and treated. Even if such treatment were beneficial for the subject, a claim many of the social protectionists would question, this would still not justify the deprivation of his liberty were it not also the case that he posed an immediate threat of direct harm to other persons. This view follows from a complete rejection of all forms of "strong" paternalism, and while certain instances of "weak" paternalism are acceptable to the social protectionists (for example, even Mill would accept the legitimacy of rendering emergency medical aid to an unconscious or delirious accident victim) they are highly suspicious of the therapeutic claim that the "mentally ill" are incompetent to freely choose treatment or nontreatment.

Nicholas Kittrie, one of the strongest critics of the therapeutic argument, believes that the state must clearly distinguish between its role as a promoter of individual health and welfare and its role as protector of individuals from harm threatened by others. The former role, he maintains, must be totally voluntary, including the protection of persons from harm to themselves. It must be carried out as much as possible outside of the framework of coercive "total institutions." Only the latter role can be compulsory, and then under the severe limits and protections of due process similar to the criminal law. Kittrie, therefore, would permit commitment of persons to mental institutions against their will only to protect other persons in society from the immediate dangers posed by their actions.[3]

Those who hold, with Kittrie, that only social protection from harm can justify the involuntary commitment of individuals believe that if it cannot be shown that the state has the right to commit persons involuntarily even when it cannot treat or cure them, then it is questionable whether the state has the right to commit involuntarily at all, even if there is treatment and cure. For them, the basic issue in civil commitment is not mental illness but dangerousness. The social protectionists tend, therefore, to rely more on predictions of dangerous behavior than upon psychiatric diagnoses of the patient's particular mental disability or prognoses for remission or cure. They also are more inclined to prefer a legal, adversary procedure for civil commitment to the medical or psychiatric diagnostic procedure called for by the therapeutic view of commitment. The former procedure emphasizes legal due process and protection of the civil rights of the potential inmate against arbitrary and capricious actions, while the latter emphasizes the prerogatives of the medical expert to decide what is best for his or her patient. The legal procedure looks for the legally relevant evidence of dangerousness (e.g. previous commission of dangerous or harmful acts, explicit threats of harm to others) while the psychiatric procedure follows the accepted canons of medical evidence for the various mental syndromes (e.g. neuroses, psychoses, schizophrenia, paranoia, etc.).

The social protectionists view civil commitment on the model of criminal punishment rather than the medical model of "treatment." One writer puts the view this way: "If involuntary psychiatry is 'punishment', then it should only be involved where accompanied by the substantive and procedural protections of the criminal law; and if it is 'treatment', then it has *no* application to a nonconsenting patient."[8] This poses a very serious dilemma for the social protection view. If civil commitment is a form of punishment rather than treatment, how can punishment be justifiably imposed upon a person who either is so mentally incompetent as to be irresponsible for his dangerous acts, or who has not committed any criminally harmful acts? Punishment in the former case violates a central principle of legal justice, which stipulates that punishment is appropriate only for those who are able to understand the moral and legal nature of their actions and were capable of choosing to act otherwise. If a person is in fact mentally incompetent, then to "punish" him for his potentially or actually dangerous behavior by depriving him of liberty (but not treating his illness) seems to work a grievous injustice against him.

On the other hand, if the individual is not mentally incompetent but is fully capable of acting responsibly, then the civil commitment procedure is an option only if the subject has not *actually* committed a harmful, criminal act but is only thought to be highly likely to do so. If he has committed a criminal act, then the usual route of trial, conviction, and punishment is appropriate, not civil commitment. If he has not yet committed a criminal act, however, the civil commitment on grounds of social protection amounts to nothing more than preventive detention, or punishment where there has been no crime. This violates another equally important principle of legal justice.

The only way out of this dilemma for the social protectionist would seem to be an admission of the therapeutic view that civil commitment of the mentally disturbed can be justified only if it includes treatment or care of them as patients, rather than punishment alone (i.e. deprivation of liberty) as criminals. In contrast to the therapeutic view, however, the social protectionists would have to insist that such coercive treatment is defensible only when the patient (1) is so mentally disturbed as to be incompetent, (2) poses a clear and immediate threat of harm to others, and (3) has already committed a criminal, dangerous act. In this "modified" social protection view the only legitimate *ground* for involuntary commitment is dangerousness to others, but such commitment must include effective treatment of the patient's incapacitating condition or, at least, proper custodial care. It must not be "punitive."

Many proponents of the therapeutic view find the social protection view, especially the "modified" form, completely irrational. For example, Dr. M. A. Peszke argues that if mental illness really is a disease entity, as he believes, then to restrict involuntary commitment only to the *dangerous* mentally ill is like saying, "Only the belligerent victim of an accident will be treated. The quiet and unconscious ones will be allowed to lie and die, since they cause no trouble and since they cannot give informed consent."[11] The social protectionist can respond to this argument only, it would seem, by maintaining that the involuntary treatment of even mentally incompetent persons is not a good that society has a right to impose on them unless it is made *necessary* by the interest society and its members have in protecting themselves from harm.

Reform of the civil commitment statutes in most states and in the provinces of Canada over the past decade indicate a strong trend in the direction of the social protection view that restricts commitment to the dangerous mentally ill and limits the type and severity of harm that can be considered dangerous.[8] The 1978 reform of the Ontario Mental Health Act is a good example of developing statutes. It requires a showing that the subject of the proceeding has:

a) threatened or attempted or is threatening and attempting to cause bodily harm to himself;

b) behaved or is behaving violently towards another person or has caused or is causing another person to fear bodily harm from him; or

c) shown or is showing a lack of competence to care for himself;

and... in addition the physician is of the opinion that the person is apparently suffering from a mental disorder of a nature or quality that will likely result in

d) serious bodily harm to the person;

e) serious bodily harm to another person; or

f) imminent and serious physical impairment of the person.[12]

This statute requires an actual threat of harm or harmful act *prior* to commitment, as well as a finding of "mental disorder" that "will likely result" in bodily harm in the future. In these respects it follows the social protection view. However, it departs from the social protection view in that it permits paternalistic intervention to prevent bodily harm to one's self. Further, it does not require a finding of incompetence, but only of the existence of a "mental disorder." This presumably would include mild neuroses as well as more severe disorders.

While the therapeutic argument tends to be most popular among mental health professionals, the social protection view finds strongest support in the legal community, especially among lawyers who are concerned for the protection of the civil rights of individuals against the powers of the therapeutic state. Indeed, the social protection view is sometimes referred to as the "civil libertarian" view,[13] because of its close association with the legal concerns for due process in civil commitment proceedings.

Although this view may be less accepted within the psychiatric social work profession than the therapeutic view, for the reasons cited earlier, it nevertheless appears that the role of the psychiatric social worker is more central to the social protection model than it is in a purely therapeutic model. This is due to the fact that under the therapeutic model the decision whether or not to commit is for the most part a *psychiatric* one—based on the prevailing criteria for the diagnosis of mental diseases and the recognized therapies appropriate for the condition diagnosed. The basic questions are simply "Is the subject mentally ill and, if so, what disease does he suffer, and which treatment is likely to be most beneficial?" These questions the professional psychiatrists or psychologists consider themselves most competent to answer. The information and expertise possessed by the medical social worker may provide important input into the psychiatric evaluation, but the decision itself remains basically a medical one.

However, in the social protection model, the considerations relevant to the commitment decision are not primarily psychiatric but *social.* When the basic issue is "dangerousness" rather than "illness," the information and expertise possessed by the social worker becomes much more crucial in the commitment decision. The social worker is probably best acquainted with the subject's interaction with family, friends, community, and legal institutions (police, courts). The social worker's assessment of the reports gathered from these sources is bound to carry great weight. The picture she paints of the subject's behavior patterns may be more influential in the commitment decision of a judge or certification board than the diagnosis of a specific mental syndrome by a psychiatrist, if the central question is the "dangerousness" of the subject.

This may place the psychiatric social worker in a difficult dilemma. According to the National Association of Social Workers *Code of Ethics,* "The social worker's primary responsibility is to clients." "The social worker should avoid relationships or commitments that conflict with the interests of clients."[14] However, if the psychiatric social worker's primary function is the assessment of his deviant client's "dangerousness" to others in the community, he appears to be representing the interests of that community in preference to those of his client. Indeed, it might justifiably be said that in the social protection model the society being protected is the social worker's primary client, not the deviant, "dangerous" individual whose liberty is at stake. This may explain why social workers tend to prefer the therapeutic model of commitment: it avoids the dilemma by turning the commitment decision into a paternalistic "doing what is best" for the person usually perceived as the client, the person being committed. Of course, the question is whether the paternalism of the therapeutic model is anything more than social protection in a benevolent disguise. If this is the case, as both social protectionists and the abolitionists of involuntary commitment maintain, then the psychiatric social worker is in fact an agent of the family or community despite his or her paternalistic intentions.

THE ABOLITIONIST VIEW

Finally, there are many writers who have argued that there can be no justification at all for the involuntary commitment of persons to mental institutions, and that the practice ought to be abolished altogether. The abolitionist argument is based upon a denial of the claims made by both the therapeutic model and the social protection model. With respect to the therapeutic model, it is denied either that there is such a thing as mental illness to be treated, or, if there is, that it is legitimate for therapy to be involuntarily imposed upon the sufferers. With respect to the social protection model, the abolitionist denies either that "mental patients" really do pose a danger to others sufficient to justify the deprivation of their liberty or, if they do, that civil commitment is the proper means of dealing with this danger.

The abolitionists of involuntary commitment are joined by the social protectionists in their rejection of the idea that society can justifiably impose psychiatric treatment upon unwilling subjects merely for their own good. As we have already seen, this rejection stems in part from a skepticism about the medical model of mental illness and the concomitant claims made by mental health professionals about both its diagnosis and cure.

A leading challenger of this medical model of mental illness has been the psychiatrist Thomas Szasz. Szasz has argued in a flood of books and articles that there is no such thing as mental illness in the medical sense of "illness." What psychiatrists call "mental illness" is not a biological or physiocochemical disorder as the terms "illness" and "disease" suggest, rather it is a personal or social difficulty—a departure from psychosocial or ethical standards.[5] In short "mental illness" is a medical label for social deviance in individuals.[5] Most so-called "mental diseases" manifest themselves as mental or behavioral "symptoms" (e.g. hallucinations, fears, depression, odd behavior), which are considered to be either diseases of the "mind" or caused by some deeper organic, neurophysiological dysfunction.

However, Szasz and other critics of "mental illness" are fond of pointing out that few "mental diseases" are traceable to discernible organic dysfunctions (e.g. brain lesions, tumors, or other neuro-physiological dysfunctions) despite the claim of some scientists that some day this will be possible.[15] While they do not dispute the fact that some behavioral deviance is traceable to or caused by organic dysfunctions, most deviance classified as "disease" by psychiatrists is *just* deviance and nothing more. Szasz has no objection to treating organic brain disorders or diseases but claims that when these patients are involuntarily hospitalized the primary purpose is to exercise social control over their behavior rather than treatment of the disease, which is, at best, a secondary consideration.[5] Even if treatment of the organic disease were the primary consideration, the treatment ought to be voluntary, just like treatment of non–mental illnesses.

In short, these critics argue, mental illness is a myth.[5] It is a misplaced medical label for what is not disease but a "problem in living" for the individual or, as is usually the case when civil commitment is at issue, a problem of social control of the deviant individual. Most of these opponents of "mental illness" do not discount the value of psychiatric help when it is freely requested by persons who experience emotional or behavioral difficulties. They insist that this help ought not to be viewed within the perspective of the "medical model" (see above) but as a form of helping distressed individuals to clarify and achieve their own goals. The function of psychiatry, says Szasz, is more ethical than medical.[5]

It is only when mental health professionals place medical labels on these problems that they overstep the proper boundaries of psychiatric care, say these critics. Labelling persons as "paranoid," "schizophrenic," etc., in most cases stigmatizes them in ways that often prove very socially detrimental; it is also a means of exercising effective control over them. It not only serves as a signal that their behavior is unacceptable, it identifies the behavior as "sick" and, hence, appropriate for "therapeutic" intervention by professionals. When buttressed by the additional assumption that the mentally sick person is not able, by virtue of his *mental* disease, to exercise free choice, the medical labels become grounds for controlling his behavior coercively. Of course, this control is viewed as "treatment."

The critics of mental illness agree with the social protectionists to the extent that the latter recognize involuntary commitment to be a form of social control over deviant individuals, in the interest of persons other than the committed individual. Both agree that the therapists are wrongly carrying out this social control under the benevolent guise of "treatment" for "disease." The "disease," however, is nonconformity to social standards of behavior or belief such as "squandering finances," "reviving one's reputation in the community," or "thinking the mafia is after him," which "diseases" a recent head of the Ontario Medical Association: Psychiatric Section cited as grounds for civil commitment.[8]

Thomas Szasz has pointed out that everyone from Barry Goldwater to Woodrow Wilson to Jesus has been diagnosed by one psychiatrist or another as "paranoid schizophrenic," "psychopathic personality," "born degenerate," or "suffering from a fixed delusional system."[5] Usually the diagnosis reflects the political or religious views of the psychiatrist rather than any illness suffered by the subject of the diagnosis, he claims. The political bias built into psychiatric diagnosis was illustrated by one study, which found evidence that the mental health professionals viewed patients who expressed radical political views as more severely ill than patients with identical symptoms but more "acceptable" political views. The authors of this study concluded that mental health professionals are the "high priests of the middle class,"[16] i.e. they are the guardians of middle class values.

The anti-medical model psychiatrists are not surprised at the results of many studies indicating that there are high levels of disagreement among professional therapists when "diagnosing" the type of "illness" present in the same case, or cases with nearly identical symptoms.[8] This is because they are not objective assessments of organic dysfunction, but subjective judgments, reflecting the values of the therapist.

If involuntary treatment of the "mentally ill" is merely a form of social control in a benevolent, therapeutic disguise, can this social control be justified? As we have seen, the social protectionists maintain that it is justified only when it is a means of protecting other people from the immediate threat of direct, usually physical, harms, but not as a means of controlling other, harmless forms of social deviance. The abolitionists, however, reject even the use of involuntary commitment to control "dangerous" individuals. Their argument, simply put, is as follows: If individuals really have proven themselves dangerous by committing criminally harmful acts, then they should be dealt with as criminals within the system of criminal law. They should be *punished,* not treated. If they have done nothing to merit criminal punishment, then it works a gross injustice against them to deprive them of their liberty coercively.

Hence, the abolitionists join forces with the therapeutic viewholders in rejecting the practice of committing persons involuntarily in order to protect the interests of others, including their interest in protection from harm. Both views find support from many studies that indicate the gross inaccuracy of most psychiatric or other predictions of dangerousness.

One of these studies involved a follow-up of nearly 1,000 former patients in hospitals for mentally ill prisoners who were ordered released by the U.S. Supreme Court in 1966.[17] The mental health professionals involved in these hospitals had predicted dire consequences for society upon release of the patients, based upon their assessment of the patients as among the most dangerous persons in the state. The follow-up study found that only twenty-six of these patients subsequently committed acts serious enough to warrant their return to incarceration,[18] hardly a greater percentage than among the general population. This study is consistent with the conclusion reached by many others, that predictions of dangerousness are not only highly inaccurate but are inaccurate in the direction of over-prediction. Further, diagnosis of "mental illness" is itself a very poor indicator of dangerousness, since dangerous behavior is no more prevalent among those so diagnosed than among the general population.[8]

Even were it possible to predict dangerousness with an acceptable degree of accuracy, most abolitionists would not accept these predictions as legitimate grounds for civil commitment. With many holders of the therapeutic view, they see this as a form of punishment where there has been no crime, or "preventive detention," which is generally considered unfair in our system of justice. At this point the "therapeutist" says, "Do not commit unless there is a mental disease that can be treated." The abolitionist, who is just as suspicious of the "mental disease" as he is of the "dangerousness" criterion says, "If you can't convict and punish for criminality, do not commit at all."

In the abolitionist view the function of the psychiatric social worker is in effect a police function, carried out in a benevolent, therapeutic guise. Perhaps more accurately, the psychiatric social worker is an agent of the deviant individual's family or community who are embarrassed or overburdened by the bizarre behavior of the deviant. While these groups seldom would openly espouse the incarceration of their friends or relatives as a way of "getting rid of the problem," and would be hesitant to call the police or to make criminal charges, they would be less hesitant to call into play the cadre of benevolent mental health professionals who will "do what is best for him."

The social worker plays a crucial role in the commitment decision, whether in the social protection model, as we have seen, or the therapeutic model. In the latter model it is the social worker who investigates the social background of the "problem" including accounts of the subject's "sick" behavior as viewed by relatives and acquaintances. This report of the "symptoms" may carry significant weight in the "diagnosis" of the "patient's" condition of "mental disease." (The quotation marks indicate medical model terms that the abolitionists would reject as inappropriate.) The social worker's report is, therefore, the major vehicle by which the values and interests of family and community enter into the commitment decision. In this respect the social worker is performing a crucial function as the guardian of social values, by identifying the nonconformists to these values and assisting in their removal from society through civil commitment. If the abolitionists are correct, it calls into serious question the self-image of the psychiatric social worker as one whose primary role is helping the sick, the needy, and the powerless.

CONCLUSION

The debate over the moral justifiability of involuntary commitment does not appear to turn only upon disagreements over basic ethical viewpoints but also upon other philosophical questions. Among the most fundamental of these philosophical questions are (1) the question of what is health and disease (is there such a thing as "mental" illness"?) and (2) the question of the nature of free choice (when is a person incompetent to make free choices?).

As we have seen, the therapeutic view of civil commitment is based on a positive answer to (1) while the abolitionist view stems from a negative answer. While the therapists believe that at least the *seriously* "mentally ill" are incompetent to choose their own therapy, the abolitionist argument seems to assume the competency of everyone to choose treatment or reject it, regardless of their emotional state.

The social protection view has adherents who fall on both sides of both questions. This viewpoint seems to rest upon an answer to a third question, which is a clear moral question: (3) Is paternalistic treatment of individuals justifiable? As we have seen, the social protection view of commitment rests upon a rejection of paternalism, apparently of both the "weak" and "strong" variety. The therapeutic view rests upon an acceptance of, at least, "weak" paternalism. Abolitionists and social protectionists may well accept the justifiability of "weak" paternalism in principle, but if they deny the incompetence of deviant individuals they do not believe it is justifiable to override their refusal of psychiatric care. Some abolitionists, on the other hand, may base their view upon a rejection of any kind of paternalism, "strong" or "weak," while admitting that some emotionally disturbed individuals may be incompetent as well.

It is impossible in this chapter to deal adequately with these three questions at the heart of the involuntary commitment issue. However, there are several things that can be said in a summary way about each of them, which point towards an answer.

With respect to question (1) the abolitionists, it seems to me, have played an important role in pointing out the abuses of the concept of mental illness by the mental health professions. It cannot be denied that psychiatric labels have been used purely as instruments of social and political control—that a great deal of behavior labelled "sick" is really nothing more than social deviance. There is still a great deal of work to be done clarifying the concept of mental illness before psychiatric diagnoses and treatments can be safely relied upon, especially when used as grounds for coercive treatment of individuals. Yet, the "anti-psychiatrists" like Szasz seem to go too far in denying the existence of functional mental illness altogether. Surely there are forms of serious disabling psychological breakdown that are appropriately treated as disease, but just as surely many of the current psychiatric labels from "empty nest syndrome" (suffered by women when their children leave home) to "paranoid schizophrenia" are often used to refer to persons or behaviors that are not sick in any sense. These behaviors may be, in fact, healthy responses to extremely "unhealthy" situations.

With respect to question (2), concerning free choice, it seems clearly apparent that there are cases of emotional or behavioral disturbances so debilitating as to deprive their bearers of the possibility of free rational choice, including especially the choice between treatment and nontreatment. If free choice has to do with the ability to act in ways that facilitate the realization of one's own goals, including the ability to perceive the world and events in a minimally coherent and reasonable way, then surely the severe cases of "psychotic" fears, paranoid beliefs, or mental disability (e.g. retardation, senility) call into question the ability of persons to exercise their own freedom of choice. This is the basis upon which we act paternalistically towards children and the severely mentally retarded, cases in which most people, including presumably Szasz, would accept its legitimacy.

Great danger lies, however, in the assumption that because a person may not be able to choose freely in one situation or at certain moments, his choice ought not to be trusted or respected in other situations or moments. One of the legitimate criticisms of the medical model of mental illness is that the application of labels like "psychotic," "schizophrenic," or "manic depressive" to a person easily becomes a basis for the ascription of complete mental incompetence in all areas of choice. The case of Mrs. Lake, above, is an example of this kind of error. The contention of the psychiatrist at the trial, that since she suffered an illness that led to periods of confusion and memory loss she was incompetent to decide where she should live, was questionable. Even if she were incompetent during these lapses it does not follow that she was incompetent *at other times* to decide how she wanted to be treated.

Finally, it does not seem reasonable to answer question (3) with an unqualified "No." If there are clear cases of inability to choose freely, as has just been argued, then it is hard to see why paternalism in its "weak" form would not be justified in these cases in order to prevent harm to the individual concerned or to promote what is unquestioningly his own good. Paternalism always carries with it great risks of violating real personal liberty because it is so easy to view another person's choice as "unfree" merely because it is bizarre. The growing tendency in our society to see all unorthodox behavior as "sick" rather than merely "odd" or "bad" makes the perils of paternalism even greater. In those cases where the ability to choose freely is clearly lost, it would be wrong not to act to protect the interests of the person who cannot choose to protect them for himself.

The psychiatric social workers are at the center of the civil commitment proceedings. If their role is primarily that of representing the client's interest, then they bear a special responsibility to see that the client is not the victim of arbitary or capricious diagnoses of "mental illness" or "incompetence" and that they are not being used as undercover agents of the prevailing political and moral mainstream in the garb of "helping professionals." It is important to remember that, as Charles Reich has said, in the benevolent, therapeutic welfare state, "the poor are all too easily regulated. They are an irresistible temptation to moralists, who want not only to assist but to 'improve' by imposing virtue. They are subject to social workers' urges to prescribe 'what is best.' "[19] The same caution must be observed with the deviant, the nonconforming, and the troublesome, who, if they are also poor, are most likely to become entangled in the tentacles of the therapeutic welfare state.

REFERENCES

1. Beauchamp, Tom L. and Childress, James F.: *Principles of Biomedical Ethics.* Oxford, Oxford U Press, 1979.
2. Lake v. Cameron, 267 F. Supp. 155 (D.D.C. 1967).
3. Kittrie, Nicholas N.: *The Right to be Different.* Baltimore, Johns Hopkins U

Press, 1971.

4. Feinberg, Joel: *Social Philosophy.* Englewood Cliffs, Prentice-Hall, 1973.

5. Szasz, Thomas: *Ideology and Insanity.* Garden City, Doubleday, 1970.

6. Szasz, Thomas: *The Myth of Mental Illness.* New York, Hoeber, 1961.

7. Laing, R. D.: *The Politics of Experience.* New York, Ballantine Books, 1967.

8. Anand, Raj: Involuntary civil commitment in Ontario: The need to curtail the abuses of psychiatry. *Canadian Bar Review, 57:*250–280, June 1979.

9. Rosenhan, D. L.: On being sane in insane places. *Science, 179:*150–158, Jan 1973.

10. Mill, J. S.: On liberty. In *Essential Works of John Stuart Mill.* New York, Bantam Books, 1961.

11. Peszke, M. A.: *Involuntary Treatment of the Mentally Ill.* Springfield, Charles C Thomas, 1975.

12. Ontario legislation: *The Mental Health Act. Statutes of Ontario.* 1978.

13. Chodoff, Paul: The case for involuntary hospitalization of the mentally ill. *American Journal of Psychiatry, 133:* May 1976.

14. NASW: *Code of Ethics.* Washington, D.C., National Association of Social Workers, 1980.

15. Mark, Vernon and Ervin, Frank: *Violence and the Brain.* New York, Harper and Row, 1970.

16. Braginsky and Braginsky: Psychologists: High priests of the middle class. *Psychology Today,* p. 15, Dec. 1973.

17. Baxstrom v. Herald, 383 U.S. 707 (1966).

18. Diamond, : The psychiatric prediction of dangerousness. *Pennsylvania Law Review, 123:*440–443, 1975.

19. Reich, Charles: Individual rights and social welfare: The energing social issues. *Yale Law Journal, 74:* 1245, 1246, 1965.

Chapter 14

HUMAN SUBJECTS FOR
RESEARCH AND EXPERIMENTATION

SHANKAR A. YELAJA

INTRODUCTION

The ethical problems and issues concerning human subjects for research and experimentation are endemic to the research enterprise. They follow from the very nature of scientific inquiry using human beings as principal subjects. When science takes man as its subject, tensions arise between two values basic to Western society: freedom of scientific inquiry and protection of individual inviolability. Scientific research has given man some, though incomplete, knowledge and tools to tame his environment, while commitment to individual worth, dignity, and autonomy, however wavering, has limited man's intrusion on man. When humans become the subject of research and experimentation, allegiance to one value invites neglect of the other. At the heart of this conflict lies an age-old question: when may a society, actively or by acquiescence, expose some of its members to harm in order to seek benefits for them, for others, or for society as a whole?[1]

Recent experience with research involving human subjects in a variety of disciplines has led to renewed concern among the scientists and the public that present regulation of the research process is unsatisfactory. Some critics call for increased government controls, more stringent monitoring of codes of ethics by investing more authority in professional review committees, more detailed and specific ethical codes, and more active participation of lay people in adjudicating ethical conflicts and decision making. Others fear that these steps and controls will hinder the advancement of scientific knowledge through research.

The essential question is: Do researchers have an ethical responsibility for protecting human rights when these conflict with their commitment to knowledge advancement? If so, what is the nature of that responsibility, and what principles/guidelines might be useful to suggest? Ethical principles and guidelines cannot be considered unless we clarify the ethical issues concerning participation of human beings in research and experimentation. In this chapter I would like to focus on significant ethical issues concerning human subjects for research and then consider guidelines for possible resolution of those issues. We are concerned here with conflict resolution, not with the advocacy of ethical absolutes.

THE ETHICS OF SCIENTIFIC OBLIGATION

The purpose of any scientific research is to contribute toward the advancement of new knowledge or the refinement of existing knowledge or theories. Researchers as scientists are committed to make a distinctive contribution to human welfare through the development of knowledge and its intelligent, creative application to the solution of human problems. Ethically then, they are bound by this scientific obligation. If researchers are constrained in the pursuit of their research and scientific inquiry, the progress toward science and its advancement is impeded. Researchers wish to exercise autonomy in their judgment with regard to research topics, methods, and procedures. They want to be free from constraints in order to live up to their scientific obligation.

However, there are ethical constraints to this obligation. Scientific knowledge and methods that can be used for human well-being and development can also be turned to manipulation, exploitation, and destruction (e.g. research on nuclear power and technology). Scientific knowledge and the research methods used to develop it are a double-edged phenomenon. The ethical dilemmas arise because of both potential and real contributions of science and research to human welfare as well as detriment. The potential for misuse of knowledge is just as great, if not greater, as the potential use for constructive purposes. Herein lies the ethical responsibility of scientists and researchers to what they do.

Social scientists whose research involves human beings are confronted with an additional set of ethical dilemmas. Their scientific obligations to advance significant aspects of human experience and social dynamics are very likely to impinge upon recognized and established human rights. Their research often deals with those aspects of societal functioning and human experience that are sensitive. They use research methods that invite controversy because these may violate acceptable social values and norms. Observations of human beings may sometimes violate norms of privacy. Deception may be used to collect information. Control groups in research study-experimentation may not be informed about the deleterious effects of research; in some cases the negative effects may be discovered only years later. The halo and placebo effects of some research experimentations may create new problems or complicate existing ones. Social scientists face additional ethical problems when human subjects are children, minority groups, mentally or physically disabled, individuals experiencing personal stress due to death, illness, etc, and communities and groups living outside the mainstream of society (e.g. gay).

In short, ethical issues and concerns in research with human subjects arise in several areas: the very choice of research questions and hypotheses, research procedures and methods used, choice of dependent and independent variables, experimental and control group research designs, and the dependent and/or captive populations used for study. These are rather unique to social science research. It can be argued, therefore, that ethical dilemmas are intrinsic to the very nature and purpose of social science research.

Ethical conflict is unavoidable when human subjects participate in research. Conflict resolution is possible when social scientists take their ethical obligation seriously and do not treat it with a cavalier attitude. Furthermore, social scientists cannot make their decisions without weighing the pros and cons of the ethical impact of their research. The question "What should take priority: advancement of science and methods or protection of human rights?" is a complex one and it cannot always be left to the ethical consciousness of the social science researcher or the institutions supporting research. These decisions need to be defended by researchers and brought before public bodies for scrutiny and appraisal.

FACTORS CONTRIBUTING TO AWARENESS OF ETHICAL ISSUES

A number of factors have directly and indirectly contributed to an increasing awareness of ethical issues concerning research with human subjects. These can be categorized as the results of post-hoc research studies, the civil rights movement of the 1960s, the self-regulating impulse of professional associations, and the impact of legal decisions on the issues.

Research studies documenting ill effects on human beings of earlier research and experimentations on them are growing in number.[2-8] When human beings who participated in research ten or twenty years ago are revisited, they appear still to suffer from the negative consequences and ill effects, which can be directly attributed to their research participation. Some subjects suffered psychological damage while others experienced pain and stress well beyond the experimentation stage. For still others participation in research and experimentation resulted in side effects they were neither aware of nor fully informed of, or could only dimly comprehend. It is now well recognized that not all research results in positive benefits. For some individuals, the negative effects, ill benefits, and side effects were more than what they had bargained for.

The ethical consequences and implications of such research studies are increasingly debated in professional meetings and journals. For example, an article appearing in an issue of *American Psychologist* expresses concern that certain behavior modification techniques are manipulative, dehumanizing, and easily abused by researchers.[9] Former research participants are resorting to legal intervention in greater numbers in an attempt to redress their grievances and to right the wrong. They are seeking compensation and wish to fix liability for the damage done to them. The results of post-hoc research studies continue to heighten the twin concerns of formulating ethical policy and guidelines and of closely monitoring them to ensure their adherence in practice.

The civil rights movement in the 1960s and 1970s led to our conscious awareness of the blatant, and in some cases not so blatant, violation of the civil rights of minority groups and members of society. Protection of civil rights of those who are especially vulnerable and can become easy targets for exploitation and manipulation, consequently causing them harm, became a rallying cry resulting in an organized movement. The effects of this movement were to be seen in the passage of new legislation protecting and guaranteeing the rights of racial minority groups whose rights were violated in wide-ranging situations of human conduct. If the 1960s was the decade of protecting the civil rights of racial minorities, the decade of the seventies may be seen as an extension of those rights to children, women, older people, physically and mentally disabled, and sexually victimized. Legislation protecting the personal rights of these groups was passed. Legislative protection and the guarantee of civil rights helped raise social awareness further to identify and recognize institutions where rights may be violated. The research enterprise was one such institution that came under increasing public scrutiny.

Professional associations, partly out of their impulse for self-regulation and partly out of sensitivity to possible violation of human rights, responded to ethical concerns. The movement appears to have gathered momentum in such professional associations as the American Psychological Association, medical research councils, National Association of Social Workers (U.S.), and many others. Impetus seems to have been added to this trend by the research fund granting agencies, both public and private, that took the initiative in developing ethical guidelines to deal with the issues. Institutions providing research funds under public auspices began to acknowledge their responsibility toward the rising awareness of the ethics of scientific obligation. Governmental agencies supporting research formulated ethical guidelines, established review boards to monitor them, and required a greater accountability on ethical standards and behavior from researchers using public research funds.

Private foundations disbursing research money also responded to protect human rights when these might be in jeopardy due to acts of commission or omission by researchers whose projects involved risk, pain, or injury to human beings. The impetus for ethical responsibility in private foundations appears to have come, in the main, from civil liberty associations and interest groups advocating protection of human rights. Leo Alexander, author of the *Nuremberg Code*, which outlines the requirements for the conduct of ethical and legal experiments on human beings, specifies that it is the right of the subject to understand the exact nature and consequences of the experiment, and to have assurance that no harm will befall him.[10]

Finally, the intervention of law courts in adjudicating conflicts and disputes arising out of possible violation of human rights appears to have been a very significant factor in focusing public attention on ethical issues with regard to research on human subjects. Consider, for example, the recent precedent-setting Supreme Court and lower federal court cases on human rights issues in the United States. The courts ruled that individuals held against their will have a right to treatment (Rouse v. Cameron, 373 F. 2d 461, 1966). The court ruled that a mental hospital patient should be released if he was not receiving treatment as provided by statute. Court rulings on cases similar to this one have had enormously severe implications for research designs with control groups in which individuals were denied treatment as part of a research experiment. In another case (Wayatt v. Stickney, 344 F. Supp.373, 1972), the court ruled that the individual has a constitutional right to treatment implicit in the Fourteenth Amendment. The court further ruled in favor of specified minimum standards for treatment in order to satisfy that right. In still other cases the courts handed out judgments interpreting as "cruel and unusual punishment" what had earlier been justified as a necessary condition for treatment.[11]

A related issue is protection from treatment. Francis A. Allen writes: " ... the problem today is one of regulating the exercise of power by men of good will whose motivations are to help, not injure. ... There is a tendency for such persons to claim immunity from such forms of restraint and to insist that *professionalism and devotion to science* provide sufficient protection against unwarranted invasion of individual rights." (emphasis added)[12] In this area, the law courts have been rather slow to act. Legal precedents are still developing. Some states in the U.S.A. have statutory regulations limiting the use of psychosurgery, electric shock therapy, and some therapeutic drugs. These forms of treatment in effect have come under strict professional and legal scrutiny. Thus, the impact of the law courts on raising the level of awareness is of no small consequence.

DEFINITION OF HUMAN SUBJECTS

The definition of human subjects is not without ethical and/or moral controversy. Differing interpretations and consequent lack of complete unanimity on this have caused problems in enforcing ethical guidelines. Some of the more significant issues have to do with rights of infants in "embryo"; of the deceased; of individuals unable to exercise their legal and other rights because of age, mental disability, socioeconomic and cultural conditions, confinement to institutions, etc.; of human beings conceived in test tubes as a result of genetic engineering and manipulation; and last but not least, of human beings whose lives were terminated even before they were born. There are no precise and clear definitions as to who should be included and who should be excluded from ethical considerations. Where these do exist, ethical/moral controversy continues. We shall next consider this issue as it pertains to intrinsic ethical issues of research with human subjects.

ETHICAL ISSUES CONCERNING RESEARCH
WITH HUMAN SUBJECTS

Of the many ethical issues in research with human subjects the following five are selected for consideration: informed consent, deception, risk/benefit, privacy, confidentiality, and anonymity of subjects.

Informed Consent

The researchers' ethical obligation to involve people as research subjects/participants only if they give their informed and free consent is the cornerstone of all the ethical principles governing their participation. This principle rests on well-established traditions of research ethics and on strong rational grounds. The primary reason for requiring consent arises out of the belief that all persons must be allowed to make decisions on matters affecting their lives. Their autonomy to participate or not to participate, or to withdraw from participation after consent is given, is central to the personal freedom guaranteed in society. The refusal to participate may be based on any grounds, whether rational or not. The individual's right of free choice requires that he/she is entitled to adequate and accurate information. There is in essence an implied contractual obligation between the researcher and the person who consents to participate.

Ethical problems arise, however, because of a number of factors inherent in research with human subjects. How much information and what kind(s) of information is considered adequate for making an informed decision? Would giving out certain information be counterproductive to maintaining the integrity of research designs? Who is capable of making the decision? What about those subjects who are unable to give their consent? Who should give consent in cases of children, captive persons, and mentally incompetent individuals? While the safest procedure may be to select only those individuals who can give informed consent, in some situations it is acceptable for parents or guardians to give consent when there is reason to believe that the results of the research will benefit the individual.[13] Under what conditions can consent be withdrawn? Does financial compensation for research create an undue inducement for subjects and act as a coercive element in seeking and influencing consent? These ethical problems require careful consideration.

The structure of the relationship between the researcher and the subject is inherently imbalanced because the researcher has advantages over the subjects who know little or nothing about their participation in the initial stages of research. The ethical obligation of a researcher to provide information about research that allows individuals to make a free choice is based on the recognition of this relationship. However, most individuals simply are unable to comprehend technical and/or complex information about research design and procedures. Yet, their ability to process complex information is a key to making a free choice and giving their informed consent.

In some cases giving out of information may put the research design in jeopardy, especially if deception is to be used (we shall discuss this issue separately). Researchers may be unaware or only dimly aware of the consequences of their research in terms of its short-term and long-term negative effects on people. There may be reasonable grounds for withholding some information from the participants. Researchers, therefore, are caught in an ethical conflict. It is now a generally accepted principle that the "subject should be informed as fully and fairly as possible, with due concern for the limitations of his comprehension, about the purpose, procedures, and reasonably foreseeable consequences of the research and his participation in it."[14]

This principle works effectively, however, only in those cases and situations where the subjects are most knowledgeable. It is often more difficult fully to inform persons with whom communication is limited. However, the suggestion has been made that, in some cases, patients least able to give informed consent are most in need of the benefits of research.[15]

Problems in communication can be caused by differences in language between the researcher and the subject, by a lack of explanatory skills on the part of the person explaining the research, by some peculiar characteristic of the subject (e.g. illiteracy), or by physical or mental impairment. Under these circumstances researchers have an even greater ethical obligation toward their subjects.

Ethical issues concerning freedom of choice and consent require special attention when the subjects are powerless and vulnerable due to their age, socioeconomic conditions, race and ethnic background, dependent status, or residence in institutions. Here again, the ethical obligation arises out of the unequal balance of power and authority between the researcher and the subject participating in research.

In situations where informed consent cannot be obtained from individuals themselves (children, mentally retarded, or mentally ill), researchers are obligated, both legally as well as ethically, to obtain the consent of the legal guardians. In the case of children, the consent of parents is required. Under these circumstances, parents must be fully informed about research procedures and purposes, and parental consent ceases to be valid when a child demonstrates adequate capacity for informed choice.[16] In the case of institutionalized persons, it is necessary to have the consent of both the individual and those in whose care he is. The heart of the ethical principle here is *that free and informed consent should be obtained from a person whose primary interest is in the participant's welfare.* Researchers are obligated to supply subjects with all the necessary information and create conditions conducive to the participant's free choice.

Giving consent to participate, however, does not constitute an irrevocable act that cannot be withdrawn. This is especially important if the subjects, after giving their consent, wish to withdraw their participation because new information has come to light or because the very nature of their participation led them to change their mind. If reasons for their withdrawal are of no consequence (except in cases where financial inducement is involved), then should a researcher allow this to happen? On the surface, it would appear that researchers carry ethical as well as moral responsibility for letting the participants withdraw from research and/or experimentation. There are, however, additional ethical considerations. The fear of reprisal and/or punishment exists in those cases where the participant has a continuing relationship with the researcher. Ethically then, researchers are required to indicate *a priori* that there are no consequences for subjects who terminate their participation in midstream. There are horrendous problems for researchers, no doubt, when they lose their subjects, but subjects cannot ethically be bound to a contract.

This issue, however, is much more complex when research participation is financially rewarded. More and more researchers are now able to offer financial rewards and compensation for defraying the time, inconvenience, and other cost incurred by participants (e.g. transportation). Very few people are prepared to participate in research without "sufficient financial compensation." The ethical issues arise when undue financial benefits are offered as an inducement to participate and, furthermore, when the subject's participation is blinded by monetary consideration affecting his/her judgment and the inability to see the risks involved in participation.

Ethically, researchers are required to ensure that compensation is not so great that it is an excessive or undue inducement. It is difficult to arrive at specific guidelines for operationalizing this ethical principle. If after some participation the subject chooses to withdraw, he/she cannot be denied appropriate compensation, nor should he/she be penalized in any way. Furthermore, researchers cannot let their participants give consent solely because of financial rewards/compensation especially when the risks outweigh the benefits. However, it is not always easy to help subjects make these decisions. The ethical responsibility of the researcher is even greater when the subjects are poor and economically dependent.

Deception

It is sometimes necessary in social science research that the subject be less than fully aware of the purposes, procedures, and some significant aspects of the research. Deception is "the withholding of essential information and/or the intentional misleading of subjects to believe that the procedures and purposes of a research project are not what they actually are."[17] Deception limits the informed consent of the individual participating in research and thus presents an ethical dilemma to the researcher who must employ it for scientific considerations. The ethical problem here is that the subject is uninformed or is misinformed with respect to one or more aspects of the research. The following case material is illustrative of the problem:

In a research study designed to measure and test the hypothesis that social agencies were more favorably disposed to racially matched adoption than interracial adoption, a researcher would make phone calls to the agency twice, once posing as a prospective adopting father wishing to adopt a child of his racial background and the second time indicating his choice for a racially different child. The phone interviews were to be taped without the knowledge and consent of social agencies. Information thus gathered was to be used in either confirming or rejecting the hypothesis.

Both researchers and the subjects involved in the deception method are affected by the problem. Sharp differences exist in the use of deception in social science, particularly in behavior research. Clearly, research that uses deceptive practices has ethical implications for both the individuals served and for the profession itself. The use of deceptive practices can build distrust among subjects as to the intentions of the researcher. This can lead to the refusal of some to participate in other experiments, plus the formulation of expectations in those who do participate that confound the results.[18] Many view the deception issue as part of the more general issue of informed consent, whereas others treat it as a qualitatively different kind of ethical issue. For those who hold the view that an open, honest, nonmanipulative, and noncoercive relationship is an absolute ethical necessity in any research with human subjects, deception is considered as violating the basic values of human dignity and respect. Widespread objection to the use of deception exists and is continuing to grow as the abuse and harmful effects of deception are brought to public awareness. Researchers employing this method must, therefore, cope with a very complex ethical responsibility.

The guidelines on deception in the *Handbook on the Use of Human Subjects*[14] seems to offer a mediating point of view between those who are totally opposed to its use and those who advocate its ethical use in research. The guidelines acknowledge that the scientific purpose of research may invite the use of deception for a variety of reasons. However, it should be used only if (1) the deception is absolutely necessary to the research design; (2) the research is not of such a nature that, if the subject realized what was under study, he could be foreseen to refuse to participate; (3) the subject is to be informed of the true character of the study immediately upon its completion. The subject may have been misinformed, but he must never feel he has been exploited, tricked, or put in a situation where he has acted in a way he regrets.[14]

The guidelines further acknowledge that the subject may, in exceptional circumstances, be incompletely informed of research purposes, but "he should never be less than fully informed about what he will be asked to do and what will be done to him."[14] The Canadian Social Sciences and Humanities Research Council's ethical guidelines appear to be far more stringent with respect to use of deception in research. It states:

> ... deception [can] never be permitted when there is any foreseeable risk of harm to the subject or when debriefing is not possible; Where deception is to be used the researcher shall be required to satisfy the review committee that no other methodology would suffice and that significant scientific advance could result from the research; that if deception is to be used, the researcher be able to satisfy the review committee that nothing has been withheld from the subject which might, if divulged, have caused him to refuse to participate; that when deception is employed, debriefing take place as soon as possible.[17]

The American Psychological Association in its handbook on *Ethical Principles in the Conduct of Research with Human Participants* acknowledges the ethical and moral controversy surrounding the use of deception in psychological research. Ethical principle #4, however, is stated in such a way that it allows greater freedom to researchers than to participants. The principle states:

> Openness and honesty are essential characteristics of relationship between investigator and research participant. When the methodological requirements of a study necessitate concealment or deception, the investigator is required to ensure the participant's understanding of the reasons for this action and to restore the quality of the relationship with the investigator.[19]

Diana Baumrind disagrees with the compromising position of the APA on the deception and risk/benefits issues. She advocates that the protection of individual rights should be a guiding principle. She writes:

> [This is] an issue that has been of special concern to me, namely, the misuse of the trust that the subject places in the investigator and the research enterprise to deceive, manipulate and devalue him as a person and to violate his basic human rights. . . . It is my view that these are times when the objective and commitments of the investigator directly conflict with the well-being of the subject, and the code of ethics should contain provisions that at such times unequivocally protect the subject from the investigator. Especially, in the case of children, the subject's rights not be harmed, or alienated from the power structure, must supercede the rights of the investigator to know and to report.[20]

Ethical guidelines on the use of deception in research vary, and there appears to be no easy solution to this very intricate problem.

Risk/Benefit

It is now a well-recognized fact that participation by human subjects in any research activity has both risks and benefits. Certain risks to individuals, groups, and communities are inevitable in the pursuit of research culminating in theories and knowledge beneficial to society or in devising innovative methods for solving human problems. The benefits of such research should offset risks to human beings participating in research. Any negative effects on the subjects from participation in research should be offset by the positive results accruing from the research. In essence the benefits to the individual should outweigh the risks.

The possible benefits of the research not only to the subject but to science itself are also important to consider. If the research is unlikely to produce results that are compelling and worthwhile, it is not justifiable to ask or require subjects to give their time or to undergo procedures that may cause risk to their physical, mental, or social well-being.

The ethical problems in weighing and calculating the ratio of risks and benefits arise from a number of considerations. Researchers are not always able to calculate the unintended consequences of what they had set out to do. Many professionals have had the sincere conviction that, in doing their research, they were engaged in an activity that benefited some individual or society at large.[21] While not planned, risk factors may occur as a result of unintended consequences. It is, therefore, difficult to include this information in the calculus. Furthermore, the benefits of research may be long-term and yet short-term benefits do not provide any immediate hope or encouragement. Should these benefits be seen in the short-term or in the long-term? An experiment conducted in the Stanford prison concluded that while subjects suffered pain and humiliation, the experiment was of great benefit in that the subjects learned a number of things about themselves and there were no persisting negative reactions.[22] Additionally, the risk factors might be distributed unevenly among different sectors of society. Past research experience has shown that the poor, inarticulate, captive, and dependent groups in society took the risks. They were considered as suitable risk groups because their participation was seen as benefiting them directly, benefit thus outweighing risk. Yet the information on the basis of which decisions were made was in itself derived from untested claims. In short, the potential and actual risks to particular individuals and groups continue to exist. A rational process of calculating risk/benefits seems to occur against the self-interest of participants.

The ethical guidelines formulated by various professional groups and research granting organizations are still somewhat broad and vague on these issues. They seem to rest on a key principle that "the possible benefits to the individual and society accruing from the research should be greater than the risks for the individual."[23]

Privacy

Although there still are varying definitions and interpretations of what constitutes individual privacy, it appears that the individual's right to privacy extends to all information relating to the person's physical and mental condition, personal circumstances, and social relationships that is not already in the public domain. "It gives to the individual or collectivity the freedom to decide for themselves when and where, in what circumstances and to what extent their personal attitudes, opinions, habits, eccentricities, doubts and fears are to be communicated to or withheld from others."[17] This definition of privacy is inclusive of a number of matters over which the individual alone can exercise his/her right to control its treatment.

Ethical issues in research with human subjects arise when the individual's right to privacy is either invaded or is in danger of being invaded for research purposes. For example, there is a long history of controversy over issues of confidentiality at crisis phone centers. The question remains: Does the taping of calls to aid in training and quality service invade the caller's privacy?[24] Invasion of privacy can occur in a variety of ways. The following case examples are illustrative of types of ethical conflict.

CASE 1: It was proposed that a researcher collect data on the interactions of a group of subjects through a one-way mirror. It was agreed that the subjects would be informed that they would be under observation, though it was not required that they be told when the investigator would be watching them and when not.[14]

CASE 2: Students enrolled in a university human sexuality course were asked to undertake a research project as part of their course assignment. It involved interviewing people in their own homes in a small community to collect data/information on their sexual activities, including their extramarital relations, activities, etc., and to share this information with the student interviewer. The student interviewers ensured that the information would be reported on an aggregate basis and no information identifying the research subjects was being recorded or quoted in their report.

The key ethical problem in both cases above is the invasion of privacy without the individual's consent. In this sense, the privacy issue is tied in very closely with ethical issues of informed consent discussed earlier. Informed consent of individuals is essential if their right to privacy is to be infringed upon for valid and legitimate research purposes and activities. However, there are at least two significant issues requiring further consideration: first, the ways and means the researcher adopts in ensuring privacy; and second, the variations in the concept of privacy from one culture to another, especially when there are differences in the cultural background of the researcher and the subjects under study.

Is it enough to promise that the privacy of subjects will be protected? Is the intent and promise of researchers enough of a guarantee in ensuring that no violations will occur? Given the freedom of researchers in formulating and adopting their own methodologies, including research procedures, violations of privacy may occur unintentionally or inadvertently. Data on sexual response, for example, may leak out if extreme care is not taken to protect individual identity. Copies of research questionnaires may wander, unauthorized persons may stumble upon the raw data accidently, and there are always nosey individuals who are looking for sensational subject matter for gossip or vicarious pleasure. The accidental dangers to individual privacy are many. The good intentions and promises of researchers to protect privacy are not always adequate insurance for participants. Actual acts of protection have to be more generous than the promise. The *Commission of Inquiry into the Confidentiality of Health Information* in Ontario in 1980 made a number of recommendations that would ensure that, where research is involved, the protection of clients is more than just a promise.[21]

Diana Baumrind expresses another ethical concern in terms of legitimizing deviant social norms as acceptable ones: "...when an investigator invades the privacy of another person...he contributes to legitimizing these indignities and therefore to their acceptance as normal forms of interpersonal behavior. I am among those who believe that by such practices behavioral research is contributing to the moral ills of society and that the influence is a direct one."[20]

Since the concepts of privacy vary from culture to culture, the question of invasion of privacy ought to be considered in a cultural context. An ethical problem arises when there are significant cultural differences between the researcher and the participants in a study. Whose values and norms are to be taken into account?

Should the researcher be guided by his/her own values and norms of privacy or by those of the participants? The risks of invading and violating individual privacy are too great if researchers base their judgment on their own values. Cultural values around privacy held by the participants should be respected. This principle certainly puts an extra but worthwhile burden of responsibility on researchers. Without it the participants would end up giving uninformed consent to open up their private world for study, observation, and experimentation.

Confidentiality and Anonymity

The ethical obligations with regard to protecting confidentiality and anonymity derive from a well-established rule of human conduct. That every person has a right to privacy regarding most aspects of life which only that person can give permission to violate is now widely accepted in law and in professional ethics. Threats to this right of privacy can and do occur in research with human subjects. The research investigator may obtain private information about people without their knowledge and/or consent. Additionally, the investigator, having obtained information about human beings through his research, with their informed consent, may later pass it on to others. In so doing the researcher may violate the expectations and norms of confidentiality. The following cases are illustrative of the ethical problems.

CASE 3: A researcher proposed to record interviews with persons over 65 in a small town in Manitoba. He proposed to publish his findings, identifying the subjects by initials only.... [14]

CASE 4: Details of the unidentified case history of a person suffering from a very rare disease were to be published in a medical journal. The subject was the only person on record in Canada as having suffered this illness, and was known to researchers in the field.... [14]

CASE 5: It was necessary to obtain a parental permission to test school children. After the research several parents requested their child's scores on the intelligence tests. But we had promised the children that no one outside the research group would be told about their scores, and so we had to refuse to discuss individual children's results with their parents, even in a general way.... [19]

CASE 6: A psychologist who was a full-time employee of a company conducted an attitude survey in one of the company plants at the time of a union organizing drive. The announced purpose of the survey was to disclose many sources of dissatisfaction with employment in the plant. The usual guarantee of anonymity was given to the participants. In the course of the study the psychologist was able to identify certain individuals or groups with strong pro-union feelings. This information, if furnished to the plant manager, could have been of value in combating the organization drive. The essential ethical question is the responsibility of the psychologist to his employer versus his responsibility to the individual employees who participated in the survey under a guarantee of anonymity. The psychologist concluded that the guarantee of anonymity covered not only non-identification in terms of specific statements but also in terms of identifying individuals as pro-union. . . . [19]

CASE 7: Members of the minority communities in this city feel that any research that involves intelligence testing is almost sure to show their mean lower than that of the majority ethnic group's. Therefore, the minority members are demanding a moratorium on intelligence testing (or at least on reporting of racial differences) for 10 years so as to give present ameliorative steps a chance to show an effect. . . . [19]

CASE 8: An in-depth study was done of a small village whose inhabitants were well known to each other. Detailed case reports were published with some attempt to disguise the individuals and incidents, without substantially reducing their scientific meaningfulness; it seemed clear, however, that any villager who read the book would identify the sources of most of what was in it and that much conflict and hard feelings would result. . . . [19]

CASE 9: In a clinical study involving projective testing of college students it became evident that certain subjects, especially one young man, exhibited pathology to the extent that the researchers were concerned. I do not know whether anyone tried to communicate with the young man to the extent of attempted suicide—which raised the issue for the researchers of what their ethical responsibility is (or how far it goes) when pathology is picked up in the course of fairly routine studies.[19]

The 1980 Ontario *Commission of Inquiry into the Confidentiality of Health Information* recommended that in cases like case 9, where a professional " . . . had reasonable cause to believe that a patient is in such mental or emotional condition as to be dangerous to himself or others . . . the health-care provider may disclose to the police or others, information about the patient without the consent of the patient."[19]

There are several facets to the confidentiality and anonymity of individual information. Maintaining confidentiality is more important for certain types of information than for others. Information on religious beliefs, sexual practices, income, racial prejudice, and other personal attributes such as intelligence and honesty is more sensitive than the type of information that does not help to reveal individual identity. For example, there is an increasing sensitivity toward identifying one's age, marital status, and ethnic origin.

There are, without a doubt, enormous individual differences in the degree of resistance people have toward disclosure of what they consider private information. Researchers, therefore, must be guided by their subjects' norms of confidentiality rather than their own. Also, people's attitudes to the relative importance of confidential information change with time.

Another facet of the problem has to do with revealing and passing on the information collected by researchers with the informed consent of the participants. Disclosure of such information invites serious ethical consideration. Researchers are sometimes caught in a double bind situation. An ethical decision has to be made whether divulging of confidential information to others is in the best interest of the person. There has to be a compelling reason and evidence to support this principle (e.g. physician requiring the health information for diagnosis and treatment). In other circumstances those requesting information may stand to use it against the best interest of the person. The intention of those requesting such information is, of course, an important consideration in resolving the ethical conflict. However, demands for divulging confidential information may come from such diverse and disparate sources that it may be difficult reasonably to judge the true intent of the requests.

The 1980 Ontario *Commission of Inquiry into the Confidentiality of Health Information* recommended very stringent procedures dictating the storage, retrieval, and destruction of health records. In addition it recommended that legislation be passed that a hospital or health-care facility may collect only information required for the care, assessment, examination, or treatment of the patient unless he or she consents to the collection of information for other purposes.[21]

Still another ethical problem of divulging confidential information arises when the researcher must make a decision on publication of the results. Some people regard the publication of confidential research information obtained via informed consent as a breach of confidence. They would argue that had they been aware of this decision they would not have given their consent. However, researchers cannot always predetermine the future course of the publication of results.

Finally, there is yet another difficult ethical problem arising out of accidental discovery of private information about research participants. Information such as a participant's drug abuse, criminal record, suicidal thoughts, anxiety, fear, depression, etc., uncovered in the course of an unrelated topic of investigation puts the researcher into a very difficult bind. Should this information be revealed for his own protection or for the protection of others?

Although the following ethical guidelines adopted by the Canadian Social Science and Humanities Research Council are helpful in resolving some of the aforementioned ethical issues, they are still inadequate in dealing with the complexities involved in confidentiality and anonymity. The guidelines state:

> ... that if confidentiality or anonymity cannot be guaranteed, participants be made aware of this limitation and its possible consequences before becoming involved in the research;
>
> that there be a clear understanding between the investigator and subjects whether, and the extent to which, information they divulge will be kept confidential in both the original use of the data and their deposit for future use;
>
> that unless there is an explicit statement by the researcher to the contrary, to which the subject agrees, it be understood that personal information given by the subject will be regarded as confidential and that the researcher will explain the steps to be taken to ensure that confidentiality and anonymity will be maintained;
>
> that steps be taken to guard against the indirect or unwitting disclosure of the identity of subjects by association or combination of information;
>
> that the researcher has an obligation in terms of third-party risk;
>
> that obtaining access to confidential institutional records respect the individual's rights to confidentiality, anonymity and informed consent.[17]

ETHICAL REVIEW PROCEDURES

There appear to be at least four ways of monitoring and enforcing ethical principles and guidelines governing research with human subjects: government control, institutional control, professional associations exercising control, and individual researchers monitoring their ethical behavior. Controversy regarding the most effective mechanism(s) for monitoring behavior and enforcing guidelines is still rife. There are two diametrically opposed views on the subject. The first holds that decisions concerning ethics should be left to the conscience and common sense of the individual researcher because he/she is likely to be best informed about the steps required for implementing the ethical principles. The second view asks the investigator to share the ethical responsibility for monitoring and enforcement and specific steps to be taken in this regard with some other responsible person or body.[25] Practices to fulfill the ethical mandate, therefore, vary.

Government Intervention and Control

The state (government) has intervened in the ethical review procedures in an attempt to exercise some control over the enforcement of ethical guidelines. This has occurred particularly in cases where research is funded out of public revenue. The United States Department of Health, Education and Welfare, for example, formulated an ethical policy statement and established ethical review boards for implementing the policy. The HEW's ethical policy sharply limits the participation of children, prisoners, and the mentally infirm in certain types of clinical research. Ethical review boards organized within federal agencies examine ethical issues in proposed projects. Further review groups called *Protection Committees* are established at institutions that receive federal research grants. The main function of these committees is to assess the validity of consent given by, or on behalf of, the subjects. In prisons, the committee membership consists of at least one prisoner or prisoner representative. The committee oversees the selection of prisoners for research, reviews information given, visits research sites regularly, and insures that any continued consent is given freely without coersion or undue inducement. The ethical review boards examine research proposals submitted for funding under federal government auspices.

The effectiveness of state intervention in ethical review is a mixed blessing. While the state-dictated procedures have forced researchers to acknowledge greater responsibility for ethical behavior and have mandated their public accountability, they have also created a bureaucratic monster. Researchers must now cope with enormous paper flow, complex procedural hurdles, and time delays before they can move ahead. In some instances the procedures have become counterproductive in protecting ethical standards and behavior. In still other cases the ethical review bureaucracy has itself become a problem because no agreement could be reached on how to resolve certain ethical conflicts. Under these circumstances, researchers can be discouraged in their research effort because of the incredible hurdles they go through in getting their research project approved for funding.

Research Institutions

An institution that sponsors research very often expects that researchers using human subjects in their investigation will observe the ethical guidelines. Institutional review boards function as a safeguard against inhumane treatment of clients, as a training mechanism for staff, and as a communication link to community-based programs.[26] A university, for example, expects an explicit obligation from its researchers to observe the policies formulated by its senate. All universities in North America now have a statement indicating either an explicit or implicit policy on this subject.

Public research funding bodies, such as the Canadian Social Science and Humanitarian Research Council and National Medical Research Council, require that all research projects involving human subjects be reviewed by an institutional ethical review committee before they are funded. These organizations have also formulated ethical guidelines, which are used by the review committee in adjudicating problems and conflicts.

In order to fulfill the mandate for monitoring and enforcing ethical guidelines, research institutions both within and outside of universities have established ethical review committees. The review committee is primarily concerned with protection of the human subject. It also acts with concern for the investigators and the sponsoring/funding institution. Membership on review committees, generally speaking, is made up of peer groups, the research director or his designates, and occasionally human rights groups. The review committee acts as a sounding board for the investigator when there are specific ethical problems and the investigator is unsure or uncertain about the best way to resolve the problem. It also acts as a medium for resolving ethical conflicts. Approval of a research ethics review committee is often mandatory before research is undertaken.

The effectiveness of this mechanism for enforcement of ethical guidelines has been questioned. Critics argue that peer group review is ineffective because of a conflict of interest. Researchers might hesitate to oppose their peers for fear that they will be going through the same procedure and examination at a future date. Stringent enforcement of guidelines, it is argued, would create too many hurdles in research, creating a disincentive for researchers and a hostile climate for research activities. Critics further point to ethical violations and abuse that went unnoticed without any remedial or preventive action.

The institutional ethics review committees, it seems, are caught up in a triad of conflict. They are obligated by law and ethical mandate to enforce guidelines; the research peer groups still exercise enormous power in practical application of the guidelines; and the research institutions maintain a vested interest in ensuring an adequate flow of research dollars. Strict and stringent enforcement of guidelines may threaten research productivity and consequently the flow of research funds from public/private bodies into universities. Despite these problems, it is only fair to acknowledge that the review committees have made an important contribution toward refinement of policies and procedures for dealing with ethical conflicts. They have made a significant contribution toward raising the level of awareness on issues.

Professional

Professional organizations have become increasingly cognizant of their responsibility in protecting human rights when these may be violated by their members in the conduct of their research. Ethical statements in the form of codes and guidelines are provided for by the professional organizations to protect the members as well as the public. A committee structure is usually used for monitoring and enforcing the ethical research standards. It is suggested that a committee on ethical standards reflects, but does not resolve, conflicts of interests and values among researchers. A researcher who is accountable to his peers may not easily violate the basic rights of subjects. These committees also serve the latent functions of protecting institutions, judging proposed research in terms of possible social policy impact, and of considering proposed research from the standpoint of community acceptability.[27]

Experience shows that only extreme violations and abuse come before the professional ethics review committee. Much of the emphasis is on prevention and raising the consciousness of members about research ethics. The professional organizations respond to complaints by individuals or groups in society if there is reasonable evidence. The extent of their power over the individual researcher is, however, somewhat limited.

Bernard Barber comments on the record of one professional organization, namely, The American Association of Sociologists. He states:

> It is our impression that professional sociologists have not been overly zealous in this first of our ethical responsibilities. While the ASA has made fitful and partial efforts during the last ten years toward institutionalizing ethical codes and procedures, there remains, what may be considered, at best, widespread ambivalence toward them among the researching members of the profession and, at worst, considerable indifference and hostility. Certainly, professional sociologists have not been innovative and intensively energetic in this ethical concern in a way of which we could be rightly proud. . . . [28]

Individual Researcher

A research investigator, like his peer group and colleagues, has a responsibility to protect persons with whom he/she deals from untoward effects of his/her research with them. No one is better equipped to exercise ethical responsibility than the individual research investigator. It is found that protecting human subjects from abuse or negative effects from research is infinitely better when the major responsibility is thrust upon researchers themselves. This may be due to increasing ethical consciousness among researchers and perhaps a recognition that self-policing is better than outside regulation and control. Clearly, individual researchers are becoming increasingly aware of the need to monitor their own research behavior insofar as enforcement of ethical guidelines formulated within their own institutions and professional organizations is concerned.

CONCLUSION

Ethical issues concerning research and experimentation with human subjects are complex. They invite yet another consideration of the age-old dilemma of human rights in conflict. They remind us that science and scientists, with all their good intentions and positive contributions to human well-being and welfare, are not immune from ethical responsibility to protect human rights, which are always in danger of being violated by acts of commission as well as omission. The scientist's ethical obligation extends not only to his/her primary task of advancing knowledge but equally, and under certain circumstances to a greater extent, to make every attempt to protect those human rights for which society has fought for recognition and acceptance.

REFERENCES

1. Katz, Jay: *Experimentation with Human Beings.* New York, Russell Sage Foundation, 1972.
2. Zimbardo, Philip G. et al.: *Influencing Attitudes and Changing Behavior: An Introduction to Method, Theory, and Applications of Social Control and Personal Power.* Reading Ma., Addison-Wesley, 1977.
3. Zimbardo, Philip G.: *Influencing Attitudes and Changing Behavior: A Basic Introduction to Relevant Methodology, Theory, and Applications.*
4. Zimbardo, Philip G.: *The Cognitive Control of Motivation: The Consequences of Choice and Dissonance.* Glenview Il, Scott Foresman & Company, 1969.
5. Milgram, Stanley: *The Individual in a Social World: Essays and Experiments.* Reading Ma, Addison-Wesley, 1969.
6. Milgram, Stanley: *Obedience to Authority: An Experimental View.* Scranton Pa., Harper and Row, 1974.
7. Milgram, Stanley and Shotland, R. Lance: *Television and Antisocial Behavior: Field Experiments.* New York, Academic Press, 1973.
8. Warwick, Donald: Deception in psychological research. *Psychology Today,* 1975.
9. Stolz, Stephanie B., Weinchowski, Louis A., and Brown, Bertram, S.: Behavior modification: A perspective on critical issues. *American Psychologist,* 30(11):Nov. 1975.
10. Alexander, Leo: Ethics of human experimentation. *Psychiatric Journal of the University of Ottawa,* 1:1-2, Oct. 1976.
11. Dickson, Donald T.: Law and social work. In *Encyclopedia of Social Work,* vol. 1. Washington, National Association of Social Workers, 1979.
12. Allen, Francis A.: *The Borderland of Criminal Justice.* Chicago, University of Chicago Press, 1964.
13. Pryce, I. G.: Clinical research upon mentally ill subjects who cannot give informed consent. *British Journal of Psychiatry, 133:* Oct. 1978.
14. Matsubara, Victoria Conlin (Ed.): *Handbook on the Use of Human Subjects.* Toronto, University of Toronto, 1975.
15. Cole, Jonathon O.: Research barriers in psychopharmacology. *American*

Journal of Psychiatry, 134(8): Aug. 1977.

16. Ferguson, R., and Lucy, R.: The competence and freedom of children to make choices regarding participation in research: A statement. *Journal of Social Issues, 34(2):* Spring 1978.

17. *Ethical Guidelines for Research with Human Subjects.* Ottawa, Social Sciences and Humanities Research Council, January 1979.

18. Weinrach, Stephen A., and Avey, Allen E.: Science, psychology and deception. *Bulletin of the British Psychological Society, 28:* June 1975.

19. Report of the Ad Hoc Committee on Ethical Standards in Psychological Research: *Ethical Principles in the Conduct of Research with Human Participants.* Washington, D.C., American Psychological Association, 1973.

20. Baumrind, Diana: Principles of ethical conduct in the treatment of subjects: Reaction to the draft report of the Committee on Ethical Standards in Psychological Research. *American Psychologist, 27(11):*887, Nov. 1972.

21. Krever, The Hon. Mr. Justice Horace: *Report of the Commission of Inquiry into the Confidentiality of Health Information.* Ontario, J. C. Thatcher, Queen's Printer for Ontario, 1980.

22. Zimbardo, Philip G.: On the ethics of intervention in human psychological research: With specific reference to the Stanford Prison Experiment. *Cognition, 2(2):* 1973.

23. Wilfrid Laurier University Senate Policy: *Ethics in the Conduct of Research with Human Subjects.* Ontario, Wilfrid Laurier University, adopted May 20, 1976.

24. Hayward, Charles H.: Human rights and accountability of crisis intervention services: Background on the taping of crisis calls. *Crisis Intervention, 7(2):* 1976.

25. Report of the Advising Research Committee: The ethics review of research involving human subjects. *Queen's Gazettee* [Queen's University], *IV(4):* Jan 30, 1974.

26. Treadway, Jerry T., and Rossi, Robert B.: An ethical review board: Its structure, function and province. *Mental Retardation, 15(4):* Aug. 1977.

27. Gray, Bradford: The functions of human subjects review committees. *American Journal of Psychiatry, 134(8):* Aug. 1977.

28. Barber, Bernard: Research on research on human subjects: Problems of access to a powerful profession. *Social Problems,:* 103–112, 1974.

Chapter 15

CONFIDENTIALITY

Suanna J. Wilson

Confidentiality has become a highly complex ethical and legal issue. Those professionals uninitiated to its complexities generally function with a few simple guidelines such as, "don't talk about clients outside work" and "when a subpoena arrives, you have to answer it." Unfortunately, numerous sticky situations arise in daily practice, and clinicians, administrators, and those concerned with personnel matters often find the standard guidelines inadequate. There may be no single, definitive answer to tell the confused practitioner what should be done. Various sources can be consulted for guidance, but in the end, the individual must often exercise professional discretion, consult his malpractice policy to determine the extent of coverage, and stick his ethical neck out and do what he thinks best under the circumstances. If the troublesome problem is researched intensively, conflicting guidelines and mandates often emerge. For example, to determine whether it is wise for a social worker to disclose sensitive medical and psychosocial information when a patient has no guardian yet is not really alert, the following sources might be consulted: licensing and accreditation standards, state and federal laws, articles on the concept of informed consent, privileged communication issues, legal aspects of guardianship, requirements of third party payers, accountability and peer review mandates and so forth. The chances are excellent that most of these sources will indicate clearly that only mentally alert individuals can give consent, and when the person is not mentally competent, the legal guardian must give the consent. Therefore, should the medical social worker keep the patient hospitalized indefinitely waiting for either of these conditions to materialize before obtaining permission to disclose information to a nursing home and bring about a discharge plan? Of course not. Thus, in reality, most practitioners do what they feel best and hope that no one looks too closely at what they are doing or challenges their actions.

A short chapter of this nature cannot attempt to present comprehensive, definitive guidelines for resolving complex confidentiality dilemmas; other sources[24] should be consulted. However, it is possible to open the "Pandora's Box" and examine a few of the more common problems that arise in practice, through a series of questions and answers. The questions that follow represent issues raised repeatedly by persons attending workshops given by the author.

QUESTION 1: *Why all this emphasis on confidentiality — you're making a mountain out of a basic, ethical molehill. We studied the subject adequately in school. Aren't we all sufficiently knowledgeable to function effectively in our practice? Why are you assuming we're all so uninformed?*

I have been collecting thousands of questionnaires from social workers (and members of other disciplines) across the country during the past three years. A preliminary review of the responses reveals that fully 90 percent or more of respondents cannot answer this question accurately: "What is meant by the term 'privileged communication'? Do you and/or your clients have this coverage?" Some social work respondents indicate that they practice in states authorizing privileged communication to social workers, and yet they do not even know they have the coverage. Many practitioners with more than ten years post-MSW experience indicate they have never received formal training on the subject of confidentiality. A number of administrators as well as line staff admit they do not know if their employer has written guidelines on confidentiality or state they have not read them. Well over half the respondents indicate they have never read state laws or Joint Commission on Accreditation of Hospitals (JCAH)[15,16] accreditation standards (when appropriate) governing their area of practice. Even when staff members work in the same facility or in similar facilities governed by rather standardized policies, there is considerable inconsistency in response to "What would you do if. . . . " questions.

For example, a recent workshop was attended by professionals concerned with the maintenance and protection of medical and psychiatric records. A special questionnaire asked questions taken

TABLE 15-I

Responses to Questions Based on JCAH Accreditation Manual
N = 50

Question	Number answering "True"	Number answering "False"	Correct Answer*	Percent Respondents who answered correctly
1. Unfortunately, there is no requirement that medical record staff have any special knowledge of how to maintain the confidentiality of records.	32	18	False	.36
2. The source of payment for a patient's medical care does not have to be treated confidentially—it is one of the permissible exceptions.	26	24	False	.48
3. Patients must be granted access to their medical records.	40	10	False	.20
4. A patient's informed consent must be obtained for disclosure of confidential information to outside parties not involved with his/her medical care.	48	2	False	.04
5. Most hosptials and outpatient programs have to abide by selected portions of the Federal Privacy Act of 1974.	42	8	False	.16
6. When a subpoena requests a medical record, the medical record custodian *must* produce the record.	33	17	False	.34
7. Once a subpoena has been received, nothing can be removed from the record.	29	21	False	.42
8. The American Hospital Association provides special confidentiality requirements/safeguards for the protection of personnel records.	29	21	False	.42

---

*Number 1 is "False" because special knowledge in this area is mentioned specifically in the list of competency areas required of medical records personnel. Number 2 is "False" because the Manual specifically mentions that this must be treated as confidential. Number 3 is "False" because the JCAH Manual does not actually state that patients must be granted access to their records; this is merely implied through discussions of patient rights to information about their diagnosis, prognosis, and treatment. Thus, this information could be made available to the patient in a variety of ways—the Manual does not specify that it must be through direct patient access to medical records (though many state laws do mandate this form of access). Number 4 is also "False" because the Manual discusses the need for patient consent for various kinds of disclosures, but does not mandate that the consent must be "informed" (though it does specify that consent for certain medical/surgical procedures must be "informed"). Number 5 is "False" as the existing Federal Privacy Act of 1974 applies only to federally funded and administered programs. Number 6 is "False" since there are various ways to fight a subpoena and avoid some disclosures. Number 7 is "False." State law may forbid some disclosures such as privileged information recorded in the record. Number 8 is "False" because no such guidelines currently exist for general medical facilities, and personnel records are among the least protected of all records maintained in such facilities.

directly from two chapters in the 1980 JCAH Manual for general medical facilities.[15] The answers given by fifty respondents can be broken down as shown in Table 15-I.

Thus, even when written guidelines exist clearly stating procedures for certain kinds of disclosures, staff affected by the procedures either do not realize they exist, are not familiar with them, do not understand them, or for some reason, chose not to follow them.

QUESTION 2: *We recognize that client access to clinical records is desirable. We know that the Federal Privacy Act of 1974 permits clients to have photocopies of their records. Our program receives some Medicare and Medicaid funds; do we need to abide by the Privacy Act?*

Many programs are under the impression that they must abide by the Federal Privacy Act of 1974.[12] In fact, I have seen several confidentiality policies that begin with "According to the Federal Privacy Act of 1974 . . . " and then go on to state that "as a result, we must do so and so." In reality, the Federal Privacy Act of 1974 applies *only* to federally funded and administered programs such as Veteran's Administration hospitals and the Social Security Administration. State and local governmental programs are not affected and even those programs receiving some federal grant monies or Medicare and other funds are not required to abide by the Act. Such programs are governed instead by state and local laws, general accreditation requirements, and so forth. However, some programs treating substance abusers are affected by special federal legislation,[10] unrelated to the Privacy Act.

Several important bills concerning privacy of medical and psychiatric records have been introduced in Congress. They were developed in an attempt to extend the basic provisions and intent of the Federal Privacy Act of 1974 to state and local governmental programs and private programs receiving certain forms of federal funding. One such bill was the "Federal Privacy of Medical Information Act."[20] This legislation would have affected some private hospitals, skilled and intermediate care facilities receiving Title XIX funding; outpatient programs receiving federal funding under title III, IV, X, XI, XII, or XIII of the Public Health Service Act, title V of the Social Security Act, the Community Mental Health Centers Act, the Comprehensive Alcohol Abuse and Alcoholism

Prevention, Treatment, and Rehabilitation Act of 1970, or the Drug Abuse Prevention, Treatment, and Rehabilitation Act; and state facilities, if the state passes a statute requiring such facilities to come under the Act. The proposed Act would have mandated patient access to records (including the right to photocopies), but included important exceptions for some mental health records and instances whereby a patient could be harmed by such access. It would also have mandated informed consent for disclosures. While this particular bill may not be the one that becomes federal law, there is a strong feeling among some congressmen and professional organizations that similar legislation is needed and will eventually be implemented. In any event, the trend toward increasing consumer right of access to records, the concept of informed consent for disclosure of confidential information, and increased protection of confidential data has been well established, and many programs are keeping a close watch on federal proposals and developing internal policies that reflect the principles of the Privacy Act and related legislation.

QUESTION 3: *I am a therapist in private practice. My client is involved in divorce proceedings, and I just received a subpoena asking me to appear in court and also provide my clinical record. I'm not worried about the records—my notes are rather informal and I plan to destroy them and tell the court I don't have any records to provide, but I want to give as little information as possible when I appear on the witness stand. What can I do?*

You should seek legal consultation immediately—*before* you destroy any records! Obviously, someone already suspects you have records and if they were to discover that you destroyed them to avoid compliance with the subpoena, you might find that you need your attorney to represent you—not just to provide consultation on how to respond to the subpoena.

The real question is: "Do I have to respond to the subpoena, and how much information do I have to provide?" You do not have to respond automatically to a subpoena by providing everything it requests. You have two basic choices: answer the subpoena without question, or challenge it by presenting arguments (through your attorney) as to why you and/or your client do not want to provide the record or oral testimony. (Arguments that can be used to challenge a subpoena are available.[25]) If you and/or your client are covered by privileged communication in the state in which you practice, you would be required by state law to fight the subpoena—to refuse to disclose the data. Failure to do so could carry stiff legal penalties. Privileged communication statutes protect sensitive data from disclosure in legal proceedings, and records containing entries made by professionals who come under privileged communication statutes (or those acting as their agents) may not make disclosures in response to subpoenaes unless the client has given permission for the disclosure. In a few states (i.e. Illinois) the professional may refuse the disclosure, even if the client has authorized it, if he feels maintaining confidentiality would be in the client's best interests.

Many practitioners overreact and treat the subpoena with more reverance than it deserves. Consider this description of a subpoena offered by Maurice Grossman:

> If the recipient (of a subpoena) knew how easy it was to have a subpoena issued; if he knew how readily the subpoena could demand information when there actually was no legal right to demand the disclosure of information; if he knew how often an individual releases information that legally he had no right to release because of intimidation—he would view the threat of the subpoena with less fear and greater skepticism. A lawyer may merely attest that he believes a certain individual has certain information that is relevant to the issue at court to get a subpoena issued. These forms are transmitted to the office of the clerk of the court routinely and the clerk of the court has a staff that routinely makes out the subpoena to be served by organized processors. No one reviews the request for the subpoena. No one examines the basis for the request. No one discusses with anyone else whether there is a legal right for disclosure. No one raises the question whether information is protected by law against disclosure before the subpoena is issued.[13]

Thus, the party receiving the subpoena is responsible for studying it carefully and determining if it is valid and whether disclosure of the data sought is legal, ethical, desirable, or appropriate. If a decision is made to contest the subpoena, arguments are presented to the court, and the court then makes a ruling declaring that all or part of the data need not be produced, or ordering it be disclosed.

QUESTION 4: *My elderly client is not fully alert mentally but certainly isn't psychotic. In order to get a guardian, my client must be disoriented as to time, place, and person. But, he isn't — he's forgetful sometimes and has short periods of confusion; he is very stubborn and sometimes downright uncooperative, but he'd never meet my state's definition of legal incompetency. His nearest family member lives over 1000 miles away. Some decisions are going to have to be made regarding my client's need for medical care (though it's not a life-saving emergency) and he's going to need a change in living arrangements. I need to disclose and also gather information about him to make adequate arrangements. Yet my facility says only competent adults can sign consent forms; otherwise a guardian must authorize the disclosure. What can I do?*

I once asked this question of a hospital attorney and his reply was essentially "Let's not even ask this question. If someone raises it and demands a formal answer, we'll be forced to put into writing unworkable restrictive procedures that will make it virtually impossible to make disclosures and get patients discharged." Unfortunately, subsequent knowledge has not produced a more effective answer to this dilemma. If we are forced to obtain informed consent from individuals who fall in the gray area between competency and incompetency, social work activity could come to a screeching halt. Some persons who might meet the legal description of incompetency have no money to pay a guardian and no relatives available to serve in this capacity. Many communities have no provisions for attorneys to perform this service at little or no fee, making it virtually impossible to secure a guardian for indigent clients. In the absence of any *clear, specific* mandate requiring informed consent and/or authorization from a legal guardian, it is not too difficult to interpret social work ethics in the interest of expedience and in what would appear to be the best interests of the client. Indeed, the revised *NASW Code of Ethics*[19] challenges social workers to contest and try to change policies and practices that are detrimental to consumers. If informed consent and guardianship policies appear iron-clad and void of flexibility for the quasi-alert client, social work ethics could be interpreted as requiring the professional to abide by agency policy. However, a differing interpretation could also be applied, enabling the professional to close his eyes to stated policies and plunge ahead with what appears best for all concerned, until such time as the practice is challenged. Indeed, many practitioners operate in just this fashion. Many have never been challenged, and thus make some disclosures without patient or guardian consent. This brings us back to the attorney's statement quoted earlier. It is comparable to asking one's superior for permission to do something. Once you've been told not to do it, it's a clear violation of policy and supervisory instructions to proceed without permission. Sometimes it's better not to ask permission, do what you feel needs to be done, and worry about employer policies versus professional ethics only if someone discovers you are doing something controversial and makes a formal issue of the matter.

QUESTION 5: *The nature of my work puts me in contact with children who have suffered abuse or neglect and I sometimes work with the child abusers themselves. The abuse or neglect may be only a small part of my total involvement with the client. Thus, my records contain information regarding the abuse or neglect and also other information that is not related to this phenomenon. Our state requires that all cases of suspected abuse and neglect be reported to Protective Services, and our setting complies with this mandate. However, after we've made the referral— sometimes several month's later—Protective Services frequently contacts us asking for our entire record. Do I have to give it to them?*

You will need to study your state statutes pertaining to child abuse and perhaps also consult with your attorney for a definite answer. However, if the information that Protective Services is seeking is related to their investigation of the abuse or neglect, you will probably have to share your information. Most states provide for a rather free disclosure of information when protection of minors is involved. (A number of states also have similar provisions for protection of the aged and the developmentally disabled.) Thus, even if you said "no" when asked to share your records, Protective Services could probably obtain them rather easily through a subpoena process. Even if privileged communication statutes seem to apply to your records, most state laws exempt abuse and neglect data from privileged communication coverage, rendering it admissible in court without any penalties for violation of confidentiality. In addition, most child abuse laws provide some special protections regarding the identity of individuals reporting child abuse or neglect, permitting them to remain anonymous if desired. Professionals rarely chose to remain anonymous; indeed, the special information in their records often proves invaluable in helping the courts and Protective Services render decisions that are in the best interests of those involved in the abuse or neglect. However, if you feel that Protective Services is requesting irrelevant or excessive data, you may want to resist disclosing that portion of your record. If a subpoena is involved, you can work closely with your attorney as he responds to the subpoena by arguing that certain data should not be provided based on its lack of relevancy to the matter the court is examining.

QUESTION 6: *Three years ago I received outpatient services from the program where I now work. Our facility keeps all records for at least ten years. I don't want anyone here to know that I was once a patient; I didn't even tell my employer this when I applied for the job, for fear I'd be discriminated against. How can I protect myself in this situation?*

It may be somewhat naive to assume that your employer would never stumble upon your old record by accident. Should he learn of your prior contact with the agency, he might take offense at your dishonest approach during the employment interview. On the other hand, I have encountered several employees who have suffered significant personal and professional damage because someone gained unauthorized or accidental access to a past treatment record. In each instance, I have referred them to their attorney and/or to their professional organization, strongly urging them to initiate a grievance and/or lawsuit against the employer.

Opportunities for abuses to staff who are or have been consumers of the system that employs them appear much more widespread than acknowledged. Many human services staff who work with individuals applying for and receiving food stamps, Medicaid, AFDC, and special services, including protective services, do come across records on relatives, friends, and neighbors. It is not unusual for human services staff to be receiving financial assistance themselves, or be known to the agency as recipients prior to obtaining their present employment. Staff members in hospitals often become patients of their employer's facility when they need medical or psychiatric care, especially if the facility involved is a large teaching-research hospital, a highly specialized facility, or simply the only place to go for medical care in the community. Supervisors and administrators in such programs normally have the right of access to every record in the house—yet, they should not be looking up former or current patient records on staff out of mere curiosity. A social worker may have access to every record in the outpatient clinic yet should not be permitted to review the record of a colleague who is in therapy. Thus, the "need to know" concept must apply: only those staff with a need to know—who are directly and professionally involved in the treatment of the patient or the provision of services—should have access to the individual's record. This concept must apply to all clerical and supportive as well as professional and management staff. Thus, special precautions must be taken to prevent inappropriate access. The following basic guidelines are recommended:

A. A special written policy should be developed, covering closed and current records on current and former staff, and records on persons known to be relatives or close friends of employees.

B. All such records should be stored in a separate location from all other records.

C. Such records should be kept under lock and key at all times, even while the individual is actively receiving services or hospitalized as an inpatient.

D. Special policies should govern access to all records pertaining to employees. Ideally, persons seeking access should be required to sign for the record, giving their name, position, relationship to the client/employee, and the date of access. Some mechanism must be used to determine that each person seeking access is in fact directly involved in providing professional treatment or services to the patient. A simple statement that the individual is a nurse, a psychiatric aide, or the individual's supervisor is not adequate. It may be necessary to explore the reason for the desired access.

E. If any questions arise regarding the appropriateness of someone's request for access to an employee's record, the employee/client should be advised who desires access and encouraged to express his wishes or feelings about the proposed access.

F. All staff should be informed of the special policies in force which protect their records should they become consumers of their employer's facility or organization. Staff/consumers should be encouraged to put into writing a list of persons in the system whom they would not want gaining access to their record. This could be kept with the record and would serve as an additional safeguard against harmful disclosures.

QUESTION 7: *My employer, a private agency, is rife with politics. I even suspect that money is passing under the table as outside parties strike deals with some staff to get referrals for certain kinds of follow-up services. Everybody seems to be related to everyone else and boat rockers are disliked. I am trying to do my social work job in the best professional manner. I'm trying to keep out of the politics as much as I can. However, I'm getting hints that some of my superiors are not happy with my performance. We don't have regular written performance evaluations, but all my verbal evaluative feedback has been positive. They can't just fire me can they? They won't let me see my personnel file—don't I have a right to know what's in there?*

Most progressive facilities require periodic written performance evaluations on all employees. These usually are done upon completion of a probationary period and every year thereafter. Modern personnel practices, including NASW's personnel standards[19] allow employees access to personnel records. Ideally, oral performance evaluation feedback should be ongoing and reasonably accurate, so that written evaluations hold no surprises for the employee. Likewise, there should be nothing in the personnel file that the employee has not already seen, received a copy of, or had shared with him in some manner. All evaluations should be signed by the supervisee, indicating that a copy has been shared and received.

Unfortunately, many small agencies and numerous interdisciplinary facilities (such as hospitals) have few guidelines governing hiring, firing, and other personnel practices, other than the ones they choose to adopt. Often these policies are not expressed in black and white, thus allowing for irregularities to occur accidently or when convenient for the employer. Thus, an employee who feels he is being dismissed without adequate cause often finds that the facility has covered itself by having nothing in writing that he can use to prove that dismissal was unwarranted, based on discriminatory practices, or political in nature. A lack of written performance evaluations over a period of time can prove frustrating to the concerned employee. However, the employer's failure to keep appropriate documentation also means that the agency or department will have difficulty defending its position should an employee bring legal action against them.

Thus, to answer your question, you may find that your employer is free to set up its own personnel policies, and even fire you according to those policies, and yet be in violation of what would be considered appropriate personnel practices by others outside your system. You should consult personnel standards and recommendations of appropriate professional groups (such as NASW), licensing or accrediting bodies, and also review local laws for anything that might be useful in forcing your employer to comply with external standards. Unfortunately, neither the American Hospital Association, the Society for Hospital Social Work Directors, or the JCAH Manual on hospital accreditation offer any meaningful guidelines or standards—they simply fail to address the issue. You might choose instead to turn to the National Labor Relations Board (chapters exist in most urban areas), the American Management Association, the American Civil Liberties Union, and the National Association of Social Workers for guidance or direct action. Federal programs such as the Office of Equal Employment Opportunity can also be consulted. Unfortunately, there may be little incentive for your local facility to abide by the personnel standards promulgated by these organizations and no way of forcing them to do so, unless violation of union regulations or laws are involved. Your final recourse may be to exhaust whatever greivance or appeal mechanisms are available in your own facility, and then file a grievance through NASW for violation of its recommended personnel practices.[19] You might also find that the facility is violating one or more provisions of the NASW Code of Ethics as well. Should the NASW Committee on Inquiry find your employer in violation of NASW standards, your facility can be sanctioned publicly. NASW could, for example, warn social workers not to accept employment in your setting, and advise schools of social work not to send students there for training. It could also file a complaint with appropriate licensing and accrediting bodies and arrange for publicity in local news media as well as in the *NASW Newsletter.* (See Appendix C for Grievance Procedures) Legal action is always an alternative, and personnel records can be obtained through the subpoena process.

QUESTION 8: *I am a supervisor/administrator. I just fired an MSW social worker for incompetency and falsification of records. My other supervisees liked this individual and are demanding to know what happened to him. The grapevine is very active with various versions of what happened, and it appears that he has been telling other staff that I fired him because I didn't like him. I'd like to defend myself and deal with the staff's reactions before the situation gets out of hand, but I also feel a committment to preserving the confidentiality of information pertaining to my former employee's performance. What can I do?*

There have been several interesting lawsuits over this very issue, and in a number of instances, the courts have ruled that a supervisor is free to tell other employees why someone was dismissed or asked to resign. For example, in *Deaile v General Telephone Co of California*,[29] an employee called in sick. When the supervisor attempted to call her at home and could not reach her, he became suspicious and subsequently learned that the employee had falsified her use of sick leave, using the time instead to vacation in the mountains. There were indications that this was not the first time this employee had abused her use of sick leave. The supervisor decided to fire the employee, giving her a choice of retirement, quitting, or being fired. The employee chose to retire. She brought suit against her employer for defamation, intentional infliction of emotional distress, and wrongful discharge from employment when she learned that some of her former co-workers had been told the reasons for her forced resignation. The employer had indeed shared the real reason for her retirement with several supervisors, and one in turn passed the information on to the plaintiff's former co-workers. The employer was concerned about misconceptions circulating among staff regarding the supposed reason for the plaintiff's departure. The following statement summarizes the court's ruling on the issue of libel and slander allegedly occurring from the supervisor's sharing of confidential information:

> An employer is privileged, in pursuing its own economic interests and that of its employees, to ascertain whether an employee has breached his responsibilities of employment and, if so, to communicate, in good faith, that fact to others within its employ so that appropriate action may be taken against the employee, so that danger of such breaches occurring in

the future may be minimized, and so that present employees might not develop misconceptions that affect their employment with respect to certain conduct that was undertaken in the past.[29]

Numerous other suits have also been brought by former employees who objected to disclosures to various co-workers and others of the reasons for their dismissal. In many instances, the courts have supported the employer's actions; in others, the courts have ruled for the former staff member. Thus, you might want to consult with your attorney on this matter. A review of prior cases testing this issue could help you prepare for any possible repercussions from the action you decide to take in this matter.[23]

QUESTION 9: *My employer has very sloppy practices for maintaining the confidentiality of client records. They often lie around all over the office and are easily read or picked up by anyone who walks by a desk or table. I've heard about and also experienced situations where outside people have just walked in and read the records — there seem to be no controls to prevent this. As a result, I make my recorded entries as skimpy as possible. Much of the information I gather from working with clients concerns emotional content and sensitive, or problematic, family relationships. Unfortunately, my employer is starting to get after me, claiming that my documentation is inadequate, and I can see that my boss is becoming increasingly dissatisfied with my performance. This matter of recording has become a real bone of contention between us, and I feel it's even caused him to lose objectivity in evaluating other areas of my performance. I'm actually afraid I could end up losing my job. What can I do?*

You are facing a real dilemma: there is an obvious conflict between your employer's expectations and the requirements of the NASW Code of Ethics. Obviously, the first step would be for you to point this out to your employer and do all you can to correct the conditions you have described. If that fails, you will be faced with a choice of doing as your employer asks in spite of the obvious ethical problems, or face disciplinary action for insubordinate behavior.

You could bring a grievance against the agency through NASW. If your employer is primarily a social work agency, a grievance ruling against the agency and the resulting negative publicity could force them to correct identified violations of the Code of

Ethics. However, if the program employs only a few social workers, it may ignore the entire grievance process, considering it little more than a nuisance.

You could seek legal redress should you actually lose your job. In fact, two social workers in California were faced with a similar problem and did just that—took their employer to court when they were fired. In the case of *Belmont v California State Personnel Board,*[27] the social workers were asked to feed sensitive psychiatric data into a computer system that they believed lacked adequate confidentiality safeguards. Their refusal to submit data to the computer cost them their jobs and they sued, claiming, among other things, that if they were required to obey their employer's request, they would be forced to violate the NASW Code of Ethics. Unfortunately, the court ruled against them and even went so far as to state that "In case of conflict between allegiance by psychiatric social workers employed by Welfare Department to code of ethics and social workers' duties as employees of state, social workers were legally bound to fulfill duties of their employment or suffer disciplinary action.[27] However, it is interesting to note that when a physician has been in a similar dilemma, the court has ruled that he could not be asked to violate the American Medical Association Code of Ethics.[28, 32] It would appear discriminatory for the courts to ignore one profession's code of ethics and yet insist on compliance with the code of another discipline. Hopefully your attorney will point this out should he represent you in action against your employer.

It is important to determine if your employer's request is a lawful one—would you be breaking any laws if you were to do as he asked? In the case of *Parrish v Civil Service Commission of the County of Alameda,*[30] a social worker refused to comply with what he believed to be an illegal order on the part of his employer. This situation involved a welfare worker who was asked to participate in "midnight raids" on the homes of randomly selected, non-suspect AFDC recipients. The social worker expressed his refusal to participate in this activity in writing to his employer and was fired for insubordination. A lower court ruled against the staff member; however the Supreme Court determined that the employer did not have a constitutional right to order the search of recipients' homes and stated that "Insubordination, as ground for discharge of county employee, can be rightfully predicated only on refusal to obey some order which superior officer is entitled to give and entitled to have obeyed."[30] Thus, you may want to review the fine points in your state's laws regarding record-keeping practices, disclosures to others, and all related areas to determine if your employer is in fact violating a law as well as the NASW Code of Ethics. Put your concerns in writing to your employer and state clearly your reasons for refusing to do as he requests, quoting specific portions of state or federal laws and/or the Code of Ethics that are being violated. Should you suffer disciplinary action, your written statement could become an important part of your defense in any legal actions.

In Conclusion

The resolution of sticky situations having no agreed upon answers requires personal and professional judgment and risk. The decision to take a controversial or unprecedented action to resolve a confidentiality problem must follow a careful review of all pertinent laws, guidelines, policies, and ethical codes that might have a bearing on the situation. The informed practitioner will also make certain he is aware of all possible repercussions before making the decision that he or she feels is in the best interests of all concerned.

REFERENCES

1. Aldrich, Robert F.: *Health Records and Confidentiality: An Annotated Bibliography.* Second Edition. Washington, D.C.: National Commission on Confidentiality of Health Records, May, 1979.
2. American Medical Record Association: *Confidentiality of Patient Health Information: A Position Statement of the American Medical Record Association.* Chicago, Illinois: American Medical Record Association. Adopted by AMRA Executive Board in December 1977. [Copies may be ordered from the AMRA, 875 N. Michigan Ave., Suite 1850, Chicago, Illinois 60611.]
3. American Psychiatric Association: *Confidentiality and Third Parties.* Task Force Report 9. Washington, D.C.: APA, 1975.
4. Barbre, Erwins: Annotation: Communication to social workers as privileged. 50 *American Law Reports* 3d 563–582 and the August, 1979 supplement.

5. Bernstein, Barton E.: Privileged communications to the social worker. *Social Work, 23(4):*259–263, July 1977.

6. Bernstein, Barton E.: The social worker as a courtroom witness. *Social Casework, 25(9):*521–525, Nov. 1975.

7. Bernstein, Barton E.: The social worker as an expert witness. *Social Casework, 58(7):*412–417, July 1977.

8. Best, B. W.: Annotation: Privilege, in judicial or quasi-judicial proceedings, arising from relationship between psychiatrist or psychologist and patient," 44 *American Law Reports* 3d, 24–162 and the August, 1979 Supplement.

9. *Confidentiality of Health and Social Service Records: Where Law, Ethics and Clinical Issues Meet.* Proceedings of the Second Midwest Regional Conference, December, 1976. Chicago: University of Illinois at Chicago Circle, 1976.

10. Department of Health, Education and Welfare, Public Health Service: Confidentiality of alcohol and drug abuse patient records—general provisions. *Federal Register, 40(127):* Part IV, July 1, 1975.

11. Family Educational Rights and Privacy Act of 1974. Amends Public Law 93-568, effective November 19, 1974 (The Buckley Amendment).

12. Federal Privacy Act of 1974. Public Law 93-579, enacted December 31, 1974, and effective September 27, 1975. *Federal Register,* Parts V–VI (Wednesday, October 8, 1975).

13. Grossman, Maurice: The psychiatrist and the subpoena. *Bulletin of the American Academy of Psychiatry and Law, 1(4):* 245–253, December 1973.

14. IBM's guidelines to employee privacy: An interview with Frank T. Cary. *Harvard Business Review,* pp. 82–90, September 10, 1976.

15. Joint Commission on Accreditation of Hospitals. *JCAH Standards for General Medical Hospitals.* Chicago: JCAH, 1980. See especially the chapters concerning "Medical Record Services", "Social Work Services" and "Rights and Responsibilities of Patients."

16. Joint Commission on Accreditation of Hospitals: *JCAH Consolidated Standards for Accreditation of Psychiatric Facilities.* Chicago: JCAH, 1979. See the chapter on "Patient Records."

17. Levine, Richard Steven, Child protection records: Issues of confidentiality. *Social Work, 21(4):* 323–326, July, 1976.

18. Mironi, Mordechai, Confidentiality of personnel records: A legal and ethical view, *Labor Law Journal,* 25:270–292 May 1974.

19. National Association of Social Workers. *NASW Code of Ethics.* Adopted by the 1979 NASW Delegate Assembly, effective July 1, 1980. Washington, D.C.: National Association of Social Workers, 1980. [Copies may be ordered from NASW, 1425 H St., N.W., Suite 600, Washington, D.C. 20005. *Also see* Appendices.]

20. "Federal Privacy of Medical Information Act." H.R. 5935, introduced into the House of Representatives in March of 1980. Rejected during the session.

21. "Privacy Rights of Parents and Students," Part II. Department of Health,

Education and Welfare, Office of the Secretary. Final Rule on Education Records. *Federal Register* (June 17, 1976), pp. 24662–24675.

22. Slovenko, Ralph: Psychiatrist-patient testimonial privilege: A picture of misguided hope. *Catholic University Law Review, 23:*649–673, 1974.

23. Spivey, Gary D.: Annotation—libel and slander: Privileged nature of communication to other employees or employees' union of reasons for plaintiff's discharge." *American Law Reports,* 3d, 1080–1122.

24. Wilson, Suanna J.: *Confidentiality in Social Work: Issues and Principles.* N.Y.: Free Press, 1978.

25. Wilson, Suanna J.: Confidentiality: Some legal and ethical dilemmas. In Rosenblatt, Aaron and Waldfogel, Diana (Eds.): *Handbook of Clinical Social Work.* San Francisco: Jossey-Bass. In press.

26. Wilson, Suanna J.: *Recording: Guidelines for Social Workers.* N.Y.: Free Press, 1980.

Cases

27. *Belmont v California State Personnel Board,* 36 Cal App. 3d 518, App. III Cal. Rptr. 607 January 3, 1974.

28. *Re Cathey,* 55 Cal. 2d 679; 12 Cal. Rptr 762; 361 P2d 426 (1961).

29. *Deaile v General Telephone Co. of California,* 40 Cal. App 3d 841; App 115 Cal. Rptr. 582. July 22, 1974 p. 583.

30. *Parrish v Civil Service Commission of the County of Alameda* 57 Cal. Rptr. 623; 425 P2d 223 (March 27, 1967).

31. *Perlman v Perlman,* Index No. 5105, N.Y. Supreme Court, Bronx County, June 20, 1930. In an initial court ruling, a social worker convinced the court of the merits of confidentiality, and no disclosure was required; however, the ruling was later reversed (see *In the Matter of the City of New York* (February 1, 1931) Sup. Court, Bronx County, 91 N.Y.L.

32. *Ritt v Ritt,* 98 NJ Super 590, 238 A2d 196, rev'd on other grounds, 52 NJ 177, 244 A2d 497 (1968).

Part IV

Values and Ethics in Professional Education

Chapter 16

VALUES AND ETHICS
IN SOCIAL WORK EDUCATION

Shankar A. Yelaja

INTRODUCTION

A serious commitment to values and ethics in professional practice cannot occur unless the subject matter has received adequate emphasis during the educational preparation of professionals. Indeed, the professional schools can ill-afford to treat this with a cavalier attitude and then expect a wholehearted commitment by practitioners to ethical standards in professional behavior. In short, values and ethics must receive serious consideration in professional education if professional ethics are to be maintained.

In social work education the significance of values and ethics content has long been recognized. The accreditation standards of the U.S. Council on Social Work Education, for example, require the schools to include such content which is clearly organized into specific learning objectives and is supported by a methodology for realizing those objectives. However, despite some degree of consensus on the importance of teaching values and ethics in social work education, educators have found it difficult to infuse the content into the curriculum. The inclusion of this content is also problematic because the curriculum standards and expectations surrounding values and ethics vary enormously across the U.S. and Canada; there are still considerable and sharp differences on the best strategy to address the issues involved.

Significant curriculum issues regarding objectives, learning outcomes, content areas, location of content in the classroom/field components, teaching methods and evaluation of teaching/learning are far from resolved. Consideration of some of the issues hopefully will help clarify the place of professional values and ethics in social work education.

PROFESSIONAL SOCIAL WORK VALUES AND ETHICS

The values and ideology of social work grew out of the Judeo-Christian tradition in Western societies. So much of early social work was influenced and motivated by religious and moral values associated with Judeo-Christian tenets that social work and religious morality were inseparable. The humanitarianism of eighteenth century philosophers and the liberalism of nineteenth century social thinkers helped to moderate the religious influence. Although philosphical influences from positivistic and humanistic schools of thought did not take away the central influence of religion and charity on social work, they paved the way for more secularization of social work values. As social work became more concerned with a science-based, technologically oriented profession, and consequently increasingly secular in its value orientation, it was required to eliminate religious bias from its basic assumptions.

Some have argued that science as a value-free discipline cannot adopt a set of moral values. Professional values, therefore, have become paradoxical. On the one hand, social work is a normative profession that has been founded upon religious/humanistic values; on the other hand, it is a scientifically oriented profession committed to a technology of finding better methods for helping people. Social work grew out of a value tradition, but in acquiring a scientifically based professional status it must confront its heritage and deal with it. Others have argued that social work has and will always remain a value-based, normative profession.

The value assumptions of social work have been discussed at length in Chapters 1 and 2 of this book. Whereas each social worker is free to base his or her commitment on the values derived from a personal philosophical and/or religious ideology, the profession has attempted to make the value assumption the *terminus a quo* of its ideological system (Bloch and Bonovich, 1981).

Social work has, by choice, commited itself to being a profession. The choice now is a foregone conclusion. As all other professions, it is accountable to society; functionally delimited in terms of purpose, goals, etc.; socially sanctioned; and required to maintain ethical standards of behavior, as well as collective responsibility for acts of commission and omission (Bloch and Bonovich, 1981). Professionals enjoy power and privileges, but there are sanctions if these are abused. Professional ethics, which are defined as values in action, essentially consist of the *rules of professional conduct* that guide the action of social workers. They represent ideal behavior expectations or preferred behavioral patterns. The ethics are derived from the values with which social workers have identified. While values are concerned with what is good, ethics are generally concerned with what is right.

According to Charles Levy there are three functions for professional ethics in social work: to serve as a guide to professional conduct; to serve as a set of principles that the social worker can apply in the performance of professional duties; and to serve as a set of criteria by which social workers' practice can be evaluated (Levy, 1976). Professional ethics is also a prerequisite for competent practice. The current ethical codes of social work professional associations in Britain, Canada, and the United States appear in the appendix of this book. Implicitly, the codes assume that a commitment to ethical standards and behavior in practice is a *sine qua non* of a competent, effective, and responsible social worker.

VALUES AND ETHICS IN SOCIAL WORK EDUCATION

Should social work education be value free or value laden? Dilemmas surrounding this question arise in a number of educational issues including curriculum policy, objectives, and educational style. Those supporting a value free philosophy and approach to social work education argue the need to place more emphasis on cognitive development than on developing allegiance to persons, groups, or a set of specific beliefs. Gross, Rosa, and Steiner (1980) write: "The paramount value for persons who support a value-free educational style is to develop the rational, cognitive capacities of students so that they come to know more about the world as it is. This focus on cognitive is sometimes referred to as valuing 'truth for its own sake'." The essential emphasis in educational philosophy is to help social work students understand and develop a picture of the social work context as it is and not as one might wish or prefer it to be.

Those supporting the value-laden educational philosophy and style argue that science is not value-free. Our notions of rationality, truth, and the scientific methods used to discover these are quite clearly influenced by values. Furthermore, it is suggested that rationality and truth are not the ultimate end-goals. They are only a means to some other goals self-determined by individuals and groups. Finally, the very purpose of university education is questioned by supporters of the value-laden philosophy. Cognition, according to them, is secondary to affective types of objectives one must seek through an educational experience. Social work education, according to this view, should emphasize instruction on values and ethics. An educational environment and milieu that allows students to develop affective responses to personal and professional values is seen as an essential element of social work educational philosophy.

A state of continuing tension between various educational philosophies and doctrines has positive effects on social work by clarifying the values and ethical code of behavior expected of its members. Social workers' commitment to values and ethics will continue to be tested in the context of the debate on varying educational philosophies and doctrines. Social work is a profession of many faces and therefore a clash in educational philosophy is inevitable.

Most social work educators would agree that without an implicit reference to values and ethics, it is impossible to prepare effective social work practitioners. However, there are strong and divergent opinions on the explicit emphasis, the relative importance of this curriculum content, on whether there should be specialized courses on values and ethics or if the content should be integrated into various parts of the social work curriculum, and whether the content should be required or left to students' needs and interests.

A survey of social work curricula on values and ethics conducted by this writer in 1979 revealed that only a dozen graduate schools in the U.S.A. and Canada had specialized courses on values and ethics. In these schools the courses were listed with a specific title, the content was clearly defined, the credit hours were listed, and the students were expected to take the course for meeting degree requirements. In a majority of schools the content was not identified in a separate course but was referred to in a number of courses pertaining to foundation (core) knowledge curriculum, social work methods courses, and practicum instruction. Some schools offered an elective on social work values and ethics, and still others cited in their calendar courses offered in other disciplines (e.g. philosophy); students had the option of taking these courses. This state of affairs has not substantially changed since the curriculum study report by Muriel Pumphrey (1959), who noted that the content on values' and ethics was frequently omitted from specific compilations of essential learning components. Joseph Vigilante's (1974) observation that "values have received only superficial attention from scholars, theory builders and curriculum designers" reinforces the current state of affairs regarding the place of values and ethics in social work education.

The Council on Social Work Education's accreditation standards governing values and ethics content reflect the uneasiness and tension among social work educators. The statement on standards, which is derived from a curriculum policy for the Master's degree program in graduate schools of social work, is broad enough to allow freedom to individual schools of social work to develop this curriculum content. The policy states:

> Professional competence in social work derives from the acquisition of knowledge, values and skills learned in the basic curriculum.... The professional curriculum for social work draws broadly and selectively from the humanities, from other professions and scientific disciplines, as well as from the knowledge and experience developed by social work. Application of this context to social work involves ethical as well as scientific commitment. The study and analysis of ethical considerations is an important component of the social work education. (Council of Social Work Education, 1971)

Current standards allow considerable discretionary judgment on how values and ethics content ought to be interpreted by individual schools of social work. Two of the 1979 revised accreditation standards state:

> A dean or director of a school of social work shall bring to the post demonstrated...commitment to the ethical values of the social work profession, and
>
> The focus of examination of a program of basic professional social work education shall include an assessment of adherence to the ethical values of the profession of social work.... (Commission on Accreditation Activities Report, 1979)

The standards, however, do not spell out the concept of social work values, nor do they state the criteria to be used for evaluating adherence to professional ethics. In summary, then, educational policy statements adopted by individual schools of social work across the U.S.A. and Canada represent diversity rather than uniformity in adhering to the curriculum standards.

The educational policy statement of the Canadian Association of Schools of Social Work makes an implicit reference to values and ethics. Thus the C.A.S.S.W. (1972) educational policy on social work education at the second (Master's degree) level states: "The curriculum shall emphasize the acquisition of skills in the analysis and criticism of social work values, goals, policies, theories and practices." The current curriculum differences can be traced to sharply differing views on the relative importance of this curriculum as compared to other curriculum areas.

Social work educators do not share a consensus on the issue of the central importance of values and ethics content in the professional curriculum. Several reasons can be cited for this. These are well summarized by Bloch and Bonovich (1981):

(1) Ethics is based on religion and we must take care to maintain separation between religion and secularism.
(2) Given the pluralistic nature of our society, we run the risk of highlighting certain values and ethical systems and fail by ignoring or underemphasizing others.
(3) Students must exercise their right to moral freedom.
(4) If we teach ethics as secular, we may be undercutting its religious roots.
(5) Educators will "push" private ethics and "pull" their students toward their own private morality.
(6) In teaching the content on values and ethics, there is a perennial fear of indoctrination.
(7) The very selection of ethical problems and the choice of emphasis within the content may be influenced by a "teaching bias."
(8) If values and ethics are not taught as indoctrination, the curriculum content becomes wishy-washy.
(9) If a deliberate attempt is made to steer away from indoctrination, then who decides on the issues, problems etc. to be examined in the course?
(10) If ethics is taught value free, its teaching can become a misleading and distorted educational experience for the student.

There is no doubt that support for one or more of these reasons can be found among social work educators who feel uneasy about giving this content a central or explicit significance in the social work curriculum.

If the content on values and ethics were left entirely to the discretion of students, chances are that it would end up becoming a chaotic experience in their professional education. This writer believes that an implicit reference to values and ethics is not sufficient insurance for effective professional practice. Ethical problems and value conflicts are inherent in social work practice. Therefore, students must be provided knowledge, methods, and skills in approaching problem resolution in their professional education.

Callahan and Bok (1980) argue that morality and moral rules are part of professional life. How they are perceived, understood, and responded to can make a difference to professional life and there are better and worse ways of dealing with them. The consideration of ethical problems and issues is necessary in professional education. Charles Levy underscores the significance of teaching ethics:

> The objective is not to equivocate about social work ethics and about the values on which it is premised, but to open the door of the student's mind to those factors bearing on the ethical issues confronted in social work practice so that the student will consider them adequately before choosing a course of action. The very nature of the student's educational experience should reflect the humility, contemplation, sensibility, yes even torment— that may be necessary before the student can feel confident that he has thought about everything he should think about and done all that he can do in fulfilling his ethical responsibilities in his work and in his relationships with clients, colleagues, employees, society and anyone or anything else that might be affected by his action or inaction. (Levy, 1976)

Ruth Smalley holds a similar point of view:

> The purpose of social work education is to give the student the opportunity both to understand *social work purposes and values and to deepen his commitment to them,* even as he becomes knowledgeable and skillful about ways of working toward this realization with the purview of his profession and through the use of its distinctive method. (emphasis added) (Smalley, 1967)

A further argument for giving explicit, special, and central attention to values and ethics in social work education can be made on the following grounds:

- Whether we like it or not, students are already exposed to and are assimilating values from a variety of sources during their professional education.
- Values and ethics cannot be disassociated from what students do in their field practice.
- Students need help in clarifying values, sorting out the complex issues, understanding the ambiguities, dilemmas, paradoxes, and controversies.
- Students benefit from faculty expertise in understanding and hopefully in resolving ethical conflicts as they are encountered in a number of practice situations and contexts during their educational period.
- Failure to impart instruction in values and ethics can result in poorly preparing students to face the real world in which value and ethical conflicts abound. They are expected to act on them. Their own personal and professional conduct is always under scrutiny.

Although one can understand the discomfort among social work educators in giving a central emphasis to values and ethics in the social work curriculum, they can ill afford to avoid the professional responsibility and obligation to students learning to become competent professionals. The content cannot be left to an accidental discovery by students; they would have missed a very valuable aspect of professional education, namely self-awareness and growth through resolving value conflicts and ethical problems.

WHAT ARE THE LEARNING OBJECTIVES?

Learning objectives for this curriculum content can be separated for graduate and undergraduate social work curriculum. Five graduate educational objectives identified by Callahan and Bok (1980) would be useful to consider:

i *To stimulate the moral imagination of students.*
... to recognize that there is a moral point of view ..., that human beings live their lives in a web of moral relationships, that a consequence of moral theories and rules can be either suffering or happiness..., that the moral dimensions of life are as often hidden as

visible, and that moral choices are inevitable and often difficult.

ii *To stimulate the student to recognize ethical issues.*

. . . the goal of a recognition of ethical issues [is] to be a conscious rational attempt to sort out those elements in emotional response that represent appraisal and judgement, however inchoate at first. Part of such an attempt will require the examination of concepts, of prescriptive moral statements and of ethical principles and moral rules.

iii *To elicit a sense of moral obligation that will lead to action.*

. . . a major point of ethics is that of the guidance of conduct, not only how I ought to direct my behavior toward others, but also what I ought to be able to claim from others in terms of their behavior toward me (and those to whom I am professionally responsible). A necessary condition for moving outside of our minds and emotions into the realm of behavior is that (1) we recognize action as an outcome of ethical judgement . . . , and (2) that we *will* to act on the basis of our judgement.

iv *To develop the student's analytical skills.*

As much as anything else, the development of analytical skills will be simply the development of logical skills. Coherence and consistency are minimal goals. . . .

v *To develop in the student the ability to tolerate and reduce disagreement and ambiguity.*

Disagreements exist in all fields, and uncertainty is not confined to ethics. But ethics takes most of the prizes in that respect, and if students are not prepared to accept and live with that reality, they will not be able to make the progress that is possible in ethics.

Muriel Pumphrey (1959), on the other hand, suggests slightly different learning objectives, citing the following educational objectives for this curriculum area:

(1) comprehension of values, and ethical judgments as human phenomena —understanding of the philosophic-spiritual component in every life situation;

(2) appreciation of different values systems, including one's own;

(3) awareness of typical professional positions with respect to values and ethics;

(4) ability to interpret social work value positions;

(5) ability to withstand pressures to change value positions and ethical judgments;

(6) recognition of classic conflict positions in a social work situation;

(7) ability to use professional procedures and channels in solving conflicts;

(8) appreciation of common ultimate goals of many branches of the profession and recognition of the unity of purpose in these diverse efforts;

(9) ability to use one's own value systems in a helping relationship; and,

(10) use of common professional goals as motivation for professional creativity.

The content of the curriculum and of the total school experience, according to the report, must provide for such patterns of thinking and acting in students so that professional social workers can be counted on ordinarily to behave in these ways. Objectives should include material needed to acquaint the prospective social worker with the nature of professional interchange with the general culture, colleagues, and clientele.

There is a fair degree of consensus among social work educators that values and ethics should be included in the undergraduate social work program. For example, the Canadian Association of Schools of Social Work (1972), in specifying curriculum standards applicable to the first university level (B.S.W.), among other items states "The curriculum shall offer the student opportunities to acquire the ability to identify value issues and assumptions which are associated with the human behavior, social problems, and the act of professional intervention." It is important to note, however, that no explicit reference to a professional ethical code is implied here. The exclusion of this content in the undergraduate social work curriculum is a significant omission.

I suggest that curriculum learning objectives for undergraduate programs need to be clearly articulated and differentially separated from the graduate program. Social work students must acquire skills for practical application of critical thinking. They need also to develop their abilities for analyzing ethical problems and deciding upon relevant principles for professional action. Frank Lowenberg (1978) argues that undergraduate social work students should be introduced to existing professional codes of ethics. Professional education, no matter where it is offered, must concern itself with socialization to professional ethics. He goes on to argue that teachers should attempt to structure learning conditions in order to create situations that will enhance learning and foster the internalization of professional ethics. Conditions and situations that are conducive to achieving this objective include:

1. new situations in which the student cannot cope using only his or her present knowledge and behavior guides;
2. situations characterized by conflicting demands or cross-pressures aris-

ing out of social inconsistencies for which the student's present knowledge and behavior guides are inadequate;

3. conditions where the student must associate with people who utilize entirely different behavioral guides, particularly when the student's own reference group is far away or prescribes norms that are not relevant in the present situation. (Lowenberg, 1978)

Specific content on values and ethics in undergraduate curriculum ought to be geared to a level that is less abstract and more concrete to avoid confusion and chaotic thinking. As one law educator succinctly stated, it is very easy to produce mushy heads with instruction on professional ethics.

Learning objectives at the undergraduate level ought to emphasize experiential learning because students are able to learn, clarify, and sort out values through directly experiencing them. Koerin (1977) suggests that special consideration be given to students who question social work values. It is very tempting to label these students as early professional deviants who are not playing the social work game. Yet these questioning students might pave the way for considering and examining issues the profession may have ignored or totally neglected.

The learning objective and content areas listed below can serve as focal points for consideration and attention in the graduate as well as undergraduate curriculum. The main differential between the two levels of education would center around the depth to be realized in these objectives and the theoretical/conceptual level of sophistication required for pursuing them. Some of the more important educational objectives follow:

To—

- Enhance capacity to identify and conceptualize characteristic values, value controversies, and value dilemmas in social work practice and for the social work practitioner
- Sharpen conceptual understanding of values and professional ethics and the capacity to use such understanding in analysis, criticism, and discussion
- Develop awareness of and ability to come to terms with one's own value positions and conflicts, in the direction of integrity and integration as a professional practitioner
- Appreciate the complexity in the resolution of value dilemmas and ethical conflicts and to anticipate means to resolution of

such dilemmas and possible consequences for clients, professional, and society

Possible objects of attention in the curriculum may include the following:

- Basic theoretical concepts, definitions, theories of ethical reasoning
- Distinction between facts and values
- Comparative value systems
- Professional ethics, and ethical code of social work profession
- Value considerations in various aspects of social work practice including fields of service, methods of intervention, etc.
- Values and ethical issues in social policy, such as abortion, work ethic, privacy, euthanasia, discrimination
- Ethical problems for social work professionals such as manipulation, confidentiality, advocacy, client participation, racism, use of conflict
- Examination of the ethical code to determine possible areas and points of conflict in practice
- Attributes of ethical social work practice
- Comparative review of ethical codes of allied helping disciplines and professions

VALUES AND ETHICS IN FIELD INSTRUCTION CURRICULUM

The importance of values and ethics in field instruction arises out of the notion that field teachers serve as models for professional practice. Field teachers have a direct impact on the social work student in applying knowledge, values, and skills to practice situations. This is where the value dilemmas and ethical conflicts are transformed into real, concrete issues and concerns. In a total educational experience the student moves from a classroom world of esoteric knowledge concepts and theories to the concrete reality of testing these in practice. Field teachers, therefore, have a crucial professional responsibility in assisting students to establish linkages between various parts of the curriculum, including values and ethics.

In a classroom context social work educators can emphasize behavioral expectations of professional ethics. They can transmit knowledge about professional ethics, about specific material describing the code, and about review procedures for monitoring, etc. However, this knowledge remains ineffective unless and until the students have had an opportunity to test it in practice situations. When students experience and test newly learned ethics and different behavior styles, the knowledge becomes personally meaningful:

> Teachers and field instructors would be derelict if they did not present their students with people and groups whose behaviors, life styles, and problems are quite different from those which they have been accustomed to work with in the past. It is precisely these types of new experiences that will facilitate the testing and adoption of professional ethics. (Lowenberg, 1978)

The onus of professional responsibility on field teachers for providing practice opportunities to test out ethical conflicts is so great that not all field teachers and social agencies can do it. Selection of teachers and agencies capable of fulfilling this responsibility and expectation is therefore one of the key elements in the overall strategy of improving the quality of field instruction.

One of the problems in integrating values and ethics between classroom and field agency has to do with compatible teacher models. Eleanor Judah draws our attention to this problem. In a study on the values of social workers and the effect of education on professional socialization, Judah found that there was incongruence between campus and field faculty. On three of the four values, namely equal rights, service, psychodynamic mindedness, and universalism;

> ... the two groups of mentors had contrasting value profiles. Campus faculty scored highest and field instructors lowest on both Equal Rights and Universalism while field instructors scored highest and campus faculty lowest on psycho-dynamic mindedness ... it appears that the class and field faculty presented different models for socialization. ... (Judah, 1979)

Clearly incompatible models will lead to further ambiguities and inconsistencies in developing role/behavioral models for students. Without the congruence between classroom and field faculty on ethical behavior, there is the perennial danger of one being pitted against the other, leaving the student confused in his search for a professional ethical model.

WHO SHALL TEACH VALUES AND ETHICS?

Teaching resources for this curriculum content are an important element in the overall strategy for quality improvement. One of the resources is the teacher/educator. Who ought to teach the courses on values and ethics? This is an intriguing question mainly because the content does not fall neatly within the traditional divisions of social work curriculum, nor does it follow the usual patterns of teaching assignments in schools of social work. For example, most schools of social work organize their curriculum on the basis of methods of practice (direct service to individuals, families and groups; community work; social policy; administration); fields of practice (micro-macro); or fields of service (aging, child welfare, minority groups, health, justice, poverty); core knowledge and specific practice competency knowledge, methods of professional intervention and skills, etc. Faculty assignments follow the pattern of curriculum organization. It is fair to say that faculty members have developed their teaching experience along the lines suggested above. There are relatively few faculty members willing to stake their claim on values and ethics as their area of primary teaching interest and competence.

Should this content then be taught by adjunct faculty members drawn from other departments, such as philosophy? Should it be taught by the social work faculty? If so, by whom? Faculty members in micro areas or macro areas? What kinds of special preparations are needed for the social work faculty? Some schools of social work have managed to attract faculty from philosophy departments to teach values and ethics courses. This is encouraging, but the problem is that social work students often feel that philosophers cannot always connect to the practical world of social workers. According to them, philosophers tend to be esoteric and somewhat removed from the level of their vantage point of inquiry and thinking on ethical issues. On the one hand, social workers must have the grounding in specialized knowledge of philosophy in such areas as metaethics, theories and methods of philosophical reasoning, inquiry, etc., but on the other hand, the students also require help in translating these theories into practice realities. We cannot leave it to philosophers to establish for us connecting linkages with practice issues. Team-teaching is one answer for integrating the theory and practice areas. It is not only a question of educational pedagogy, but also of integrating the knowledge and methods for problem solving in social work.

Faculty members teaching the course content and drawn from macro as well as micro areas of social work curriculum require specialized preparation to teach this content. The preparation for teaching values and ethics would include such areas as grounding in theories and methods of value education; approaches to moral values education; values clarification methods; teaching methods for clarifying ethical conflicts (e.g., use of decision making theory); approaches to teaching professional ethics; use of case studies and case material in teaching values and ethics; and innovative approaches to teaching values awareness.

One of the other significant aspects of teacher preparation has to do with helping teachers develop self-awareness about their own personal and professional values and ethics. Teachers cannot always do this by themselves. In-service training programs and continuing education opportunities can be immensely helpful in expanding the limits of self-awareness. Milton Rokeach (1973) suggests that value education programs will turn out to be illusory or self-deceptive if the role focus is on the students' own values. Self-awareness and self-understanding are but the opposite sides of the coin of social awareness and understanding.

Although there is no empirical evidence, it may well be that a majority of educators teaching the courses are from macro areas. Furthermore, the faculty teaching this content may not necessarily have received specialized instruction, although increasing numbers of faculty members are updating their skills through curriculum development workshops, in-service training, etc. There is a growing awareness among social work faculty interested in teaching the content for the need to receive specialized instruction, as witnessed by some doctoral programs geared to fulfilling this need. Without special preparation through in-service training in cooperation with philosophy departments, centers for the study of ethics, and curriculum institutes and workshops, it would be impossible to expect anything approaching quality. A small but significant number of social work faculty members have already begun to approach preparation for teaching as a top priority. What is also needed, however, are innovative and imaginative ways and means of organizing the curriculum.

INNOVATIONS FOR QUALITY IN CURRICULUM

If there is one area in the social work education that urgently calls for innovation, it is that of values and ethics. Innovations for upgrading quality and curriculum improvements can be considered along these lines:

Involving university philosophy departments in inter-disciplinary teaching holds considerable promise and can pay rich dividends to social work students and faculty alike. Social workers are not alone; they do not have to rediscover the wheel. Other professions experience similar ethical problems. We can learn from each other. Social workers need tools and methods for understanding values and ethics. Philosophers can help us acquire these.

Organizing debating societies in schools of social work can help immensely. Controversies are better understood when subjected to rational thinking through a debating process. When a controversial topic is discussed or examined through a debate, differing arguments become alive. Application of debate method as a teaching format in imparting instruction on social work values and ethics has been successfully demonstrated in a course that the writer has taught for the past several years (Yelaja, 1980). Further innovations along this line need to be considered and explored.

Liaison with institutes and centers on applied ethics (e.g. Hastings Institute) being established in and outside of universities can be useful resources in providing training for social work faculty.

Continuing education and in-service training of faculty teaching the courses help them become better prepared and equipped to teach the subject matter.

Building and developing social work literature on values and ethics is essential, since much of the literature currently used comes from outside the mainstream of social work (e.g. this writer had to depend on a medical ethics text for a social work ethics course until Charles Levy's book, *Social Work Ethics* (1976), became available).

CONCLUSION

Social work is a professional service through which society attempts to actualize its human welfare values. Social workers have emphasized the value base of their profession. Their practice is based on value assumptions. In one of her eloquent writings on values in social work education, Helen Perlman (1976) forcefully argues that values give a sense of purpose and direction to what social workers believe, but as soon as social workers move from belief to action, from the abstract to the concrete, and from ultimate to proximate values, then the conflicts, the differences, and the varied interpretations of values begin. She further states that a value has small worth if it cannot be transmitted from idea or conviction into some form, quality, or direction of behavior. Because of the inevitability of such conflicts, some guidelines for choosing and deciding among values cannot be left to an accidental discovery in social work education.

A professional ethical code is helpful in two ways: it provides the social worker with a set of guides or principles that can be applied in practice; and, it is designed to protect present and future clients who have no way of evaluating the competence and integrity of social work service. Students must be given a structured and organized experience in clarifying value conflicts and ethical problems during their professional education if we hope to prepare them as effective and competent social workers to face a real practice world. Failure to do so, or anything short of this expectation, is unethical for social work educators.

REFERENCES AND BIBLIOGRAPHY

Aptekar, Herbert H.: Basic values in North American social work. *International Social Work*, November 1967.

Bartlett, Harriett: Toward clarification and improvement of social work practice. *Social Work*, p. 3–9, April 1958.

Becker, Howard J.: The nature of a profession. In *Education for the Professions.* Chicago, University of Chicago Press, 1962.

Biestek, Felix J.: *The Casework Relationship.* Chicago, Loyola University Press, 1957.

Bisno, Herbert: *The Philosophy of Social Work.* Washington, D.C., Public Affairs Press, 1952.

Bloch, Mary and Bonovich, Robert: Material prepared for the Curriculum Development Institute on Ethics in Social Work. Annual program meeting of the Council on Social Work Education, Louisville, Kentucky: March 8, 1981. (Unpublished.)

Boehm, Werner: The role of values in social work. *The Jewish School Service Quarterly*, 26, June 1950.

Boehm, Werner: Value Issues in Social Work—Perspectives on Curriculum Development. Paper delivered at the annual program meeting of the Council on Social Work Education, Philadelphia, March 1. 1976.

Bosh, Samuel J. and Rehr, Helen: *A Professional Search into Values and Ethics in Health Care Delivery.* Doris Siegal Memorial Colloquium, New York City, May 1977.

Bowers, Swithun, O.M.I.: Social work as a helping and healing profession. *The Social Worker* (Canada), 24, October 1956.

Buhler, Charlotte: *The Values in Psychotherapy.* Glencoe, Illinois, Free Press, 1962.

Callahan, Daniel, and Bok, Sissela: *Ethics Teaching in Higher Education.* New York: Plenum Press, 1980, pp. 64–68.

Canadian Association of Schools of Social Work: *Manual of Standards and Procedures for the Accreditation of Programs of Social Work Education.* Ottawa, C.A.S.S.W., 1972.

Cohen, Nathan: Humanitarianism in search of a method. In *Social Work in the American Tradition.* New York, Holt, Rinehart & Winston, 1958.

Commission on Accreditation Activities Reported. *Social Work Education Reporter,* 27:14, January, 1979.

Costin, Lela B.: Values in social work education: A study. *Social Service Review,* 38, September 1964.

Council on Social Work Education: *Manual of Accrediting Standards for Graduate Professional Schools of Social Work.* New York, Council on Social Work Education, April 1971.

de Schweinitz, Karl: Social values and social action—The intellectual base as illustrated in the study of history. *The Social Service Review, 30(2):*June 1956.

Emmet, Dorothy: Ethics and the social worker. *British Journal of Psychiatric Social Work, 6:*4, 1962.

Frankel, Charles: Social philosophy and the professional education of social workers. *Social Service Review, 33:*345–359, 1959.

Frankel, Charles: Social values and professional values. *Journal of Education for Social Work, 5(1):*29–35, 1969.

Gordon, William E.: A critique of the working definition of social work practice. *Social Work,* October 1967.

Gordon, William E.: Knowledge and value; Their distinction and relationship in clarifying social work practice. *Social Work,* July 1965.

Gow, Kathleen: *Yes Virginia There is Right and Wrong.* Toronto, John Wiley & Sons, 1980.

Gross, Gerald M., Rosa, Linda and Steiner, Joseph: Educational doctrines and social work values: Match or mismatch? *Journal of Education for Social Work, 16(3):*13–24, Fall 1980.

Halmso, Paul: *The Faith of the Counsellors.* New York, Schocken Books, 1966.

Halmos, Paul (Ed.): *Moral Issues in the Training of Teachers and Social Workers.* Keele, Staffordshire, University College of North Staffordshire, 1960.

Handler, Joel: *The Coercive Social Worker.* Chicago, Markham, 1974.

Hartmann, Heinz: *Psychoanalysis and Moral Values.* New York, International Universities Press, 1960, p. 121.

Hart, Gordon M.: *Values Clarification for Counsellors.* Springfield, Illinois, Charles C Thomas, Publishers, 1978.

Hays, Dorothy, and Varley, Barbara: Impact of social work education on student's values. *Social Work,* p. 401, July 1965.

Howard, Donald: *Social Welfare: Values, Means and Ends.* New York, Random House, 1969.

Judah, Eleanor H.: Values: The uncertain component in social work education. *Journal of Education for Social Work, 15(2):*79–86, 1979.

Keith, L. A.: Ethics in social work. In *Encyclopedia of Social Work.* Washington, D.C., National Association of Social Workers, 1971, pp. 324–329.

Kendall, Katherine A. (Ed.): *Social Work Values in an Age of Discontent.* New York, Council on Social Work Education, 1970.

Klenk, R. W. and Ryan, E. M.: Philosophy and values in social work practice. In *The Practice of Social Work.* Belmont, California, The Wadsworth Publishing Co., 1970.

Koerin, B.: Values in social work education: Implications for baccalaureate degree programs. *Journal of Education for Social Work, 13(2):*84–90, 1977.

Kohs, S. C.: *The Roots of Social Work.* New York, New York Association Press, 1966.

Laycock, Joseph E.: Values and operating principles of the profession. *The Social Worker* (Canada), 35, September 1967.

Levy, Charles: The context of social work ethics. *Social Work, 17(2):*95–101, March 1972.

Levy, Charles: The value base of social work. *Journal of Education for Social Work, 9(1):*35, Winter 1973.

Levy, Charles: *Social Work Ethics.* New York, Behavioral Publications, 1976.

Lewis, Harold: Morality and the politics of practice. *Social Casework,* p. 404, July 1972.

Lowenberg, Frank: Values and ethics in social work education. In *Educating the Baccalaureate Social Worker.* Cambridge, Mass., Baillinger Publishing Company, 1978.

Lundberg, George A.: Can science validate ethics? *Bulletin of the American Association of University Professors,* 36, Summer 1950.

McCormick, Mary J.: *Enduring Values in a Changing Society.* New York, Family Service Association of America, 1971.

McCormick, Mary J.: Professional codes and the educational process. *Journal of Education for Social Work,* 2, Fall 1966.

McCormick, Mary J.: Professional responsibility and the professional image. *Social Casework,* p. 635, December 1966.

McCormick, Mary J.: The role of values in social functioning. *Social Casework,*

February 1961.

McCormick, Mary: The role of values in the helping process. *Social Casework,* January 1961.

McCormick, Mary J. (Ed.): *The Social Workers' Code of Ethics: A Critique and Guide.* New York, National Association of Social Workers, 1964.

McCormick, Mary J.: Dimensions of social work values in the United States: Implications for social work education. *International Social Work, 12(3):*14–28, 1969.

N.A.S.W.: *Values in Social Work: A Re-examination.* New York, National Association of Social Workers, 1967.

Perlman, Helen H.: Believing and doing: Values in social work education. *Social Casework, 57(6)z:*381–390, 1976.

Plant, Raymond: *Social and Moral Theory in Casework.* London, Routledge and Kegan Paul, 196.

Pumphrey, Muriel W.: *The Teaching of Values and Ethics in Social Work Education,* vol. XIII of the Curriculum Study. New York, Council on Social Work Education, 1959.

Pumphrey, Muriel W.: Transmitting values and ethics through social work practice. *Social Work,* 6, July, 1961.

Raths, Louise B., Marmin, Merrill, and Simon, Sidney: *Values and Teaching: Working With Values in the Classroom.* Columbus, Ohio, Charles E. Merrill Publishing Company, 1966.

Report of the Intercultural Seminar, The East-West Centre, Hawaii: *An Intercultural Exploration Universals and Differences in Social Work Values, Functions, and Practice.* New York, C.S.W.E., 1966.

Rokeach, Milton: The e of human values and value systems. *The Nature of Human Values.* New York, The Freeman Press, 1973, pp. 3–25.

Rokeach, Milton: *Understanding Human Values: Individual and Societal.* New York, The Free Press, 1979.

Romanyshyn, John: *Social Welfare: Charity to Justice.* New York, Random House, 1971.

Schneiderman, Leonard: The value commitment of social work: Some underlying assumptions. In Klenk, Robert W., and Ryan, Robert M. (Eds.): *The Practice of Social Work.* Belmont, Calif., Wadsworth, 1974.

Simon, Sidney, Howe, Leland W., and Kirschenborum, Howard: *Values Clarification: A Handbook of Practical Strategies for Teachers and Students.* New York, Hart Publishing Company, Inc., 1972.

Siporin, Max: Social work philosophy. In *Introduction to Social Work Practice.* New York, Macmillan, 1975.

Smalley, Ruth Elizabeth: *Theory for Social Work Practice.* New York, Columbia University Press, 1967.

Stein, Herman: Reflections on competence and ideology in social work education. *Journal of Education for Social Work,* p. 81–90, Spring 1969.

Stein, Herman et al.: Teachability and application of social work. *International*

*Social Work, 12(1):*23–25, 1969.

Tillich, Paul: The philosophy of social work. *Social Service Review, 36(1):*13–16, March 1962.

Turner, F. J.: A comparison of procedures in the treatment of clients with two different value operations. *Social Casework, 45:*273–277, May 1964. (Also in Turner, *Differential Diagnosis,* p.p. 615–627.)

Turner, Francis J.: Effect of value re-evaluation on current practice. *Social Casework,* May, 1975.

Vigilante, Joseph: Between values and science: Education for the professional during a moral crisis or is proof truth. *Journal of Education for Social Work,* 10, 1974.

Yelaja, Shankar A. (Ed.): *Authority and Social Work: Concept and Use.* Toronto, University of Toronto Press, 1971.

Yelaja, Shankar A.: Teaching Values and Ethics Through a Debate Format. Paper presented at the Educational Innovation Exchange Session, annual program meeting, Council on Social Work Education, Los Angeles, California, March 1980. (Unpublished.)

Younghusban, Eileen: *Social Work and Social Values.* London, Allen and Unwin, 1967.

Younghusban, Eileen: Intercultural aspects of social work. *Journal of Education for Social Work, 2(1):*59–65, Spring 1966. (Also in Klenk and Ryan: *The Practice of Social Work.*

Appendices

CASE STUDIES

This set of case studies has been constructed in order to provide the reader with a situation in which he/she may test his/her individual awareness of the ethical considerations brought to bear in specific chapters of this text. The author/authors of each chapter is not responsible for the production or content of these case studies. These cases were specifically designed to contain as much information as possible on the basis of which the social workers must make their professional decisions. The cases, therefore, include essential ingredients of an ethical problem or a conflict situation. Any similarity between these cases and actual cases is accidental, even though these cases are intentionally designed to reflect real cases. In each case, there is an attempt to present different positions or viewpoints derived from the standpoint of differing ethical values. Some artificiality may creep into the construction of these cases, but it is hoped that the reader will overlook this in favor of setting up a useful comparison between these case studies and the situations he/she encounters in his/her day-to-day practice. It is impossible to come up with one case that will cover all possible variations in individual cases; therefore, it is hoped that the reader will employ these cases as useful models for analyzing ethical problems and in arriving at a professional decision that is ethically responsible and defensible.

HOMOSEXUAL CLIENTS

As a social worker for a city welfare agency I have constantly been amazed by the range and diversity of new cases I am asked to deal with each week, but this case was the first occasion in which I was faced with dealing with one aspect of the "homosexual problem," or as some radical homosexuals preferred to call it, the "heterosexual problem." In the university I had been confronted by a group of outspoken "gays" whose flamboyant behavior and radical social/political views stretched my liberal tolerance to its limits. Sexual preference and activity had always seemed to me to be inherently "private." This was at least the norm and any violation of these publicly avowed standards seemed a clear violation of a sense of public decency. But, now I was faced with a case involving a homosexual male who had decided to "come out of the closet." At the very least, then, in my professional capacity I must stress "tolerance" in my appraisal of the situation.

John Marcus and his wife Dianne has been married for eight years. She was thirty-two years old, and he was thirty-five years old. They had two sons, aged seven and five. John had decided to "come out" publicly as a practicing homosexual. For over a year he had been involved in a homosexual relationship. John was worried about making this move. First, he was a school teacher and thus in the eyes of the school administration, and some of the public, functioned as a moral role model for his students. In this situation, it seemed as if the only acceptable moral role model was a heterosexual one. Second, he was a father and a public avowal of his homosexuality would change some people's perception of his relationship with his two sons. How could fathers function adequately as fathers and as practicing homosexuals? There had been a lot of publicity lately surrounding male homosexual advocacy of pedophelia and child molestation. This kind of publicity enhanced the stereotypical view of male homosexuals as "limp wristed" body-builders with a desire to seduce young boys in parks or public washrooms. John could understand why some homosexuals felt it necessary to take a high political profile in order to force the public to change their attitudes to the practice.

John told me that he had opted for this homosexual relationship as much for the caring and compassion he felt as for the sexuality it expressed. His relationship with Dianne had been, from the beginning, a sort of "cop out" to what he perceived as "conventional mores" and not a genuine expression of his emotional needs. He felt trapped and unfulfilled in this relationship. The relationship had gradually deteriorated to the point where he felt that he was functioning poorly as a father as well as a husband.

In our counselling session, John pointed out that he desired to separate and eventually divorce Dianne but that he wanted to maintain his relationship with his sons. He knew that Dianne would suffer considerably from his decision. She would feel personally responsible for the fact that he was unfulfilled as a husband in this heterosexual relationship. He did not know how to tell her that she was not to blame, that his desires in favor of homosexuality had been latent for years, and that he had not been seduced by anyone into this life-style.

It looked to me as if John had everything working against him. I knew exactly what would happen when I went into family court with him. Questions would be raised about whether or not John had opted for a deviant "me first" attitude at the expense of his family. His adequacy as a father and teacher "figure" would surely be questioned. Here were two high profile heterosexual male roles he was not only failing to fulfill but openly declaring he could not and would not fulfill. The deterioration of our Christian (family centered) moral code would be cited in the press; these sorts of open declarations of "sexual deviancy" were viewed by some as the beginning of the end of civilized society.

What was I going to put in my report to the court? John was willing to amply support his wife and sons. From conversations with Dianne and others, it appeared as if he was a good father. His teaching appraisals rated him as excellent. I had a copy of a report which pointed out that he had sought therapy for his "problem" earlier in his life, but that the therapy had not proved a success in changing his sexual orientation. Should I recommend to John that he not proceed with the divorce and stay in this hypocritical relationship in order to protect his family from scorn and harm? Or, should I recommend that he proceed with his initial decision, defending this decision on the basis of his right to the free expression of his sexuality? Was the general welfare of society threatened by the exercise of this right—the same society that permitted the free expression of Neo-Nazi groups proclaiming genocide for certain minorities? The relationship John was opting for was unconventional, but was it dangerous to society as well? Overt expressions of homosexuality practices are somewhat offensive to standards of public decency, but so are open, public expressions of heterosexual practice. The possible harm to impressionable children seems inherently equal. The debate over whether the right to a sexual preference included the right to publicly disseminate this preference was unresolved in my mind, as was the debate over whether or not John's sexual preferences could be separated from other important aspects of his character.

I decided in favor of "tolerance." I would recommend that John, in my considered opinion, should make public his declaration and should be given visitation rights. The possible harm to the general welfare was, I thought, minimal.

1. What sorts of ethical concerns should one bring to bear against individuals who openly/publicly promote homosexual life-styles and practices, when such practices offend general public sentiments? Would it make any difference if the individual doing the promotion was in a very visible position, a teacher for example?

2. Should any sexual practice be prohibited when there is no immediate psychological harm to the participants?

CHILD MISTREATMENT

Whenever I am faced with assessing a possible case of child mistreatment, I take two steps backwards to stabilize my emotional state. I had to face one such case last year and the memory of the case remains with me.

Mr. and Mrs. Johns had a son, Jonas, nine years of age, who the neighbors had reported was being physically abused. Mr. Johns was not reluctant to let me into his extremely spartan home and introduced me to his wife and son. Jonas was pale in color and seemed to walk with a slight stoop. He was short for his age, and although he did not seem unfriendly, intimidated, or fearful, he only answered the questions I put to him and did not attempt any conversation on his own.

In my discussion with Mr. Johns, I discovered that he ran his household in a very stoic manner, in strict compliance with what he took to be some vaguely defined religious edicts. The family ate a sparse diet of rice and beans. Each member was required, in a ritualistic manner, to perform a number of hours of physical labor and read from a religious text for a period of several hours. This particular religious text was unknown to me.

My discussion with Mrs. Johns disclosed that as a family they had a unique life together, each working to free themselves from some sort of communal sin and modelling their day-to-day life-style after some more primitive situation. They donated a very substantial part of their income to overseas charity and lived on as little money as possible. In order to sustain this life-style, they intentionally kept their distance from the rest of society.

It seemed to me that there was a delicate balance between each member of this family; they had one goal they all agreed to and they all worked toward this goal. This life-style was so all-pervasive that it seemed as if no one member could survive on their own very long outside of this situation.

I was troubled by this life-style, however. That it was an unusual life-style did not bother me, but the effect of the diet and working schedule on young Jonas seemed to be severe. I did not have the immediate opportunity to consult with a psychiatrist on the possible adverse psychological effects this situation was having on Jonas' mental development, but I suspected the worse. At the very least, it looked as if the development of his individual autonomy was in jeopardy.

Still, it did not seem as if any family member was intentionally trying to directly harm Jonas. Was this particular family care insufficient for Jonas' well-being? Barring some possible nutritional problems, the answer to this question was somewhat hard to determine since Jonas seemed not overly joyful but very content. He did not appear fearful of either of his parents, and I had no evidence that he had ever been beaten and suspected I would not find any. There was the religious (or was it pseudo religious) aspect to the case as well. These people did have the right to follow their religion, but did this right also include possible abuse of their child? This was not necessarily a case of *mal*-treatment, although it could still be a case of *mis*-teatment.

To take Jonas from this protective environment against his will and the will of his parents could prove detrimental to this family unit and traumatic to the child. This life-style had in some significant ways shaped his personality and outlook on life. I knew that the parents were unlikely to alter their somewhat dogmatic and severe life-style—it was a cocoon, their protection against the verities of the outside world.

The identification of this situation as a case of child abuse was going to involve a lot of individual factors, not the least of which would be the introduction of a set of liberal social values into this family, values they would likely find very alien to their world view.

1. Does it make any ethical difference whether a case of child mistreatment shows evidence of *intentional* harm/neglect or not?
2. How far should the agents of society allow deviant life-styles to extend into areas of which some possible psychological harm may result to the children of these families, especially when these life-styles are based on some form of religion?

ASIAN MINORITY

I had been working with the Asian minority in our community for a number of years before the "Ying case" was added to my case load. This case was given me by the director of the agency because of my past experience and with the proviso that I consider very carefully any recommendations concerning the case.

In my research of the case, I discovered that the set of problems facing this family seemed to center around Mr. Ying, the father. The family had emigrated to this country two years earlier and the father continued to hold to the traditional values, while his two teenage daughters objected to these values and his young son seemed caught somewhere in the middle. Mrs. Ying seemed to comply with her husband's authority and shared his somewhat fatalistic world view, in opposition to the materialist outlook of their North American neighbors. Mr. Ying had taken a low paying "low profile" job as a dishwasher in a restaurant rather than a better paying executive position for which he was qualified. He took the lower position because he knew that in order to fit into the better paying position he would have to undergo some fundamental changes in outlook, attitude, and life-style. He loved his family and felt that this possible change would involve the loss of the traditional values he felt were so important for his family. This family, which had been a close knit unit to the benefit of all of the members, was beginning to break apart. All the children were encountering problems of social integration in their school. Their wearing of the traditional clothing and following the "old ways" caused a psychological segregation from their peers and precipitated a certain amount of intolerant discrimination.

The Ying's neighbors had brought the case to the social agency. One year earlier, a proud Asian father who felt threatened in his new environment, insulted and demeaned by well-meaning neighbors who sought to free his wife and children from his autocratic control, had killed his wife and three children, before committing suicide himself. The neighbors felt that the ingredients for such a repeat situation were present now in the case of the Yings.

The situation seemed pervaded by a common conflict of the "old ways" in opposition to the "new ways"—this same conflict occurred in the Asian minority community itself, with some families going one way or the other. These kinds of cases tested my own liberal attitudes. These children are and would always be Asians with a long and honorable history, they would always carry this history and tradition with them, and to deny it seemed somehow wrong. On the other hand, I wondered whether the father was stubbornly refusing to learn the new ways, stubbornly refusing to give up any of his entrenched authority. Was this simply a self-interested attempt on his part to hold onto power? For, he had wielded considerable power over his family before the breakdown began. I do not agree that the maxim "When in Rome, do as the Romans do" should be uncritically followed by Asian immigrants in North American society. What did seem to me to be universal was the notion that offspring in any society should be encouraged to become autonomous individuals, fully capable of making their own self-determined choices. How could one encourage this desirable goal while at the same time not denegrating traditional values, values that involved a rigid hierarchical family structure? My task was not going to be an easy one, but somehow I had to convince both Mr. Ying and his family that there was some sort of compromising yet not demeaning middle ground, involving some integration (not uncritically) into North American ways and some retention of traditional values and ways, which would not involve the denegration of these old ways. It almost looked as if I was back in the conflicts of the 1960s, with its revolt of the "new morality" against the more traditionally conservative "old morality"—this analogy made me even more squeamish about the choice I must make concerning a course of action in the Ying case.

1. What ethical problems could Asian immigrants face, if they uncritically accepted the maxim "When in North American society, do as the North Americans do"?
2. Should every family, in every society, encourage the development of self-determined, autonomous offspring, despite incursions on traditional values?
3. Construct or research a case, similar to the one presented above, but different in one or more ethically relevant respects. Show how an approach to both cases would or would not be similar.

OLDER PEOPLE

"Cost/benefit analysis"—the term was beginning to get under my skin. Everywhere I went lately people were using the term as a device for determining viable administrative procedures for dealing with people—especially older people. Today was the last straw. One of my students had introduced a "cost/benefit analysis" appraisal of procedures designed to deal with a hypothetical case study I had introduced in class. My response was somewhat less than fully rational, so I decided to introduce some of my students to a real case I was in the process of resolving.

Mrs. Jennings was a seventy year old patient at the local hospital. She was about to be released after some major surgery and a psychiatric examination. The psychiatric examination had been requested by her daughter. The patient had not been told why the examination was conducted; it was simply stated that this was standard procedure. The daughter had requested the examination to determine whether or not her mother was mentally incapable/senile and thus qualified for institutionalization after the operation. The operation was successful and the psychiatric examination had not shown that Mrs. Jennings was mentally incapable. The situation was in a holding pattern at the moment, as Mrs. Jennings' daughter had hoped her mother would be institutionalized and the burden for her care permanently removed. I was brought in to assess the situation as Mrs. Jennings had now discovered that her next home might be an institution, and she was objecting to this possibility.

In our first meeting at the hospital, the doctor talked incessantly about the cost/benefits of Mrs. Jennings staying in a particular institution, her daughter's home, or some other situation. The daughter talked of her mother as an emotional and economic burden in the way one speaks of a subhuman object that can be stored in one place or another—until such time as the inevitable end occurs. This convenient way of viewing Mrs. Jennings began to offend me. The pattern was not unfamiliar to me. First, you start by talking in vague terms about the "quality of life" (that is the life that is "worth living") and then you start talking about "population control" of those deemed "socially useless." At the bottom line, talk turns to "cost/benefit" analysis and "efficient social management" of the population because of scarce resources. The whole line of argument gets off the ground initially and gains some plausibility when one starts by conceptualizing people not in terms of their inherent worth or dignity, not in terms of their inherent rights and their self-determined autonomy, but rather as objects to be manipulated in favor of the overall social good.

The doctor protested to me that we could never underestimate calculations in terms of "social good," since decisions always had to be made concerning the most efficient distribution of a limited amount of these goods. I pointed out to both Mrs. Jennings' daughter and the doctor that it appeared as if the quality of life enjoyed by Mrs. Jennings did not seem to play an important role in their calculations, since her lifespan was likely to be short and her social productivity either low or nonexistent. It looked to me as if Mrs. Jennings had been "written off" in this social calculus. The daughter protested that I ought not try to create excessive guilt in her, since she was already feeling such "pangs." I pointed out to her that this was not my intention, but that her mother had some human rights that should serve to protect her against unwarranted paternalistic considerations made purportedly on her behalf by others.

I pointed out to my social work students that my conversation with Mrs. Jennings showed her to be fully lucid with only some minor lapses in memory. She thought herself to be a valuable member of both the family and society, although she was not quite sure how to measure her contributions. She was sure that her life would be much worse in an institution with a subsequent loss of privacy, dignity, and an enforced detachment from her grandchildren and friends. She asked me to speak to her daughter and the doctor on her behalf. My class was almost equally divided on what I should say on Mrs. Jenning's behalf, but I had to make a decision on my own, one not based solely on the majority view.

1. If you were faced with a similar situation, what sorts of ethical considerations would you bring to bear either in favor of the daughter and doctor's position or in favor of Mrs. Jennings views?
2. In what other areas of social work practice do considerations of cost/benefit analysis and quality of life calculations play a significant role in ethical decisions? What loss to human dignity is or is not suffered in these situations?
3. Is "geriatric genocide" ever likely to become an acceptable social policy in the future or are there moral/ethical safeguards against such a possibility?

DEVELOPMENTALLY DISABLED INDIVIDUALS

I suppose as social care workers we are constantly asking ourselves just how far we can go in the area of paternalistic guardianship of the developmentally disabled. How far can developmentally disabled persons be trusted to make reasonable decisions for themselves? Conflicts develop between the choices made for the disabled by his/her parents/family/guardian and the actual choice made by the patient himself/herself. We seek to promote the autonomy of these individuals, but at what ultimate expense? A case brought to my attention recently focused on many of the issues surrounding the integration of the developmentally disabled into society.

I was attached to a mental institution and had, as part of my caseload, two patients in their late twenties who had expressed a desire to get married and live a "normal" life outside of the institution. The director was in favor of integrating these two into the outside world, but doubted that they could cope with the range of problems most of us face in society. I was asked to assess the situation and make my recommendations along with the institute's psychologist.

Males and females in the institution were segregated, but Mary and George, since they both had been in the institution from a very early age and had no living relatives, had found occasions to work together and form a bond of friendship and perhaps even love. After forming this bond, each of them began to show a marked improvement in their behavior and general outlook. Both seemed to have developed a sense of responsibility beyond their respective stages of intellectual development but perhaps not at the stage of most people in their late twenties. They both expressed a desire to leave the institution and get married. Would both of them be capable of handling the full responsibilities of marriage and perhaps child rearing?

In conjunction with the psychologist, I recommended that these two individuals be discharged from the institution and allowed to marry. The director agreed that this would be a good test case for the new integration program, would alleviate the over-crowding in the institution, increase the therapist: client ratio, and subsequently improve overall patient care. He also stipulated that close monitoring and support be given this couple for at least a year.

It all looked as if the experiment would work—at least on paper it looked as if it would work. George and Mary were married and began domestic life with George getting a part-time job and Mary looking after the apartment. Within six months Mary became pregnant and newspaper reporters heard that two retarded individuals were living in their community and about to raise a child. George was badgered by co-workers in his job and became increasing irritable. Mary was having some difficulty coping with pregnancy, but support staff served to help her through this difficult period. The baby was born and both parents seemed enthusiastic about their new situation for about the first six months. At about the seventh month after the baby's birth, the in-city social worker attached to the case began to get telephone calls from concerned neighbors that there were loud arguments taking place in the apartment and that the baby's physical health might be in danger.

Again, the local newspaper took up the case, citing local clergymen who were outraged that the institution should condone not only the marriage of two retardates but also the birth of a child to these "irresponsible parents." People were asking why these two had not been sterilized and who would be responsible for the care, safety, and long-term expenses for this child. It looked like the integration program had backfired on all of us, and I was worried about the overall effect of this possible reversal, as well as the effect on George and Mary.

The director was also worried. Such an integration program depended heavily on public support and the possibility of the institution in some way contributing to the creation of another institutional child greatly disturbed him. We reviewed the case again and finally made our decision. It was not an easy decision and it would not satisfy everyone.

1. As a social care worker in a similar situation, what sort of decision would you make in this case?
2. How far should we push the development of autonomy within developmentally disabled individuals who have been institutionalized for a good part of their lives?

TERMINALLY ILL PATIENTS

It was one of those depressing days in which I knew that as a social work counsellor, I must make a decision, an ethical decision involving a case with a multitude of dimensions and no clear solution. No one likes to play Solomon, especially me.

Dr. Enge and Chaplain Peters had asked me to counsel a patient in the hospital with what had been diagnosed as a terminal illness.

As Dr. Enge began to describe the case, the complications immediately became obvious. It seems Mr. Marshall, age forty, husband and father of one living son, had been admitted to the hospital and initially diagnosed as terminal by Dr. Enge. This diagnosis had been confirmed by two other doctors. This same patient had been admitted a year earlier with the same terminal diagnosis, but on subsequent remission had been released in a month. Dr. Enge was the man's physician in this case as well. The doctor had attributed part of the man's previous remission to an "increased and almost ferocious will to live" that had overtaken his patient when told the news of his illness. The man's wife and two sons had been supportive at this time.

Now, however, the situation was somewhat different. Mr. Marshall's oldest son had died six months ago as a result of an uncommon drug reaction. This death had caused a profound change in Mr. Marshall's demeanor. Where previously he had been resigned to dying, but at the same time a tenacious fighter for the continuation of his own life, now he seemed to "cling to life fearfully," to the extent that he seemed not to admit to himself that he was even sick, but rather "simply over-tired."

It was suggested by the doctor that this patient was engaged in some sort of self-deceptive, self-delusory behavior—a strategy designed to systematically keep his conscious awareness away from the truth of the situation. Should this be brought to the patient's attention? Should he be made to face up to or spell out his real situation to himself? The doctor did not normally approve of such self-deception, but in this case it seemed to have a calming effect on the patient and actually seemed to enhance his will to live in a strange sort of way. Dr. Enge generally disapproved of deception. He felt that, especially in his position as a medical doctor, he had a duty to tell his patients the truth about their conditions. With the truth, the patient, his family and friends could, within the general timetable of the terminal disease, live their life together. They could piece together loose ends and make amends for past sins, while planning the future. The doctor thought that it might be nice if he were given this chance, the chance those who die instantly are never given at the end. He liked the previous attitude expressed by Mr. Marshall because he hated the fatalistic "What's the use there is nothing we can do anyway" attitude. He hated this attitude because he knew that the defeatist decreased his own chances of survival and increased the likelihood that he would undergo a more painful illness. Sometimes he felt as if this defeatist attitude, this premature giving up of life, was a means of committing suicide. The doctor believed that patients had a moral duty to do everything they could to continue to survive and that medical professionals have an overriding moral duty to do everything that they can to aid this continued survival. Therefore, in this case, the doctor had decided to override his objections to comply with a lie, but even after all this pondering, he still was not sure.

If I was not puzzled enough by this description of the case, the Chaplain's description added some new twists. He agreed, in general, with Dr. Enge's description but disagreed with the doctor's approach. First, the Chaplain was worried that an unexpressed fear on the part of the doctor that in one or even both hospitalizations there had been a misdiagnosis of a terminal illness affected the doctor's decision not to tell either the patient or his family the negative results of the tests. The doctor had rationalized not telling the family of his negative findings on the grounds that they might inadvertently destroy the patient's fabricated view of his situation. I had to agree with the chaplain that one should not push a fabrication too far, especially since this lie was now affecting two more innocent people. But, I also felt some kinship with the doctor, since my responsibility (like his) was to the welfare of my client, his patient, Mr. Marshall.

I could also sympathize with the doctor's reluctance to fix a patient's timetable for life. It was like playing God, or at least it gave the appearance to some people that you had insight into God's plan for a particular individual. Chaplain Peters urged that all parties concerned should be made aware of the true situation. I agreed. My client was Mr. Marshall, but I also had some responsibility to his family. Sometimes a lie has the effect of ensnaring a lot of people in its web of deceit and that seemed to be what was happening in this case. I decided to share the realization of the truth of his situation with Mr. Marshall and his family. Perhaps Mr. Marshall was envious of the living or simply fearful of death and this is why he was engaged in this self-deceptive strategy, but, whatever the rationale for his denial defense, only a full confrontation with the truth would give peace to Mr. Marshall and his family in the long run.

1. Is it ever ethically justified to lie to a patient about his illness or impending death, if it could be argued that the successful execution of such a lie would make the patient's last few hours of life more comfortable?

2. Dying involves adverse consequences not only to the patient but also (less severe) to the patient's family and friends. Is it ever ethically justified to lie to a patient's family and friends, even if it could be argued that such a lie would be in their immediate best interests?

WOMEN SEEKING ABORTION

The problems that surround the question of abortion are so enmeshed with issues involving religion, ethics, social policy, and health that counselling necessarily involves a careful consideration of the circumstances that surround each case.

A case I confronted last week, in my capacity as the social worker attached to the local hospital, served to highlight some of the considerations surrounding this issue.

A mother and her daughter were admitted to the hospital and it was diagnosed that both the unmarried eighteen-year-old daughter and the forty-year-old mother were pregnant. Both were in the early stages, so an abortion was deemed medically safe for both women. The problem was that both were having some problems making a decision as to whether or not to have an abortion, and I was called in to offer my services.

The mother had a job at which she had been working for about a year. The job meant a lot to her, since it finally presented her with the chance to achieve some independence from her somewhat domineering husband. She was achieving a kind of autonomy she had never experienced before. Her children had matured to the stage where they were measurably independent. We discussed the possible loss of independence she would experience as a result of having to care for a small infant and the chances of her bearing a child with Down's syndrome or other serious disorders. Psychologically she seemed prepared to accept her fate whatever decision she finally made. She seemed aware of the difference between "quality of life" calculations in her favor and "sanctity of life" calculations in favor of the fetus. She knew her daughter was in the same hospital and currently contemplating the same operation and was worried that she might not set the "right" example for her daughter. She wanted to make a decision that was well thought out so that, if need be, she could explain her choice clearly and without guilt to her daughter.

The daughter had not talked to her mother yet. Her boyfriend wanted her to keep the baby and argued that it was as much his decision and responsibility as hers, pointing out that he had a job and could support them both. He had taken her to a "sanctity of life" meeting in which she had been shown slides of young fetuses and had been told that ultimately abortion was just another form of murder and that she had an obligation to support life rather than take it. She was not deeply religious but had been affected emotionally by the slides. She was now very confused and felt trapped by her situation. She loved her boyfriend but was not sure she wanted all the responsibilities that were attached to child rearing. She knew her mother had had an earlier abortion and somehow felt cheated that she had never known this child. She knew that in many respects the quality of her life would suffer emotionally, economically, and even psychologically, but she also worried about the sanctity of the life she carried within her. Was this fetus human? Was it just a biological organism with none of the developed characteristics of a person, like an appendix or a cancerous growth as some people suggested? Would the fetus suffer pain as a result of the operation? Would she later regret this decision, haunted by nagging and guilt-ridden doubt?

Finally, the three of us met for three hours and discussed all of the pro and con issues surrounding both cases. Each of them would have to make an independent decision, and each choice would affect both of them for some time after it was made. Both mother and daughter seemed drawn together by this choice, but it also seemed as if both could be at odds with each other depending upon how they made their choices.

1. Outline the reasons cited by the mother in favor of her ultimate choice (in the case in which she chooses to have the abortion and the case in which she chooses not to have the abortion).

2. What weight should be placed on quality of life and on sanctity of life considerations by the daughter in her ultimate decision?

3. To what extent should a social worker make his/her own position on this issue known to those faced with making the decision?

4. To what extent should population control arguments be brought into a individual decision regarding an abortion?

BEHAVIOR MODIFICATION

Alfie (aged 14) moved nervously about the room, like a caged animal about to attempt an escape. Mr. and Mrs. Caine looked on apprehensively. Mr. Dean, Alfie's teacher, and Mr. Grimes, the social worker called in as a consultant, both had hopes that this meeting would lead to the introduction of a behavior modification program designed to deal with Alfie's inappropriate behavior in the classroom. Both Mr. Dean and Mr. Grimes were in agreement that the program would help Alfie only if his parents were brought in as an integral part of the program, since the targeted behavior occurred both at home and in the classroom. Alfie seemed a bright, intelligent boy who continually interrupted the class at inappropriate times, had been truant on many occasions, and responded well on tests in class only when he wanted to. At home he spent most of his time watching television or playing chess with some of his friends. He did his homework assignments only when it interested him; as a result, his grades were plummeting and his parents were disturbed. Alfie was given an allowance just for staying at home and "being a good boy"—his father believed he owed his son this allowance regardless of his son's behavior. Mr. Caine opened the discussion:

Gentlemen, as you know, I am an art instructor at the local college and as such I am not as concerned about social conformity as you social scientists or "social engineers" seem to be. I am more concerned that my son be allowed to develop his capacity for autonomous, responsible decision-making. In the development of this capacity, he will be confronted by the mistakes he has made and will continue to make and he will be confronted by the anxiety that accompanies any personal choice. I'm worried that your program seems designed to deal with some sort of mechanistic man whose responses are neither rational nor irrational but rather simply *automatic*. You have suggested a practical solution to Alfie's problems based on some fundamental changes in his behavior, so that it more appropriately matches what you think his behavior ought to be in these circumstances. You seek out the most efficient program to deal with his behavior. But, is not the most efficient program, from your point of view, the one that unfairly generalizes about what Alfie's tastes, desires, dispositions, and opinions *ought to be* and not *what they are*—irrespective of the degree of social deviancy? You seek out conformity in behavior at the expense—the very great expense— of individual autonomy. Considerations of efficient technology supercede considerations of personal morality.

MR. GRIMES: The view you present is an interesting one, but I believe that both Mr. Dean and myself can allay some of your fears; I am sure that you are aware that, at the very least, we are operating in your son's best interests. All of us will sign a contract in which we agree to a program that targets for change, timetables the changes, outlines how the changes are to be brought about and what each of us must do as part of the program. Each of us will sign the agreement, binding for a specified period of time, and outlining the ultimate achievement of certain specified goals. What could be fairer than this approach? We are not using "adversive techniques," like those used to alter the behavior of cigarette smokers or sexual deviants, but rather positive conditioning in a program that involves the voluntary cooperation and participation of all involved.

MRS. CAINE: I am not so sure as you that we are so far removed from the kind of reprehensible social utopias, the kind of "go with the flow group think," that I, for one, want to avoid at all costs. You two, for example, seemed to have weighted the consequences of our not agreeing to the program so high that we are in fact left with no other choice than to agree to it. You have told us that if we do not agree to the full implementation of this program, then our son faces expulsion from school and possible institutionalization. It looks to me as if we are being unduly coerced by you people into signing this therapy contract document. How is this situation substantially any different from the similar situation of those people in institutions, asked by the social workers responsible for their care and release to sign such documents? The coercion may be somewhat more subtle in this case, but it is coercion nonetheless. Have you thought about whether or not this coercion is morally justified, and what about possible psychological/emotional harm done to my son as a result of this token economy bribe you propose?

MR. DEAN: If you read the contract, you will see that the token economy procedure is used only for a limited period of time; ultimately it is phased out. We are, after all, not "buying" immoral behavior from your son but rather encouraging appropriate behavior with a material means your son finds valuable. As to the coercion, a significant change in your son's behavior is required for his sake as well as the rest of the class. We need an environment in which thirty children will best be able to learn and this puts some clear restrictions on the autonomous self-expressive tendencies of every one of these children. As well, it seems necessary for the well-being of society and each member in it that our educational system provide a model for cooperative enterprise.

MR. GRIMES: I think I am beginning to see the basis for some of your disagreements Mr. and Mrs. Caine. You seem to believe that what we have here is a simple case of "conflict of will" and that, in opposition to the implementation of this program, everyone ought to be more tolerant of your son's behavior—so that *he* sees that *he* must change it himself, consistent with *his* social development.

MR. DEAN: I can see clearly that my responsibility is to Alfie. In talking earlier with Alfie, he suggested that he would sign the document if the rest of us signed it as well. I can give you no guarantees that Alfie will not lose some of his creative, self-expressive qualities (admired of artists) as a result of his participation in this program. I do know that Alfie, himself, seems to believe that he needs help and that this program seems less offensive to individual autonomy than the other available option. On the basis of all that I have heard today, I think I must recommend in favor of the implementation of this program with the inclusion of both parents. No one is proposing a *Walden II* here, nor is it likely that this program is the thin edge of a wedge designed to pave the way for involuntary social engineering.

1. What sort of coercion is ethically justified when a social work professional seeks approval for a program designed in the client's best interests? Are there, for example, degrees of coercion or limits of coercion beyond which no further pressure is justified?

2. How important is it for a client to voluntarily agree to participate in a behavioral modification program; that is, important from the point of view of the enhancement of the client's autonomy?

GENETIC COUNSELING

I was a product of the 1960s. Remember the sixties? Flower children. Peace and Love. Ban the Bomb. As a product of this era, I had developed the attitude that human life was intrinsically valuable and any taking of this life ought to be considered seriously. Now, as a social worker, I had to face the task of discussing the possibility of sterilization with a woman who was referred to me by Dr. Herman.

Anne was a pleasant enough woman, thirty-two years old, of such low intelligence that she could be considered mildly retarded. She was newly married and had no children. She wanted children, but adopting agencies did not consider her a suitable candidate for a parent. For various reasons Anne was incapable of employing the usual range of contraceptive devices. I had some previous contact with Anne, so Dr. Herman asked me to talk to her and explain to her that there was some evidence that her baby would suffer from Down's syndrome. From my previous experience with Anne, I was convinced that, with some outside help, she was capable of looking after a child. But, was she capable of looking after a child with Down's syndrome? This was a more difficult question to answer. She and her husband were in a low income bracket and already required some social assistance to stay alive. Her husband's parents were dead and Anne's parents lived some distance from them. What immediate help could they be to this expanded family?

Initially, what she ought to do seemed obvious. My previous conversations with Dr. Herman seemed to reinforce this view. We had talked at some length about similar problems in the past. We talked about the need for any society to protect the best quality of life for all of its members. We talked of the massive amounts of monetary expenditures and time consumed in any society in which there was no control over possibly defective individuals. In this context, several examples were mentioned of the social and economic havoc wrought by the lack of social control in some underdeveloped countries. What was technology for, anyway, if it was not used to make the majority of the population of any society better off? If any society were to be "swamped with incompetence," would we not all be worse off? Was it not our duty to aid in the creation of the best possible society, a society in which the most number of people could make the maximum use of a limited set of resources? After all, in order to bring about the greatest good for the greatest number, was it not sometimes necessary to eliminate potential or even actual people even though these "people" are in fact innocent of intentionally causing harm to anyone else? That is, we would not be condoning the elimination of these people because they themselves were unhappy or made someone else unhappy but because they could not participate in the benefits of our culture. They could not appreciate beauty. They were incapable of learning like the rest of us, or of contributing to the advancement of society.

However, there seemed to be something wrong with this view. Perhaps it was just my flower child past resurfacing, but somehow there seemed to be something basically wrong with a view that could condone an unjustified harm against an innocent minority of the population. Was there no dignity, worth, or value to life itself? I began to recall cases of eugenic control that seemed to have "gone sour": the excesses in Nazi Germany, the sterilization of some American prison inmates against their will, and other cases of sterilization of the mentally incompetent. Were these excesses not also justified in the name of social expediencey or good fiscal policy? What about the "right to procreate," the "right to form a family"? How far can we extend arguments favoring paternalistic intervention into the lives of individuals?

What began to trouble me the most was that I firmly believed that Anne and her husband would love this child. In all our calculations, it seemed as if we often overlooked this very important emotional bond. Also, the external means needed to support Anne seemed minimal. Sometimes it seemed best to consider each situation on its own merits and act from a spirit of loving concern rather than from a set of rules or principles.

Treating each individual separately and each new situation individually seems on the face of it a fair approach. Of course, it has some drawbacks: it is hardly scientific; how would we go about convincing someone that they ought to have this "spirit of loving concern," since, it is obvious that not everyone does have this concern. Treating every case strictly on its own merits on the face of it was consistent but to do so seemed to make too much of the difference between cases and not enough of their similarities.

The decision must involve complex personal and social ethical factors.

1. To what extent should parents faced with the prospect of producing genetically defective offspring be allowed to bring such offspring into a society with limited social assistance resources?

2. Is there such a thing as a "right to procreate," and does it make any sense to

suppose that an unborn child would not want to be born if he/she could know that he/she would lead a dreadful life of misery?

INVOLUNTARY COMMITMENT

Joan and Barry's son, Roger, came home late Sunday night after spending a three week summer vacation with friends up north. Roger's behavior, however, began to trouble and disturb both parents. His bland monosyllabic responses to questions seemed strange for the normally bright, bubbly, and very talkative Roger. He sat in the corner for hours on end mumbling something in a language that neither parent could understand. All the while, he was rocking back and forth and seemed to be in some sort of a trance—completely oblivious to what was going on around him. What troubled them more was that he refused to eat anything but what he called "purified seeds" and refused to drink anything but water.

The concerned parents called their family doctor who, after a thorough examination, suggested that he could find nothing physically wrong with the boy—at least nothing that could count as the cause of this strange behavior. The doctor suggested further tests be performed at the hospital, but the boy refused to be moved. The doctor surmised that the cause of the boy's behavior could be some sort of mental disorder and that a competent professional be called in to assess the situation.

Before calling a psychiatrist, the boy's parents called some of his friends and asked them to come over to the house to try to reason with him. All attempts by his friends to either reason with him or to offer an account for his strange behavior failed.

At this point, the boy's behavior changed again. He confronted his mother, angrily, on several occasions demanding that she "keep the house clean and free of unpurified elements." He added that if she and his father did not "keep the house free from these unpurified elements" all of them would suffer some unspecified "dire consequences." This was the only conversation the boy engaged in with his parents.

Joan called a friend of theirs who was a lawyer, and a psychiatrist recommended by their family doctor.

After an appraisal of the situation, the social worker pointed out to the parents that—in his view—the boy ought to be admitted to the local psychiatric clinic for further appraisal and possible treatment for his disorder. He pointed out to the parents that the boy had refused to admit himself to the clinic.

A discussion ensued about what to do with Roger.

JOAN: Well doctor, I am at my wits end. What are we going to do about Roger? I want to help my son, but I don't know what to do.

SOCIAL WORKER: Has Roger ever behaved this way before?

JOAN: No, he has always been quite normal, outgoing, lively, loving to his parents and others. I cannot explain what has happened to him. None of his friends seem to know where he went on his vacation, but this is not unusual because we have always respected his right to privacy and know that sometimes he likes to get away from it all for awhile.

SOCIAL WORKER: I think that Roger ought to be admitted right away to the clinic, and that we ought to set the necessary machinery in motion before the situation deteriorates any further. He must be committed, even if it means involuntarily committing him.

LAWYER: Wait a minute. What reason could you have for involuntarily committing Roger? I do not see that he poses any real threat to society, his parents, or even to himself. On the grounds of his behavior alone, he could not even be forcibly admitted to a medical hospital let alone a mental institution.

SOCIAL WORKER: First of all, Roger's behavior is somewhat threatening to his parents.

LAWYER: If we locked up everybody who was at some time threatening to his parents we would have to incarcerate half the population of this city. These sorts of grounds for taking away an individual's liberty seem shaky, at best.

SOCIAL WORKER: It is also clear to me that Roger represents a clear threat to his own well-being. We cannot refuse to help Roger on the grounds that we will violate some abstract legal rights he has, even if in his current state he is unaware that he has them. I am not harming or infringing on anyone's liberty by attempting to treat this individual, so that he may return to a normal state where he will be aware of and act in regard to what is in his best interests. I have tried to warn him of the dangers associated with his behavior, but he does not respond to my warnings or even acknowledge that I am talking to him. I am obliged to help Roger and placing him in the clinic for further tests and possible treatments is the only way I can follow through on my obligations. He cannot be treated here and he requires treatment. I have a professional responsibility to help those who are in need of my help—just as you have a professional responsibility to help those in need of legal assistance.

BARRY: I am having some problems following all of this. First of all, it is not at all clear to me that Roger does not know what he is doing or what is in his best interests. Although his mental state seems to be deteriorating, he has not done himself any physical harm so far. I admit his behavior is strange, and he is an inconvenience. But, how can we know for sure that he does not know what he is doing? How do we know that this behavior will continue and that he will not—on his own—snap out of it? How do we know that we are not just getting rid of Roger for our own sakes and not his well-being? We have all read horror stories of people being institutionalized because they were spastic, suffering from nervous disorders, suffering from speech or language defects, or were political dissidents. Look Joan, if we sign Roger into an institution, then only a psychiatrist (sometimes the same one who admits him) can decide when he has recovered enough to be released. Both the appraisal of the mental disease and the success of the treatment involve more subjective interpretation than the medical practitioners' diagnosis of a medical disorder. If Roger were terminally ill from cancer, he could still sign himself out of the hospital. He cannot sign himself out of the place we are contemplating sending him to, even if *he* believed he was cured. Besides, oftentimes people are not cured of these sorts of mental dysfunctionings but merely brought to the state where they can live with them or learn to cope.

LAWYER: I agree with Barry. What is of central importance, here, is that there is no agreed-to standard definition of what is to count as normal in all cases and in all situations. Legal and psychological definitions vary and determinations of what is to count as normal change over time. What if Roger has simply gone through a personality change that has made him no better or worse than he was before? Perhaps it is just that Roger is different from what he was before, and we are having trouble coping with this difference. We are assuming that we can operate from what is in his best interests, but what if his interests—his autonomously chosen concept of the good—have undergone a change? Often in these situations, we tend to operate from a conservative stance, assuming the worse possibilities are likely to occur. That is, with minimal information, we assume that Roger will harm himself or others. We place an inordinately high value on social conformity and employ legalistic moves: if the law allows me to involuntarily commit Roger, then this move is morally justified. But, this is a way of defaulting on our moral responsibility. We cannot just commit people against their will for treatment on the basis of a "potential threat" to themselves or others.

PSYCHIATRIST: Well, obviously, if we wait until he is an actual threat to himself or to others we may be too late to save him from harm to himself or others. I will not argue with you about whether or not we ought to equate a medical disorder with a socio/psychological dysfunction. What is clear is that we have evidence that Roger is not fully responsible for his actions. From a legal point of view, this would seem to be all we need to begin proceedings to have Roger involuntarily committed.

LAWYER: Yes, but what prior evidence do you have of Roger's violent behavior to himself or others? If you have no such evidence, then your presentation before the court may flounder. I know you do not agree to the need for this prior evidence. But, try to imagine Roger's situation or your situation or mine in a society in which none of our individual human rights were protected by an independent judiciary. We both, after all, want to protect Roger from harm.

At this point the lawyer and the psychiatrist had to leave. Joan and Barry were left to ponder what to do about Roger, knowing the full weight of their ultimate decision.

1. To what extent should the right to refuse treatment override considerations in favor of the patient's mental health? Does it make that much difference when we introduce considerations of the patient's physical health instead of his/her mental health?

2. When an individual is involuntarily committed on the basis of a perceived threat to society, should there be procedures involving some form of "due progress" so that the individual can defend him/herself against the claim that he is a bona fide threat to others?

RESEARCH AND EXPERIMENTATION USING HUMAN SUBJECTS

In many situations it is useful and even necessary to employ human subjects in social work experiments. As in all situations using human subjects, the experimenter is accorded a special responsibility for these subjects. He/she is more directly responsible for their welfare than he/she might be even in a clinical situation. The adverse consequences on the subjects of certain experiments may be both immediate and long-term.

I had an occasion to take the proposed design for an experiment, using children in a nursery school setting, to my supervisor for approval and appraisal. In the course of our discussion, he suggested that we discuss a case he had dealt with earlier in his career. Without getting into the specifics of the case, he mentioned that it involved the use of college students in role-playing situations in which decisions were forced on the subjects against their will, by the circumstances of the experiment. The adverse psychological effects of this individual experiment was felt by these voluntary subjects well after the experiment was over—for many years thereafter as a matter of fact. The supervisor lapsed into a pensive mood, so I decided to try to draw out of him what his views were about such experiments now. He spoke first, almost in response to my unasked question.

SUPERVISOR: Each of us involved in this kind of experimentation is in a very delicate situation. As experimenters we could be suspect as interested parties in any appraisal of the ethical constraints that need to be put on a particular experiment. We, after all, have a vested interest in the progress of scientific knowledge, in our own particular scientific project, and also in the enhancement of progress in our careers in the social work field.

SOCIAL WORKER: I think I understand what your concern is with the ethical appraisal of these situations. Subjects in these experiments are in a sense letting themselves be used as a means not necessarily towards their own good but to some other more abstract "social good." Even though they voluntarily choose to partic-ipate and even receive some compensation for this participation, the overall gain, if the experiment is successful, may be to the progress of science or some other goal external to them.

SUPERVISOR: I suppose we all know the danger of employing individuals from a minority group in these experiments. The real danger seems to be in our think-ing of human subjects not as human beings but rather as the objects of an experiment or things or samples. It is easy to slip from this kind of characteriza-tion into talk of experimental manipulation, which seems to neglect that we are dealing with human beings with a fundamental set of human rights.

SOCIAL WORKER: Yes, I suppose this is possible—as we try to become more scientific in our approach we lose sight of the fact that we are dealing with human beings. But, it seems to me that each of us is being repaid now in some ways by the results derived from the outcomes of past experiments.

SUPERVISOR: This is true, but we must be careful in weighing any present foreseeable harm to a small number of human subjects against a possible large gain to future generations. If we think of individuals as having human rights, then these rights accord protection to an individual that override claims made in favor of future gains to a particular society. Dictators, politicians, and even some scientists in the past have tried to justify (or is it rationalize?) mistreatment of human subjects by claiming great social benefits would accrue in the future.

SOCIAL WORKER: I am beginning to see now some of the *human* concerns that must be incorporated in the design and implementation of any experiment in the social sciences involving human subjects. I might start by conceiving of myself as the human subject, in my own experiment, and try to consider all of the possible physical, psychological, and even ethical consequences that might result from my participation in this experiment. Of course, I must design this experiment in such a way that the subjects are not fully aware of all that will take place and even here I may be engaged in an element of deception. At the very least I will be witholding information and at the very most I will be deceiving them. This gets more complicated by the minute.

SUPERVISOR: When it appears less complicated, then you will know that either you are dealing with "objects" rather than human beings or your design and implementation requires closer strutiny.

1. What sort of special ethical safeguards should be employed when children are used as the subjects in social experiments?

2. Should there be an external ethical review board, composed of different members of the community, to assess the participation of human subjects in social science experiments? What sort of mandate should this ethical review board be given? What sorts of special problems would social scientists face when subjected to the review of such a board?

CONFIDENTIALITY

I had just moved to this city and taken up employment with a new social agency when, for the first time in my career, a deep conflict seemed to be developing between my ethical standards and those of the social agency that employed me. This was one of those tricky ethical situations that had to be resolved to both my satisfaction and the satisfaction of the social agency and its director.

At the former agency, where I had been in both an administrative and field position, the policy on the use of client's confidential records was quite explicit. Before any person, other than the social worker directly responsible for the case, could obtain access to these confidential records, written approval from the director in consultation with the ethics committee was required. Specific reasons documenting the exact nature of the information sought and the need for this information was required in writing and assessed by the director and the committee.

In this agency, the situation was much more lax, with people from within and even without this agency embarking on "fishing expeditions," purportedly seeking information in one area and then "snooping" through the files to gain other information to be used for another purpose entirely. This first time it happened, I was somewhat shocked. The second time it happened, I was more troubled than shocked. I could not go to the director, since it was partly due to his lax policy that this situation was allowed to take place, and I could not go to my fellow workers since I feared being labelled as a trouble maker.

The first case involved a client of mine who had trouble adjusting to his homosexuality. Within his file there was some reference to a situation that was a borderline case of child abuse. A subpoena had been shown the director and he complied with it, without fully reading the vague terms of reference contained in it. My client was outraged when he discovered that certain specific information regarding his problems with both homosexuality and child abuse had been leaked during police questioning of some of his friends and his employer. This had served to alienate his friends and jeopardize his job. He wondered why I had not scrutinized the subpoena carefully, assessed it in conjunction with legal advice and an appeal to the Social Work Code of Ethics whether an objection to the subpoena could not be gained on ethical grounds. I had to admit that I had done none of these things but merely followed the director's policy. He wondered whether he had any individual right to privacy at all, given that it appeared as if the police had no case against him at all but were merely "fishing" for suspects without substantial prior evidential grounds. I wondered to myself whether this new trouble would precipitate a new set of psychological/social problems for my client, which would serve to reactivate a file I had hoped was closed. It looked like this case was one in which the interests of society were somewhat in conflict with the interests of my individual client.

The second case involved a situation in which the director, in my absence, had allowed an investigator from the Social Welfare Department access to a file of one of my clients. The investigator had said he wanted information regarding my client's marital status and place of employment. But, the subsequent fishing expedition he actually went through turned up information used to disqualify my client from social assistance benefits. There is, obviously, a need for close cooperation between the Social Welfare Department and our agency, but this case caused me to think through my own ethical policy toward divulging information about my clients. Should I minimize the information I put into the files, so that only I know the full version? No, this would not do, since my caseload could be taken over by someone else who would need all pertinent information. Should I put my client's interests/well-being above the law and put myself in jeopardy? I had to sort these considerations out quickly before another "fishing expedition" occurred.

1. How far should a social work professional go in objecting to the use made of information derived from his/her client's confidential file?

2. Are there other situations in which a social work professional could be legally forced, against his/her own ethical standards, to divulge information that could be detrimental to his/her client's interests and well-being?

ETHICAL CODES OF SOCIAL WORK PROFESSIONAL ASSOCIATIONS

Alberta Association of Social Workers

SOCIAL WORK CODE OF ETHICS

(approved in principle by the Canadian Association of Social Workers on October 2, 1977 and adopted by the Council of the Alberta Association of Social Workers on October 3, 1977)

Preamble

VALUES The profession of social work holds the worth, dignity and creative individuality of every human being as of primary value. Therefore, social workers shall not discriminate against anyone on the basis of race, color, language, religion, age, sex, marital status, physical and mental handicap, economic condition or national ancestry and they shall work towards preventing and eliminating such discrimination in rendering service, in work assignments and in employment practices. The profession of social work affirms that society has an obligation to ensure that all people have access to resources, services and opportunities they require to promote their well-being; and that each person has the right to self-determination with due regard to the interests of others.

PURPOSE In accordance with these values the profession of social work is committed to fostering human welfare through its' professional services and activities, and to developing or changing social and economic institutions or systems towards this end. Social work practice focuses on the relationships among people in their social environment. The social worker endeavors to enhance the problem solving and functioning capacities of people to help people better utilize personal and environmental resources, and to effect changes in society towards social justice for all.

ACCOUNTABILITY Social workers have an obligation to protect and promote the interests of clients through professional services delivered with integrity and competence. This can only be achieved by establishing and maintaining high standards of social work practice. The following Declaration sets out the fundamental ethical principles to which social workers should adhere in professional relationships and practice. It is understood that failure to fulfill the following

Reprinted with permission.

obligations to the best of one's ability may result in disciplinary action by the Professional Association.

Social Work Declaration

As a member of the profession of social work I commit myself to fulfill to the best of my ability the following obligations:

1. I will regard the well-being of the individuals, the groups and the communities I serve as my primary professional duty.
2. I will fulfill my obligations and responsibilities with integrity.
3. I owe a duty to clients to be competent in the performance of the services and functions I undertake on their behalf.
4. I will serve clients in a conscientious, diligent and efficient manner.
5. I will respect clients in my professional relationships with them.
6. I will protect the privacy of clients and hold in confidence all professionally acquired information concerning them. I will disclose such information only when authorized by clients or when obligated legally or professionally to do so.
7. I will not allow outside interests to jeopardize my professional judgment, independence or competence.
8. I will assume responsibility for the total operation of my private practice and I will adhere to the guidelines established by my Professional Association in this regard.
9. I will work for the creation and maintenance within agencies employing social workers of conditions and policies which are consistent with the values and obligations of this code.
10. I will endeavour to promote excellence in the social work profession.
11. I will attempt to effect social change fostering human well-being.

Commentary on the Code of Ethics

Preface

The profession of social work is dedicated to improvement of human welfare. Therefore, the basic ethical principles in social work are necessarily extremely wide and quite general. The purpose of a statement of professional obligations is to provide a guide and a framework for the individual social worker and the profession within which to practice. It is not possible to foresee every situation which a social worker may encounter and therefore, it is not intended that this code will stand for all time but will require periodic revision.

The preamble identifies the philosphy, values and objectives of the profession in general terms. The declaration attempts to provide a guide for practice while recognizing that social workers must exercise personal judgement and ethical reflection. The obligations, therefore, are qualified by the words "to the best of my ability", and in some instances may become extremely individualized when attempting to fulfill certain obligations such as, contributing to social change and to the development of the social work profession. In such instances the willingness of social workers' to give of their best is recognized.

Declaration

PRIMARY OBLIGATION

1. I will regard the well-being of the individuals, the groups and the communities I serve as my primary professional duty.

   Commentary

   This principle is fundamental and self-explanatory. The following obligations are intended to aid the worker in fulfilling this primary professional duty. It is also noted that in order to fulfill this obligation the statement on discrimination in the preamble is applicable.

INTERGRITY

2. I will fulfill my obligations and responsibilities with integrity.

   Commentary

   (1) Oxford English Dictionary, "Integrity, . . . soundness of moral principle especially in relation to truth and fair dealing; uprightness, honesty, sincerity."

   (2) Integrity is an integral part of social work practice and therefore underlies each point of the Code of Ethics.

   (3) Public announcements (advertising, etc.) relating to social service made by social workers shall be clear and true and not misleading.

   (4) If a conflict arises in professional matters, the standards declared by this Code take precedence. Such conflicts may occur because of demands from the social worker's employer or from a particular service requested by the client. In the latter instance the social worker must inform the client that the service cannot be provided.

   (5) The social worker is expected to observe this Code of professional conduct in spirit as well as in the letter. Therefore, it is expected that a social worker will report to the appropriate professional body any instance involving or appearing to involve a breach of this Code. In all such cases a report should be made in good faith.

   (6) In private life or professional activity the social worker's behavior reflects upon the profession as a whole. If the behavior is such that knowledge of it would be likely to impair the client/worker relationship, the Council will consider a complaint and take suitable action. Examples of such behavior include the committing of a criminal offence which indicates a potential threat to a client (child molesting), taking improper advantage of a client, and gross disrespect for human beings (racial bigotry).

   (7) It is noted that this Code is not meant to imply a standard of perfection. Even though it might be actionable under law, a mistake would not necessarily constitute a failure to maintain the standards set by this Code. However, evidence of gross neglect in a particular matter or a pattern of neglect or mistakes may be evidence of such a failure regardless of civil liability.

COMPETENCE AND QUALITY OF SERVICE

3. I owe a duty to clients to be competent in the performance of the services and functions I undertake on their behalf.

4. I will serve clients in a conscientious, diligent and efficient manner.

Commentary

(1) Competence goes beyond formal qualifications. Social workers should strive continuously to upgrade and use effectively their knowledge, skills and abilities in professional service.

(2) Social workers should not undertake a matter unless they honestly believe they are competent to handle it. If they cannot become competent without undue delay, risk, or expense to their clients, they should either decline to act or obtain the client's agreement to consult, collaborate with or refer to a social worker who is competent in that field. This standard of care is apart from that which a court would invoke for purposes of determining negligence. It is noted, however, that the above should not be construed to mean that a social worker when lacking specialized expertise should decline to help a client when there is no one more competent in that particular field of practice available to the client. Such instances can become common in rural areas and with large caseloads.

(3) Social workers should recognize that competence for a particular task may require advice from or collaboration with experts in other professional fields, and they should seek their client's agreement to consult in such situations.

(4) Part of professional social work competence is to maintain one's own wellbeing so as to be able to be effective with clients.

(5) Social workers will provide a quality of service which is at least equal to that which they would expect to receive on their own behalf in a like situation.

(6) The following list is illustrative of attributes and conduct which meet the competence and quality of service required:

   a) possess an adequate knowledge and understanding of human behavior and development, environmental factors affecting human life and the interaction between them;

   b) hold a working knowledge of treatment methods, change strategies and community resources;

   c) know the organizational objectives, resources, policies, procedures and limitations of the employment setting;

   d) have an awareness of the applicable laws and legal processes related to the client situation;

   e) respond appropriately in a crisis situation;

   f) shall not fail or cease to provide a service except for just and reasonable cause among which are
   —the loss of a client's confidence,
   —prolonged failure of the client to benefit from the services,
   —conflict of interest.

g) when withdrawing from service facilitate the orderly transfer of the
client to a social worker or other professional with a minimum amount
of expense and other inconvenience;

h) attempt to keep clients informed of all relevant committments and
possible implications of their situation;

i) when unable to meet a request notify the client within a reasonable
interval;

j) refrain from the use of intoxicants or drugs which interferes with
service to the client;

k) make a prompt and appropriate report when required;

l) attempt to keep appointments with clients and answer all verbal and
written communication within a reasonable time;

m) arrange for adequate coverage of service in times of absence;

n maintain adequate office staff and facilities.

SOCIAL WORKER/CLIENT RELATIONSHIP

5. I will respect clients in my professional relationships with them.

Commentary

(1) Social workers should respect their clients as individuals and attempt to
ensure through advocating and other appropriate measures that their dignity, individuality, rights and responsibilities are safeguarded.

(2) The social worker/client relationship requires that the social worker be
trustworthy. Therefore, a social worker should be open, honest, nonjudge-
mental, empathetic, congruent and accepting.

(3) The focus within the professional relationship is on the client and the
mutually agreed upon planned change. This focus assumes that social workers
maintain a high degree of self-awareness so that they can recognize when
personal needs, feelings, values and limitations interfere with the process of
planned change and/or termination of the professional relationship.

(4) The social worker must take into account the client's motivation, capacity
and opportunity for change at any given time during the change process to
appropriately guide the interaction ("Start where the client is").

(5) A social worker's involvement with voluntary and involuntary clients
must be based on the clients' consent to work upon mutually agreed goals. In
the case of the involuntary client such consent and agreed goals may be
minimal but they are conditioned by statutory legislation and/or the rights
of the community and others to protection. The social worker must be aware
of the parameters of authority involved in the relationship and ensure that
the clients' agreements are based only on relevant information, to protect
them from coercion by use of power or expert position. Whenever it becomes
apparent that clients have misunderstood or misconceived their position, the
social worker should explain and renegotiate so that clients are fully advised
of their true position.

(6) Recognizing the intense level of affective involvement inherent in a
professional relationship, the social worker must ensure that the difference
between professional and personal involvement with clients is explicitly

understood and respected and that the social worker's behavior is appropriate to this difference.

(7) When making agreements with and working with clients the social worker must be mindful of the parameters established by the worker's abilities and values, and the breadth and scope of the worker's activities.

CONFIDENTIAL INFORMATION

6. I will protect the privacy of clients and hold in confidence all professionally acquired information concerning them. I will disclose such information only when authorized by clients or when obligated legally or professionally to do so.

Commentary

The committment to confidentiality fosters open communication and is essential to effective social work practice. Most social work agencies and organizations have policies concerning agency confidentiality and it is the duty of social workers to abide by these policies if sound or to work for the creation and maintenance of effective policies and procedures.

Concerns about privacy and confidential matters arise throughout the entire professional relationship-from intake to after the case is closed.

Receiving Information

(1) Clients should be the primary source of information about themselves and their problems. Exceptions to this occur when small children, the ill, the retarded and so forth are the clients.

(2) Social workers have the obligation to ensure the clients understand what is being asked, why and to what purposes the information may be used. Generally, persons seeking social service go to an agency, not a worker. Therefore, social workers should ensure that their clients understand agency confidentiality.

(3) Where confidential information is required by law social workers must help their clients to understand the possible consequences of refusal to give such information.

(4) When information is required from other sources, social workers should explain this to clients and where possible decide with the client what other sources are to be used and the method for obtaining the needed detail.

(5) Social workers should take extreme care in accepting for safekeeping personal papers belonging to clients.

(6) Social workers have the obligation to impress upon employees, students and associates the importance of confidentiality both during their employment and thereafter.

Recording Information

(1) Social workers should ensure that all information recorded is either demonstrably related to the solution of the client's problem or required by agency administrative accountability or research needs.

(2) As a general rule, a minimum amount of personal information should be recorded.

(3) Preliminary diagnosis and treatment plans should not form part of the

permanent record and should be destroyed once their usefulness is passed.

(4) Before tape recording or video taping an interview, social workers must obtain the client's permission.

Client Accessibility to Records

(1) As a general principle clients have the right to know what their records contain and should be allowed the opportunity to check the accuracy of all factual data.

(2) Exceptions to this principle may occur for just and reasonable causes when a case involves different family members and client access to the records could mean divulging family confidences or when recorded language could be misunderstood and prejudicial to the client. In such instances only appropriate parts of the record should be made available to the client.

Disclosure

(1) As a general rule social workers should not disclose that clients have consulted them or the source of information about clients unless the nature of the matter requires it (examples of this follow).

(2) The obligation to maintain confidentiality continues indefinitely after social workers have ceased contact with their clients.

(3) Social workers should avoid unnecessary conversations regarding clients and their affairs as matters overheard by third parties may be detrimental to clients.

(4) Confidential information may be divulged with the express authority of the client concerned.

(5) The transferring of case records and related files to another agency or individual may only occur with the express consent of the client or guardian and then only with assurance that the receiving agency provides the same guarantee of confidentiality.

(6) Disclosures of confidential information required by law or the policies of the agency should be explained to the client, where at all possible, before such disclosure is made.

(7) Social workers practicing group therapy should notify the participants of the likelihood that aspects of their private lives may be revealed in the course of treatment and therefore, require a committment from each group member to respect the private and confidential nature of the communications within the group.

(8) Social workers practicing conjoint or family therapy must safeguard the right to confidentiality of members of the couple or of the family.

(9) Disclosure by social workers may be justified to defend themselves, their colleagues or employees against allegations of malpractice or misconduct or to collect fees. However, such disclosures should occur only to the extent necessary for such purposes.

(10) Disclosure of information necessary to prevent a crime, to prevent clients doing harm to themselves or to others is justified. Such disclosure should not be made without great care and without the client's knowledge, unless informing the client would impede the due process of law or endanger someone.

(11) When disclosure is required by law, by order of a court of competent jurisdiction or by the work setting, social workers should not divulge more information than is required and when possible notify the client of this requirement.

(12) Social workers must take care to thoroughly disguise client identity in making use of confidential information for teaching, public education, accountability and research purposes.

Retention and Disposition of Information

(1) Social workers should destroy case records over which they have jurisdiction within a reasonable period of time after the case is closed. The retention of certain documents required by law or for teaching and research purposes may be retained with discretion.

(2) Where applicable social workers should promote the adoption of sound and reasonable policies concerning retention and disposition of client information within their employing agency.

OUTSIDE INTERESTS AND THE PRACTICE OF SOCIAL WORK

7. I will not allow outside interests to jeopardize my professional judgement, independence or competence.

Commentary

(1) Social workers must make clear the capacity in which they are acting.

(2) A social worker's committment to professional values does not exclude the social worker from participating in outside interests such as politics, another profession, occupation or business enterprise. The term "outside interests" covers the widest possible range and includes activities which may or may not overlap with the practice of social work.

(3) Ethical considerations will usually not arise from outside interests unless conduct brings the social worker or the profession into disrepute, or the activities impair competence. An example of this is when the outside interest so occupies the social worker's time that clients suffer from inattention or poor service.

(4) Whenever an outside interest might influence the social worker's judgement, the social worker should disclose and explain the nature of the conflict to the client and his employer. In some instances it may be necessary to withdraw from the case.

PRIVATE PRACTICE

8. I will assume responsibility for the total operation of my private practice and I will adhere to the guidelines established by my Professional Association in this regard.

Commentary

(1) The fees charged by a private social work practitioner should be fair and reasonable and reflect the customary charges of other practitioners of equal standing in the locality in like matters and circumstances.

(2) The social worker may properly make social work services available by charging a reduced fee or no fee at all to a client who would have difficulty in paying the fee.

(3) When social workers are engaged in private practice as well as social work employment in an agency or an organization, they shall communicate fully and completely their intentions and activities to their employers. It is recommended that there be a detailed written agreement between the employer and the private practitioner with regard to such things as: use of office space and other facilities, conflict of interest. Caution must be taken to ensure that there is a clear distinction between referrals to the employing organization and to the private practitioner.

(4) The private practitioner is expected to carry adequate liability insurance.

RESPONSIBILITY TO EMPLOYER

9. I will work for the creation and maintenance within agencies employing social workers of conditions and policies which are consistent with the values and obligations of this code.

Commentary

(1) Social workers are accountable and responsible for the efficient performance of their duties to their employers.

(2) At times the responsibilities to the employer and the client may be in conflict and the social worker should bring this situation to the attention of the employer. In some instances it may be necessary to enlist the support of professional colleagues in an attempt to safeguard client rights and promote changes in the procedures of the agency which will be consistent with the values and obligations of this code. It may also be required by social workers to subordinate the employer's interests to the interests of clients as it must be remembered that frequently clients lack the necessary power to ensure their rights. In extreme circumstances, the social worker may have to resign from that employment and when so doing should inform the Professional Association.

RESPONSIBILITY TO THE PROFESSION

10. I will endeavour to promote excellence in the social work profession.

Commentary

(1) The individual social worker should assist the profession to function properly and effectively by participation in such activities as influencing social policy, continuing in and contributing to social work knowledge and education, liaison with colleagues and other professions, and the activities of the Professional Association.

(2) The profession has a public responsibility to provide competent social work services. Therefore, the individual social worker should be prepared to advise the profession through appropriate channels on a complaint involving another social worker.

(3) Social workers must be careful in expressing their views on the findings, opinions and professional conduct of colleagues, confining such comments to matters of fact and matters of their own knowledge.

RESPONSIBILITY TO SOCIETY

11. I will attempt to effect social change fostering human well-being.

Commentary

(1) Social workers should make social work services available to the public in an efficient and convenient manner. This could include such activities as participating in referral services, welfare appeal boards, education and advice concerning social welfare matters, and engaging in programs for public information.

(2) A social worker who is aware of unmet needs should be prepared to advocate for change in policy and/or legislation. In such activities the social worker should recognize the value of enlisting professional and other support.

(3) Social workers are expected to take steps to protect the community from individuals or groups purporting to offer or provide welfare services, but whose services are incompatable with the well-being of those to whom the services are offered.

British Association of Social Workers

A CODE OF ETHICS FOR SOCIAL WORK

Objectives

1 Social work is a professional activity. Implicit in its practice are ethical principles which prescribe the professional responsibility of the social worker. The primary objective of the code of ethics is to make these implicit principles explicit for the protection of clients.

Foreword

2 Membership of any profession entails certain obligations beyond those of the ordinary citizen. A profession's code of ethics sets down in general terms, these special obligations, and specifies particular duties which follow from them.

3 Members of a profession have obligations to their clients, to their employers, to each other, to colleagues in other disciplines and to society.

4 In order to carry out these obligations, the professional has complementary rights which must be respected for him to work effectively.

5 Any professional association has the duty to secure as far as possible, that its members discharge their professional obligations; and that members are afforded in full necessary professional rights.

Statement of Principles

6 Basic to the profession of social work is the recognition of the value and dignity of every human being, irrespective of origin, status, sex, sexual orientation, age, belief, or contribution to society. The profession accepts a responsibility to encourage and facilitate the self-realisation of the individual person with due regard for the interest of others.

7 Concerned with the enhancement of human wellbeing, social work attempts to relieve and prevent hardship and suffering. Social workers thus have a responsibility to help individuals, families, groups and communities through the provision and operation of appropriate services, and by contributing to social planning and action. Social work has developed methods of practice, which rely on a growing body of systematic knowledge and experience.

8 The social worker has a commitment to serve these purposes with integrity and skill. He acknowledges a professional obligation, not only to increase his personal knowledge and skill, but also to contribute to the total body of professional knowledge. This involves the constant evaluation of methods and policies in the

Reprinted with permission.

412

light of changing needs. He recognises that the competence of his particular discipline is limited, and that the interests of the client require co-operation between those who share professional responsibility for the client's welfare.

9 The social worker's responsibility for relief and prevention of hardship and suffering is not always fully discharged by direct service to individual families and groups. He has the right and duty to bring to the attention of those in power, and of the general public, ways in which the activities of government, society or agencies, create or contribute to hardship and suffering or militate against their relief. Social workers are often at the interface between powerful organisations and relatively powerless applicants for service. Certainly social workers are accountable to those under whose authority they work, and responsible for the efficient performance of their professional task and for their management of the organisation's resources. In view of the applicant's lack of power, social workers have a special responsibility to ensure the fullest possible realisation of his rights and satisfaction of his needs.

Principles of Practice

10 In accepting the statement of principles embodying the primary obligations of the social worker, each Member of the Association undertakes that, to the best of his ability.

1 He will contribute to the formulation and implementation of policies for human welfare, and he will not permit his knowledge, skills or experience to be used to further inhuman policies.

2 He will respect his clients as individuals and will seek to ensure that their dignity, individuality, rights and responsibility shall be safeguarded.

3 He will not act selectively towards clients out of prejudice on the grounds of their origin, status, sex, age, belief or contribution to society.

4 He will help his clients increase the range of choices open to them and their powers to make decisions.

5 He will not reject his client or lose concern for his suffering, even if obliged to protect others against him, or obliged to acknowledge an inability to help him.

6 He will give precedence to his professional responsibility over his personal interests.

7 He accepts that continuing professional education and training are basic to the practice of social work, and he holds himself responsible for the standard of service he gives.

8 He recognises the need to collaborate with others in the interests of his clients.

9 He will make clear in making any public statements or undertaking any public activities, whether he is acting in a personal capacity or on behalf of an organisation.

10 He acknowledges a responsibility to help clients to obtain all those services and rights to which they are entitled, both from the agency in which he works and from any other appropriate source.

11 He recognises that information clearly entrusted for one purpose should not be used for another purpose without sanction. He respects the privacy of clients and confidential information about clients gained in his relationship with them or others. He will divulge such information only with the consent of the client (or information) except: where there is clear evidence of serious danger to the client, worker, other persons or the community, in other circumstances, judged exceptional, on the basis of professional consideration and consultation.

12 He will work for the creation and maintenance in employing agencies of conditions which enable social workers to accept the obligations of this code.

Commentary on the Code of Ethics

1 The primary objectives of the Code are stated in para 1 'objectives'. It attempts to be generally applicable, but not to stand for all time. New ideas about social work and changes in its environment will necessitate revision of the Code from time to time. The Code now presented is seen as an initial statement.

2 The Foreword (paras 2–5) is a statement about the purpose of the Code. The Statement of Principles attempts to make explicit the values implicit in the practice of social work, and the Principles of Practice attempt to set out a basic Code for the individual social worker.

3 The Code of Ethics cannot be a manual of practice guidance. It must be couched in general terms, without being so general as to be incapable of application.

4 The Foreword expresses the view that the acceptance of special ethical obligations is part of the definition of any professional worker. This is the basic assumption which underlies any code of professional ethics (para. 2). Paragraph 3 challenges, as being oversimplifications, suggestions that the professional's only obligation is to his client, or that the employed professional's only obligations are to the employer who hires him. Paragraph 4 refers to the rights of professionals. Chief among these is the right to exercise professional discretion.

Statements of Principles

ON PARAGRAPH 6.

Basic ethical principles in social work are necessarily extremely wide in view of the wide focus of social work. A narrower basis than 'recognition of the value and dignity of every human being would not be adequate. The social worker's basic values must relate to individuals, whether he works with individuals, groups or communities, since it is the welfare of the individuals in a group or community which is the social worker's basic concern even if indirectly. The phrase 'irrespective of origin, status sex, sexual orientation, age, belief or contribution to society' is intended to be interpreted widely. 'Origin' includes national, racial, social, cultural and class origins, distant or recent. 'Status' refers to an individual's current situation and includes social status, citizenship status and status in an institution or organisation. 'Age' does not mean old age only. 'Belief' is not confined

to religious beliefs and includes beliefs which might be regarded as delusions.
The second sentence avoids the term 'self-determination, which sounds a little too open-ended and attempts to recognise the limitations which real-life situations impose Social workers are often concerned with trying to harmonise conflicting interests and failing harmony, to arrive at the least damaging solution for all concerned. It is, therefore sometimes not possible to ensure that there will be no detriment to the interests of others, or to the client's interests. Hence the phrase with due regard for the interests of others'.

ON PARAGRAPH 7:
In the first sentence, limits to what social work can achieve have to be recognised. Being concerned with the enhancement of human well being implies a responsibility to promote social functioning as well as to relieve suffering. The Codes of Ethics of the American and Canadian Associations state that the social worker renders appropriate service in a public emergency. All citizens are expected to do this and it is unnecessary to make this point specifically in relation to social workers. It is, however, covered in a general way by the reference to the relief of hardship and suffering.

ON PARAGRAPH 8:
In statements about obligations, commitments or responsibilities, it is important not to impose obligations which cannot be fulfilled. It is reasonable and proper to demand that social workers have integrity and skill. It would not be reasonable to demand, for example, that a social worker should feel sympathy for a particular client, since feelings cannot be summoned at will. At the same time, it would be reasonable to expect the social worker to declare his position if the client aroused in him feelings which obstruct his capacity to help.

ON PARAGRAPH 9:
The first two sentences in this paragraph relate back to the statement in paragraph 7 about social planning and action. The paragraph then comments on the social worker's own particular position in relation to planning, policy-making and the giving of service. The word 'interface' is intended to denote a place where contacts take place, contacts which may be active or passive and which may lead to harmony or to conflict. The paragraph goes on to try to balance the social worker's responsibility to his employers against his responsibility to his client. The client's frequent lack of power must be taken into account in weighing these responsibilities.

Principles of Practice

6 The Principles of Practice are based on and derived from the Statement of Principles, but are more personal and in more concrete terms. They move from general principles to principles to guide practice, while recognising that social workers must exercise personal judgment. The preamble identifies the Statement of Principles as giving the primary, underlying or basic objectives of the social worker. All the undertakings which follow are qualified by the words 'to the best of his ability'. It is therefore, recognised that, to take the first principle as an example, the opportunity to contribute to the formulation of policies may in a

particular case be extremely limited. The social worker's willingness to give of his best is also recognised.

Principles

1 The Principle is fundamental. Observance of it may lead the social worker to resign his post in certain circumstances.

2 This Principle has general implications, but particular attention should be paid lest a person suffers loss of dignity or rights by the very act of becoming a client.

3 This Principle recognises that acting selectively is a morally neutral concept; in other words there are good reasons and bad reasons for acting selectively. It also recognises that no-one is entirely free from prejudices. Objections can be taken only to selective or discriminatory action founded in prejudice. See also the comment on paragraph 6.

4 This Principle holds good in all circumstances but it is sometimes necessary to help the client to abandon pseudo- or fantasy-choices so that effective choices may be made.

5 This Principle raises the problem of what can legitimately be said about the worker-client relationship. It is not possible to lay down requirements about the social worker's feelings, but 'rejection' includes action as well as feeling. Rejecting the client is, of course, different from closing the case. The reference to the need to protect others against the client does not cover all the situations in which the client may be in danger of rejection.

6 This Principle recognises the opportunities for conflict between personal interest and professional responsibilities. It places on the social worker an obligation not to pursue personal interests at the client's expense. It does not imply that at all times the social worker must put his responsibility to a client above his other responsibilities, for example, as a citizen, as a parent.

7 This Principle recognises that qualifying training does not complete a social worker's education. The importance of continuing education is also increased by the need to keep abreast of changing social factors. The assumption of personal responsibility for one's work is crucial to professionalism. A completely bureaucratised service cannot be a professional one.

8 This Principle places an obligation on social workers not only to be alert to the need to collaborate, but to take appropriate action.

11 This Principle has been distilled from the Associations Discussion Paper No. 1 on Confidentiality in Social Work, and for full considerations of the issues involved readers are referred to that Discussion Paper and subsequent statements.

The sanction referred to in the first sentence of the Principle is the sanction of the person giving the information to the social worker.

The multi-purpose agency, in particular, has to consider what administrative arrangements should be made to guard against the misuse of information.

The paper on confidentiality, after outlining situations in which the client's right to confidentiality might be over-ridden, states: 'In all the foregoing circumstances the breach of confidence must remain limited to the needs of the situation at that time and in no circumstances can the worker assume a carte blanche to reveal matters which are not relevant to that particular situation'.

12 There is a clear implication in this Principle that employers should recognise the whole code. The Principle also acknowledges the difficulties of the employed professional, especially the social worker who works in an agency whose role is not specifically therapeutic.

(The Code was adopted by BASW at the Annual General Meeting, Edinburgh 1975. All members of the Association are required to uphold the Code.)

Canadian Association of Social Workers

CODE OF ETHICS

(First approved by the C.A.S.W. Board of Directors, October, 1977; reaffirmed June 9, 1979—that members must adhere to *no less than* the **Preamble** and the **Social Work Declaration**. The **Commentary** which includes a small preface is a guideline to the provinces for their future development as necessary.)

Preamble

Values

The profession of social work holds the worth, dignity and creative individuality of every human being as of primary value. Therefore, social workers shall not discriminate against anyone on the basis of race, color, language, religion, age, sex, marital status, physical and mental handicap, economic condition or national ancestry and they shall work towards preventing and eliminating such discrimination in rendering service, in work assignments and in employment practices. The profession of social work affirms that society has an obligation to ensure that all people have access to resources, services and opportunities they require to promote their wellbeing; and that each person has the right to self-determination with due regard to the interests of others.

Purpose

In accordance with these values the profession of social work is committed to fostering human welfare through its' professional services and activities, and to developing or changing social and economic institutions or systems toward this end. Social work practice focuses on the relationships among people in their social environment. The social worker endeavors to enhance the problem solving and functioning capacities of people to help people better utilize personal and environmental resources, and to effect changes in society towards social justice for all.

Accountability

Social workers have an obligation to protect and promote the interests of clients through professional services delivered with integrity and competence. This can only be achieved by establishing and maintaining high standards of social work

---

Reprinted with permission.

practice. The following Declaration sets out the fundamental ethical principles to which social workers should adhere in professional relationships and practice. It is understood that failure to fulfill the following obligations to the best of one's ability may result in disciplinary action by the Professional Association.

Social Work Declaration

As a member of the profession of social work I commit myself to fulfill to the best of my ability the following obligations:

1. I will regard the well-being of the individuals, the groups and the communities I serve as my primary professional duty.
2. I will fulfill my obligations and responsibilities with integrity.
3. I owe a duty to clients to be competent in the performance of the services and functions I undertake on their behalf.
4. I will serve clients in a conscientious, diligent and efficient manner.
5. I will respect clients in my professional relationships with them.
6. I will protect the privacy of clients and hold in confidence all professionally acquired information concerning them. I will disclose such information only when authorized by clients or when obligated legally or professionally to do so.
7. I will not allow outside interests to jeopardize my professional judgement, independence or competence.
8. I will assume responsibility for the total operation of my private practice and I will adhere to the guidelines established by my Professional Association in this regard.
9. I will work for the creation and maintenance within agencies employing social workers of conditions and policies which are consistent with the values and obligations of this code.
10. I will endeavour to promote excellence in the social work profession.
11. I will attempt to effect social change fostering human well-being.

Commentary on the Code of Ethics

Preface

The profession of social work is dedicated to improvement of human welfare. Therefore, the basic ethical principles in social work are necessarily extremely wide and quite general. The purpose of a statement of professional obligations is to provide a guide and a framework for the individual social worker and the profession within which to practice. It is not possible to foresee every situation which a social worker may encounter and therefore, it is not intended that this code will stand for all time but will require periodic revision.

The preamble identifies the philosophy, values and objectives of the profession in general terms. The declaration attempts to provide a guide for practice while recognizing that social workers must exercise personal judgement and ethical reflection. The obligations, therefore, are qualified by the words "to the best of my ability", and in some instances may become extremely individualized when

attempting to fulfill certain obligations such as, contributing to social change and to the development of the social work profession. In such instances the willingness of social workers to give of their best is recognized.
(Copies of the remainder of this commentary available on request)

Suggested Guidelines for Dealing with Alleged Violations of the Code of Ethics

1. Provincial Associations of Social Workers in provinces where the law itself does not contain provision or does not set out procedures for dealing with ethical problems, will need to develop a policy for the treatment of alleged violations of the Code. (In provinces where there is a Registration Act, the Registration Boards will be governed by provisions of their respective Acts.) In setting out such policies and in taking action by reason of a breach of the Code of Ethics, Provincial Associations must recognize that statements concerning a member carry with them certain risks and serious responsibilities. The Code of Ethics relates closely to personal character and conduct and an allegation or a finding against a member would, of necessity, carry with it an imputation of misconduct and could affect the individual's ability to continue in his profession.

2. The greatest accuracy is imperative and the utmost care must be exercised in discussing allegations of violations of the Code and in reporting on actions taken to the membership, to the public or to an Association in another province. It should not follow automatically that action taken by the Association should be reported to any person or persons or any group either inside of or outside the Association. Neither should it follow that the Association take action because another group, such as a Registration Board, has done so.
   Policies and procedures should be clear and should be adhered to by both the Association and its officers and by those laying complaints.

3. As a minimum requirement, the following procedures for laying all complaints would appear to be desirable.
   a) All complaints, to be considered, should be made in writing and in a specified manner, and include supporting evidence.
   b) If a complaint by any member or non-member is made in the proper manner, the Board of Directors, within a specified time, *must* set up an enquiry to report to the Board.
   c) The enquiry must hear all parties involved, or their representatives. The member complained of may name another member of the Association to represent him.
   d) If either the person laying the complaint or the member against whom the complaint is made is not satisfied with the decision of the enquiry, the Board must provide for an appeal at which all evidence is reviewed by the Board *but no new* evidence introduced.
   e) The Board of Directors takes such action, if any, that it deems appropriate.

4. For each formal complaint filed a tribunal of members of the Association be

appointed, as follows:

One named by the Board of the Association;
One named by the member against whom the complaint is made;
A third selected by the above two members.

In the event that the two representatives cannot agree on the third member, the Board of Directors assists in finding a third person (not a Board Member) acceptable to both parties.

The tribunal must hear all witnesses, review all evidence, and recommend to the Board of the Association only as to whether the member is guilty or not guilty of the alleged violation.

5. If a member is found guilty of a violation or violations of the Code of Ethics, disciplinary measures should be determined by the Board of Directors of the Association. Depending on the seriousness of the infraction or infractions various measures might be considered, such as: (a) verbal warning (b) letter of warning (c) letter of censure (d) fine (e) suspension for a specified period (f) suspension until such time as certain conditions are met (g) permanent cancellation of membership.

This code to be reviewed and modified as necessary every three years.

National Association of Social Workers (U.S.A.)
As adopted by the 1979 NASW Delegate Assembly,
effective July 1, 1980.

CODE OF ETHICS

Preamble

This code is intended to serve as a guide to the everyday conduct of members of the social work profession and as a basis for the adjudication of issues in ethics when the conduct of social workers is alleged to deviate from the standards expressed or implied in this code. It represents standards of ethical behavior for social workers in professional relationships with those served, with colleagues, with employers, with other individuals and professions, and with the community and society as a whole. It also embodies standards of ethical behavior governing individual conduct to the extent that such conduct is associated with an individual's status and identity as a social worker.

This code is based on the fundamental values of the social work profession that include the worth, dignity, and uniqueness of all persons as well as their rights and opportunities. It is also based on the nature of social work, which fosters conditions that promote these values.

In subscribing to and abiding by this code, the social worker is expected to view ethical responsibility in as inclusive a context as each situation demands and within which ethical judgement is required. The social worker is expected to take into consideration all the principles in this code that have a bearing upon any situation in which ethical judgement is to be excercised and professional intervention or conduct is planned. The course of action that the social worker chooses is expected to be consistent with the spirit as well as the letter of this code.

In itself, this code does not represent a set of rules that will prescribe all the behaviors of social workers in all the complexities of professional life. Rather, it offers general principles to guide conduct, and the judicious appraisal of conduct, in situations that have ethical implications. It provides the basis for making judgements about ethical actions before and after they occur. Frequently, the particular situation determines the ethical principles that apply and the manner of their application. In such cases, not only the particular ethical principles are taken into immediate consideration, but also the entire code and its spirit. Specific applications of ethical principles must be judged within the context in which they are being considered. Ethical behavior in a given situation must satisfy not only the judgement of the individual social worker, but also the judgement of an

Reprinted with permission.

unbiased jury of professional peers.

This code should not be used as an instrument to deprive any social worker of the opportunity or freedom to practice with complete professional integrity; nor should any disciplinary action be taken on the basis of this code without maximum provision for safeguarding the rights of the social worker affected.

The ethical behavior of social workers results not from edict, but from a personal commitment of the individual. This code is offered to affirm the will and zeal of all social workers to be ethical and to act ethically in all that they do as social workers.

The following codified ethical principles should guide social workers in the various roles and relationships and at the various levels of responsibility in which they function professionally. These principles also serve as a basis for the adjudication by the National Association of Social Workers of issues in ethics.

In subscribing to this code, social workers are required to cooperate in its implementation and abide by any disciplinary rulings based on it. They should also take adequate measures to discourage, prevent, expose, and correct the unethical conduct of colleagues. Finally, social workers should be equally ready to defend and assist colleagues unjustly charged with unethical conduct.

Summary of Major Principles

I. *The Social Worker's Conduct and Comportment as a Social Worker*

    A. PROPRIETY. The Social worker should maintain high standards of personal conduct in the capacity or identity as social worker.

    B. COMPETENCE AND PROFESSIONAL DEVELOPMENT. The social worker should strive to become and remain proficient in professional practice and the performance of professional functions.

    C. SERVICE. The social worker should regard as primary the service obligation of the social work profession.

    D. INTEGRITY. The social worker should act in accordance with the highest standards of professional integrity.

    E. SCHOLARSHIP AND RESEARCH. The social worker engaged in study and research should be guided by the conventions of scholarly inquiry.

II. *The Social Worker's Ethical Responsibility to Clients*

    F. PRIMACY OF CLIENTS' INTERESTS. The social worker's primary responsibility is to clients.

    G. RIGHTS AND PREROGATIVES OF CLIENTS. The social worker should .make every effort to foster maximum self-determination on the part of clients.

    H. CONFIDENTIALITY AND PRIVACY. The social worker should respect the privacy of clients and hold in confidence all information obtained in the course of professional service.

    I. FEES. When setting fees, the social worker should ensure that they are fair, reasonable, considerate, and commensurate with the service performed and with due regard for the clients' ability to pay.

III. *The Social Worker's Ethical Responsibility to Colleagues*

    J. RESPECT, FAIRNESS, AND COURTESY. The social worker should treat colleagues with respect, courtesy, fairness, and good faith.

    K. DEALING WITH COLLEAGUES' CLIENTS. The social worker has the responsibility to relate to the clients of colleagues with full professional consideration.

IV. *The Social Worker's Ethical Responsibility to Employers and Employing Organizations*

    L. COMMITMENTS TO EMPLOYING ORGANIZATIONS. The social worker should adhere to commitments made to the employing organizations.

V. *The Social Worker's Ethical Responsibility to the Social Work Profession*

    M. MAINTAINING THE INTEGRITY OF THE PROFESSION. The social worker should uphold and advance the values, ethics, knowledge, and mission of the profession.

    N. COMMUNITY SERVICE. The social worker should assist the profession in making social services available to the general public.

    O. DEVELOPMENT OF KNOWLEDGE. The social worker should take responsibility for identifying, developing, and fully utilizing knowledge for professional practice.

VI. *The Social Worker's Ethical Responsibility to Society*

    P. PROMOTING THE GENERAL WELFARE. The social worker should promote the general welfare of society.

The NASW Code of Ethics

I. *The Social Worker's Conduct and Comportment as a Social Worker*

    A. PROPRIETY — The Social worker should maintain high standards of personal conduct in the capacity or identity as social worker.

    1. The private conduct of the social worker is a personal matter to the same degree as is any other person's, except when such conduct compromises the fulfillment of professional responsibilities.

    2. The social worker should not participate in, condone, or be associated with dishonesty, fraud, deceit, or misrepresentation.

    3. The social worker should distinguish clearly between statements and actions made as a private individual and as a representative of the social work profession or an organization or group.

    B. COMPETENCE AND PROFESSIONAL DEVELOPMENT — The social worker should strive to become and remain proficient in professional practice and the performance of professional functions.

    1. The social worker should accept responsibility or employment only on the basis of existing competence or the intention to acquire the necessary competence.

    2. The social worker should not misrepresent professional qualifications, education, experience, or affiliations.

C. SERVICE—The social worker should regard as primary the service obligation of the social work profession.

1. The social worker should retain ultimate responsibility for the quality and extent of the service that individual assumes, assigns, or performs.

2. The social worker should act to prevent practices that are inhumane or discriminatory against any person or group of persons.

D. INTEGRITY—The social worker should act in accordance with the highest standards of professional integrity and impartiality.

1. The social worker should be alert to-and resist the influences and pressures that interfere with the exercise of professional discretion and impartial judgement required for the performance of professional functions.

2. The social worker should not exploit professional relationships for personal gain.

E. SCHOLARSHIP AND RESEARCH—The social worker engaged in study and research should be guided by the conventions of scholarly inquiry.

1. The social worker engaged in research should consider carefully its possible consequences for human beings.

2. The social worker engaged in research should ascertain that the consent of participants in the research is voluntary and informed, without any implied deprivation or penalty for refusal to participate, and with due regard for participants' privacy and dignity.

3. The social worker engaged in research should protect participants from unwarranted physical or mental discomfort, distress, harm, danger, or deprivation.

4. The social worker who engages in the evaluation of services or cases should discuss them only for the professional purposes and only with persons directly and professionally concerned with them.

5. Information obtained about participants in research should be treated as confidential.

6. The social worker should take credit only for work actually done in connection with scholarly and research endeavors and credit contributions made by others.

II. *The Social Worker's Ethical Responsibility to Clients*

F. PRIMACY OF CLIENTS' INTERESTS—The social worker's primary responsibility is to clients.

1. The social worker should serve clients with devotion, loyalty, determination, and the maximum application of professional skill and competence.

2. The social worker should not exploit relationships with clients for personal advantage, or solicit the clients of one's agency for private practice.

3. The social worker should not practice, condone, facilitate or col-

laborate with any form of discrimination on the basis of race, color, sex, sexual orientation, age, religion, national origin, marital status, political belief, mental or physical handicap, or any other preference or personal characteristic, condition or status.

4. The social worker should avoid relationships or commitments that conflict with the interests of clients.

5. The social worker should under no circumstances engage in sexual activities with clients.

6. The social worker should provide clients with accurate and complete information regarding the extent and nature of the services available to them.

7. The social worker should apprise clients of their risks, rights, opportunities, and obligations associated with social service to them.

8. The social worker should seek advice and counsel of colleagues and supervisors whenever such consultation is in the best interest of clients.

9. The social worker should terminate service to clients, and professional relationships with them, when such service and relationships are no longer required or no longer serve the clients' needs or interests.

10. The social worker should withdraw services precipitously only under unusual circumstances, giving careful consideration to all factors in the situation and taking care to minimize possible adverse effects.

11. The social worker who anticipates the termination or interruption of service to clients should notify clients promptly and seek the transfer, referral, or continuation of service in relation to the clients' needs and preferences.

G. RIGHTS AND PREROGATIVES OF CLIENTS—The social worker should make every effort to foster maximum self-determination on the part of clients.

1. When the social worker must act on behalf of a client who has been adjudged legally incompetent, the social worker should safeguard the interests and rights of that client.

2. When another individual has been legally authorized to act in behalf of a client, the social worker should deal with that person always with the client's best interest in mind.

3. The social worker should not engage in any action that violates or diminishes the civil or legal rights of clients.

H. CONFIDENTIALITY AND PRIVACY—The social worker should respect the privacy of clients and hold in confidence all information obtained in the course of professional service.

1. The social worker should share with others confidences revealed by clients, without their consent, only for compelling professional

reasons.

2. The social worker should inform clients fully about the limits of confidentiality in a given situation, the purposes for which information is obtained, and how it may be used.

3. The social worker should afford clients reasonable access to any official social work records concerning them.

4. When providing clients with access to records, the social worker should take due care to protect the confidences of others contained in those records.

5. The social worker should obtain informed consent of clients before taping, recording, or permitting third party observation of their activities.

I. FEES—When setting fees, the social worker should ensure that they are fair, reasonable, considerate, and commensurate with the service performed and with due regard for the clients' ability to pay.

1. The social worker should not divide a fee or accept or give anything of value for receiving or making a referral.

III. *The Social Worker's Ethical Responsibility to Colleagues*

J. RESPECT, FAIRNESS, AND COURTESY—The social worker should treat colleagues with respect courtesy, fairness, and good faith.

1. The social worker should cooperate with colleagues to promote professional interests and concerns.

2. The social worker should respect confidences shared by colleagues in the course of their professional relationships and transactions.

3. The social worker should create and maintain conditions of practice that facilitate ethical and competent professional performance by colleagues.

4. The social worker should treat with respect, and represent accurately and fairly, the qualifications, views, and findings of colleagues and use appropriate channels to express judgements on these matters.

5. The social worker who replaces or is replaced by a colleague in professional practice should act with consideration for the interest, character, and reputation of that colleague.

6. The social worker should not exploit a dispute between a colleague and employers to obtain a position or otherwise advance the social worker's interest.

7. The social worker should seek arbitration or mediation when conflicts with colleagues require resolution for compelling professional reasons.

8. The social worker should extend to colleagues of other professions the same respect and cooperation that is extended to social work colleagues.

9. The social worker who serves as an employer, supervisor, or mentor to colleagues should make orderly and explicit arrangements

regarding the conditions of their continuing professional relationship.

10. The social worker who has the responsibility for employing and evaluating the performance of other staff members, should fulfill such responsibility in a fair, considerate, and equitable manner, on the basis of clearly enunciated criteria.

11. The social worker who has the responsibility for evaluating the performance of employees, supervisees, or students should share evaluations with them.

K. DEALING WITH COLLEAGUES' CLIENTS—The social worker has the responsibility to relate to the clients of colleagues with full professional consideration.

1. The social worker should not solicit the clients of colleagues.

2. The social worker should not assume professional responsibility for the clients of another agency or a colleague without appropriate communication with that agency or colleague.

3. The social worker who serves the clients of colleagues, during a temporary absence or emergency, should serve those clients with the same consideration as that afforded any client.

IV. *The Social Worker's Ethical Responsibility to Employers and Employing Organizations*

L. COMMITMENTS TO EMPLOYING ORGANIZATION—The social worker should adhere to commitments made to the employing organization.

1. The social worker should work to improve the employing agency's policies and procedures, and the efficiency and effectiveness of its services.

2. The social worker should not accept employment or arrange student field placements in an organization which is currently under public sanction by NASW for violating personnel standards, or imposing limitations on or penalties for professional actions on behalf of clients.

3. The social worker should act to prevent and eliminate discrimination in the employing organization's work assignments and in its employment policies and practices.

4. The social worker should use with scrupulous regard, and only for the purpose for which they are intended, the resources of the employing organization.

V. *The Social Worker's Ethical Responsibility to the Social Work Profession*

M. MAINTAINING THE INTEGRITY OF THE PROFESSION—The social worker should uphold and advance the values, ethics, knowledge, and mission of the profession.

1. The social worker should protect and enhance the dignity and integrity of the profession and should be responsible and vigorous in discussion and criticism of the profession.

2. The social worker should take action through appropriate channels against unethical conduct by any other member of the profession.

3. The social worker should act to prevent the unauthorized and unqualified practice of social work.

4. The social worker should make no misrepresentation in advertising as to qualifications, competence, service, or results to be achieved.

N. COMMUNITY SERVICE—The social worker should assist the profession in making social services available to the general public.

1. The social worker should contribute time and professional expertise to activities that promote respect for the utility, the integrity, and the competence of the social work profession.

2. The social worker should support the formulation, development, enactment and implementation of social policies of concern to the profession.

O. DEVELOPMENT OF KNOWLEDGE—The social worker should take responsibility for identifying, developing, and fully utilizing knowledge for professional practice.

1. The social worker should base practice upon recognized knowledge relevant to social work.

2. The social worker should critically examine, and keep current with emerging knowledge relevant to social work.

3. The social worker should contribute to the knowledge base of social work and share research knowledge and practice wisdom with colleagues.

VI. *The Social Worker's Ethical Responsibility to Society*

P. PROMOTING THE GENERAL WELFARE—The social worker should promote the general welfare of society.

1. The social worker should act to prevent and eliminate discrimination against any person or group on the basis of race, color, sex, sexual orientation, age, religion, national origin, marital status, political belief, mental or physical handicap, or any other preference or personal characteristic, condition, or status.

2. The social worker should act to ensure that all persons have access to the resources, services, and opportunities which they require.

3. The social worker should act to expand choice and opportunity for all persons, with special regard for disadvantaged or oppressed groups and persons.

4. The social worker should promote conditions that encourage respect for the diversity of cultures which constitute American society.

5. The social worker should provide appropriate professional services in public emergencies.

6. The social worker should advocate changes in policy and legislation to improve social conditions and to promote social justice.

7. The social worker should encourage informed participation by the public in shaping social policies and institutions.

ETHICAL REVIEW PROCEDURES

National Association of Social Workers
Approved by the Board of Directors, October 6, 1970.
Revised by the Board of Directors, June 22, 1972
and June 15, 1978.

Introduction

The following are procedures to be used by the National Association of Social Workers (NASW) for considering complaints of alleged violations of the NASW Code of Ethics, an agency's personnel standards, or the right of social workers to take professional action on behalf of clients. In most instances, the steps in the adjudication process are the same. Differences in them, stemming from the differences in their content, are clearly indicated.

NASW adjudication proceedings are not formal legal proceedings. Hence many legal strictures and conventions are not observed. The group conducting the inquiry has far greater discretion and latitude as to the manner in which it proceeds than does a court of law. No limitation on the manner in which proceedings are conducted is to be implied from these procedures unless expressly stated. The association, through the body to whom it delegates the adjudication of complaints, has a serious responsibility to arrive at sound and just conclusions. It must, therefore, have freedom to fulfill this responsibility.

These procedures implement the Policy Statement on the Adjudication of Grievances adopted by NASW Delegate Assembly on April 11, 1967, which is set forth on page 14 of this booklet.

A. Types of Complaints Accepted

1. *Complaints of violation of the Code of Ethics by a member.* A complaint may be filed by any individual, group of individuals, or organization (referred to as the complainant). The complainant need not be a member of NASW. The respondent must be a member of NASW.

2. *Complaints of violation of personnel practices by an agency.* A complaint may be filed by an individual NASW member or group of NASW members (hereinafter referred to as complainant) affected by the same grievance, provided the complainant was (a) employed in a social work capacity, (b) an active candidate for a social work position, or (c) a social work student in the agency or institution against which the complaint is filed at the time the alleged violation occurred. No complaints will

---

be considered against foreign agencies. The complainant(s) must be a member of NASW at the time of filing or before the complaint is accepted.

Complaints against agencies for imposing limitations on or penalities for professional action on behalf of clients. A complaint may be filed by an individual NASW member or group of NASW members (hereinafter referred to as complainant) affected by the same grievance, provided the complainant was employed in a social work capacity by, or a social work student in, the agency or institution against which the complaint is filed. No complaints will be considered against foreign agencies. The complainant must be a member of NASW at the time of filing or before the complaint is accepted.

B. How to File a Complaint

1. Declaration of Complaint forms shall be available from NASW chapters or the national office.

2. The complainant shall file *two* copies of the Declaration of Complaint and a supporting statement with the president of the chapter of which the respondent is a member or with a chapter within whose territory the alleged violation took place. The initial statement of complaint should include only such documentation as is needed to establish the eligibility of the complaint and to specify allegations being made. Persons filing complaints are responsible for complying with the time limits for filing set forth in these procedures.

3. A complaint of unethical conduct filed against a member of NASW who is not a member of any specific chapter shall be filed with the national committee.

C. When to File

1. The time limits for each category are set forth in Section H4. A complaint alleging unethical conduct shall be filed separately from any other category of complaint and must be filed within the time limit prescribed for that category. When a complaint is being filed in more than one category, the time limits for each category must be respected for that aspect of the complaint.

2. A complaint shall not be considered untimely because it was filed initially under an inappropriate category, as long as it met the time limitations for that category.

D. Acknowledgment of a Complaint

1. The president of the chapter (or the chairman of the national committee) shall, within ten days of receipt of a Declaration of Complaint, acknowledge such receipt in writing to the complainant. A copy of the Declaration of Complaint, its supporting statement, and a copy of the acknowledgment letter shall be mailed to the national office.

E. Chapter Committee on Inquiry

1. The structure, size, and membership of chapter Committees on Inquiry may vary to meet the requirements of the specific chapter involved. The chapter itself, through its formal process of decision-making, shall decide on the form of its committee, subject to approval by the national Committee on Inquiry and Board of Directors.

2. The committee shall reflect the makeup of the membership of the chapter. It should be appointed by the elected governing body of the chapter. Its roster

should include alternatives to serve in the place of a member who cannot serve or is disqualified from participating in a specific inquiry. The decision of the chapter Committee on Inquiry shall be by majority vote. An alternate who is substituting for a regular member of the committee shall have the right to vote.

3. The chapter must endeavor to insure that complaints will be handled fairly. Members who cannot be impartial about a complaint must be excluded from participating in its determination. An ad hoc hearing panel may be appointed by the chapter president to conduct a hearing and to report to the chapter Committee on Inquiry. A hearing panel shall have at least three members present at each session.

4. Both the complainant and respondent shall have the right to challenge the participation of any member of the Committee on Inquiry who they believe to be prejudiced with respect to the matter to be adjudicated. Such a challenge, stating reasons, shall be submitted in writing to the chairman of the inquiry committee who will inform the member so challenged and provide an opportunity for voluntary disqualification. If the committee member chooses not to do so, the chairman will inform the other members, and the committee will determine whether to disqualify the member so challenged.

F. National Committee on Inquiry

1. The national Committee on Inquiry shall be appointed by the president of NASW with the approval of the Board of Directors. It shall consist of at least nine persons, appointed to serve no more than two terms of three years each.

2. The national Committee on Inquiry shall act by a majority of its members or by a panel of three members to whom the committee may delegate authority to act for it. The chairperson of the national committee shall be appointed by the president of NASW.

G. Jurisdiction

1. CHAPTER ACTION

The chapter shall act on all complaints filed with it except in the following instances:[1]

a. *Complaint for alleged unethical conduct.* If the respondent is not a member of a specific chapter, the national committee shall arrange for an ad hoc group of NASW members to be convened and to act in the same manner as would a chapter Committee on Inquiry under these procedures.

b. *Complaints against agencies for alleged violation of their personnel standards.* When a complaint is filed against a multi-state organization, the chapter shall have the right either to accept the complaint for review or inquiry or may defer jurisdiction to the national Committee on Inquiry.

c. *Complaints against agencies for imposing limitations on or penalities for professional action on behalf of clients.* When a complaint is filed against a multi-state organization, the chapter may accept the complaint for review or inquiry or may defer jurisdiction to the national Committee on Inquiry.

---

[1]*Standards for NASW Chapters*, adopted by the 1962 Delegate Assembly, includes this statement: "A Chapter shall receive and determine the disposition of complaints against agencies. . . . and against members in accordance with established procedures.

d. Filing under an inappropriate chapter. If a chapter concludes that a complaint has been inappropriately filed with the chapter, it shall refer the complaint to the national committee, which shall determine the appropriate jurisdiction.

2. DEFERRAL OF JURISDICTION

A chapter may apply to the national committee for a deferral of jurisdiction when the chapter is convinced that a judicious handling of the complaint cannot be achieved by the chapter. In requesting a deferral, the chapter must give specific reasons. The national Committee on Inquiry shall determine which chapter or national committee is to proceed.

3. QUESTIONS OF JURISDICTION

All questions of jurisdiction will be determined by the national Committee on Inquiry. In the case of a member who is not assigned to a chapter, the Declaration of Complaint shall be filed with the national office. On its own determination, the national committee may assume jurisdiction at any point in the proceedings of an inquiry being conducted by a chapter when issues of national significance are involved or when irregularities in the adjudication process appear to jeopardize the rights of either party to a fair and timely hearing.

H. Accepting the Complaint

Unless otherwise specifically stated, the procedures contained in this section shall apply to chapter and national Committees on Inquiry.

1. DETERMINING THE CATEGORY

If a complaint is filed in a category (ethics, personnel standards, or professional action) deemed by the Committee on Inquiry to be inappropriate, it shall be heard in a correct category, with an extension of the time limit if necessary. If more than one complaint is filed against the same respondent or is related to the same situation, the Committee on Inquiry shall determine which to consider first or whether they should be considered concurrently.

2. REQUESTING ADDITIONAL INFORMATION

If after reviewing a formal Declaration of Complaint the Committee on Inquiry finds that the complaint has been incorrectly executed or that additional information is required, the Declaration of Complaint may be returned to the complainant for revision or a written request sent to the complainant for further information. The relevant time limits may be adjusted accordingly.

3. NOTICES REQUIRED

The complainant must be notified by the committee, in writing, of whether or not the complaint is accepted. The respondent must be notified at the same time if the complaint is accepted but is *not* notified if it is not accepted. The letter notifying the respondent that a complaint has been accepted shall include a copy of the Declaration of Complaint and its supporting statement.

The chapter shall insure that a complainant is assisted, whenever it is necessary, to identify specifically each alleged violation. On request, assistance shall be provided to a respondent to interpret and utilize these procedures.

4. CRITERIA FOR ACCEPTING A COMPLAINT

The chapter Committee on Inquiry shall accept a complaint if *all* the criteria of any category are met. If the complaint does not meet all such criteria, it shall be found not eligible for action; this finding requires endorsement by the chapter president.

a. *Category 1. Complaints against members for alleged unethical conduct.*

    a. 1. The complainant charges a violation of the Code of Ethics as specified by the complainant or by the Committee on Inquiry.

    a. 2. The respondent is a member of NASW.

    a. 3. The alleged unethical behavior complained about came to the complainant's attention no more than sixty days prior to the date the substance of the complaint was first made known to the chapter. An exception to this limit may be granted by the national Committee on Inquiry.

    a. 4. The complainant has personal knowledge of the alleged behavior complained about or is in a position to supply relevant, reliable testimony or other evidence on the subject.

    a. 5. The complainant is willing to give testimony.

    a. 6. The complainant keeps the pledge, contained in the Declaration of Complaint, to furnish additional data and to keep confidential the proceedings of the committee. The Committee on Inquiry may, at its own discretion, terminate its inquiry procedure at any stage if the complainant fails to comply with these conditions.

b. *Category 2. Complaints against agencies for alleged violation of their personnel standards.*

    b. 1. The complaint cites a violation of the agency's written standards of personnel practices. If the agency has no written standards or the action complained about is not covered by them, the complainant must cite a violation of the *NASW Standards for Social Work Personnel Practices.*

    b. 2. The complainant must have been personally and directly affected by the alleged violation. The complainant must submit the complaint in his or her own behalf, except in the event of an incapacity, when an agent may assume this responsibility. The complainant must be in a position to supply relevant, reliable testimony or other evidence on the subject and be willing to testify in person.

    b. 3. The complainant must satisfy the committee that every reasonable effort has been made to utilize the complaint machinery existing within the agency.

    b. 4. The alleged violation must have occurred no more than sixty days prior to the date of the complaint or sixty days after efforts to use intra- or extra-agency machinery have been completed. When the complainant or an NASW chapter is engaged in efforts to resolve a problem through negotiation or there are other exceptional circumstances, the committee may accept the complaint and keep it pending or accept it for study after the time limit has expired.

    b. 5. The complainant must keep the pledge, contained in the Declaration of Complaint, to furnish additional data and keep confidential the proceedings of the committee. The Committee on Inquiry may, at its own discretion, terminate its inquiry at any stage if the complainant fails to comply with this condition.

c. *Category 3. Complaints against agencies for imposing limitations on or penalties for professional action on behalf of clients.*

c. 1. The complainant charges that the agency has placed limits on or imposed penalties for professional action on behalf of clients.

c. 2. The complainant must have been personally and directly affected by the alleged violation. The complainant must submit the complaint in his or her own behalf, except in the event of an incapacity, when an agent may assume this responsibility. The complainant must be in a position to supply relevant, reliable testimony or other evidence on the subject and be willing to testify in person.

c. 3. The complainant must satisfy the committee that every reasonable effort has been made to utilize the complaint machinery existing within the agency.

c. 4. The alleged violation must have occurred no more than sixty days prior to the date of the complaint or sixty days after efforts to use intra- or extra-agency machinery have been completed. When the complainant or an NASW chapter is engaged in efforts to resolve a problem through negotiation or there are other exceptional circumstances, the committee may accept the complaint and keep it pending or accept it for study after the time limit has expired.

c. 5. The complainant must keep the pledge, contained in the Declaration of Complaint, to furnish additional data and keep confidential the proceedings of the committee. The Committee on Inquiry may, at its own discretion, terminate its inquiry at any stage if the complainant fails to comply with this condition.

5. RIGHT TO APPEAL

The committee's decision to accept or not accept a complaint may be appealed. (See Section N—Appeals.)

6. FAILURE OF CHAPTER TO ACT

"Official action" means either (1) action to accept or not accept the complaint or (2) a request for additional information from the complainant. If the chapter fails to take official action with regard to a complaint within forty-five days of the receipt of a Declaration of Complaint, the complainant may request the national Committee on Inquiry to investigate and take appropriate action including, if necessary, the assumption of jurisdiction over the proceedings. The national Committee on Inquiry may take whatever action it determines to be necessary and appropriate for this purpose.

A hearing is mandatory in every case in which the committee accepts a complaint.

I. The Hearing

Unless otherwise stated, the procedures in this section apply to chapter and national Committees on Inquiry.

1. PURPOSE

The purpose of a hearing is to determine the facts and decide whether such facts constitute a violation of the Code of Ethics or a violation of personnel standards or the right of social workers to take professional action on behalf of clients.

2. Notices Required

All parties shall be notified, in writing, by the committee as soon as possible after a complaint is accepted. They will be notified of

    a. The members of the committee who will conduct the hearing.

    b. The time, place, and other arrangements for the hearing.

    c. The scope of the hearing by a clear statement of the allegations to be heard.

    d. Their right to present witnesses.

A copy of this notice shall be sent to the national office. Any challenge of a member of the Committee on Inquiry must be made within ten days of receipt of this information.

3. Respondent's Comment

The respondent shall be requested to present a written statement outlining his or her view of the situation or conduct complained about, to enable the committee to prepare for the hearing. A copy of the respondent's statement shall be sent to the complainant by the respondent.

4. Hearing Sessions

Sessions of the hearing shall be called by the Committee on Inquiry or a designated panel of three or more members of NASW. Although the complainant and respondent shall be notified of and requested to be present at all sessions, the hearing may proceed whether or not they are present, at the committee's discretion. At least three panel members shall be present at each session.

5. Time of Hearing

The hearing shall commence as soon as possible after the decision to accept the complaint. If additional sessions are required, they shall be held as soon as possible. Hearings should be completed within sixty days of acceptance of the complaint. The report shall be completed within forty-five days of the conclusion of the hearings.

6. Representation at the Hearing

The complainant and/or respondent may seek advice from any person, including an attorney, but may not be represented by counsel at hearings of the committee or its representatives. Either party may bring to the committee hearings a member of NASW to aid them in the presentation of their case.

7. Responsibility of the Committee

The hearing panel shall have the responsibility to question the complainant and respondent and their witnesses and to examine documentary evidence in the course of the hearing to ascertain relevant facts. Should the testimony and documentary evidence fail to provide adequate information on which to base a decision, the committee shall request either the complainant or respondent or both to provide additional information. If either is unable to do so, the committee, with notice to the complainant and respondent, shall call additional witnesses or request access to pertinent documents.

8. Responsibility of the Complainant and Respondent and Witnesses

The complainant and respondent shall present at the hearing all information relevant to the complaint. They may also present pertinent documents or oral testimony of individuals who have knowledge of the situation giving rise to the compliant. The parties *may* be required by the committee to provide, in the number needed by the committee, copies of any document they wish to present. The complainant and respondent shall have the right to be present when witnesses called by the committee are heard and to question them. They shall be given the right to inspect documents examined by the committee and, when feasible, shall receive copies of such documents.

9. USE OF WRITTEN TESTIMONY

If either the complainant or respondent is unable to appear, the Committee on Inquiry may, with the consent of both, accept written statements in lieu of oral testimony, provided that each receives a copy of the other's statements and has an opportunity for rebuttal.

10. CONFIDENTIALITY

Both the complainant and respondent are required to keep the proceedings of the committee confidential, except if it becomes necessary to share information in order to provide relevant evidence. The committee shall make every effort to conceal the names of the parties to the proceedings and the identifying circumstances. The respondent may appeal to the national committee if he or she believes the chapter committee is revealing such information unnecessarily. The national committee may then take whatever action it deems appropriate. If the inquiry appeal is being conducted by the national committee, this appeal should be directed to the president of NASW for appropriate action.

11. RESIGNATION FROM NASW BY RESPONDENT

Members of NASW are pledged, by their specific affirmation on joining NASW, to submit to proceedings of NASW for any alleged violation of the Code of Ethics. If a respondent resigns from NASW or fails to appeal before or otherwise cooperate with the Committee on Inquiry, the committee shall continue its activity, noting in its final report the circumstances of the respondent's failure to cooperate or his or her resignation. Also the committee will note the difficulties occasioned by a respondent's lack of cooperation. If a complainant refuses to appear at a hearing or fails to appear without giving adequate reasons, the complaint may be dismissed with or without prejudice, at the discretion of the committee, on the application of the respondent.

12. WITHDRAWAL OF THE COMPLAINT

If the complainant wishes to withdraw the complaint, the committee must obtain the respondent's permission before terminating the inquiry. If the respondent withholds permission, the inquiry must be completed.

J. Report of the Committee

Within forty-five days of the conclusion of the hearing or hearings, the committee shall prepare a report of its findings and recommendations with respect to the complaint. Unless otherwise stated, the procedures contained in this section shall apply to chapter and national Committees on Inquiry.

1. CONTENTS REQUIRED

The report shall contain (a) a summary of the complaint; (b) the positions of the complainant and respondent as well as their respective statements of the facts; the findings of fact made by the committee regarding each allegation, including a summary of the testimony and evidence on which such findings are based; and the committee's reasons for such findings; (c) the conclusions of the committee with respect to each allegation set forth in the Declaration of Complaint; (d) its recommendations; and (e) an appendix composed of documents submitted in evidence and cited in the report.

2. CONCLUSIONS AND RECOMMENDATIONS REQUIRED

a. *Unethical behavior.* A report on a complaint against a member for alleged unethical conduct shall include the following:

1. *Conclusions.* The committee shall state whether the conduct complained of constitutes a violation of the Code of Ethics and the manner in which the Code of Ethics was violated.

2. *Recommendations and sanctions.* If the committee finds the member's conduct to have been a violation of the Code of Ethics, it may make suitable recommendations, in consultation with the chapter officers, among which are these:

- Restitution by the respondent to an individual group or organization harmed by the respondent's unethical behavior.
- Censure by the chapter.
- Censure by the National Board of Directors.
- Recommendations that membership in NASW and/or ACSW be suspended.
- Permanent exclusion from NASW and/or ACSW membership.
- Publication of the findings and penalties imposed.
- Referral to state licensing boards for disciplinary action.

b. *Violations of personnel standards.* A report on a complaint against an agency of alleged violations of their personnel standards shall include the following:

1. *Conclusions.* The committee shall state whether the subject of the complaint constituted a violation of personnel standards and the manner in which the standards were violated.

2. *Recommendations and sanctions.* If the committee finds the agency's action to have been a violation of personnel standards, it may make suitable recommendations for corrective actions, in consultation with the chapter officers, among which are these:

- Restitution by the respondent to the complainant for losses suffered as a result of the violation
- Recommendations to the agency board, executive, and staff for revision of policies and procedures related to personnel standards in conformity with *NASW Standards for Social Work Personnel Practices.* In addition, the chapter committee may offer to help the agency revise its procedures and policies.

c. *Penalties for professional action.* In the case of complaints against agencies for imposing limitations on or penalties for professional action on behalf of clients, the report shall include the following:

1. *Conclusions.* The committee shall state whether the complaint constituted a restriction on professional action and the manner in which this restriction occurred.

2. *Recommendations and sanctions.* If the committee finds the agency's action to have been a violation of the complainant's right to take professional action on behalf of clients, it may make suitable recommendations for corrective action, in consultation with the chapter officers, among which are these:

- Restitution by the respondent to the complainant for losses suffered as a result of the violation.
- Recommendations to the agency board, executive, and staff for revision of policies and procedures related to personnel practices in conformity with *NASW Standards for Social Work Personnel Practices.* Also the chapter committee may offer to help the agency revise its policies and procedures.

K. *Review by Chapter Officers*

1. The report of the Committee on Inquiry shall be submitted for review to the chapter executive officers, who shall respect the confidentiality of the parties at all times.

If the chapter officers do not agree with the findings of the committee, they may not reverse the decision but may send the report back to the committee for reconsideration explaining their reasons. If the committee after reconsideration does not revise its report, the report shall stand. The officers may modify the committee's recommendations but may not increase the recommended sanctions. When differences arise, the majority opinion of the officers shall prevail. The final report shall not be submitted to or considered by the full membership of the chapter.

L. *Sanctions*

1. The report shall specify what, if any, sanctions are to be imposed by the chapter if the respondent fails to act on the recommendations to the satisfaction of the chapter. Among the appropriate sanctions are the following:

a. Recommendations that the report be shared with community councils, funding agencies, schools of social work whose students are placed with the agency for fieldwork, national and state standard-setting bodies, and/or other appropriate bodies in a position to influence change in the agency's policies and practices.

b. Publication of the findings and penalties imposed.

c. Censure of a member of NASW.

d. Suspension or termination of membership in NASW and ACSW.

M. *Disposition of the Final Report*

Copies of the final report, including a report of actions and recommendations as well as information about when and how they may appeal the decisions, shall be sent by certified mail, return receipt requested, to (1) the complainant, (2) the respondent, and (3) the national Committee on Inquiry.

1. IF NO VIOLATION HAS BEEN FOUND

If the final report states that the respondent has not violated the Code of Ethics or personnel standards or the rights of social workers to take professional action on behalf of their clients, after the time to appeal has expired, a copy of the report shall be sent to all witnesses and every member of the chapter Committee on Inquiry who heard the case. The respondent is free to make known the disposition of the case and to use the report as he or she sees fit, except that it may not be made public without authorization by the NASW national Board of Directors.

2. IF A VIOLATION HAS BEEN FOUND

If either the complainant or the respondent has not appealed the chapter's decision within thirty days of receipt of the report, the recommendations shall be implemented by the chapter. However, the chapter may not implement recommendations related to NASW or ACSW membership status, which shall be implemented by the national office at the request of the chapter, or recommendations for making the report public, which require approval by the national Board of Directors. The report shall designate the time limit for carrying out the recommendations, and the chapter shall follow up to determine what action the respondent has taken with respect to the recommendations for restitution to the complainant or revision of personnel policies or practices. The chapter shall report its findings to the national office and send copies of its findings to the complainant and respondent. If no action has been taken (or the actions are not satisfactory to the chapter) the chapter officers shall consider what further action should be imposed.

3. PUBLICATION OR DISTRIBUTION OF THE REPORT

There shall be no publication or oral or written distribution of any part of a report, except to the complainant, respondent, and national Committee on Inquiry, unless authorization is granted by the national Board of Directors after the advice of legal counsel. The national Board of Directors shall decide in what manner, if at all, such publication or distribution shall be made.

N. Appeals

1. APPEALABLE ACTIONS

An appeal may be made of the following actions:

a. Not accepting a complaint.

b. The final report issued by a chapter.

c. The termination of an inquiry by a committee.

d. A decision of the national committee.

2. GROUNDS FOR APPEAL OF A REPORT

One or more of the following reasons are sufficient grounds for the appellant to base an appeal of a final report.

a. The Committee on Inquiry's departure from the procedures was serious enough to cause the appellant's rights to be prejudiced.

b. The findings of fact stated in the committee's report were so inaccurate as to prejudice the appellant's rights.

c. The conclusions reached by the committee were not appropriate to the findings of fact.

d. New evidence had been discovered after the final report was issued. Except for newly discovered evidence, no party may offer additional evidence in support of its position on the appeal.

e. The recommendations of the Committee on Inquiry were inappropriate to the conclusions.

f. The sanctions are not appropriate.

3. LETTER OF APPEAL

The letter of appeal shall contain the following:

a. If the appeal is based on a procedural issue, the letter of appeal must cite the procedural error and the appellant's reasons for believing that the alleged error influenced, or will influence, the results of the inquiry.

b. If the appeal is based on new evidence, the new evidence must be stated and an explanation given as to why it was not submitted during the hearing.

c. If the appeal is based on an allegation of inappropriate conclusions or recommendations, the letter of appeal must present the appellant's line of reasoning and indicate in what way the appellant disagrees with the final report.

d. If the appeal is based on serious inaccuracies in the findings of fact, the letter of appeal must state specifically the alleged inaccuracies and evidence that supports these charges as well as the reasons why such inaccuracies are serious enough to prejudice the appellant's rights.

An appellant shall furnish a copy of the appeal to any other party or parties involved as a complainant or respondent, who shall have the right to submit a written rebuttal within thirty days of its receipt.

4. APPELLATE BODIES

Appeals of actions of a chapter Committee on Inquiry shall be heard by the national Committee on Inquiry and shall be addressed to the chairperson of the national committee, at the national office, within no more than thirty days of receipt of notice of the decision or report being appealed.

In case of an appeal to the national Committee on Inquiry, the national committee shall transmit copies to the president of the chapter that made the decision being appealed. The chapter shall submit a rebuttal or explanation of any of its actions being appealed.

Appeals of actions of the national Committee on Inquiry shall be heard as arranged by the national Board of Directors. The letter of appeal shall be filed within thirty days of receipt of notice of the action being appealed and shall be addressed to the president of the board at the national office. Neither a complainant nor respondent shall have the right to appear before the national committee or the national Board of Directors.

5. ACTION ON APPEALS: NATIONAL COMMITTEE ON INQUIRY

The national Committee on Inquiry shall undertake consideration of an appeal at its next regularly scheduled meeting after an opportunity for rebuttal has been given. After considering the appeal, the national Committee on Inquiry may do one of the following:

a. Deny the appeal.

b. Request further information from the parties and/or the chapter Committee on Inquiry.

c. Issue an amended final report.

d. Return the case to the chapter for further or new proceedings.

If the national committee does not find in the report of the chapter committee sufficient information on which to base a decision, it may request the chapter to obtain such information from the complainant and/or respondent (or other sources, provided the complainant and respondent are informed) and to present the information either at a hearing at which both parties are present or in writing, provided that copies of all writings submitted shall be given to the other parties.

The chapter will then submit an amended final report incorporating the additional information and any changes in conclusions and recommendations.

6. ACTION ON APPEALS: NATIONAL BOARD OF DIRECTORS

The national Board of Directors shall undertake consideration of an appeal at the next regularly scheduled meeting after four weeks from the date opportunity for rebuttal has been given.

After considering the appeal, the national Board of Directors may do one of the following:

   a. Deny the appeal.

   b. Request further information from the parties and/or the Committees on Inquiry.

   c. Issue a final report.

   d. Return the case to a Committee on Inquiry for further or new proceedings.

The national Board of Directors may delegate its authority to act with respect to any or all appeals to a group of directors.

7. NOTIFICATION OF RESULTS

The parties, the chapter, and the Committee on Inquiry shall be notified in writing, by certified mail (return receipt requested), of the action taken by the appellate body; the notification shall include notice of any right of further appeal.

O. Closing of Cases

   1. A case shall be deemed closed by the national office when

   a. The complaint has been not accepted and the decision has not been appealed, or all appeals have been completed.

   b. A final report has been issued and has not been appealed or all appeals have been completed.

   c. A complaint has been terminated or withdrawn with no objection.

   2. Record copies of all complaints filed shall be maintained by the national office, under the supervision of the national Committee on Inquiry.

NASW POLICY STATEMENT NO. 3:
ADJUDICATION OF GRIEVANCES

(Adopted by the Delegate Assembly of the National Association of Social Workers, April 11, 1967.)

In keeping with its purpose "to promote the quality and effectiveness of social work practice in the United States of America," under conditions of nondiscrimination in personnel practices and provision of services, with respect to race, color, creed, or national origin, the National Association of Social Workers has responsibility to study and adjudicate complaints of alleged practices detrimental to this purpose and to do the following:

•Insure responsible use of facts in making judgments about agency or individual action.

•Protect its members against exploitation and injustice.

•Promote sound and equitable personnel administration.

•Protect the agency and the public from unethical practice by social workers.

•Discipline its members when unethical conduct is found to exist.

To fulfill this obligation, NASW has developed adjudication procedures governing the handling of grievances resulting from alleged violations of social work personnel practices or the Code of Ethics and alleged instances of penalties imposed as a consequence of social or political action.

These procedures shall consistently be designed to do the following:

•Make the NASW chapter the initial unit of the association to receive and act on a complaint.

•Provide for reasonable promptness in filing and adjudicating complaints for the protection of the parties to a complaint.

•Insure objective, factual, and confidential consideration of the situation under adjudication.

•Permit both parties to a complaint to be heard and to defend their positions.

•Provide for judicious handling of appeals from chapter decisions to the national Committee on Inquiry and final appeal to the Board of Directors.

•Make possible waiver of chapter jurisdiction and referral of a case to the national Committee on Inquiry in either one of two instances: when the chapter (1) chooses to disqualify itself or (2) fails to comply with the stipulated time limits for acting on a complaint.

Revisions in procedure growing out of the experience of the association shall meet these criteria as stated previously. They shall be made by the Board of Directors on recommendation of the national Committee on Inquiry with the approval of the Cabinet of the Division of Professional Standards.

Any member or group of members may initiate revision of the procedures by submitting suggestions to the Committee on Inquiry. The committee may circulate to the chapters and other groups revisions that it suggests and may ask for reactions and suggestions before making its recommendations to the division cabinet and Board of Directors. The Committee on Inquiry shall report to the membership annually on its work.

INDEX

A

Abortion, 208–31; case study in, 390–92
 on demand, and *Roe v. Wade* decision,
  211–14
 and fetal status, moral cases for and
  against, 214–19
 for genetic disease reasons, 225–27;
  ethical issues in, 263–72
 and law, 219–20; in Canada, 209–11,
  212, 213; in U.S.A., 211–14
 and public policy, 220, 222
Abortion counseling, 221–30, 265–66 (*see also*
 Genetic counseling)
Accountability, and social work as a profession, 22, 26, 27, 359–60
Adolescents, and homosexuality, 96–100
Advocacy, defined, 63
 by social workers, for developmentally
  disabled, 175; and ethical conflicts,
  26, 63–65; for homosexuals' rights,
  89–90, 101
Aged, 139–55; age categories of, 141–43
 autonomy of, vs. paternalistic intervention, 144–46, 150, 151–53
 case study on, 386–87
 home vs. institutional care of, 146–50
 terminally ill, 151–52, 198, 201–3
 utilitarian view of, 139–41, 143, 154
Alberta Association of Social Workers, code
 of ethics of, 402–11
Allen, Rodney, his decision making format,
 41ff.
American Association of Social Workers, 17
American Association of Sociologists, and
 ethical responsibilities, 335
American Bar Association, and child mistreatment, 106
American Psychiatric Association, on homosexuality, 92, 94
American Psychological Association, on use

 of deception in human experimentation,
  323–24
Amniocentesis, for detection of fetal genetic
 defects, 225, 262, 264–65, 266, 271–72
 for sex determination, 226–27
Anonymity, right to, of human experimental subjects, 328–31
Asian minorities, 121–38; case study on,
 384–86
 fatalistic social philosophy of, 130–31
 and individual identity crises, 132–34
 political importance of group for,
  134–35
 and role of family, 124–30
Association for Advancement of Behavior
 Therapy, statement on ethical issues,
 256–57
Autonomy (*see* Self-determination)

B

Badgley Committee, on abortion law, 210
Behavior, and decision making, 40
 deterministic view of, 239
 preferred modes of, as instrumental
  values, 36–37
Behavior control, aversive and positive, ethics of, 242–48, 255
Behavior modification, 232–60; case studies
 in, 246–47, 249–51, 392–94
 and developmentally disabled, 165–67
 elements of, 234–37
 ethical issues in, 238–54; regarding
  behavioral control, 240–48, 255; contracted behavioral change, 248–52;
  informed consent, 252–54
 in institutional setting, 241–48
 misconceptions of, 165–66, 232–33,
  237, 239
 in social work practice, 233–34, 243,
  248–49, 254, 255
Behavioral assessment, in behavior modifi-